Name Index, Volumes 1–12

Books by David Whitwell

Philosophic Foundations of Education
Foundations of Music Education
Music Education of the Future
The Sousa Oral History Project
The Art of Musical Conducting
The Longy Club: 1900–1917
A Concise History of the Wind Band
Wagner on Bands
Berlioz on Bands
Chopin: A Self-Portrait
Schumann: A Self-Portrait in His Own Words
Mendelssohn: A Self-Portrait in His Own Words
La Téléphonie and the Universal Musical Language
Extraordinary Women
Aesthetics of Music in Ancient Civilizations
Aesthetics of Music in the Middle Ages
Aesthetics of Music in the Early Renaissance

The History and Literature of the Wind Band and Wind Ensemble Series

Volume 1 The Wind Band and Wind Ensemble Before 1500
Volume 2 The Renaissance Wind Band and Wind Ensemble
Volume 3 The Baroque Wind Band and Wind Ensemble
Volume 4 The Wind Band and Wind Ensemble of the Classical Period (1750–1800)
Volume 5 The Nineteenth-Century Wind Band and Wind Ensemble
Volume 6 A Catalog of Multi-Part Repertoire for Wind Instruments or for Undesignated Instrumentation before 1600
Volume 7 Baroque Wind Band and Wind Ensemble Repertoire
Volume 8 Classical Period Wind Band and Wind Ensemble Repertoire
Volume 9 Nineteenth-Century Wind Band and Wind Ensemble Repertoire
Volume 10 A Supplementary Catalog of Wind Band and Wind Ensemble Repertoire
Volume 11 A Catalog of Wind Repertoire before the Twentieth Century for One to Five Players
Volume 12 A Second Supplementary Catalog of Early Wind Band and Wind Ensemble Repertoire
Volume 13 Name Index, Volumes 1–12, The History and Literature of the Wind Band and Wind Ensemble

www.whitwellbooks.com

David Whitwell

Name Index, Volumes 1–12, The History and Literature of the Wind Band and Wind Ensemble

THE HISTORY AND LITERATURE OF THE WIND BAND AND WIND ENSEMBLE, VOLUME 13

EDITED BY CRAIG DABELSTEIN

WHITWELL PUBLISHING • AUSTIN, TEXAS, USA

Whitwell Publishing, Austin 78701
www.whitwellbooks.com

Printed in the United States of America

PAPERBACK
ISBN-13: 978-1-936512-56-0
ISBN-10: 1936512564

Composed in Bembo Book

Contents

Foreword   vii

Acknowledgements   ix

Name Index, Volumes 1–12
The History and Literature of the Wind Band and Wind Ensemble

Abadie – Azerets	1
Babb – Byrd	9
C & S Thompson – Czibulka	31
d'Albert – Dyke	44
E.S.T.M.Bn. – Eytelwein	54
Fabbrucci – Fux	59
Gabetti – Gyrowetz	70
Haas – Hyrtner	84
Iacchini – Ives	98
J.S. – Jusdorff	100
K & S – Kyle	105
l'Imprimerie du Cons. de Musique – Lyttich	114
Maanen – Myslivecek	126
Naderman – Nutti	144
Oberndöffer – Ozi	148
Pacak – Pythochares	150
Quagliati – Quirici	163
R.O. – Ryembault	164
Saal – Szervánsky	176
Taaffe – Tyther	197
Uber – Utrecht	203
Vaet – Vulder	204
Wace – Wynne	209
Xenophon – Xenophon	218
Yost – Yost	218
Zabala – Zyrler	219

About the Author   221

About the Editor   223

Foreword

THIS VOLUME IS THE THIRTEENTH AND FINAL VOLUME in the series, *The History and Literature of the Wind Band and Wind Ensemble*, comprised of the following volumes:

1. The Wind Band and Wind Ensemble before 1500
2. The Renaissance Wind Band and Wind Ensemble
3. The Baroque Wind Band and Wind Ensemble
4. The Classical Period Wind Band and Wind Ensemble
5. The Nineteenth-Century Wind Band and Wind Ensemble
6. A Catalog of Multi-Part Repertoire for Wind Instruments or for Undesignated Instrumentation before 1600
7. Baroque Wind Band and Wind Ensemble Repertoire
8. Classical Period Wind Band and Wind Ensemble Repertoire
9. Nineteenth-Century Wind Band and Wind Ensemble Repertoire
10. A Supplementary Catalog of Early Band and Wind Ensemble Repertoire
11. A Catalog of Wind Repertoire before the Twentieth Century for One to Five Players
12. A Second Supplementary Catalog of Early Wind Band and Wind Ensemble Repertoire
13. Name Index, Volumes 1–12, The History and Literature of the Wind Band and Wind Ensemble

This volume replaces volume 11 of the first edition, originally an index of the first ten volumes completed in 1990. In this second edition, the index includes entries for volumes 1 to 12, with in excess of 8,000 entries.

David Whitwell
Austin, Texas

Acknowledgments

The reader is indebted for the second edition of this book
to Mr. Craig Dabelstein of Brisbane, Australia. Without his
contribution to design and all things involved as an editor this
book would never again have been available.

David Whitwell
Austin, 2012

Name Index

Abadie, ?, 19th century French composer, **IX:** 2

Abadie, Egbert, 19th century French composer, **IX:** 2

Abadie, Jacques, 19th century French composer, **V:** 214; **IX:** 2

Abbati, ?, 19th century Italian composer for band, **X:** 172

Abbiate, Charles, 19th century French composer, **IX:** 2

Abbiati, Dionigio, 19th century Italian composer for band, **X:** 172

Abdul Medjid, 19th century Turkish Sultan, **IX:** 22; **X:** 198, 244

Abel, Carl F., 1732–1787, composer, **XI:** 3, 181

Abel, Clamor-Heinrich, late 17th century German composer of dances, **VII:** 146

Abel, Giardini, 18th century English composer, **XI:** 7

Abell, Dav., 16th century composer, **VI:** 25

Abeltshauser, J. G., fl. 1812–1830, German composer, **XI:** 3, 308

Aber, Giovanni, late 18th century Italian flautist, composer, **VIII:** 362; **X:** 33

Aber, Johann, Italian composer, 1756–1783, **XI:** 3, 181

Abert, Johann, 1832–1915, German composer, **X:** 96

Abingdon, 4th Earl of, 1740–1799, composer for Harmoniemusik, **VIII:** 251

Abraham, ?, d. 1805, clarinet professor in Paris in 1788 & composer, **XI:** 127, 150

Abranyi, Emil, b. 1882, Hungarian composer, **XII:** 123

Abt, Franz, 1819–1885, German composer, **IX:** 145; **X:** 113; **XI:** 308

Accademico Filarmonico, 18th century publisher in Bologna, **XI:** 255

Acerbi, Domenico, 1842–1921, Italian composer for band, **IX:** 115; **X:** 172

Acerbi, Giuseppe, 1773–1846, Italian composer, **XI:** 127

Achleitner, Rudolf, 19th century Austrian composer, **IX:** 207

Ackermann, 19th century French composer, conductor 93e de Ligne, **IX:** 3, 263; **X:** 116ff

Adam, Charles Adolphe, 1803–1856, French composer, **V:** 63, 66, 70; **IX:** 253, 254 [*Regine*, arranged for band]

Adam, H. C., 19th century, *Messe* for chorus and band (arranged by Klosé) **IX:** 113

Adam, I. J., 18th century composer, **XI:** 3

Adams, Stephen, 1841–1913, pseud. For Michael Maybrick, English composer, **X:** 118

Adams, Thomas, 1785–1858, English composer, **IX:** 263

Addimando, Cesare, oboist in New York ca. 1905, **XII:** 212

Addison, John, 18th century English composer, **XI:** 181

Adelaide, 19th century Queen of England, **V:** 205

Adelinda, female minstrel, 1086, England, **I:** 182

Adinari, Alessandro, poet, **III:** 65

Adler, ?, late 18th century Italian composer, **X:** 34

Adler, F. B., 19th century composer, **XI:** 3

Admirall of Castile, 17th century Spanish noble, **III:** 75

Adorno, Francesco, 16th century Florentine composer, **VI:** 38

Adrien l'Aîné, 18th century French composer, **IV:** 195

Adrien, Ferdinand, solfeggio faculty of the 1792 Paris Conservatoire, **IV:** 157

Adrien, l'aîné, 18th century France, *Hymne à la Victoire,* for band, **VIII:** 268

Adson, John, d. 1640, London, composer for Duke of Lorraine, **VII:** 14

Aelianus, Claudius, 2nd century AD historian, **I:** 12, 51

Aerts, Felix, 19th century French composer, **IX:** 3

Aeschfachter, Walther, Switzerland composer, b. 1901, **XII:** 71

Aeschylus, ancient Greek playwright, **I:** 49

Agazzari, Agostino, 1603, Italian composer for voices and instruments, **VII:** 193

Agesilaus, King of Sparta, 444–361 BC, **I:** 33

Aghte, F. W., 19th century composer for the horn, **XI:** 163

Aglais of Megacles, ancient Greek trumpet player, **I:** 32

Agnola, Giacomo, 1761–1845, Italian composer for band, **X:** 172; **XI:** 256

Agostinelli, ?, 19th century Italian composer, **X:** 173

Agostini, Lodovico, 1534–1590, Italian composer, **VI:** 88

Agrell, Johann, 1701–1765, 18th century German composer, **XI:** 181

Agricola, Martin, 1486–1556, German composer at Magdeburg, **II:** 232; **VI:** 17, 76

Ahl, C., as arranger of works for Harmoniemusik, **VIII:** 89, 137; **XII:** 51 [as arranger of Paer's *Griselda*]

Ahle, Johann, 1625–1673, German composer, **III:** 214ff; **VII:** 110, 146

Aibl, 19th century publisher in Munich, **IX:** 151, 156

Aiblinger, *Die Fee und der Ritter* arranged by Sedlak, for Harmoniemusik, **VIII:** 150

Aiblinger, Johann Kaspar, 1779–1867, German composer, **V:** 18, fn. 56

Aich, Arnt von, 16th century publisher in Köln, **VI:** 61

Aichinger, Grégor, 1565–1628, German composer, **III:** 60; **VI:** 65, 78; **VII:** 110, 147, 180

Aigrette (Pseud.), (1808), English composer, **IX:** 263

Al Sfoi, 16th century composer, **VI:** 82

Alabieff, A., 19th century Russian composer, **V:** 86

Alain, Jehan, French, 20th century composer, **XII:** 72

Alamire, Pierre, 1470–1536, German/Dutch composer, **VI:** 106

Alba, A., 19th century French composer, **IX:** 3

Albanese, Luigi, b. 1859, Italian composer, **X:** 173

Albano, Marcello, 1616, Italian composer of canzoni collection, **VII:** 194

Albeniz, Enrique, 20th century Spanish composer, arranged by Strasser, **XII:** 190

Albergati, Pirro, 1663–1735, Italian composer, **III:** 14; **VII:** 185

Albert V, Duke at Munich, **II:** 97ff

Albert, 19th century Prince of England, **V:** 205

Albert, Charles, 1864–1932, German composer, **X:** 96

Albert, composer in 1650 collection of 4-part music, **VII:** 167

Albert, Duke of Prussia, 16th century, **II:** 113, 107ff; **VI:** 57

Albert, Johann, 1832–1915, German composer, **IX:** 146

Albert, Prince Consort of England, 19th century composer, **XI:** 175

Alberti, D., 19th century French composer, **IX:** 3

Alberti, Domenico, 1710–1740, Italian singer, **III:** 14

Albertin, Alphonso, 18th century Swiss composer, **VIII:** 372

Albertini, Thomas Anton, late 17th century, Vienna, composer, **VII:** 7

Albertino, Ignazio, late 17th century composer, **VII:** 7

Alberto, Duke Carlo of Piedmont, 1831 ordinance on Italian bands, **V:** 88

Albertus Alasco, Palatine of Poland, visits Elizabeth I in 1583, **II:** 44

Albinoni, Tommaso, 1671–1751, Italian composer for Hautboisten, **III:** 14; **VII:** 103, 185; **X:** 13; **XII:** 7

Albmeyer, Giorgio Cristoforo, German leader of Ital. military band in 1722, **III,** 152

Albrecht V, Duke of Bararia, **VI:** 10

Albrecht, 19th century Prince of Prussia, **V:** 25

Albrecht, trombonist in band of George IV, **V:** 203, fn. 10

Albrechtsberger, Johann, 1736–1809, **IX:** 207; **XI:** 3

Alcampo, Matteo, 19th century Italian composer for band, **X:** 173

Alcibiades, 5th century BC Statesman, **I:** 32

Alcock, John, 1715–1806, 18th century English composer, **XI:** 158

Alday, composer in repertoire of band of George IV, **V:** 201

Alday, l'aîné, b. 1763, 19th century French composer, **IX:** 3

Aldobrandini, Giovanni, on Italian military trumpets in 1601, **III:** 151

Aleppo, Giancarlo, 20th century Italian composer, **XII:** 202

Alessandri, Felice, 1742–1798, composer for Harmoniemusik, **VIII:** 3, 362

Alessandrino, Venetiano, 16th century composer, **VI:** 29

Alessandro VIII, 1610–1691, Pope, trumpets in 1689, **III:** 73

Alessandro, Michele, 1859–1918, Italian composer, **X:** 173

Alessio, Francesco, 18th century composer for Harmoniemusik, **VIII:** 163, 171ff [56 Parthias]; **XI:** 280

Aleworth, John, civic musician hired by Rochester in 1640, **III:** 180

Alexander I of Russia, **XI:** 132 [dedication]

Alexander III, 1845–1894, Emperor of Russia [his wind band of nobles], **V:** 193; **XII:** 218

Alexander VI, Pope, **II:** 117

Alexander, Friedrich, 19th century German composer, **XI:** 249

Alexandre, 19th century French composer, **IX:** 3

Alexandre, E., 19th century French composer, **IX:** 3

Alexandre, L., 19th century French composer, **IX:** 3

Alexandre-Georges, ?, 19th century French composer, **IX:** 3

Alexius, Frantisek, 18th century composer in Graf Pachta Harmonie Coll., **IV:** 22, fn. 10

Alfonso the Magnanimous, b. 1396, of Naples, **I:** 239

Alfonso V, 1416–1458, **I:** 220

Alfred, ?, 19th century German composer, **IX:** 141

Aliani, Nicola, 19th century Italian composer, **X:** 173

Alkan, Charles [Pseud. for Charles Morhange], 1813–1888, French composer, **IX:** 3; **XII:** 193

Allegri, Lorenzo, 1618 Italian composer, **VII:** 167, 194

Allen, William, 19th century English composer, **IX:** 263

Allier, Gabriel, 19th century French composer, **IX:** 3

Allmann, H., 19th century French composer, **IX:** 4

Almenraeder, Karl, 1786–1843, German composer, **IX:** 146

Aloe, Luigi, b. 1829, Italian composer for band, **X:** 173

Aloize, Giovanni, famous trombonist at Mantua, **II:** 132

Alquier, A.-L., 19th century French composer, **IX:** 4

Alsloot, Dennis, van, 17th century Dutch painter, **III:** 153, 188

Altafulla, Ubaldo-Antonio, early 19th century Italian composer, **IX:** 115; **X:** 34; **XII:** 55

Altamira, J., 19th century French composer, **IX:** 4

Altenburg, Johann Ernst, 1734–1801, writer on trumpet performance practice in 1671, **III:** 68, 117ff, 215; **IV:** 4, **VIII:** 301

Altenburg, Michael, 1584–1640 German composer, **VII:** 111, 144, 147

Amadino, Ricciardo, 16th and 17th century publisher in Venice, **VI:** 82, 89, 94, 98, 101ff, 105; **VII:** 188, 194, 201, 203ff, 206, 209

Amalie, Prinzessin von Preussen (sister to Frederick the Great), as composer, **VIII:** 301; **IX:** 143

Amantino, 18th century composer in Graf Pachta Harmonie Coll., **IV:** 22, fn. 10; **VIII:** 173 [(12) *Divertimenti* for Harmoniemusik]

Amat, José, 19th century French composer, **IX:** 4

Ambra, Francesco, d', playwright, 16th century, **II:** 130

Ambroz, Anton, 19th century German composer, conductor for K. K. Österreich 57. Linien-Inf. Reg. Grossherzog von Mecklenburg-Schwerin, **IX:** 146

Amette, Louis, 19th century French composer, **IX:** 4

Amillon, Édouard, 19th century English composer, **IX:** 263

Amirow, Fikret, b. 1922, Russian composer, **XII:** 72

Amner, composer in 17th century English pavan and galliard collection, **VII:** 20

Amon, Giovanni, 1763–1825, Italian composer, **XI:** 127

Amon, Johann Andreas, 1763–1825, German composer, **IX:** 146; **XII:** 10

Amourdedieu, Casimir, 19th century French composer, **IX:** 4

Amourdedieu, Pascal, 19th century French composer, **IX:** 4

Amsdorf, Bishop of Naumberg, [description of church music in 1542], **II:** 231

Amsfortius, Franciscus, 16th century composer, **VI:** 25

Amy, Gilbert, b. 1936 in Paris, composer, **XII:** 72

Anacker, M., 19th century Austrian composer, **IX:** 207

Ancot, Jean, 1779–1848, Belgium composer, **IX:** 259

Andreozzi, unknown composition arranged for Harmoniemusik by Courtin, **VIII:** 154

Andolfi, Guglielmo, 1847–1928, Italian composer for band, **X:** 173

André Johann, 1775–1842, German, as composer, **IX:** 146

André, Chelard, solfeggio, clarinet faculty of the 1792 Paris Conservatoire, **IV:** 156

André, Ernest, 19th century French composer, **IX:** 4

André, F., French serpent virtuoso in the Prince Regent band in London, **V:** 203

André, Johann, 1775–1842, German, as composer, **XI:** 3, 163, 181, 267

André, Johann, 18th and 19th century publisher in Offenbach, **IV:** 71, **VIII:** 4, 12, 63, 81ff, 89ff, 92ff, 94, 99ff, 103, 117ff. 135, 137, 145, 148, 158, 196, 216ff, 218ff, 220, 230, 246, 296, 304, 321, 331ff, 344, 353ff, 358; **IX:** 153, 155, 156, 163, 164, 183; **X:** 18, 100; **XI:** 14, 21, 41, 48, 54, 67, 84, 115, 127, 128, 148, 192, 209, 232, 306,321; **XII:** 10, 35, 39, 45, 51, 52, 53

André, Paul, 19th century French composer, **IX:** 4

Andreozzi, Gaetano, 1763–1826, Italian composer, **IX:** 263; **XI:** 3

Andrew, Enos, 19th century English composer, **IX:** 263

Androet, Cesare, 1827–1889, Italian composer, **X:** 174

Androux, Giovanni, 18th century Italian composer, **XI:** 181

Anfossi, Pasquale, 1727–1797, as composer for Harmoniemusik, **VIII:** 3, 362; **XI:** 4, 102

Angée, Pierre, faculty of the 1792 Paris Conservatoire, **IV:** 157

Angermaier, Christoph, early 17th Century German furniture maker, **III:** 4

Anguillar, Sante, ca. 1780–1860, Italian oboist and composer, **XI:** 102

Aniebas, J., 19th century English composer, **IX:** 263

Anna d'Orléans, niece to Louis XIV, **III:** 71

Anna-Vanni, Giuseppe, 19th century Italian composer, *Sinfonia* for band, **X:** 174

Anne of Austria, 1601–1666, queen consort of Navarre, visits Paris in 1664, **III:** 46

Anne of Prussia, 19th century, **IX:** 170

Anne of Russia, 17th century, **III:** 110

Annoscia, Enrico, 19th century Italian composer, **X:** 174

Anonymous, 15 original Italian works for Harmoniemusik, **VIII:** 362

Anonymous, 170 original English band compositions, **VIII:** 250

Anonymous, 177 opera arrangements for Harmoniemusik, **VIII:** 151

Anonymous, 18 original French works for band, **VIII:** 267

Anonymous, 194 Austrian-Bohemian original works for Harmoniemusik or band, **VIII:** 163

Anonymous, 257 original Swiss compositions for Harmoniemusik, **VIII:** 371ff

Anonymous, 275 Austrian works for band or Harmoniemusik, **IX:** 203ff

Anonymous, 454 original German works for Harmoniemusik or small band, **VIII:** 294

Anonymous, 643 German works for band or Harmoniemusik, **IX:** 143ff

Anonymous, *Alexandre et Campase de Larisse,* ballet arr. for Harmoniemusik, **VIII:** 154

Anonymous, *Ballo,* unknown arranger for Harmoniemusik, **VIII:** 158

Anonymous, *Beliebter Marsch,* unknown arranger for Harmoniemusik, **VIII:** 158

Anonymous, *Condrillon Romace,* unknown arranger for Harmoniemusik, **VIII:** 158

Anonymous, *dem bummen Gartner,* unknown arranger for Harmoniemusik, **VIII:** 155

Anonymous, *Der Quacksalber und die Zwerge*, arr. Triebensee for Harmonie, **VIII**: 156

Anonymous, *Die Eingebildenden Philosophen*, opera, arr. Wendt for Harmonie, **VIII**: 155

Anonymous, *Die Psyche*, arranged by Ruzni for Harmoniemusik, **VIII**: 156

Anonymous, *Die Tage der Gefahr*, opera arr. Triebensee for Harmoniemusik, **VIII**: 157

Anonymous, *Die Zween Anton*, opera, arranged for Harmoniemuisk, **VIII**: 157

Anonymous, four 18th century marches for band from Belgium, **VIII**: 248

Anonymous, *Fucheria e puntiglio* arr. Fuchs for Harmoniemusik, **VIII**: 155

Anonymous, *König Lear*, arranged by Blumenthal for Harmoniemusik, **VIII**: 156

Anonymous, *La Bianca e la Rolsa*, ballet, arranged by Wendt for Harmoniemusik, 155

Anonymous, *La morte di Virginia*, unknown arranger for Harmoniemusik, **VIII**: 156

Anonymous, *La Sposa Persiana*, ballet, arr. Wendt for Harmoniemusik, **VIII**: 157

Anonymous, *Le Baal Angloise*, ballet, unknown arranger for Harmoniemusik, **VIII**: 155

Anonymous, *Le Festin de Piere*, ballet, unknown arranger for Harmoniemusik, **VIII**: 155

Anonymous, *Le fête flamende*, ballet, unknown arranger for Harmoniemuisk, **VIII**: 155

Anonymous, *Le Lavandajie de Cittera*, arranged by Wendt for Harmoniemusik, **VIII**: 156

Anonymous, *Les Horaces*, ballet, unknown arranger for Harmoniemusik, **VIII**: 155

Anonymous, *Messellan*, arranged J. Wratni for Harmoniemusik, **VIII**: 156

Anonymous, *Rochus Pumpernickel*, unknown arranger for Harmoniemusik, **VIII**: 157

Anonymous, *Rundtanz aus Figaro*, ballet, unknown arranger for Harmoniemusik, **VIII**: 155

Anonymous, *Sposalizio Allegro*, unknown arranger for Harmoniemusik, **VIII**: 158

Anonymous, Valses, '*Le bon gout*,' unknown arranger for Harmoniemusik, **VIII**: 155

Anonymous, *Vénus et Adonis*, arr. Vanderhagen for Harmoniemusik, **VIII**: 157

Anschütz, Johann, 1772–1856, German composer, **IX**: 146

Anschüz, G., 19th century German composer, **IX**: 146

Ansel, M., 19th century English composer, **IX**: 263

Anselm, Carl, Prince of Thurn und Taxis in Regensburg, **IV**: 58

Anselmo, 16th century composer, **VI**: 30

Ansiaux, Hubert, 1781–1826, Belgium composer, **IX**, 259; **XI**: 6

Antegnati, ?, composer in 1608 Venetia canzoni collection, **VII**: 208

Antegnati, Const., 17th century Italian composer, **VII**: 145, 208

Anton, C., 19th century German composer, **IX**: 146

Antoni, ?, 19th century French composer, **IX**: 2, 5

Antoni, director of Prussian army music school, **IV**: 90

Antonie Brumel, 1460–1613, French composer, **VI**: 11

Antonio, Grotto, 1753–1831, Italian composer, **IX**:115

Apel, ?, 19th century composer, **IX**: 5, 146

Apel, Jakob, 16th century publisher in Leipzig, **VI**: 65

Apell, David (pseudo. Capelli), 1754–1832, German composer, **IX**: 146

Apell, Johann, 1754–1832, German, (12) *Notturni* for winds, **VIII**: 301

Apostel, Hans Erick, b. 1901, German composer, **XII**: 72

Appel, K., 19th century German composer, **IX**: 146

Appenzeller, Benedictus, 1480–1558, Franco-Flemish composer, **VI:** 120, 122

Applin, W. T., 19th century English composer, **IX:** 263

Apuleius, 2nd century AD historian, **I:** 17

Arban, J. J., 1825–1889, French composer, **IX:** 5; **X:** 65

Arbau, Thoinot, 1520–1595, French author of *Orchésographie*, 1588, **II:** 46, 80, 181ff, 252;
   III: 138; **VI:** 56

Arbuckle, John, 19th century English composer, **IX:** 264; **X:** 116

Arcadelt, Jacques, 1507–1568, Flemish composer, **VI:** 25, 30, 49, 63, 114

Archambeau, 19th century English composer, **IX:** 264

Archduke Joseph, Palatine, visits Eisenstadt in 1797, **IV:** 4

Archduke of Austria, (1716), **III:** 123

Ardemanio, Casare, Italian composer in 1617 collection of canzoni, **VII:** 204

Ardespin, Melchior, 1643–1717, German composer of 2 ballet suites, **VII:** 147

Arezzo Della Targia, Giambattista, 19th century Italian composer, **X:** 174

Argoin, G., 19th century French composer, **IX:** 5

Aria, Giuseppe, 19th century Italian composer for band, **X:** 174

Aribert, Archibishop of Milan, 11th century, **I:** 121

Arici, Marco, 1778–1827, Italian composer, **X:** 34

Ariosto, Ludovico, 1474–1533, Italian poet, **III:** 46

Aristides Quintellianus, Music theorist, 2nd – 3rd century AD, **I:** 45

Aristophanes, ancient Greek playwright, **IX:** 27

Aristotle, 4th century BC, **I:** 29, 30, 33, 34, 39, 45

Armon, ?, 19th century composer, **XI:** 6

Arnaud, C. T., 19th century French composer, **IX:** 5

Arnaud, J., 19th century French composer, **IX:** 115

Arnaud, P.-J., 19th century French composer, **IX:** 5

Arnaud. E., 19th century French composer, **IX:** 5

Arndt, C., 19th century German composer, **IX:** 147

Arnkiel, T., auther of a 1683 treatise on the use of horns in music, **XI:** 164

Arnold, F. W., 19th century German composer, **IX:** 147

Arnold, Johann, 1652, German composer, music for 5 winds, **VII:** 111

Arnold, Samuel, English composer, 1740–1802, **XI:** 6

Arnoldi, Joseph, 19th century French composer, **IX:** 6

Arnould, Eugene, 19th century French composer **IX:** 6

Arnoux, A., 19th century French composer, **IX:** 6

Arrivabene, Andrea, 1540 publisher of 4-part ensemble music, **VI:** 92

Arsaut, Gabriel, 19th century French composer, **IX:** 6

Arscott, Julius, 19th century English composer, **IX:** 264

Arsinoe, Queen of Egypt, 3rd century BC, **I:** 17

Artaria, 18th and 19th century publisher in Vienna, **VIII:** 6, 112ff, 209, 218ff, 226; **IX:** 246;
   XI: 48, 58, 64, 73, 80, 84, 134, 138, 234, 247

Arthopius, Balthasar, ca. 1490–1534, German composer, **VI:** 63

Artique, P., 19th century French composer, **IX:** 6

Artôt, ?, 19th century French composer, **XI:** 286, 309

Artus, ?, composer in 1660 German collection of dance music, **VII:** 145

Artus, Alexandre, 19th century French composer, **IX:** 1, 6

Arundal, Earl of, 17th century English noble, **II:** 46, **III:** 91

Arundall, Robert (Gallway, Lord Viscount), 18th century composer for Harmoniemusik, **VIII:** 251

Asch, Georg, 19th century English composer, **IX:** 264; **X:** 118

Asche, W., 19th century German composer, conductor 1st Hanseatischen Regiment, Hamburg, **IX:** 147

Aschenbrenner, ?, composer in Erlebach collection of Hautboisten music, **VII:** 156

Aschenbrenner, Christian Heinrich, 1654–1732, composer, **VII:** 7, 147

Aschenbrenner, Georg, 1673, German composer of ensemble dance music, **VII:** 147

Ascher, Joseph, 1829–1869, English composer, **IX:** 264

Ascherl, ?, *Marsch* for Harmoniemusik, **VIII:** 174

Ascolese, Raffele, 1855–1923, Italian composer for band, **X:** 174

Ashley, John, 18th century English composer, **XI:** 182

Ashley, Josiah, *Royal Dorsetshire March*, 1797, for Harmoniemusik, **VIII:** 252

Ashton, Hugh, d. 1522, composer of Hornpype, **VI:** 35ff

Ashton, T., 19th century French composer, **IX:** 6

Ashwell, 16th century composer, **VI:** 35

Asioli, Bonifazio, 1769–1832, Italian composer, **IX:** 115; **X:** 175

Asioli, Luigi, 18th century composer, **XI:** 6

Asioli, Raffaele, 1817–1899, Italian composer, **X:** 175

Asioli,Bonifazio, 1769–1832, Italian composer, **XI:** 256

Asopodorus of Palius, ancient Greek professional aulos player, **I:** 39

Aspelmayr, Franz, 1728–1785, composer in Bohemia, **IV:** 22, fn. 9 & 10, 24, 41; **VIII:** 163, 174ff [76 Partittas]

Asselin, Th., 19th century French composer, **IX:** 6

Assman, Ernest, timpani, clarinet faculty of the 1792 Paris Conservatoire, **IV:** 156

Assuni, Ghillini, late 18th century composer, **XI:** 6

Astoin, ?., 19th century French composer, **IX:** 6

Astorga, Jean, 18th century English composer, **XI:** 183

Athalanta, Greek goddess, **VII:** 196

Athenaeus, 2nd century BC historian, **I:** 16, 29, 39, 40 [on lost aulos treatises], 49

Attaingnant, Pierre, 1494–1552, Paris publisher, **II:** 67ff, 180; **VI:** 38ff, 40, 42ff, 44ff,47, 50ff

Atterburg, Kurt Magnus, b. 1887, Swedish composer, **XII:** 123

Attwood, Thomas, b. 1765, English, (6) works for Harmoniemusik, **VIII:** 252

Atys, ?. 18th century French composer, **XI:** 228

Au grand magazine de musique, 18th century publisher in Amsterdam, **VIII:** 159

Auber, Daniel François Espirit, 1782–1871, French composer, **V**: 63, 70, 73, 134, 148; **IX**: 28; **XII**: 218

Auber, Daniel, 1782–1871, composer of works arranged for Harmoniemusik, **VIII**: 3 [*La Bergère Châtelaine*]; 4 [*La Maçon, Emma, La Maçon, La Muette de Portici, La Neige*]; 5 [*Le Duc d'Olonne, Le Philtre, Le Serment*], Unidentified works, 151

Auber, Daniel, 1782–1871, composer of works arranged for band, **IX**: 163 [*le concert à la Cour*]; 173 [*La Fiancée*]; 196 [*la Muette de Portici*]; 254 [Fra Diavolo]; unidentified works arranged for band, 142, 166, 174; **X**: 105 [unidentified work arranged by Lindpainter]

Auberlen, Louis, 19th century German composer, **X**: 95

Aubert, Aug., 19th century French composer, **IX**: 6

Aubert, Charles, 19th century French composer, **IX**: 1, 6

Aubert, Jacques, 1689–1753 French composer, **XI**: 183

Aubin, ?, 19th century French composer, **IX**: 7

Aubréy du Boulley, Prudent, 1796–1870, French composer **IX**: 7

Aubry, Abel, 19th century French composer, **IX**: 7

Audoir, Barthélemy, 19th century French composer, **IX**: 7

Audran, ?, composer included in 19th century English band collections, **X**: 115, 116

Aufschnaiter, composer in Erlebach collection of Hautboisten music, **VII**: 156

Aufsess., B., 19th century German composer, **IX**: 147

Augé, Claudo, 19th century French composer, **IX**: 7

August der Starke, 1670–1733, King of Poland, **III**: 124, 126

August, Elector of Saxony, 16th century, **II**: 113

August, Prince, 19th century, as composer, **IX**: 141

Augustanus, Jacobus Ellendus, merchant, collector of instruments, **II**: 144

Augustin de Verona, cornettist, 16th century, **II**: 90

Augustine of Augsburg, 15th century trombonist, **I**: 125

Augustus II of Poland, d. 1735, **III**: 110

Augustus, Rudolphus, 17th century Duke of Braunsweig und Lüneburg, **VII**: 148

Aulagnier, 19th century publisher in Paris, **IX**: 25

Auzende, Ange-Marie, 19th century French composer, **IX**: 7

Avalione, Vincenzo, 19th century Italian composer, *Sinfonia* for band, **X**: 175

Avenarius, Thomas, German composer of dance music (1630–1638), **VII**: 148

Avertal, ?, 18th century (Viennese) (6) *Parthias* for Harmoniemusik, **VIII**: 177

Avoni, Petronio, b. 1790, Italian, as arranger, **X**: 175; **XI**: 128

Avseri de Chistofano, Giuseppe, 19th century Italian composer for band, **X**: 175

Azémar, ?, 19th century French composer, **IX**: 7

Azerets, ?, 19th century German composer, **IX**: 147

Babb, 18th century publisher in London, **XI:** 208

Babell, William, d. 1722, English flautist & composer, **XI:** 6, 103

Baccherini, Francesco, 19th century Italian composer for band, **X:** 175

Bacchius, 16th century composer, **VI:** 108, 123

Bach, Chr., 19th century German composer, **IX:** 147

Bach, Johann Christian, 1735–1782, German composer in London, as composer for band,
    IV: 115; **VIII:** 302ff [(10) *Symphonies*, (6) *Divertissements*, (9) *Marches* for Harmoniemusik]

Bach, Johann Sebastian, 1685–1750, **III:** 13, 59, 66, 160, 162, 174; **X:** 5; **XI:** 6, 7, 103, 126,
    183, 228; **XII:** 89 [fugue scored for band by Holst]; 191 [arranged by Strasser]; 199 [arranged
    for band by Stokowsky]; 200, 202, 213, 214, 215

Bach, Johann Christoph Friedrich, 1732–1795, *Sepett* for Harmoniemusik, **VIII:** 302

Bach, Karl P. E., 1714–1788, **VII:** 117 [as editor]; **VIII:** 303ff (19) *Marches*, (6) *Sonatas* for
    Harmoniemusik; **XI:** 7, 103, 116, 150, 183, 243, 247, 254, 320

Bach, Otto, 19th century Austrian composer, **IX:** 207; **XI:** 254

Bach, Pierre, fl. 1800–1828, German composer, **IX:** 147

Bach, Wilhelm Friedemann, 1710–1784, German composer, **XI:** 183

Bach, Wilhelm Friedrich, 1759–1845, German composer, **IX:** 147

Bachelet, Alfred, 1864–1944, French composer, **XI:** 164

Bachimont, H., 19th century French composer, **IX:** 7

Bachmann, 19th century publisher in Hannover, **IX:** 155

Bachmann, Anton, 1716–1800, German composer for Frederick the Great, **IV:** 89;
    VIII: 303ff (9) *Marches, Allegro and Andante* for Harmoniemusik,

Bachmayer, ?, 19th century Austrian composer, **IX:** 208

Backofen, Enrico, 1768–1839, German composer, **XI:** 128

Backofen, Johann Georg, 1768–1830, works for Harmoniemusik, **VIII:** 304

Badart, Louis, 19th century French composer, **IX:** 7

Badings, Henk, 20th century German composer, **XII:** 202

Bado, Giuseppe, 19th century Italian composer for Harmoniemusik, **X:** 176

Baehr, ?, 19th century German composer, **IX:** 180

Baer, F., arr., *Pièces d'Harmonie*, a collection for Harmoniemusik, **VIII:** 158

Baethen, J., publisher of 1554 book of instrumental partitas, **VI:** 106

Bagarre, A., 19th century French composer, **IX:** 7

Bagge, Selmar, 1823–1896, German composer, **IX:** 147

Bagnat, ?, 19th century French composer, **IX:** 8

Baier, ?, composer included in a 1875 English collection of band music, **X:** 114

Baille, F., 19th century French composer, **IX:** 8

Baille, Gabriel, 19th century French composer, **IX:** 8

Baille, Martial, 19th century French composer, **IX:** 8

Bailleaux, 19th century publisher at Paris, **XI:** 286

Baillie, R. Miss, composer, 1795, for Harmoniemusik, **VIII:** 252

Baillon, Ad. Victor, 19th century French composer, conductor Musique au 127e, **IX:** 8

Baioni, Massimo, 19th century Italian composer for band, **X:** 176

Bajus, Z., 19th century French composer, **IX:** 8

Balay, Guillaume, 19th century French composer, conductor, Garde Républicaine Band, **IX:** 8

Balbi, Aloysii, 1606 Italian composer, church music for voices and winds, **VII:** 194

Baldan, Angelo, 1747–1804, *Credos* for voices and winds, 1789, **VIII:** 362ff; **XI:** 288, 304

Baldessari, Pietro, 17th century (?) Italian composer, **XI:** 159

Baldiani, F., 19th century French composer, **IX:** 8

Balduin, Noel, 1480–1530, German composer, **VI:** 63, 119

Baldwine, John, d. 1615, London, composer of ensemble works, **VII:** 29

Balfe, Michael, 1808–1870, Irish composer, **IX:** 264

Ball, S., 19th century English composer, **IX:** 264

Ballard, 18th century publisher in Paris, **VII:** 87, 93; **XI:** 47, 56

Ballay, Guillaume, 19th century French composer, **XI:** 317

Ballicourt, ?, 18th century celebrated flautist in London ca. 1744, **XI:** 8

Ballmüller, E., 19th century German composer, **IX:** 147

Balocke, E., 19th century French composer, **IX:** 8

Balzac, 19th century French novelist, **XII:** 219

Balzer, 19th century publisher in Vienna, **VIII:** 73

Banchi, Giuseppe, 19th century Italian composer for band, **X:** 176

Banchieri, Adriano, 1568–1634, Italian composer, **II:** 245; **III:** 220; **VI:** 85, 93; **VII:** 194ff

Bangratz, A., 19th century French composer, **IX:** 9

Banister, John, 1630–1679, English composer, **III:** 179; **VII:** 29

Banner, John, (1805) English composer, **IX:** 264

Banta, Frank, 19th century English composer, **IX:** 264

Bantock, Sir Granville, 1868–1946, English, composer, **XII:** 72

Banwart, Jakob, d. 1657, German composer of Tafelmusik, **VII:** 148

Baragatti, Romeo, 19th century Italian composer, **X:** 176

Barat, J. Ed., 19th century French composer, **IX:** 9

Barbandt, Carl, 1716–1775, German composer, **IV:** 105, fn. 2; **XI:** 103, 184, 235

Barbandt, Charles, German composer of 1652 ens. 'in the newest Italian manner,' **VII:** 148

Barbe, Anthony, choral master in Antwerp, 1550, **II:** 214; **VI:** 63, 119ff

Barber, Samuel, b. 1910, American composer, **XII:** 72

Barberis, Pier, 19th century Italian composer, funeral music for Ponchielli, **X:** 176

Barbet, C., 19th century French composer, **IX:** 9

Barbion, 16th century composer, **VI:** 109ff, 120, 123

Barbot, Emile, bassoonist in the 1910 Barrère Ensemble in NYC, **XII:** 214

Barclay, Alexander, author of *Ship of Fools* [1508], **II:** 148

Bardin, V., 19th century French composer, **IX:** 9

Bargaglia, Scipion, composer in 1587, **VI:** 93

Barges, composer in 1551 collection of 3-part canzoni, **VI:** 92

Bargnani, Ottavio, 1570–1627, Italian composer, **III:** 220; **VII:** 194

Bariolla, Ottavio, 16th century composer, **VI:** 93

Barley, Willim, 16th century publisher in London, **VI:** 33

Bärman, F., 18th century German clarinetist, **XI:** 128 [biographical note]

Bärmann, Carl, 1810–1885, German Clarinetist & composer, **XI:** 139 [dedication], 184

Bärmann, Heinrich, 1784–1847, German composer, clarinetist, **X:** 96

Barner, Major von, 19th century cavalry leader in Berlin, **V:** 24

Baron, 20th century publisher in New York, **XII:** 139

Baron, Ernest, 1696–1760, German composer, **XI:** 8

Baron, Eugéne, 19th century French composer, **IX:** 9

Baronville, ?, French composer (2) *Ordonnance des dragoons*, 1756, band, **VIII:** 268

Barra, political hero of the French Revolution, **VIII:** 270

Barraud, E., 19th century French composer, **IX:** 9

Barre, Antonio, 16th century composer, **VI:** 30

Barreca, D., 19th century Italian orchestrator, **X:** 205

Barrère, George, 1876–1944, flutist in Paris and New York, **XII:** 212ff, 216

Barrés, ?, 19th century French composer, **IX:** 9

Barret, 19th century oboist in London, **V:** 5

Barrett, Emmeline, 19th century English composer, **IX:** 264

Barrett, R., 19th century English composer, **IX:** 264

Barrier, A., 19th century French composer, **IX:** 9

Barrows, John, b. 1913, American hornist, **XII:** 73

Barsanti, Francesco, 1690–1772, Italian composer, **XI:** 8

Bárta, Josef, 18th century composer in Graf Pachta Harmonie Coll., **IV:** 22, fn. 10

Bartali, Antonio, late 17th century, instrumental sonatas, **VII:** 148

Bartel, trumpeter for 19th century Duke of Sondershausen, **V:** 185, fn. 2

Barth Christian, 1735–1809, as composer and arranger of works for Harmoniemusik and band, **VIII:** 59, 92, 94, 137; 304 [*Grand Sinfonie* for band]; **IX:** 9

Barth, ?, 19th century leader of the Civic Band in Leipzig, **V:** 23

Barth, Crisstiano, 19th century (?) German composer, **XI:** 104

Barth, Freiderick, b. 1813, German composer, **IX:** 147

Barthe, Adrien, 1828–1898, composer, **V:** 153

Barthel, K., 19th century German composer, **IX:** 148

Barthélémon, François-Hippolyte, 1741–1808, band composer in London, **IV:** 135; **VIII:** 252 [Prince of Württemberg March]

Barthmann, Charles, 19th century English composer, **IX:** 264

Bartholomeus, ?, 19th century English composer, **IX:** 264

Bartholomeus, P., 19th century French composer, **IX:** 9

Bartolini, composer in 1608 Venetia canzoni collection, **VII:** 208

Bartolomeas, ?, composer included in a 1875 English collection of band music, **X:** 114

Bartolomeo, P. F., 1638, bassoonist under Archduke Leopold, canzoni, etc., **VII:** 185

Bartolucci, Mariano, 19th century Italian composer, **X:** 176

Bary, A., 19th century French composer, IX: 21

Baryzehnikoff, ?, composer included in a 1871 English collection, X: 113

Baschieri, Giovanni, 19th century Italian composer for band, X: 176

Basquit, Heinrich, 19th century English composer, IX: 264

Bassano, Augustine, composer in 1613–1619 Tregian ensemble collection, VII: 13, 23

Bassano, G., composer in James I band library, 1603–1665, VII: 13

Bassano, Giovanni, d. 1617, cornettist and conductor at St. Mark's, Venice, II: 244; VI: 88ff

Bassano, Hieronymo, ca. 1600–1630, composer of ensemble works in England, VII: 29

Bassus, Jean, 19th century French/German composer, IX: 148; XI: 305, 316

Baston, Edm., 19th century French composer, IX: 10

Baston, Josquin, 1515–1576, Franco-Flemish composer, VI: 25, 107ff, 109, 114, 118ff, 123

Bate, Stanley, b. 1913, English, composer, XII: 73

Bateman, Robert, English composer in 1621 collection of ens. music, VII: 25, 166

Batiste, Édouard, 1820–1876, composer, IX: 10; XII: 202

Batka, Edvard, 19th century Czech (?) composer, XI: 311

Batley, Thomas, composer included in a 1893 English collection, X: 116

Baton, Charles, d. after 1754, French composer in 1733 ensemble Collection, VII: 84

Battagh, Mario of Rimini, 15th century, VI: 8

Battaglia, Giacinto, 1803–1861, 19th century Italian composer, X: 177

Battalus, Prince (17th century), III: 124

Batthyány, Prince Joseph von, Cardinal of Hungary, 1776–1784, IV: 33

Battiany, Graff Joseph of Hungary, 19th century [dedication] by Druschetzky, XII: 46

Battiferi, Luigi, 1762, music for cornett consort, VII: 111

Battino, ?, 18th century Italian composer, XI: 8, 184

Baucourt, A., 19th century French composer, IX: 10

Bauderuc, Jouan, 19th century French composer, IX: 10

Baudin, Henry, 19th century French composer, IX: 10

Baudron, Antoine, 1743–1834, French, 5th *Suite du Concert Militaire*, Harmonie, VIII: 268

Bauduin, ?, 1827–1835, director of civic band school in Douai, V: 148

Bauer, 17th century publisher in Nürnberg, VII: 153, 158

Bauer, Alois, 1794–1872 German composer, XI: 129

Bauer, Conrad, 17th century publisher in Nürnberg, VI: 66

Bauer, Marion, b. 1897, American, composer, XII: 73

Bauldouyn, 16th century composer, VI: 64

Baulduino, Domenico, 1711–1779, Italian composer, XI: 8

Bauller, A., de, 19th century French composer, IX: 11

Baumann, Georg, 16th century publisher in Erfurt, VI: 65, 72ff

Baumberg, J. C. 18th century, German composer, XI: 184, 271

Baumgarten, ?, German band leader in London, IV: 106

Baumgarten, C. Gotthilf, 1741–1813 works for military trumpet ensemble, VIII: 304

Baumgarten, Carl, 18th century composer, XI: 8, 104, 129, 285

Baumgärtner, 18th and 19th century publisher in Leipzig, **XI:** 35, 198

Baussnera, Waldeman, 1866–1931, composer, **XII:** 73, 123

Bausteder, ?, German Baroque composer, **X: 5**

Bavagnoli, Manlio, 19th century Italian composer, *Sinfonia Pastorale* for band, **X:** 177

Bax, Arnold, 1883–1953, English composer, **XII:** 123

Baxberg, C. L., 19th century German composer, **XI:** 278

Bayard, 18th century publisher in Paris, **VIII:** 268

Bayer, ?, composer (in Prague?) *Ländler* for Harmoniemusik, **VIII:** 178

Bazin, Emmanuel, 1816–1878, French composer, **IX:** 11

Bazin, François, 1816–1878, Italian composer, **XI:** 256

Beatrice d'Este of Ferrara, 15th century, **I:** 231, 236

Beaucé, 19th century publisher in Paris, **VIII:** 29; **IX:** 48, 61

Beaucherne, Raphaël, 19th century French composer, **IX:** 11

Beaudonck, L.-J., 19th century French composer, **IX:** 10

Beaujoyeulx, Ballthasar de, French composer for Henry III of France, **VI:** 55

Beauregard, François, French oboist in Berlin in 1681, **III:** 6

Beauvarlet-Charpentier, Jacques, 1766–1834, composer, **IX:** 11

Bécher, L., 19th century French composer, **IX:** 11

Bechler, Johann, 1784–1857, American composer, **IX:** 137

Beck, 19th century publisher in Vienna, **IX:** 247

Beck, Conrad, b. 1901, Swiss, composer, **XII:** 73, 123

Beck, Johann, German composer of 1666 collection of dance music, **VII:** 149

Beck, Peter, 19th century German composer, **IX:** 148

Becker, ?, 19th century English composer, **IX:** 265

Becker, 18th century publisher in Leipzig, **VIII:** 331

Becker, Carl, 16th century composer in German dance music ['Duke Moritz'], **VI:** 76

Becker, Dietrich, d. 1679, 1668 'Instumental Harmonia' collection, **VII:** 149

Becker, Heinrich, 19th century German composer, **IX:** 148

Becker, P., 19th century French composer, **IX:** 11

Becker, Vincenz, 19th century German composer, **IX:** 148

Beckerath, Alfred von, b. 1901, German composer, **XII:** 73

Beckford, Mons. De, 18th century French, *Marche* for Harmoniemusik, **VIII:** 253

Beckford, William, 1759–1844, student of Mozart, *March* for Harmoniemusik, **VIII:** 253

Bédard, ?, 19th century French composer, **IX:** 11

Bédard, Jean-Baptiste, 1765–1815, French, *Potpourri Connus* for Harmonie, **VIII:** 268

Bedford, Herbert, 1867–1945, English composer, **XII:** 124

Beecham, Sir Thomas, 20th century English conductor, **XII:** 217

Beecke, Ignaz, 1733–1803, (2) *Partitas* for Harmonie with flutes, **VIII:** 304

Beecke, Ignaz, as arranger of works for Harmoniemusik, **VIII:** 22, 149

Beecke, Notger, 1733–1803, German composer, **XI:** 9

Beer, Alfred, 19th century English composer, **IX:** 265

Beer, Johann, 1655–1700, Konzertmeister at Weissenfels, **III:** 60, 171

Beer, Joseph, 1744–1811 [here as Bärr], *Variatione* for Harmoniemusik, **VIII:** 178; **XI:** 129 [biographical note], 146

Beer, ?, performed Beethoven Quintet with Beethoven in 1798, **IV:** 32, fn. 67

Beethoven, Ludwig van, 1770–1827, German composer, **III:** 103; **IV:** 32 fn. 67, 52ff [on his study with Haydn]; **V:** 6, 19 fn. 61, 34, 35, 41 fn. 3 [*Siegessinfonie*], 48, 81, 86 [Rimsky-Korsakov as arr.], 97, 108, 114, 132, 150, 153, 181, 183 fn. 21, 187, 202, 203, 205; **IX:** 208ff [original works for band and winds]; **XI:** 144 [autograph score owned by Beethoven]; **XII:** 45 [unidentified march by unidentified arranger]; 61, 147, 197, 202, 213, 214, 215

Beethoven, Ludwig van, 1770–1827, composer of works arranged for Harmoniemusik, **VIII:** 5 [*Egmont Music*]; 6 [*Fidelio, Quintet,* Op. 16, *Septet,* Op. 20, *Sestetto*]; 7 [*Sonata pathétique, Symphony Nr. 1, Symphony Nr. 8, Trauer Marsch, Wellingtons Sieg*]

Beethoven, Ludwig van, works arranged for band, **IX:** 30 [*Third Symphony,* arr. Constant]; 51 [*Third Symphony* (second movement) arr. for band by R. Goueytes]; 78 [*Symphony Nr. 6,* arr. for band by Auguste Mimart]; 102 [*Quintet,* Op. 16, for piano and winds, arr. full band by F. Stoupan]; 113 [*Egmont Overture and March* (Fischer); *Leonore Overture* (Fischer); Marche Turque, *Ruines d'Athnes* (Fischer); 'Adagio,' *Sonata Pathetique* (Fischer); 'Allegretto,' *Sonate in Ut# Minor* (Lajarte); 'Andante,' *Symphony Nr. 5* (Grillet); 'Allegro,' *Symphony Nr. 6* (Fischer); 'Allegretto,' *Symphony Nr. 8* (Fischer); 180 [*Eggmunt Simphonie, Fidelio*]; 254 [*Egmont, Fidelio, Sonata,* Op. 27, *Wellingtons-Sieg*]; and unidentified works arranged for band, 28, 141, 254 [*Türkischer Marsch*]; **X:** 95 [*Septetti*]; 130 [*Symphony Nr. 1*]; 177 [*Symphony Nr. 1,* Andante; *Coriolan Overtureo, Egmont Overture, Symphony Nr. 4,* Adagio; *Symphony Nr. 5,* Andante; *Patetica Sonata,* Adagio]; 178 [*Symphony Nr. 3,* Funeral march; *Symphony Nr. 9,* first movement; *Fidelio Overture; Septet*]; 254 [*Fidelio*]

Beffroy de Regny, 19th century composer, arranged for Harmoniemusik, **VIII:** 153

Beglarian, Grant, 20th century American composer, **XII:** 202

Behr, Franz, 1837–1898, German composer, **IX:** 148

Behred, Fritz, b. 1889, Berlin composer, **XII:** 74

Behrens, trombonist in band of George IV, **V:** 203, fn. 10

Beinet, ?, 18th century French (3) *Suites* for Harmoniemusik, **VIII:** 268

Beinet, ?, as arranger for Harmoniemusik, **VIII:** 153ff

Bekker, Johannes, b. 1826, Dutch composer, **IX:** 125

Bela, ?, composer included in a 1874 English collection of band music, **X:** 113

Belcke, Friedrich, 1795–1874, German composer, **IX:** 148

Belderbusch, Kaspar Anton von, maintained Harmoniemusik in 1783, **IV:** 51

Belin, Guillaume, 16th century composer, **VI:** 44ff, 48ff

Bellanda, Lodovico, fl. 1593–1613, Italian composer, **VI:** 93

Bellasio, composer in 1600 dance collection published in Heidelberg, **VII:** 180

Belle, Jan, 16th century Italian composer, **VI:** 114

Bellère, Jean, 16th century publisher in Antwerpen, **VI:** 110, 114ff, 124

Bellermann, Konstantin, 1696–1758, composer, **XI:** 9, 125

Belli, Sandre, 19th century Italian composer, **IX:** 115; **X:** 177

Bellini, 19th century Italian opera composer, **V:** 170, 180

Bellini, Gentile, 15th century Italian painter, **I:** 127

Bellini, Vincenzo, 1801–1835, Italian composer, **IX:** 38; **XII:** 55

Bellini, Vincenzo, 1801–1835 composer of works arranged for Harmoniemusik, **VIII:** 8 [*I Capuleti e i Montecchi, La Straniera, Bianca e Gernando*; 9 [*Breatrice di Tenda, I Puritani di Scozia, La Sonnambula, Norma*]

Bellini, Vincenzo, 1801–1835 works arranged for band, **IX:** 122 [*La Sonnambula*]; 254 [*Montechi e Capuleti, Norma, I Puritani di Scozia*]; 266 [*Norma*]; and an unidentified works, 253, 254; **X:** 105 [unidentified work arranged by Lindpainter]; 170 [*Beatrice di Tenda*, unidentified arranger]; 192 [*Norma*, arranged by Petrali]; 254 [*Norma*, arranged by Vessella]

Bellinzini, Paolo, 1690–1757, Italian composer, **XI:** 9

Bellmann, 19th century publisher in Dresden, **IX:** 147, 175

Belloli, 19th century Maestro nel IR Conservatorio di Musica, Milano, as arr., **IX:** 122, 257

Belloli, Agostino, 1778–1838, Italian composer for winds and band, **VIII:** 157 [*Vitelius Maximus*, arr. for Harmoniemusik]; **X:** 177

Bellon, J., 19th century French composer, **IX:** 11

Bellonci, von Leidisdorf, 19th century composer, **XI:** 164

Bellroy de Reigny, arranged for band, **IX:** 113

Belotti, Giuseppe, 19th century Italian composer, church works with band, **X:** 179ff

Belval, E., 19th century French composer, **IX:** 11

Belville, Edward, 19th century English composer, **IX:** 265

Bém, Josef, 18th century composer in Graf Pachta Harmonie Coll., **IV:** 22, fn. 10

Bém, Vaclav, 18th century composer in Prague, *Parthia* for Harmoniemusik, **VIII:** 178

Bénard, ?, 19th century French composer, **IX:** 11

Bénard, Jean, 'king' of minstrels in Paris in 1537, **II:** 179

Benda, ?, 18th century German composer, **XI:** 249

Benda, ?, 18th century, *Dragoner-Marsch* for Harmoniemusik, **VIII:** 305

Benda, Franz, 1709–1786, Czech composer, **III:** 131

Benda, Frederic, 1752–1792, German composer, **XI:** 9

Benda, Georg, 1722–1795, German composer, **XI: 9**

Benda, Georg, Baroque German composer for voices and winds, **VII:** 122

Benda, Hans, George, d. 1757, German composer, **XI:** 9, 184

Bender, conductor of the Guides, **V:** 73, fn. 24, 155

Bender, H., 19th century German, (6) *Pièces für Kavalleriemusik*, **VIII:** 305

Bender, V., 19th century French composer, **IX:** 12

Bendinelli, Cesare, famous Baroque trumpeter, composer, **II:** 264, **III:** 227

Bendusi, Francesco, d. 1553, Italian composer, **VI:** 89

Benedict, Sir Julius, 1804–1885, English composer, **IX:** 265; **X:** 118

Benedictus, (Appenzeller?), 16th century composer, **VI:** 39,63, 109ff 113, 119

Benedikt, Walter, 20th century Austrian composer, **XI:** 9; **XII:** 74

Benegger, Antonio, 18th century German composer, **XI:** 10

Benelli, Antonio, d. 1830, Italian composer, **XI:** 10

Benjamin, 19th century publisher in Hamburg, **IX:** 182

Benleb, bassoonist in the 19th century Duke of Sondershausen Harmonie, **V:** 185, fn. 2

Bennet, C. W., 19th century English composer, **IX:** 265

Bennet, John, ca. 1599–1614, English composer, **VII:** 30

Bennett, 18th century publisher in London, **XI:** 37, 198

Benoist, G (C), 19th century French composer, **IX:** 12

Benoist, Nicolo, b. ca. 1510, composer, **VI:** 63, 92

Benoit, Petrus, 1834–1901, Belgium composer, **IX:** 259; **XI:** 10

Benser, J. D., 18th century, German composer, **XI:** 10

Benson, Warren, 20th century American composer, **XII:** 20

Bentley, W., composer included in a 1891 English collection of band music, **X:** 117

Bentzon, Jorgen, b. 1897, Danish composer, **XII:** 124

Bentzon, Niels, b. 1919, Danish composer, **XII:** 74, 125

Benz, D., 19th century Austrian composer, **IX:** 209

Beraud, G., 19th century French composer, **IX:** 12

Berault, 18th century publisher in Paris, **XI:** 96, 204

Bérault, Jean-Baptiste, père et fils, in 1768–77 Les Grands Hautbois, **IV:** 64, fn. 4

Berault, Mme, 18th century publisher in Paris, **VIII:** 268, 291, 314

Berbiguier, Tranquillo, 1782–1838 French flautist, student of Berton, **XI:** 10 [biograhical information]

Berchem, Jacob van, 1505–1567, Franco-Flemish composer, **VI:** 25,49, 92, 109ff, 114

Berdic, royal minstrel, 1086, England, **I:** 182

Beretta, Giovanni, 19th century Italian composer, **X:** 182

Beretta, Ludovico, 1604 Italian composer of canzoni, **VII:** 195

Berezovsky, Nicolay, b. 1900, Russian composer, **XII:** 74, 125

Berg & Neuber, 16th century publishers in Nürnberg, **VI:** 64

Berg, Adam, 16th century publisher in Munich, **VI:** 65, 67, 69, 73ff

Berg, Johann, 16th century publisher in Erben, **VI:** 62, 66

Bergen, 17th century publisher in Dresden, **VII:** 157

Bergen, Gimel, 16th century Dresden publisher, **VI:** 72, 74

Berger, Andreas, 1609 canzona collection, **VII:** 150

Berger, Ludwig, 1777–1839, German composer, **IX:** 148

Berger, Martin, composer in 1622 German collection of dance music, **VII:** 145

Berger, Theodor, b. 1905, Austrian composer, **XII:** 75

Bergmann, Eduard, 19th century English composer, **IX:** 265

Bergs, Johanna, widow of Dietrich Gerlach, 16th century German publisher, **VI:** 73ff

Bergson, M., 19th century English composer, **IX:** 265

Berka, Frantisek, 19th century Austrian composer, **IX:** 209

Berlioz, Hector, 1803–1869, **V:** 5, 7, 27ff, 37ff, 48 fn. 34, 66, 73, 86ff, 100, 109, 121, 138, 144ff, 164; **IX:** 12 [*Symphonie Funèbre et Triomphale* for band]; **X:** 65 [symphony for band]; **XII:** 202, 219ff

Berlioz, works arranged for band, **IX:** 196 [*Overture, Roman Carnaval*, arr. R. Lehmann]; 254 [*Damnation of Faust*]

Berlyn, Aron, 1817–1870, Dutch composer, **IX:** 125

Bernard, A., 19th century French composer, **IX:** 12

Bernard, Emile, 1843–1902, French composer, **IX:** 12

Bernardi, Enrico, 1838–1900, Italian composer, **X:** 182

Bernardi, Franz, b. 1767, Austrian flautist & composer, **XI:** 10

Bernardi, Stefano II, fl 1600–27, Verona, Salzburg, sonata for winds, **VII:** 186

Bernardi, Stefano, 1613 Italian composer for church sonatas, sinfonias, **VII:** 195ff

Bernardini, Marcello, (Marcello di Capua), *Furberia et Pontiglio*, opera?, arranged for Harmoniemusik, **VIII:** 13

Bernasconi, Andrea, 1706–1784, Italian composer, **XI:** 10

Berner, Friedrich, 1780–1827, German composer, **IX:** 148

Bernhard von Sachsen-Meiningen, 19th century, **X:** 110

Bernier, Antony, 19th century French composer, conductor, la Musique Municipale de Nantes, **IX:** 12

Bernier, René, b. 1890, Belgium composer, **XII:** 75

Bernini, Frediano, 19th century Italian composer, **IX:** 115

Bernn, Alexandre, 19th century French composer, **IX:** 12

Berr, ?, 19th century French composer, arranger, **IX:** 1, 12, 70, 183

Berr, Ennes, co-founder of the *Gymnase de Musiquec Mil.*, **V:** 62, 73

Berr, Frédéric, 1794–1848, German composer, **IX:** 148; **XI:** 129

Berr, Josef, 1744–1811, as arranger of works for Harmoniemusik, **VIII:** 5, 47, 69

Bertain, Jules, 19th century French composer, **IX:** 12

Bertali, Antonio, 1605–1669, composer, **VII:** 1, 186

Bertani, Natale, 19th century Italian composer, church works with winds, **X:** 182

Berten, Léon, 19th century French composer, **IX:** 13

Berth, ?, 19th century French composer, **IX:** 72

Berthold, ?, 19th century German composer, **IX:** 149

Bertie, Willoughby, 18th century English composer, **XI:** 184

Bertini, Ernesto, 19th century Italian composer for band, **X:** 182

Bertini, Severto, 19th century Italian composer for band, **X:** 183

Bertoia, ?, 19th century publisher in Venice, **XI:** 34

Bertolazzi, ?, 19th century Italian composer, **X:** 183

Bertoli, Giovanni, 17th century Italian composer, **XI:** 150

Berton, Henri Montan, 1767–1844, French composer, **IV:** 162, fn. 46, 206; **VIII:** 268ff

Berton, Henri, 1767–1844, composer of works arranged for Harmoniemusik, **VIII:** 9 [*Le grand Deuil, Montano et Stéphanie*; 10 [*Aline, Reine de Golconde; Féodor*]; 11 [*Françoise de Foix*]

Bertoni, Ferdinando, 1725–1813, Italian composer, church music for voices and winds, **VIII**: 363; **X**: 34; **XI**: 10, 304

Bertuzzi, A. M., 18th century Italian, church music for winds and voices, **VIII**: 363

Berwald, Franz, 1796–1868, Swedish composer, **IX**: 133

Beseda, ?, 19th century Austrian composer, **IX**: 209

Besozzi, ?, 18th century composer in Bohemia, **IV**: 41

Besozzi, Alessandro, 1702–1775, Italian composer, oboist at Turin, **IV**: 61; **XI**: 11, 104, 184, 239

Besozzi, Antonio, 1714–1781, oboist at Dresden, **IV**: 61

Besozzi, Carlo, b. 1738, 5 *Parthias* for Harmoniemusik, **VIII**: 363

Besozzi, Giuseppe, b. 1686, oboist at Turin, **IV**: 61

Bessière, ?, 19th century French composer, **IX**: 13

Betts, Arthur, 1776–1847, English composer, **XI**: 11

Betz, 18th century publisher in London, **XI**: 45

Beutheri, 17th century publisher at Freyberggae, **XI**: 285

Bevilacqua, Count Mario of Verona, **II**: 134

Bevin, Elway, d. 1615, English composer of ensemble works, **VII**: 30

Bewlay, Henry, d. 1797, English composer, **XI**: 11

Beyerbach, ? 19th century arranger, **IX**: 256, 257

Beyle, Henri ([Pseud., Stendhal)], 1816 account of a band concert in Milan, **V**: 103

Bialas, Gunter, b. 1907 in Prussian Silesia, composer, **XII**: 125

Bianchedi, Pretro, 19th century Italian composer for band, **X**: 183

Bianchi, Francesco, 1752–1810, Italian, *La Villanella rapita*, arranged for Harmoniemusik, **VIII**: 11; 101, 155 [unidentified works]; **XI**: 185

Bianchi, Giovanni, 19th century Italian composer, church music with band, **X**: 183

Biber, ?, composer in Erlebach, mss collection of Hautboisten music, **VII**: 156

Biber, Heinrich, 1644–1704, Bohemian-Austrian composer, **III**: 169, **IV**: 21; **VII**: 2, 7

Bibl, Rudolf, 1832–1902, Austrian composer, **IX**: 209

Bidet, Nicolas, member in 1768 of the Les Grands Hautbois, **IV**: 64, fn. 4

Bidgood, Thomas, 19th century English composer, **IX**: 265

Biedermann, Hans Christian, court trumpeter in Weimar (early 18th century), **III**: 162

Biefeld, Karl, 1866–1944, German composer, **XII**: 75

Bierey, Gottlob, 1772–1840, *Das Blumenmädchen*, arranged for Harmoniemusik, **VIII**: 11

Biffi, ?, composer in a 1616 Nürnberg collection, **VII**: 163

Biffi, Gioseffo, 1596, German publisher, **VI**: 79

Bigaglia, Diogenio, 1676–1745, Italian composer, **III**: 220; **VII**: 186; **X**: 6

Bignon, Paul, 19th century French composer, **IX**: 13

Bihler, Franz, 1760–1824, German composer, church music with Harmonie, **X**: 35

Billaut, A., 19th century French composer, **IX**: 13

Billaut, J.-B.-A., 19th century French composer, **IX**: 13

Billaut, Louis, 19th century French composer, **IX**: 13

Billema, ?, 19th century English composer, **IX:** 265

Billert, Karl, 1821–1875, German composer, **IX:** 149

Billi, Vincenzo, 1869–1938, Italian composer, a church work with band, **X:** 183

Billot, ?, 19th century French composer, **IX:** 13

Biloir, Joseph, 19th century French composer, **IX:** 13

Bilse, Benjamin, 1811–1902, German composer, **IX:** 149; **X:** 113

Bilton, M., composer included in a 1890 English collection of band music, **X:** 116

Bimboni, Gioacchino, 19th century Italian arranger, **IX:** 115; **X:** 107 [arranger of Meyerbeer *Fackeltanz* Nr. 3]

Binchois, Giles, 1400–1460 Franco-Flemish composer, **VI:** 8

Binder, Christlieb, 1723–1789, German composer, **XI:** 11, 185

Binet, Jean, b. 1893, Swiss composer, **XII:** 75, 126

Bingham, ?, 18th century Dutch (?) flautist in Amsterdam, **XI:** 11

Birch, Lt. Col., 18th century officer in British military, **VIII:** 252

Birchall, 18th and 19th century publisher in London, **XI:** 28, 37, 39, 190, 111, 210,235, 257, 299

Birckner, 17th century publisher in Erfurt and Mühlausen, **VII:** 147, 151, 153, 180

Birk (Birck), Charles, 19th century French composer, **IX:** 13

Birnbach, ?, 19th century German composer, **IX:** 149

Birnbaum, ?, 19th century composer, **IX:** 253

Birnstiel, 18th century publisher in Berlin, **XI:** 99, 217

Bisch, ?, 18th century French, **VIII:** 269 [original marches]; works arranged for Harmoniemusik, 103, 178, 230

Bisch, F., 19th century French composer, **IX:** 13

Bischoff, 16th century composer, **VI:** 65

Biscogli, Antonio, 18th century Italian composer, **XI:** 12

Biscogli, Francesco, 18th century Italian composer, **XI:** 185, 278

Bishop, Henry, 1786–1855, English composer, **V:** 167; **IX:** 265

Bishop, John, organist in Winchester Cathedral, early 18th century, **XI:** 185

Bisoni, Antonio, fl. 1784, Italian composer, church music with Harmoniemusik, **X:** 3

Bissoli, Mattio, 1711–1780, Italian composer, **XI:** 105

Bitterman, Carl, 19th century German composer, **IX:** 150

Bitti, Martino, 1656–1743, Italian violinist & composer, **XI:** 12, 104, 159

Bittoni, Bernardo, 1757–1829, Italian composer, a church work with band, **X:** 183

Bittoni, Mario, 18th century Italian composer, **XI:** 12

Biumo, Giacomo, 1627 Italian composer for 4–8 part canzoni, **VII:** 196

Bizet, Georges, 1838–1875, French composer, **V:** 156

Bizet, Georges, 1838–1875, French composer, works arranged for band; **X:** 242 [*Carmen,* arr. by Rosi]; 254 [*Carmen,* arr. by Vessella]

Black, English composer in early 17th century, **VII:** 22

Blackwell, J. G., 18th century English, *Divertimento* for military band, **VIII:** 253

Bláha, Filip, 19th century Austrian composer, **IX:** 209

Blake, Charles, 19th century English composer, **IX:** 265

Blanc, ?, 18th century, compositions for flute, **XI:** 12

Blanc, P., 19th century French composer, **IX:** 14

Blanchet, Thomas, 17th century engraver, **III:** 38

Blancheteau, ?, 19th century composer for church music for choir and band, **V:** 215; **IX:** 14, 265

Blanckeman, L., 19th century French composer, **IX:** 1, 15

Blanckmüller, Georg, 16th century composer, **VI:** 62ff, 76

Blancks, Edward, 16th century composer, **VI:** 36

Bland & Weller, 18th century publisher in London, **VIII:** 252, 258; **XI:** 36, 57, 127, 269

Bland, 18th century publisher in London, **XI:** 36, 43, 97, 233, 272

Bland, J., 18th publisher in London, **XI:** 14, 186

Blangy, Auguste, 19th century French composer, **IX:** 15

Blanke, John, black trumpeter, court of Henry VIII, **II:** 18

Blankes, Edward, ca. 1500–1530, English composer, **VII:** 20, 30

Blasius, Frédéric (born Matthieu), 1758–1829, French violinist and composer, including a *Messe*, and arranged works for Harmoniemusik, **IV:** 178; **VIII:** 24, 106, 269, 278; **X:** 21 [*Messe* for choir & Harmonie]; **XI:** 129, 150, 243, 250, 256, 280

Blasius, Ignace, bassoon faculty of the 1792 Paris Conservatoire, **IV:** 156

Blasius, Pierre, violinist, 1793 faculty of Paris Conservatoire, **IV:** 162

Blasius. F., 19th century French composer, **IX:** 1, 15, 253

Blavet, Michel, 1700–1768, French composer, **XI:** 12, 185

Bléger, A., 19th century French composer, **IX:** 15

Bléger, Michel, 19th century French composer, **IX:** 15

Blemant, Louis, 19th century French composer, **IX:** 16

Bleyer, Nikolaus, German composer in 1621, 1628 collections, **VII:** 24, 150

Blieck, Ad., 19th century French composer, **IX:** 16

Blockwitz, Johann, Baroque German composer, music for Hautboisten, **VII:** 111

Blon, Franz von, 1861–1945, German composer, **IX:** 150

Blondel, famous Trouvère with Richard Coeur de Lion, **I:** 184

Blow, John, 1649–1708, English composer of *Glorious Day* for voices and winds, **VII:** 14; **XI:** 185 [a work dedicated to Purcell]

Blühmel, claimed to invent the valve for brass instruments in 1805, **V:** 4

Blum, Robert, b. 1900, German composer, **XII:** 75

Blumenfeldt, Aron, b. ca. 1827, German composer, **IX:** 150

Blumenthal, ?, 19th century composer, **V:** 183, fn 21

Blumenthal, C., 19th century Austrian composer, **IX:** 209

Blumenthal, J. von, arr., *Grosser Marsch aus König Lear* for Harmoniemusik, **VIII:** 156

Blumenthal, Leopold, 19th century Austrian composer, **IX:** 209

Blummer, Martin, 1827–1901, German composer, **IX:** 1, 50

Bo & Ma, 20th century publisher in London, **XII:** 106

Boara, Giovanni, 19th century Italian composer, **IX:** 116; **X:** 183 [church works with winds]

Boccherini, Luigi, 1743–1805, Italian composer, **X:** 35; **XI:** 12, 185

Bocchorone, R., 19th century Austrian composer, **IX:** 209

Bocchoroni, ?, *Hamlet* (original unknown), arranged for Harmoniemusik, **VIII:** 11

Bochsa, ?, 19th century French composer, **IX:** 1

Bochsa, 19th century publisher in Paris, **IX:** 17; **XI:** 164

Bochsa, Charles Nicholas, 1789–1856, French composer and harpist, **V:** 143; **VIII:** 46ff [as arranger of Haydn Symphonies for Harmonie]; **IX:**17 [*Requiem for Louis XVI* for chorus and band]; **X:** 65 [*Requiem* for band]; **XI:** 130, 235, 317

Bochsa, Karl, 'pere,' d. 1821, **IX:** 17, 180; **XI:** 13 [biographical note], 105, 130, 317

Bock, 18th century publisher in Berlin, **XI:** 226

Bock, Anton, hornist in Harmoniemusik of Cardinal Batthyány, **IV:** 33, fn. 71

Böckmann, 18th century publisher in Lübeck, **VII:** 157

Bode, ?, hornist, 19th century court of Mechlenburg-Schwerin, **V:** 185, fn. 4

Boehlman-Sauzeau, H., early 19th century French composer, **X:** 65

Boehm, Theobald, 1794–1881, composer, developer of the modern flute, **V:** 7; **XI:** 13

Boettge, M., conductor of the Bayreuth military band, late 19th century, **V:** 38

Bogaerde, F. L., 19th century English composer, **IX:** 266

Boggetti, Edwin, 19th century English composer, **IX:** 266

Bogria, Rodrigo, 1431–1503, Pope Alexander VI, **II:** 117

Boh, Alb., 19th century German composer, **IX:** 150

Bohemus (Martin de Boémia?), 16th century composer, **VI:** 62

Bohemus, Eusebius, mid 17th century composer, **VII:** 7

Bohm, ?, 19th century Austrian composer, **IX:** 209

Böhme, 19th and 20th century publisher in Augsburg, **IX:** 160, 217; **XII:** 103, 150, 172

Böhme, 19th century publisher in Leipzig, **XI:** 94

Böhme, J. A., 18th and 19th century publisher in Hamburg, **IV:** 71; **VIII:** 29, 73, 79, 219, 262, 275; **IX:** 147, 167, 182; **XI:** 116, 135; **XII:** 42

Böhmel, Jean August, 18th century publisher in Hambourg, **XII:** 53

Böhner, Johann, 1778–1860, German composer, **V:** 212; **IX:** 150; **XI:** 150

Boieldieu, 19th century publisher in Paris, **XI:** 319

Boieldieu, François Adrien, 1775–1834, French composer, **IV:** 17, 79; **V:** 148, 214; **VIII,** as composer of works arranged for Harmoniemusik, 11 [*Ma Tante Aurore*]; 12 [*Jean de Paris, La Dame blanch*]; 152, unidentified works; **IX:** 17; **XII:** 10 [biographical note]

Boieldieu, jeune , 19th century publisher in Paris, **XII:** 65

Boisdeffre, René, 1838–1906, French composer, **V:** 153; **IX:** 17; **XII:** 193

Boismortier, Joseph-Bodin, 1691–1765, French composer of concerti, **VII:** 84; **XI:** 13, 150, 186, 251, 267, 315

Boito, *Mefistofele,* arranged for band by Rosi, **X:** 242

Boivin & Le Clerc, 18th century publishers in Paris, **VII:** 84, 91, 94

Boivin, 18th publisher in Paris, **XI:** 64, 223

Bokemeyer, Heinrich, 1679–1751, German composer, **XI:** 235

Bolardt, Thomas, 19th century Austrian composer, **IX:** 209

Boleyn, Anne, wife of Henry VIII, **II:** 26ff

Bollius, Daniel, 17th century German composer, **III:** 215

Bologna, Jeronimo da, 16th century composer, **VI:** 92

Bolvin, 18th century publisher in Paris, **XI:** 20

Bolzoni, Giovanni, 1841–1919, Italian composer, **IX:** 116

Bona, 17th century Italian composer, **III:** 220

Bona, Valerio, 1619 Italian composer for canzoni collection, **VII:** 196

Bonacci, Francesco, late 18th century Italian composer, *Mottetti,* voices & winds, **X:** 35

Bonari, Guierriero, fl. 1812, Italian composer, *Messa* for chorus and winds, **X:** 36

Bonasegla, Carl Philipp, b. 1770, German composer, **XII:** 10

Bonasegla, Carl, b. 1779, German composer, **IX:** 150

Bonelli, Aurelio, 1569–1620, Italian composer, **II:** 245, **III:** 220; **VII:** 196

Bonenfant, F. ?, 19th century French composer, **IX:** 17

Bonferoni, Pietro, 19th century Italian composer, church works with band, **X:** 184

Bongiorno, Francesco, 19th century Italian composer, **X:** 184

Bonicioli, Riccardo, 1853–1933, Italian composer, **X:** 184

Bonicoli, Venceslao, 19th century Italian composer for band, **X:** 184

Bonifante, Francesco, b. 1576, head of music St. Marks, first introduced strings, **II:** 244

Bonnelle, A., 19th century French composer, **IX:** 17

Bonnelle, V., 19th century French composer, **IX:** 17

Bonnisseau, ?, 19th century French composer, **IX:** 17, 266; **X:** 113

Bonnot, C., 19th century French composer, conductor, 14e de Ligne, **IX:** 1, 17

Bono, Giuseppe, 1710–1788, Italian composer, **IV:** 24; **VIII,** 178ff, as composer of (11) *Parthias* for Harmoniemusik.

Bononcini, Marc, 1675–1726, Italian composer, **XI:** 13, 186

Bonvin, Ludwig, 1850–1939, German composer, **IX:** 150

Bonzanni, Giacomo, 1616 Italian composer, **VII:** 197

Boosé, Carl, conductor of the Scots Guards in 1845, **V:** 81

Boosey & Hawkes, 20th century publisher in London, **XII:** 92, 108

Boosey's Military Jounal, London, **IX:** 264

Booth, 18th and 19th century publisher in London, **VIII:** 259; **X:** 113ff

Booth, General William, founder of the Salvation Army bands, **V:** 166; **XII:** 92 [dedication]

Borchgrevinck, composer in a 1609 Hamburg collection, **VII:** 166

Borck, Edmund von, b. 1906, German composer, **XII:** 126

Bordet, ?, 18th century French flautist & composer, **XI:** 13

Bordoux, Jean Ernest, 18th century marches for Harmoniemusik, **VIII:** 269ff, 305 [a march by 'a Lewin']

Borea, Vincenzo, 19th century Italian composer for band, **X:** 184

Borel, G., 19th century French composer, **IX:** 18

Borghi, Giovanni, 1713–1796, Italian composer, **X:** 36

Borgia, Lucrezia, 1480–1519, daughter to Pope Alexander VI, **II:** 118ff

Borgo, Casare, 16th century Milanese organist, composer, **VI:** 94; **VII:** 197

Bornstädt, 18th century German General, **VIII:** 297

Borovansky, ?, 19th century Austrian composer, **IX:** 210

Borrea, Manuel, 19th century French composer, **IX:** 18

Borrel, H., 19th century French composer, **IX:** 18

Borso d'Este, 1450–1471, **I:** 229ff

Bortniansky, Dimitri, 1751–1825, composer in Germany, **V:** 18, fn. 54

Borussus, Erhardus of Dresden, famous 16th century trombonist, **II:** 263

Bosch, ?, 19th century French composer, **IX:** 18

Boscher, A., 19th century French composer, **IX:** 18

Boscka, ?, 18th century German composer, **XI:** 130

Boser, ?, German, (7) *Partitas*, ca. 1768, for Harmoniemusik, **VIII:** 305

Bosisio, ?, 19th century English composer, **IX:** 266

Bosse, 20th century publisher in Regensburg, **XII:** 120

Bossler, 18th century publisher at Speyer, **XI:** 220

Bost (Rost), ?, 19th century German composer, **IX:** 150

Bote & Bock, 19th century publisher in Berlin, **IX:** 174, 188; **XII:** 62, 82, 88

Bothe, Gustav, 19th century German composer, **IX:** 150

Botsch, 16th century German composer, **VI:** 62

Bottaccio, Paolo, 17th century Italian composer, **III:** 220; **VII:** 197, 204

Bottrigari, Hercole, 1531–1612, scholar of Italian court life, **II:**126, **III:** 13

Botz, 18th century publisher (in London?), **VIII:** 275

Bouchaudon, Clude de, 'king' of minstrels in Paris, 1575–1590), **II:** 179

Bouchel, J., 19th century French composer, **IX:** 18

Boudier, Achille, 19th century French composer, **IX:** 19

Boué, Ernest, 19th century French composer, conductor Musique de 13e Leger, **IX:** 1, 19

Bouffil, ?, clarinetist in Paris, ca. 1820, **IX:** 19

Bougon, ?, 19th century French composer, **IX:** 19

Bouillé, General, 18th century France, **IV:** 150

Bouillon, Paul, 19th century French composer, **IX:** 19

Bouin, Castagnery & Blaisot, 18th century publishers in Paris, **VIII:** 153

Boujut, ?, 19th century French composer, **IX:** 19

Boulcourt, Alfred, 19th century English composer, **IX:** 266

Boullard, Marius, 19th century French composer, **IX:** 19

Boulley, Prudent-Louis du, 1796–1870, founder of civic bands near Paris, **V:** 149

Bourbon, Louis-Joseph de, Prince de Condé, 17th century Paris, **IV:** 68, fn 241

Bourdeau, 19th century French composer, conductor 44e de Ligne, **IX:** 1

Bourdon, J., 19th century French composer, **IX:** 19

Bourgault-Ducoudray, 19th century French composer, **IX:** 20

Bourgeois, Ed., 19th century French composer, **IX:** 20

Bourgeois, Jules, 19th century French composer, **IX:** 20

Bourgoin, ?, 19th century French composer,conductor 5e Lanciers, **IX:** 2

Bourguignon, Anónim, ca. 1450–1521, Franco-Flemish composer, **VI:** 38, 43, 49

Bournigal, Léon, 19th century French composer, **IX:** 20

Bourquier, Fréd., 19th century French composer, **IX:** 20

Bourrellis, H.-J., 19th century French composer, **IX:** 20

Bousquet, Narcisse, 19th century French composer, **IX:,** 1, 20, 266

Bousquier, L., 19th century French composer, **IX:** 20ff

Bouthel, L., 19th century French composer, **IX:** 21

Bouvier, B., 19th century French composer, **IX:** 21

Bouward, ?, 18th century composer, **XI:** 186

Bow Church Yard, 18th century publisher in London, **XI:** 5, 102

Bowles, Paul, b. 1910, American composer, **XII:** 75, 126

Boyer, 18th and 19th century publisher in Paris, **VIII:** 11, 29, 269ff ; **XI:** 93, 249, 309

Boyer, Louis, 19th century French composer, **IX:** 21

Boyer, Th., 19th century French composer, **IX:** 21

Boyvin, Jacques, 1562–1633, French composer, **VI:** 44, 48ff

Boze, E. G., married in 1693, **VII:** 135

Braccini, Luigi, 18th century Italian, *Miserere* for voices and winds, **VIII:** 363

Brack, 16th century German composer, **VI:** 61ff

Bracquet, 16th century composer, **VI:** 123

Brade, William, 1560–1630, collections (1609–1619), **VII:** 150, 166, 172

Bradley, ?, composer in 1600 English collection of ensemble music, **VII:** 20

Braetel, Huldrich, 1495–1544 German composer, **VI:** 25

Braga, Giuseppe, 1829–1907, Italian composer for band, **X:** 184

Braham, Charles, 19th century English composer, **IX:** 267

Brahm, ?, composer included in a 1876 English collection of band music, **X:** 114

Brahms, Johannes, 1833–1897, **V:** 131; **IX:** 151; **XI:** 8, 183, 249 [works he owned in autograph scores]; **XII:** 202, 215

Braithwaite, Richard, author of treatise on manners in 1621, **III:** 88

Brambilla, ?, 19th century Italian composer, **IX:** 116

Bramble, Matthew, 18th century report of Vauxhall Gardens in London, **IV:** 134

Bramieri, 16th century composer, **VI:** 61; **VII:** 142

Bramley, ca. 1600 English composer of instrumental *Miserere*, **VII:** 30

Brandi, Gaetano, 18th century composer in England, **XI:** 13

Brandt, Lüdeken, 16th century publisher in Helmstedt, **VI:** 67

Brandts Buys, H. F. R., b. 1850, Dutch composer, **IX:** 125

Brandus, 19th century publisher in Paris, **XII:** 62

Brant von, Jobst, 1517–1570, German composer, **VI:** 63ff

Braquetz, 16th century composer, **VI:** 109

Brasser, Jan de, member of the Antwerp town band, **II:** 166

Brätel, 16th century German composer, **VI:** 63

Bratfisch, A., 19th century German composer, **IX:** 151

Braun, ?, 19th century French composer, **IX:** 21

Braun, Baron de [dedication by Cherubini], **X:** 66

Braun, C., 19th century German composer, **IX:** 151

Braun, Charles, b. 1868, celebrated oboist in Berlin, **XI:** 105 [biographical note]

Braun, Guillaume, 19th century (?) composer, **XI:** 235

Braun, Jean Daniel, French composer of Hautboisten music, **VII:** 84

Braun, Johann, 1753–1795, German, works for Harmoniemusik, **VIII:** 306

Braun, von, 18th century, maintains Harmoniemusik for Tafelmusik, **IV:** 41

Braunschweig, Duke, 19th century, **IX:** 141 [as composer]

Braunschweig, Sophie-Elisabeth von, VII: 178 [as composer]

Brausi, Paolo, conductor of the Modena town band in 1608, **III:** 193

Brauwer, Casin de, commissioned band music for church in Antwerp, **II:** 214

Brawas (Prowo), Pierre, 1697–1757, German composer, **XII:** 2

Breau, ?, 20th century German composer, **XII:** 75

Brecht, Erhard, German composer of 1670 music for 'Harmoniam,' **VII:** 151

Bregoli, ?, 19th century Italian composer for band, **X:** 185

Breitengraser, Wilhelm, 16th century German composer, **VI:** 62ff

Breitkopf & Härtel, 18th and 19th century publisher in Leipzig, **VIII:** 6ff, 21, 68, 83ff, 106ff, 108, 110, 199ff, 206, 216ff, 219ff, 245, 250, 295ff, 304, 341, 345ff, 354; **IX:** 17, 49, 70, 107, 150, 155, 156, 157, 162, 166, 168, 172, 173, 174, 182, 188, 209, 220, 227, 229, 236, 239, 247, 252; **XI:** 50, 51, 57, 79, 80, 86, 100, 103, 104, 105, 127, 132, 136, 138, 144, 148, 153, 157, 169, 217, 235, 247, 260, 262, 268, 278, 287, 299, 300, 304, 319; **XII:** 40, 112, 123, 184

Bremer, 17th century publisher in Lübeck, **VII:** 150

Bremner, 18th century publisher in London, **XI:** 3, 37,43, 81, 187, 211

Bremner, Rl., 18th century publisher in London, **VIII:** 250, 261

Brépsant, Engebert, 19th century French composer, **V:** 73; **IX:** 2, 21, 267; **XI:** 130

Bresciani, Pietro, as composer of works arranged for Harmoniemusik, **VIII:** 12, 13

Bresciano, Ambrogio, late 16th century Italian composer, **VI:** 93ff

Bretagne, Duke of, last grandchild of Louis XIV, **III:** 43, 45

Bretonnière, V., 19th century French composer, professor of music for the Turkish ambassador in Paris, **IX:** 1, 22

Breunich, Michele, 1699–1755 German composer, **XI:** 186

Brewer, Josiah, 19th century English composer, **IX:** 267

Brewer, Mark, 19th century English composer, **IX:** 267

Brewer, Thomas, b. 1611, English composer of ensemble music, **VII:** 30

Briant, Denis, 16th century composer, **VI:** 25, 108

Briccialdi, Giulio, 1818–1881, Italian composer, **X:** 185

Bridam, 16th century composer, **VI:** 39

Bridge, Frank, 1879–1941, English composer, **XII:** 126

Bridge, Sir John, 19th century English composer, **IX:** 267

Bridgeman, Charles, 18th century, English, (8) *Marches* for Harmonie, fifes, **VIII:** 253

Briederike, Princess, wedding in Berlin, 1791, **VIII:** 342

Briegel, Wolfgang, 1626–1712, German composer, **III:** 17; **VII:** 112, 151

Brielle, ?, composer faculty of the 1792 Paris Conservatoire, **IV:** 156

Briffaux, J. B., 19th century composer, **IX:** 267

Briggs, E. C., 19th century English composer, **IX:** 267

Brimle, John, ca. 1500–1576, English composer, **VI:** 35

Briscoli, Domenico, early 19th century Italian composer in London, **IV:** 115; **VIII:** 364 [3 *Symphonies* for Harmoniemusik with flutes]; **XI:** 13

Briscot, Charles, 19th century French composer, **IX:** 22

Brixi, Frantisek, 1732–1771, composer in Graf Pachta Harmonie Collection, **IV:** 22, fn. 10, 23; **VIII:** 179 [(4) *Parthias* for Harmonie]

Brixia, Matheus de, fl. 1412–1419 in Vicenza, composer, **VI:** 13

Brizzi & Nicolai, 20th century publisher in Florence, **XII:** 175

Brizzi, ?, famous 19th century trumpeter in the Napoli band, **V:** 195

Brock, Cameron, composer included in a 1893 English collection, **X:** 116

Brock, Othone von Den, 18th century French composer, **XI:** 164

Brod, as arranger of Weber, *Der Freischütz*, opera, for Harmoniemusik, **VIII:** 132

Brod, Henri, 19th century French composer, **XI:** 239

Broderip & Wilkinson, 18th century publisher in London, **VIII:** 261ff, 329, 355; **XI:** 26, 245

Brody, A., 19th century French composer, **IX:** 22

Broege, Timothy, 20th century American composer, **XII:** 202

Brooks, C., 19th century English composer, **IX:** 267

Brooks, E., 19th century English composer, **IX:** 267

Brooks, James, (36) *Select pieces for Military Band*, 1797, **VIII:** 253

Brösel, ?, German, (3) *Marches*, ca. 1780, for Harmoniemusik, **VIII:** 306

Brown, Jimmy, d. 2012, oboist, English Chamber Orchestra, **XII:** 207

Browne, John, 17th century London publisher, **VII:** 14

Bru, C., 19th century French composer, military conductor, 8e de Ligne, **IX:** 1

Bru, G. C., 19th century French composer, **IX:** 2

Bru, Jean (Pseud: Bellacour, Jeannette), 19th century French, **IX:** 22

Bruck, Arnold von, 1500–1554, Franco-Flemish composer, **VI:** 62ff

Bruckner, Anton, 1824–1896, his church works for choir, winds or band, **V:** 213; **IX:** 210; **XII:** 78 [unidentified melody used by Johann David]; 84 [unidentified melody used by Vinzenz Goller]; **XII:** 201

Brückner, Wolfgang, German composer, 1656 music for voices and insts, **VII:** 151

Brülow, M., composer of 1664 Bransles, **VII:** 151

Brun, ?, 19th century, French composer, **XII:** 193

Brun, François, 20th century French composer, **XII:** 76

Brun, Georges, b. 1878, French composer, **IX:** 22

Bruneau, Louis Charles, 1857–1934, France composer, **XII:** 127

Brunelli, Antonio, 1614 Italian composer of voices and winds collection, **VII:** 197

Brunet, L., 19th century composer, **IX:** 267

Brunett (Brunetti), Gaéton, 1740–1809, (2) volumes of dances for Harmonie, **VIII:** 269

Brunette, ?, 19th century English composer, **IX:** 267

Brunetti, Giovanni, 1715–1808, Italian composer, **X:** 36

Brunetti-Pasano, August, b. 1926, Austrian composer, **XII:** 76, 127

Brunetti-Pisano, August, 1870–1943, Austrian composer, **XI:** 13, 295, 317

Bruni, Antonio, 1751–1821, as composer of works arranged for Harmoniemusik, **VIII:** 13 [*La Recontre en voyage, Spinette et Marini, Toberne*]; 151, 153, unidentified works

Brun-Lavainne, ?, conductor of Lille civic band in 1814, **V:** 148

Brusek (Bruscheck), Joseph, composer for Harmonie and voices and winds, **VIII:** 179ff

Brustad, Fjarne, b. 1895, composer, **XII:** 127

Bruyer, 16th century composer, **VI:** 63

Bruyer, Victor, 19th century French composer, **IX:** 22

Bruyne, E. de, 19th century French composer, **IX:** 22

Bruzzeh (Brusek), Joseph, Austrian Baroque composer, **X:** 17

Bucalossi, Ernest, 19th century English composer, **IX:** 267

Bucalossi, Procida, 19th century English composer, **IX:** 268

Buch, Antoine, horn faculty of the 1792 Paris Conservatoire, **IV:** 156

Buchal, J., as arranger of works for Harmoniemusik, **VIII:** 63, 140, 141

Buchanan, John, 1819–1898, English composer for band, **X:** 118

Buchholz, ?, 19th century German composer, **IX:** 151

Büchler Ferd., 1817–1891, German composer, **IX:** 151

Buchmann, flutist, 19th century court at Rudolstadt, **V:** 186, fn. 8

Buchna, ?, *Todten-Marsch* for Harmoniemusik, **VIII:** 180

Buchnal, as arranger of works for Harmoniemusik, **VIII:** 91, 147

Büchner, Johann, German composer of 1614 collection of dances, **VII:** 152

Bucholtz, Johann, d. 1800, German, (3) *Partie,* 1766, for Harmoniemusik, **VIII:** 306

Bucke, John, ca. 1600, English composer of instrumental music, **VII:** 30

Budik, ?, composer included in a 1880 English collection of band music, **X:** 115

Buel, ?, composer in a 1616 Nürnberg collection, **VII:** 163

Bufalari, Carlo, 19th century Italian composer for band, **X:** 185

Buffet, 19th century publisher in Paris, **IX:** 8; **XI:** 139

Buffet-Choudens, 20th century publisher in Paris, **XII:** 76

Buffet-Crampon, 19th and 20th century publisher in Paris, **VIII:** 367; **IX:** 111

Buhl, Joseph-David, 1781–1860, French composer, leader of the Versailles trumpet school, **V:** 57; **IX:** 22; **XI:** 159, 278, 307; **XII:** 10 [biographical note]

Bühler, Franz, 1760–1824, German church work for voices and Harmoniemusik, **VIII:** 306

Bulan, Charles, 19th century French composer, **IX:** 22

Bull, John, 1563–1628, English composer, **VII:** 25, 31

Bülow, General, German, 18th century, **VIII:** 301

Bülow, Hans von, 1830–1894, **V:** 22, 108 [reviews a band concert in 1858, conducted by Piefke], 114, 194; **IX:** 151; **X:** 96

Bultel, Jacob, 16th century composer, **VI:** 25

Bum, Michael, clarinetist in Harmoniemusik of Cardinal Batthyány, **IV:** 33, fn. 71

Buona (Bona?), Valerio, b. 1560, composer, **VI:** 94

Buonamente, Battista, 1636 Italian composer of canzoni and 6-part sonata, **VII:** 197

Buonavita, Antonia, late 16th century organist in Pisa, composer, **VI:** 104

Buot, Victor, 19th century French composer, conductor, Musique de l'Artillerie de la Garde, **V:** 215; **IX:** 2, 23

Burald, ?, 19th century English composer, **IX:** 268

Burbure de Wesembeek, 1812–1889 Belgium composer, **IX:** 259

Burck, Joachim, composer in 1575, **VI:** 65

Burckart, Franz, 17th century composer of Hautboisten music, **III:** 19

Burckart, J. V., 17th century, German composer, for Hautboisten, **VII:** 112

Burckhardt, ?, 19th century English composer, **IX:** 268; **X:** 113, 114

Bureau des arts et d'industrie, 19th century publisher in Vienna, **IX:** 220; **XI:** 149; **XII:** 39, 44

Bureau, Joseph, member in 1777 of the Les Grands Hautbois, **IV:** 64, fn. 4

Buresch, Adalbert, as 19th century arranger, **IX:** 256

Bürg, R., 19th century German composer, **IX:** 151

Bürgerl, ?, 19th century Austrian civic militia composer, **V:** 126

Bürgl. Noten und Kupferdruckery, 19th century publisher in Linz, **XII:** 42

Burgmann, ?, 19th century French composer, **IX:** 24

Burkhard, Willy, b. 1900, Swiss composer, **XII:** 76, 127

Burmeister, Paul, 19th century German composer, **IX:** 151

Burney, Charles, 1726–1814, English historian & composer, **IV:** 85, 87, 89, 91ff, 100, 119ff; **V:** 13ff; **XI:** 186

Burns, Felix, Sr., 19th century English composer, **IX:** 268

Burrowes, John, b. 1787, English composer, **XI:** 14, 267

Bury, ?, 19th century French horn player & composer, **XI:** 164

Busby, Thomas, 1755–1838, English composer, (3) *Marches,* **VIII:** 2536ff

Buschmann, ?, German, (2) *Partitas,* c. 1760, for Harmoniemusik, **VIII:** 306

Bush, Alan, b. 1900, English composer, **XII:** 76

Busi, Alessandro, 19th century Italian composer, **XI:** 159

Busino, Horatio, Venetian ambassador in London in 1618, **III:** 86ff

Buskies, Rudolph, 19th century German composer, **IX:** 151

Busnois, Antoine, 1430–1492, French composer, **VI:** 31

Busscher, Albert de, oboist in the 1910 Barrère Ensemble in NYC, **XII:** 214

Busser, Henri, b. 1872, French composer, **XII:** 76, 127

Bütner, Crato, German composer of 1662 music for voices and winds, **VII:** 152

Butten, Jacob, German composer, 1702 music for voice and winds, **VII:** 122

Búttner, Max, 1873–1956, German composer, **XII:** 77

Buttstett, Franz, 1735–1814, German, *Quintet,* 1793, for Harmoniemusik, **VIII:** 307

Buus, Jacques, 1500–1565, Franco-Flemish composer, **VI:** 82, 94

Buxtehude, Dieterich, 1637–1707, composer in Germany, **III:** 215ff; **VII:** 112

Buys, 16th century composer, **VI:** 107ff

Buzzolla, Antonio, 1815–1871, Italian composer, **IX:** 116; **X:** 185

Bynneman, Henry, Baroque publisher in London, **VII:** 19

Byrd, William, 1543–1623, English composer, **VII:** 20, 22, 23, 25, 26, 31ff

C. & S. Thompson, 18th publisher in London, **VIII:** 250

Cabillau, 16th century composer, **VI:** 107, 109, 122ff

Caccavaio, Luigi, 19th century Italian composer for band, **X:** 185

Caccavajo, Salvatore, 19th century civic band conductor in Naples, **V:** 157

Caccini, ?, Italian composer in a 1614 collection, **VII:** 197

Cadéac, Pierre, fl. 1530–1558, French composer, **VI:** 45, 109ff, 114

Caesar, Johann Melchior, German composer of 1682 *Lustige Tafel-Musik*, **VII:** 152

Caffare, Giuseppe, Italian composer, **XI:** 105

Cagliero, Giovanni, 1838–1926, Italian composer, **IX:** 116

Cagnola, Emilio, 19th century Italian composer, **X:** 185

Cahusac, 18th and 19th century publisher in London, **XI:** 4, 202

Cahusac, T. & W. M., 18th century publisher in London, **VIII:** 264

Cahusac, Thomas, 18th century English composer, **XI:** 14

Caietain (Cajetan), Fabrice Martin, (fl. ca. 1570–1578), **VI:** 56

Cajani, Giuseppe, 19th century Italian composer for band, **X:** 186

Calabr, Andreas Tallafangi, fl. 1440–1450, composer, **VI:** 13

Calamara, Gregorio, 19th century Italian composer, **X:** 186

Calcott, J. W., 19th century English composer, **IX:** 268

Caldara, Antonio, 1670–1736, composer, **VII:** 2

Calecari, G. F., 19th century Italian collection for 8 trumpets, **X:** 186

Calenberg [Gallenberg], ?, *Hamlet*, Overture, unknown arr. for Harmoniemusik, **VIII:** 13

Calenius, Gerwinus, 16th century publisher in Köln, **VI:** 67

Calesstani, ?, composer in a 1614 Brunelli collection, **VII:** 197

Cali, Girolamo, 19th century Italian composer, *Sinfonia* for band, **X:** 186

Califano, ?, German Baroque composer of Hautboisten music, **X:** 6

Califfi, ?, 19th century Italian composer, **IX:** 116; **X:** 186

Calvi, ?, 19th century Italian composer, a church work with band, **X:** 186

Calvi, Girolamo, d. 1848, numerous works for Harmonie and band, **X:** 186

Calvisius, Sethus, 1556–1615, German composer of instrumental works, **VII:** 152

Camas, A. de, 19th century French composer, Capitaine au 2e de Chasseurs à pied, **IX:** 1

Cambart, A., 19th century French composer, **IX:** 46

Cambiagho, Italian composer in 1626 collection of canzoni, **VII:** 205

Cambier, Victor, 19th century French composer, **IX:** 24, 268

Cambini, Giovanni, 1746–1825, Italian composer, **IV:** 195ff; **VIII:** 269ff [(11) works, voices and Harmonie, & *Marche*]; **XI:** 14ff, 186

Cambridge, Duke, creates Kneller Hall in 1856 in England, **V:** 83

Camomille, J., 19th century French composer, **IX:** 24

Campagnoli, Bartolomeo, 1751–1827, Italian composer, **XI:** 15

Campbell, 18th century publisher in London, **XI:** 97

Campenhaut, François, 1779–1848, Belgium composer, **IX:** 259

Campini, Giuseppe, 1746–1825, Italian composer, **XI:** 15

Campion, Thomas, 1567–1620, English masque composer in 1607, **III:** 85

Campioni, Carlo, 1720–1793, Italian composer, **XI:** 187

Canal, Giuseppe, 1703–1779, Italian composer, **XI:** 15, 187

Canale, Floriano, 17th century Italian composer, **III:** 220; **VII:** 197

Canaple, Henri, 19th century French composer, **IX:** 24

Candeille, Pierre, 1744–1827, French composer, **XI:** 234, 282

Cangiasi, Giovanni, 1614 Italian composer of scherzi forastieri, **VII:** 198

Canis, Cornelius, 1510–1561, Franco-Flemish composer, **VI:** 25, 107ff, 118ff, 122

Canivez, L., 19th century French composer of works, **IX:** 24

Cannabich, Christian, 1731–1798, German composer, **XI:** 15

Cannabich, Johann, 1731–1798, German, *March* for band, **VIII:** 307

Canobbio, Carlo, 1741–1822, Italian composer, **XI:** 16

Cantelo, ?, 18th century English collector, (24) *American country dances,* **VIII:** 254

Cantelo, Hezekiah, trumpeter at Vauxhall in 1785, **IV:** 131, note on pgs. 132–133

Canteloube, Joseph, b. 1879, French composer, **XII: 127**

Canthal, ?, composer included in a 1888 English collection of band music, **X:** 116

Canti, 19th century publisher in Milano, **XI:** 272

Canti, Antonio, 19th century Italian composer for band, **X:** 188

Cantone, Serafino, Italian composer in 1617 collection of canzoni, **VII:** 204

Canus of Rhodes, famous aulos player, 3rd century AD, **I:** 11

Capanna, Alessandro, 1814–1892, 19th century Italian composer, **XI:** 159

Caparelli, ?, 18th century Italian horn player and composer, **XI:** 164, 256

Capati, R. D., 19th century English composer, **IX:** 268

Capelli, ?, [see Apell, David]

Caphisias, aulos teacher, court of Alexander the Great, **I:** 41

Caplet, André, 1878–1925, French composer, **XII:** 77, 128, 192, 214

Caporali, Luigi, 19th century Italian composer for band, **X:** 188

Cappa, G. A., composer included in a 1893 English collection of band music, **X:** 116

Cappelli, Oreste, 19th century Italian composer for band, **X:** 189

Cappi, 19th century publisher in Vienna, **XI:** 41, 48, 79

Cappon, A., 19th century French composer, **IX:** 1

Capricornus, Samuel, ca. 1629–1665, German composer of dance works, **VII:** 152

Capua, Marcello, b. ca. 1740, *Furberia et Pontiglio,* arranged for Harmonie, **VIII:** 13

Carafa, Michele, 1787–1872, co-founder of the Gymnase de Music Mil., **V:** 62ff; **VIII:** 14, as composer of works arranged for Harmoniemusik; **IX:** 24; **X:** 65; **XI:** 130, 164, 257; **XII:** 202

Caravaglios, Raffaele, 1860–1929, civic band conductor in Napoli, **V:** 158

Carbon, ?, 19th century English composer, **IX:** 268

Carcani, Giosoffo, 1703–1749, Italian composer for Hautboisten, **VII:** 186; **XI:** 188

Carcassone, Georges, 19th century French composer, **IX:** 24

Card, W., 18th century English flute professor in England in 1825, **XI:** 16

Cardew, Phil., 19th century English composer, **IX:** 268

Cardon, 16th century composer, **VI:** 107, 109

Cardonne, Jean, 1730–1792, French composer, **XI:** 105

Carducci, Aristodemo, 19th century Italian composer for band, **X:** 189

Carini, Cesare, b. 1841, 19th century Italian composer for band, **X:** 189

Carisch, 20th century publisher in Milan, **XII:** 159

Carl August of Weimar, 19th century, **IX:** 227

Carl Friedrich, 19th century Grand Duke of Baden, **V:** 188ff

Carl, Carl, 1830–1898, German composer, **IX:** 151ff

Carl, Günther Friedrich, 19th century Prince of Schwarzenburg, **IX:** 184

Carl, Gustav, 19th century German composer, **IX:** 152

Carli, 19th century publisher in Paris, **VIII:** 93, 107ff, 110ff, 276

Carlini, *Rintocco della mezzanotte,* arranged for band by Vessella, **X:** 254

Carlino, 17th century publisher in Napoli, **VII:** 194

Carnicer, Ramon, 1789–1855, Spanish composer, **IX:** 131

Carolina, 19th century Empress of Austria, **IX:** 226

Caroubel, Francis, Baroque French composer for crumhorn consort, **VII:** 84

Carpentier, Raymond, b. 1880, composer, **XII:** 128

Carr, John, 18th century English composer, **XI:** 164

Carr, Robert, 17th century English composer, **XI:** 16, 188, 267

Carraut, L., 19th century French composer, **IX:** 25

Carre, 19th century publisher in Paris, **IX:** 7

Carrié, Louis, 19th century French composer, **IX:** 25

Carstens, ?, 17th century publisher in Hamburg, **VII:** 177

Cartellieri, Antonio, 1772–1807, Bohemian composer, Harmoniemusik composer, **IV:** 19,
    42; **VIII:** 180 (11) works, voices and Harmonie, & *Marche*; **XI:** 16

Carter, Henry, 19th century English composer, **IX:** 268

Carteron, Alexandre, 19th century French composer, **IX:** 25

Carulli, Benedetto, 1797–1877, Italian composer, arranger, **VIII:** 8; **IX:** 116; **X:** 189;
    XI: 176; **XII:** 55

Casadesus, François Louis, 1870–1945, French composer, **XII:** 77, 128

Casamorata, Luigi, 1807–1881, Italian composer, works for Harmoniemusik, **X:** 189

Casanova, Giacomo, 1725–1798, Italian author, **IV:** 65

Casare, Rinaldo, German composer, early 18th century, **XII:** 2

Casato, Francesco, Italian composer in 1617 collection of canzoni, **VII:** 204

Casella, Alfredo, 1893–1947, Italian composer, **XII:** 77, 129, 202

Caselli, Giuseppe, 18th century (?) Italian composer, **XI:** 16

Casimir von Brandenburg, wedding music in 1518, **II:** 230

Casquil, ?, 19th century French composer, **IX:** 25

Cassard, L., 19th century French composer, **IX:** 25

Castagnery, 18th century publisher in Paris, **VIII:** 267

Castaud, 19th century publisher in Lyon, **VIII:** 160

Castela, A., 19th century French composer, **IX:** 25

Castelbarco, conte Cesare, 19th century Italian composer, **XI:** 16, 131

Castellani, Margherita of Florence, ca. 1465, **VI:** 14

Castello, Dario, 1590–1658, Italian leader of Venice wind band and composer, **III:** 220; **VII:** 186

Castiglione, 16th author of *Il Cortegiano*, **I:** 175

Castil-Blaze, François, d. 1857, French composer, **IX:** 25

Castileti, Johannes, 1512–1588, Flemish composer, **VI:** 25, 120

Castnis, Fran. de, 18th century (?) composer in Vienna, **XI:** 235

Castro, Jean de, 1540–1611, Belgian composer, **VI:** 124

Catel, Charles-Simon, 1773–1830, French composer on faculty of the 1792 Paris Conservatoire, **IV:** 156, 160, 164ff, 165, 188, 196ff, 199ff, 205; **V:** 197; **VIII:** 269ff [(9) works for voices and band, (2) *Overtures* (2) *Symphonies*, (6) *Marches* for band]; **XI:** 131, 297, 299; **XII:** 45

Catel, Charles-Simon, as composer of works arranged for Harmoniemusik, **VIII:** 14 [*l'Officier enlevé, Sémiramis, Wallace*]; 15 [*Zirphile et Fleur de Myrte*]

Catherine de Medici, 16th century, **II:** 73ff

Catherine II, 1729–1796, Empress of Russia, **IV:** 77

Cato, ?, composer in 1600 dance collection published in Heidelberg, **VII:** 180

Caton, Diomedes, 17th century Polish instrumental works, **VII:** 217

Catrufo, Giuseppe, 1771–1851, *Félicie*, opera, arranged for Harmoniemusik, **VIII:** 15

Catullus, 1st century BC Roman poet, **I:** 58, 59

Cauchie, F., 19th century French composer, **IX:** 25

Cauciello, Prospero, 18th century Italian composer, **XI:** 188

Caudron, L., 19th century French composer, **IX:** 25

Caulery, Jean, 16th century composer, **VI:** 107ff, 123

Caussinus, V., 19th century French composer, **IX:** 25

Causton, Thomas, early 16th century English composer, **VI:** 35

Causy, ?, 19th century French composer, **IX:** 25

Cavaccio, Giovanni, 1556–1626, Italian composer, **VI:** 95; **VII:** 198

Cavailini, P., 19th century English composer, **IX:** 268

Cavaillé-Massenet, F., 19th century French composer, **IX:** 26

Cavalari, Francesco, 18th century Italian composer, **XI:** 16

Cavalieri, Bonaventura, b. 1598, Milan, treatise on military music, **VII:** 187

Cavalli, Francesco, 1602–1676, composer, **III:** 74; **VII:** 187 [5-part hunting fanfares]

Cavallini, Ernesto, 1807–1874, Italian composer for band, **X:** 189

Cavazzoni, Hieronimo, 16th century composer, **VI:** 92

Cavelier, 18th century publisher in Paris, **VII:** 95

Caveron, Robert, 1st official leader of minstrels in France, 14th century, **I:** 146

Cavos, ?, 19th century German composer, **IX:** 141

Cayron, J., 19th century French composer, **IX:** 26

Cazzati, Maurizio, 1620–1677, Italian composer for trumpet sonatas, **VII:** 187; **XI:** 160

Cebedem, 20th century publisher in Brüsel, **XII:** 159

Cecere, Carlo, 18th century Italian composer, **XI:** 16, 188

Cejka, Valentin, 18th century composer in Graf Pachta Harmonie Coll., **IV:** 22, fn. 10; **VIII:** 180 [(3) *Divertimenti* for Harmoniemusik]

Çelebi (Efendi), Evilya, author on travels in 17th century Ottoman Empire, **III:** 107ff

Celestino, Eligio, 1739–1812, German, untitled work for Harmoniemusik, **VIII:** 307

Cellesi, Luigi [dedication], *Quintets* by Ghardeschi, 18th century, **VIII:** 365

Cellier, Alexandre-Eugene, b. 1883, French composer, **XII:** 77

Cellier, Alfred, 19th century English composer, **IX:** 268

Cellier, Jacques, artist drawings of the taille in 1660–1695, **III:** 226

Cellini, Benvenuto, 1500–1571, goldsmith, diarist, **II:** 112, 198; **IV:** 12

Centroni, Professor B., XI: 117 [dedication of a work by Raffaele Parma]

Cerclier, Jules-H.-L., 19th century French composer, **XI:** 307; **IX:** 26

Cerone, Domenico Pietro, 1566–1625 Italian composer, theorist, **III:** 4, 15

Cerquetelli, Giuseppe, 1848–1931, Italian composer, **X:** 190

Certon, Pierre, 1510–1572 French composer, **VI:** 38, 43ff, 49ff, 119

Cervetto, Giacobbe, 18th century Italian composer, **XI:** 17

Cesare, Giovanni, ca. 1590–1667, trombonist at Günzburg; Baaria; Fugger, **VII:** 113

Cesari, Pietro, 19th century Italian composer for band, **X:** 190

Cesti, Pietro, 1623–1669, Florentine composer, **III:** 62, 74

Chabrier, Emmanuel, 1841–1894, French, arr. Grovlez, **XII:** 193

Chabril, 16th century composer, **VI:** 82

Chailley, Jacques, 1910–1936, French composer, **XII:** 129

Chambroux, J., 19th century French composer, **IX:** 26

Champein, Stanislas, 1753–1830, works arranged for Harmoniemusik, **VIII:** 15, 153

Champein, unidentified work arranged by Ozi, **XII:** 51

Champernowne, Sir Richard, maintained wind band with Holborne, **II:** 59; **VI:** 33

Chanel, 19th century publisher in Lyon, **IX:** 1

Chanel, 19th century publisher in Lyon, **XII:** 70

Chao-hao, Emperor of China, 2,598 BC, **I:** 9

Chapdevielle, Pierre, b. 1906, French composer, **XII:** 77, 128

Chapelle, Ed., 19th century French composer, **IX:** 26

Chapelle, unnamed composition arranged by Ozi for Harmoniemusik, **VIII:** 153

Chapman and Beaumont, Baroque playwrights with wind band, **III:** 184

Chapman, 18th century publisher in London, **XI:** 11, 23, 104, 193, 215

Chapman, Richard, 18th century English, *Royal Circus* music, **VIII:** 254

Chappell, 20th century publisher in New York, **XII:** 92

Chardiny, unnamed composition arranged by Ozi for Harmoniemusik, **VIII:** 153

Chargnioux, Marie, 19th century French composer, **IX:** 26

Charigny, J.-A.-L, 19th century French composer, **IX:** 26

Charlemagne, I: 261; **X:** 108 [dedication]

Charles I, 1600–1649, King of England, **III:** 79, 90ff

Charles II of Spain, d. 1699, **III:** 151

Charles II, 1630–1685, King of England, **III:** 92ff, 148, 204; **IV:** 105; , **XI:** 190

Charles III of Spain, **III:** 152

Charles III, 1543–1608, Duke of Lorraine, **III:** 27ff

Charles IX of France, reigning 1560–1574, **II:** 73ff, 84, 217

Charles the Bold, Duke of Burgundy, **I:** 256ff

Charles V, 1500–1558, Emperor, Holy Roman Empire, **I:** 213; **II:** 24ff, 63, 88ff, 123,

Charles VI, 1380–1422, **I:** 213

Charles VI, Emperor, 1717–1740, **III:** 227

Charles VII, 1422–1461, **I:** 214

Charles VIII, 1483–1498, **I:** 216

Charles X of France, **IX:** 43, 149

Charles, ?, 18th century English composer, **XI:** 188, 257

Charles, ?, 19th century French composer, **IX:** 26

Charles, 18th century archduke of Austria, **X:** 27

Charles, Prince of Baviere, 19th century, **IX:** 187

Charlotte de Saxe, 19th century Princesse, **IX:** 170

Charlotte von Preussen, 19th century German composer, **IX:** 152

Charlotte, 18th century English Princess of Wales, **X:** 28

Charon of Lampsacus, 5th century BC historian, **I:** 37

Charpentier, Jean François, in 1777 of the Hautbois et Musettes du Poitou, **IV:** 64,

Charpentier, Marc-Antoine, 1643–1704, French composer, **III:** 217, 228; **VII:** 85

Chartrains, ?, 18th century composer, **XI:** 188

Chassain, Raoul, 19th century French composer, **IX:** 26

Chasseigneau, Paul, 19th century French composer, **IX:** 26

Chassin, A., 19th century French composer, **IX:** 26

Chastelain, Joannes, 16th century composer, **VI:** 25, 107, 123

Chastellain, Georges, Burgundian historian, 15th century, **I:** 215, 246

Chaucer, I: 80ff

Chaulier, Cyriaque, 19th century French composer, conductor, Musique au 6md de Ligne, **IX:** 27

Chaumont, Lambert, 1630–1712, on his use of winds in church, **III:** 199

Chaussee, Nivelle de la, owned a Chansonnier, 15th century, **VI:** 8

Chausson, Ernest, 1855–1899, French composer, **IX:** 27

Chavatte, Henri, 19th century French composer, **IX:** 27

Chavez, Carlos, b. 1899, Mexican composer, **XII:** 129

Checci, Rene, 18th century Italian composer, **XI:** 17

Chechi, ?, 18th century composer, **XI:** 188

Chedeville, Espirit Philippe, 1696–1762, French composer, **XI:** 17

Chédeville, Nicolas, French composer and member in 1777 of the Les Grands Hautbois, **IV:** 64, fn. 4; **VII:** 85ff; **XI:** 17, 228, 273

Chédville, Espirit Philippe, 1696–1762, member in 1768 of the Les Grands Hautbois, **IV:** 64, fn. 4; **VII:** 85

Cheisser (Reinhard Keiser), German composer, early 18th century, **XII:** 2

Chelard, Hippolyte, 1789–1861, German composer, arranger, **IX:** 152, 196

Chelleri (Keller), Fortunato, b. 1668, Italian composer in Germany ca. 1725, **VII:** 114; **XII:** 2

Chemin, Nicolas du, 16th century publisher in Paris, **II:** 71, 181; **VI:** 49, 54ff, 56

Chemin-Petit, Hans, b. 1902, German composer, **XII:** 129

Chemische Druckerei, 19th century publisher in Vienna, **VIII:** 7, 12, 122, 125, 137, 229ff, 235; **IX:** 211, 220, 218, 241, 243; **XI:** 31, 198

Chénier, Marie-Joseph, 1764–1811, leading French poet of the Revolution, **IV:** 159, 178ff, 194, 197

Cheron, André, 1695–1766, French composer, **XI:** 17, 188

Cherubini, Luigi, 1760–1842, composer in 1794 Paris Conservatoire, **IV:** 156, 162 fn. 46, 195, 198, 201, 203ff, 206, 214; **V:** 182, 197, 203; **VIII:** 273ff [(9) original works for voices and band]; **IX:** 27; **X:** 66

Cherubini, Luigi, 1760–1842, as composer of works arranged for Harmoniemusik, **VIII:** 16 [*Élisa oder der Bernhardsberg, L'Hôtellerie Portugaise, Médée*]; 17 [*Anacréon, La Prisonniére, Les deux Journées*]; 18 [*König Saul von Israel*]; 152 unidentified work; **X:** 66 [*Lodoiska*, anonymous arranger]; **XII:** 45 [*Faniska* arr Sedlak; *Die Tage der Gefah*, unidentified arranger]; 46 [*Lodoiska*, unidentified arranger for Harmoniemusik] 218

Cherubini, works arranged for band, **IX:** 141 [*les 2 Journées*]; 196 [Overture from *Der Wasserträger* arr. Geo. Schmitt]; 197 [Overture from *Demophon*), arr., S. J. Weber]; one unidentified work, 245

Cheryl Bishop, granddaughter to Georges Longy, **XII:** 193

Chés les fréres Meyn, 18th century publisher in Hambourg, **XII:** 53

Chevalier, R., 19th century French composer, **IX:** 27

Chevardiere, 18th century publisher in Paris, **XI:** 92, 187, 195

Chez Tournier, 19th century publisher in Paris, **XII:** 63

Chezam, Alexander, composer in 1621 German pub. of English ens. music, **VII:** 24

Chiapareli, ?, 18th century Italian composer, **XI:** 17

Chiaula, Mauro, 1544–1603, composer, **VI:** 105

Chic, Léon, 19th century French composer, conductor 66e de Ligne, **IX:** 1, 2, 28

Chiesa, Melchierre, 18th century Italian composer, **XI:** 189

Chiesa, Natale, 19th century (?) Italian composer, **XI:** 282

Chilese, ?, composer in 1608 Venetia canzoni collection, **VII:** 208

Chinelli, Giovani, 1610–1677, century Italian composer, **III:** 220; **VII:** 187

Chinzer, Giovanni, 18th century Italian composer in England, **XI:** 189

Chomel, L., 19th century French composer, **IX:** 28

Choquard, E., 19th century French composer, **IX:** 29

Choudens, 20th century publisher in Paris, **XII:** 76

Christenius, Johann, German composer of 1619 collection of instr. suites, **VII:** 153

Christian I of Saxony, 1560–1591, **II:** 114, 115 [instrument collection]

Christian III, King of Denmark, 1534–1559, royal wind band library, **II:** 110; **VI:** 24, 57

Christian IV, 1588–1648, King of Denmark, visits England in 1606, **III:** 79, 82; **VI:** 29

Christian Ludwig II, 1683–1756, Duke of Mecklenburg-Schwerin, **IV:** 59

Christian of Weissenfels, Duke, 1712–1736, **III:** 60

Christian von Hessen, 18th century Prince, **VIII:** 298

Christian, Prince of Saxony, 1702, **VII:** 112

Christianus dem Spelmann, cornettist in the Jacobkirche, Hamburg, **III:** 208

Christman, Harry, clarinetist in the 1910 Barrère Ensemble in NYC, **XII:** 214

Churchill, John, 1650–1722, Duke of Marlborough, **IV:** 109

Cianchi, Emilio, 19th century Italian composer, **IX:** 116

Cifra, ?, canzona composer in Venice, 16th century, **II:** 245

Cifra, Antonio, 1615 Italian composer of canzoni, ricercaras, **VII:** 198

Cigler, ?, *Parthia* in F for Harmoniemusik, **VIII:** 181

Cilea, *Gloria,* opera, arranged for band by Vessella, **X:** 254

Cima, Andrea, Italian composer in 1616, 1617 collections, **VII:** 198, 204

Cima, Giovanni, 1616 Italian composer of collections of instr. music, **VII:** 198, 205

Cimarosa, Domenico, 1749–1801, Italian composer, **IX:** 122; **XI:** 17, 189

Cimarosa, Domenico, 1749–1801, operas arranged for Harmoniemusik, **VIII:** 18 [*Giannina e Bernardone, L'Impresario in Augustie*]; 19 [*Il Matrimonio segreto*]; 20 [*Gli Orazi ed i Curiazi, Le Astuzie femminili*]; 21 [*Amor rende Sagace, I Nemici generosi, I Zingari in Fiera, Matrimonio per Raggiro*]; 22 [*Bohémiens en foire*]; unidentified works, 11, 21, 101, 155; **XII:** 46 [*Orazi e Curiazi* (opera) arr. by composer for Harmoniemusik]

Cimaroso, works arranged for band, **X:** 175 [unidentified work arranged for band by Petronio Avoni]

Cimino, Gabride, 19th century Italian composer, *Sinfonia* for band, **X:** 190

Cimoso, Domenico, 1780–1850, Italian composer, **IX:** 116

Ciotti, Francesco, 19th century Italian composer, *La Desolata. Elegia* for band, **X:** 190

Cipriani, 19th century publisher in Firenze, **XI: 138**

Cirri, Giovanni, 18th century Italian composer, **XI:** 17

Cisler, ?, *Parttia* for Harmoniemusik, **VIII:** 181

Citizen Vivazza [Rossini], **V:** 87

Ciuffolotti, Vincenzo, 18th century Italian, *Motetto,* 1796, for voices and winds, 364

Ciurache, Giovanni, 18th century Italian composer, **XI:** 18

Clagget, Charles, 19th century London inventor, **V:** 4

Clam-Gallas, Christian Philipp Graf, of Prague, 1748–1808, **IV:** 24ff

Clapisson, Louis, 1808–1966, French composer, **IX:** 29 [biographical note]

Clark, C., 19th century English composer for band, **X:** 119

Clarke, Jeremiah, ca. 1674–1707, suite for winds, **VII:** 15

Clarke, Nigel, 20th century English composer, **XII:** 202

Claus Schall, 1757–1835, Danish composer of horse ballet music in 1791, **IV:** 5

Cleland, James, author of treatise on manners in 1607, **III:** 89
Clemens non Papa, Jacques, 1510–1556, Flemish, composer, **II:** 121, 231; **VI:** 25ff , 45, 49, 84, 107ff, 109ff, 114, 118ff, 120, 122ff
Clement, J., 19th century English composer, **IX:** 268
Clement V, pope, 14th century, **I:** 187
Clement VII, pope, 1478–1534, **II:** 121ff; **IV:** 12
Clemente IX, 1600–1669, pope, trumpets in 1667, **III:** 72
Clemente X, 1590–1676, pope, trumpets in 1670, **III:** 73
Clemente XI, 1649–1721, pope, trumpets in 1700, **III:** 73
Clementi, 19th century publisher in London, **XI:** 47, 108, 245
Clementi, Muzio, 1752–1832, Italian composer, **XI:** 18, 212 [unidentified music, arr. Neilson]
Clendon, Hugh, 19th century English composer, **IX:** 268
Cleopatra, Egyptian queen, **VII:** 196
Cleopatra, X: 208 [dedication]
Clerico, Francesco, 1755–1838, works arranged for Harmoniemusik, **VIII:** 22
Cleton, 18th century publisher in Rome, **XI:** 95
Cleves, Anne, wife of Henry VIII, **II:** 27
Clodomir, P., 19th century French composer, **IX:** 29
Cobbold, W., 1560–1639, English composer of ensemble music, **VII:** 23, 33
Cocchi, Gioachino, 1715–1804, Italian composer, **X:** 36; , **XI:** 189
Coccon, Nicolo, 1826–1903, Venetian composer, **IX:** 116; **X:** 190 [church music with winds]
Cocconi, ?, 19th century Italian composer, church music with winds, **X:** 191
Coccurullo, Felice, 19th century Italian composer for band, **X:** 191
Coch, Johann, 18th century German composer, **XI:** 189
Cochet, 19th century publisher in Paris, **XI:** 129
Cocke, Arthur, d. 1604, English composer of ensemble music, **VII:** 33
Cocq, Gerard de, 16th century composer, **VI:** 26, 108
Codivilla, Filippo, b. 1841, Italian composer, **IX:** 117
Coenen, Johannes, 1824–1899, German composer of a *Tone Poem* for band, **X:** 96
Cohen, Karl, 1851–1938, German composer, **IX:** 152
Cohn, Arthur, b. 1910, American composer, **XII:** 78
Cohn, Irving, oboist in the 1910 Barrère Ensemble in NYC, **XII:** 214
Col. Joseph, 19th century French composer, conductor 66e de Ligne, **IX:** 1, 29
Cole, James, creator of a writing sampler illustrating a Wait band in 1742, **III:** 178
Coleman, Charles, d. 1664, English composer of ensemble music, **VII:** 33ff
Coleridge-Taylor, Samuel, 1875–1912, English composer, **XII:** 129
Colerus, Valentin, German composer, 1604, 1605 works for winds, **VII:** 114, 153
Colin, Pierre, 16th century composer, **VI:** 56
Collaert, Adrian, artist in Italy, 16th century, **II:** 205
Collardo, ?, 19th century composer, **IX:** 141
Collauf, ?, 19th century American composer, **IX:** 137

Collection Époques, 18th century publisher in Paris, **VIII:** 272ff, 283ff

Collection of military marches in Berlin, 1867–68, **X:** 95

Collection, 20 Italian *Märsche* for military band, **IX:** 115

Collection, anonymous Polish group of 71 works without titles, 1800–1868, **IX:** 129

Collection, anonymous Polish, ten *Polonoises,* 1800–1868, **IX:** 130

Collection, US, 11th US Infantry, 1862, for band, **IX:** 137

Collection, US, 25th Mass. Regiment band books, 70 works for band, **IX:** 137

Collection, US, 26th Regimental Band, NC, c. 1862–1865, parts for band, **IX:** 137

Collection, US, 3rd New Hampshire Infantry band books, 50 works for band, **IX:** 137

Collection, US, *Brass band Journal*, 1854, **IX:** 137

Collection, US, of dances, marches, 65 full scores, **IX:** 137

Collection, US, Stratton *Military Band Journal*, 1866–1871, 150 works, **IX:** 137

Collet, 19th century publisher in Paris, **IX:** 36

Collier, Alexandre-Eugene, b. 1883, French composer, **XII:** 129

Colline, Victor, 19th century English composer, **IX:** 269

Colloredo-Waldsee, Anton Theodor, 1777–1811, Archbishop at Kromeriz, **IV:** 22

Colman, ?, composer in 1613–1618 ensemble collection, **VII:** 22

Colman, John, 18th century English composer, (24) Marches, 1796, for band, **VIII:** 254

Colmier, L., 19th century French composer, **IX:** 29

Colombani, Orazio, 1535–1595, composer, **VI:** 105

Colonne, 19th century French composer, **XII:** 212

Comettant, ? 19th century French reviewer of the Distin Quintet, **V:** 164

Comina, W., 19th century French composer, **IX:** 29

Commer, Franz, 1813–1887, German composer, **IX:** 152

Compere, composer in *Odhecaton*, 1501, **VI:** 17

Compini, Leopoldo, Italian composer ca. 1850, **V:** 89

Comtesse de Wallerstein, 18th century, **VIII:** 194

Condé, 18th century Prince de, **VIII:** 281

Conforti, Giovanni, 1560–1608, Italian composer, **VI:** 96; **VII:** 198

Coniac, Pieter de, Dutch instrument maker, 16th century, **II:** 165

Connor, Bill, 20th century English composer, **XII:** 202

Conor, Léon, 19th century French composer, **IX:** 29

Conradi, A., 19th century English composer, **IX:** 269

Conradi-Carlshall, W., (1864) German composer, **IX:** 152

Conseil, Jean, 1498–1534, French composer, **VI:** 63

Constant, H., 19th century French composer, **IX:** 30

Constantini, Francesco, 1789–1854, Italian composer, **IX:** 117

Conterno, G.E., b. 1866, English composer for band, **IX:** 269; **X:** 119

Conti, A., 19th century French composer, **IX:** 30

Conway, 20th century American band conductor, **XII:** 201

Cook, H.J., 19th century English composer, **IX:** 269; **X:** 117

Cooke, 18th century publisher in Dublin, **VIII**: 258
Cooke, Arnold, b. 1906, English composer, **XII**: 78
Cooke, B., 18th century publisher in London, **XI**: 5, 80, 190, 200, 236
Cooke, Grattan, 19th century English composer, **IX**: 269
Cooke, Henry, 1615–1672, English composer, **VII**: 15
Cools, Eugene, 1877–1936, French composer, **XII**: 78, 130
Cooper, 18th century publisher in Edinburgh, **XI**: 62
Coote, ?, editor of a 19th century English band journal, **V**: 82
Coote, Charles, Jr., 19th century English composer, **IX**: 269
Coote, Charles, Sr., 19th century English composer, **IX**: 269
Cope, W., 18th century English composer, **XI**: 189
Copland, Aaron, 20th century American composer, **XII**: 202
Coprario (Cooper), John, ca. 1570–1626, English composer, **VI**: 36; **VII**: 20, 22, 23, 25, 26, 28, 34ff, 73
Coqquelin, G., 19th century French composer, **IX**: 30
Coqueterre, 19th century French arranger, conductor, 13e Artillerie, **IX**: 2
Coqulet, O., 19th century French composer, **IX**: 30
Coquterre, François, 19th century French composer, **IX**: 30
Corbin, Alexandre, member in 1777 of the Hautbois et Musettes du Poitou, **IV**: 64, fn. 5; **IX**: 30
Cordeilles, Charles, fl. ca. 1540–1548 French composer, for Lyons wind band, **VI**: 56
Cordier, 19th century publisher in Paris, **IX**: 5
Corelli, Arcangelo, 1653–1713, Italian composer, **III**: 16, 19; **XI**: 18
Coreria, Cherubino, 18th century Italian composer, **XI**: 190
Cormier, Carlo, 19th century (?) Italian composer, **XI**: 271
Cornale, Lodouico, cornettist in Venice in 1608, **III**: 194; **VII**: 203
Cornazzani, Phileno, 1543–1628, lost work for Emperor Ferdinand I, **VI**: 77
Cornet, Christoph, German composer of 8-part canzon, **VII**: 143, 163
Cornet, Séverin, 1530–1594, Franco-Flemish composer, **VI**: 121
Cornu, Jacques, serpent, 1793 faculty of Paris Conservatoire, **IV**: 162
Cornysh, 16th century composer, **VI**: 35
Corradini, Nicolò, 17th century, Italian composer of ricercare and canzoni, **VII**: 187, 199
Corrette, Michel, 1709–1795, French composer, **XI**: 18, 190, 239, 257, 267
Correvon de Ribaucourt, Marie-Louise, 19th century French composer, **IX**: 31
Corri, Dussek, 18th century publisher in London & Edinburgh, **XI**: 214, 216
Cortazar, M., 19th century French composer, **IX**: 31
Corteccia, Francesco, 1502–1571, Italian composer, **VI**: 104
Corvinus, Georg, 16th century publisher in Frankfurt, **VI**: 72
Coryat, Thomas, on church music in Venice in 1608, **III**: 219
Cosimo I, Duke of Florence, 1519–1574, **II**: 127ff; **III**: 74; **VI**: 104
Cossart, Leland, b. 1877, German composer, **IX**: 152; **XII**: 78, 193
Costa, 17th century canzona composer, **VII**: 180, 208

Costa, Antonio, 19th century Italian composer, **X:** 191

Costa, *Histoire d'un Pierrot*, arranged for band by Vessella, **X:** 254

Costallat, 19th and 20th century publisher in Paris, **XI:** 50, 122, 170; **XII:** 139

Cotes, Ambrosio, ca. 1550–1603, Seville, composer, **VI:** 125

Cotischau, 19th century German composer, **IX:** 180

Cotté, E., 19th century French composer, **IX:** 31

Couldery, Claudius, 19th century English composer, **IX:** 269

Couleuvrier, 19th century French composer, **IX:** 31

Count de Monterey, 17th century Spanish noble, **III:** 75

Count Palatine of Germany, music for marriage in 1612, **III:** 69

Couperin, François (le grand), French composer for Hautboisten, **VII:** 94

Couperin, Louis, 1626–1661, French composer for Hautboisten, **VII:** 86

Coupigny, 18th century French poet, **IV:** 205

Cour, Claude, de la, member in 1777 of the Hautbois et Musettes du Poitou, **IV:** 64, fn. 5

Courbet, Admiral [dedication], **IX:** 28

Courteville, Raphael, 18th century French composer, **XI:** 190

Courtin, ?, 19th century French composer, **IX:** 31

Courtin, 18th century arranger of a collection of Harmoniemusik, **VIII:** 154

Courtois, Jean, 16th century composer, **VI:** 26, 63, 119

Cousin, H., 19th century French composer, conductor, 2nd Rég. Da Génie, **IX:** 1

Cousin, Jean, 1425–1475, Flemish composer, **VI:** ix

Cousser, Johan, Baroque German composer, for Hautboisten, **VII:** 114

Couthier, E., 19th century French composer, **IX:** 31

Covalovsky, in an anonymous 18th century arrangement for Harmoniemusik, **VIII:** 151

Cowen, Sir. Frederic, 19th century English composer, **IX:** 269

Cowper, 16th century composer, **VI:** 31, 35

Cox, 18th century publisher in London, **XI:** 81

Coyon, Emile, 19th century French composer, **IX:** 31

Cozzi, Gaetano, 19th century Italian composer, church music with band, **X:** 191

Cramer, 20th century publisher in London, **XII:** 136

Cramer, Carl, 1752–1807, prof. at Keil, reports on Harmonie in Bonn and Vienna, **IV:** 17, 36, 51

Cramer, Johann, 1771–1858, English composer, *March from Divertimento*, arr. Triebensee, **VIII:** 22ff; **XI:** 18ff

Cramer, Wilhelm, 1746–1799, *Rondo* for Harmoniemusik, **VIII:** 307

Cranford, William, ca. 1500–1530, English composer of ensemble music, **VII:** 25, 41; **VII:** 26

Cranz, 19th century publisher in Hamburg, **XI:** 51, 73

Cranz, 19th century publisher in Leipzig, **XI:** 50

Cras, Jean, 1879–1932, French composer, **XII:** 130

Creatore, Luigi, 20th century band conductor, **XII:** 201

Cremitasch, ?, *Parthia* for Harmoniemusik, **VIII:** 181

Crémont, Pierre, 1784–1846, French composer, **IX:** 31

Crémont, Pietro, 19th century, German professor of clarinet in Vienna in 1825, **XI:** 131

Crequillon, Thomas, 1505–1557, Franco-Flemish composer, **VI:** 26, 63ff, 82, 84ff, 107ff, 109ff, 117ff, 122ff

Crespel, Jean, fl. mid-16th century, French composer, **VI:** 26, 107ff, 109, 120, 122ff,

Cressonnois, Jules, 19th century French composer, **IX:** 32

Cressonois, ?, conductor of a French band in the 1867 competition, **V:** 117

Creste, W., 19th century French composer, **IX:** 32

Crisanti, Vincenzo, b. 1813, Italian composer under Pio X, for band, **X:** 192

Crispin, Eugene, 19th century French composer, **IX:** 32

Cristoforo Colombo, [dedication] **X:** 202

Croce, Giovanni Dalla, 16th century composer, **VI:** 105

Croce, Giovanni, 17th century Italian composer, **XI:** 219

Croebelis, Domingo, 18th century composer in Denmark, *Quartet* for flutes, **VIII:** 249

Croes, Henri-Joseph, 1758–1842, composer for Harmonie at Regensburg, **IV:** 58; **VIII:** 307ff [(30) *Partitas* for Harmonie]; **IX:** 180

Croft, Frederick, 19th century English composer, **IX: 269**

Croft, William, 1678–1727, English composer, **XI:** 18, 190

Croisez, ?, 19th century English composer, **IX:** 269

Cross, 18th century publisher in London, **XI:** 31

Crotti, Archangelo, fl. 1608, Ferrara, vocal chant with wind canzona, **VII:** 188, 199

Crotti, Giovanni, 19th century Italian composer, **X: 192**

Crowe, Alfred, 19th century English composer, **IX:** 270

Crüger, Johann, 1598–1662, German composer, **III:** 215; **VII:** 114

Crusell, Bernard, 1775–1838, Swedish clarinetist, **VIII:** 5 [arranger of the Beethoven *Septet*, Op. 20 for band]; **XI:** 131 [biographical note]

Ctesibius, 3rd century BC inventor, **I:** 17

Culliford, Rolfe & Barrow, 18th century publisher in London, **VIII:** 251ff, 263; **XI:** 210

Cumberland, Earl of, 17th century English noble, **III:** 88

Curci, Giusuppe, 19th century Italian composer for band, **X:** 192

Curschmann, Karl, 1805–1841, German composer, **IX:** 153; **X:** 96

Curtenbosch, Arent van, member of the Oudenaarde town band, 16th century, **II:** 168

Curtois, 16th century composer, **VI:** 85

Cushing, Charles, 20th century American composer, **XII:** 202

Cyrano de Bergerac, 20th century composition by Herberigs, **XII:** 145

Czapek, Leopold, 1792–1840 Bohemian composer, **XI:** 19

Czar of Russia, 18th century, **VIII:** 352

Czermak, ?, composer included in a 1870 English collection of band music, **X:** 113

Czerny, 19th century pianist, **XII:** 80 [unidentified melody, used by Edouard Flament]

Czerny, Gaspard, 18th century, **XI:** 126 [biographical note]

Czerwenka, Franz, bassoonist in Harmoniemusik of Cardinal Batthyány, **IV:** 33, fn. 71, and Imperial Harmoniemusik in Vienna, **IV:** 35, fn. 77

Czeyka, Valentin, b. ca. 1769, Polish, works for band and Harmoniemusik, **VIII:** 181, 369; **X:** 41 [*Ländler* for Harmoniemusik]

Czibulka, Alphons, 1842–1894, Austrian military band leader, **V:** 43; **IX:** 153, 270

d'Albert, Eugen, 1864–1932, Scottish-German composer, **XII:** 123

D'Auxerre, 16th century composer, **VI:** 45, 48

d'Indy, Vincent, 1851–1931, French composer, **V:** 121, fn. 53; **IX:** 57; **XII:** 91, 194, 212, 213, 214, 215

Dacci, Gusto, 1840–1905, Italian composer for band, **X:** 192

Daddi, Giuseppe, 19th century Italian composer for band, **X:** 192

Dagnelies, D., 19th century French composer, **IX:** 32

Dal Vasco, Agostino, Italian composer, **IX:** 117

Dalayrac, Nicolas, 1753–1809, composer of works arranged for Harmoniemusik, **VIII:** 22, 54 [*Nina*]; 23 [*Azemia, Camille, Les deux petits Savoyards*]; 24 [*Gulistan, Gulnare, La jeune Prude*]; 25 [*Corsaire, Die Nacht in Walde, La Tour de Neustadt, Poëte et le Musicien*]; 26 [*d'une Heure de Marriage, La Boucle de Cheveux, Picaros et Diègo, Sargines*]; unidentified works, 13, 153ff

Dalayrac, Nicolas, 1753–1809, composer of works arranged for band, **IX:** 197 [*Adolphe et Clara, Nacht im Walde, Maison a Vendre*]

Dale, 18th and 19th century publisher in London, **VIII:** 252, 259, 302; **IX:** 263; **XI:** 7, 89

dall'Abaco, Felice, 1675–1742, Italian composer, **III:** 14

Dall'argine, Luigi, 19th century Italian composer, church works with winds, **X:** 193

Dalla Casa, Girolamo, 1530–1601, leader Doge's wind band, Venice, author of *Il Vero Modo de Diminuir,* for wind ensemble, **II:** 201ff, 241, 243, 253ff, 262, **III:** 12; **VI:** 83, 105

Dalla Casa, Nicoló, d. 1617, Italian composer, **II:** 243; **VI:** 105

Dalla Casa, Zuanne, II: 243

Dallée, ?, 19th century French composer, **IX:** 2, 32

Daman, Wm., composer in 1613–1619 Tregian ensemble collection, **VII:** 23

Dambert, 16th century composer, **VI:** 123

Damian, François, 19th century French composer, **IX:** 32

Dampierre, Marc Antoine, French composer for Hautboisten, **VII:** 86

Damrosch, Walter, 20th century conductor of the New York Symphony, **XII:** 213

Danckelmann, 19th century German composer, **XII:** 68

Danckerts (Dankers), Ghiselin, 1510–1565, Dutch composer, **VI:** 30, 63

Danese, Domenico, 19th century Italian composer, *Elegia funebre* for band, **X:** 193

Daniero, Francisco, 19th century Italian composer for band, **X:** 193

Danvaux, Jean, 1742–1822, French composer, **XI:** 273

Danzi, Franz, 1763–1826, German composer, *Sestetto* and *Pot-pourri* for Harmoniemusik, **VIII:** 27 [*Freudenfest,* arr. Sartorius for Harmoniemusik]; **VIII:** 309 [*Sestetto* and *Pot-pourri* for Harmoniemusik]; **X:** 24; **XI:** 19, 105, 151, 232, 247

Dard, Antoine, member in 1768 of the Les Grands Hautbois, **IV:** 64, fn. 4

Darius III, King of Persia, **I:** 11

Daroudeau, ?, *Rosier,* arranged for Harmoniemusik, **VIII:** 27

Darthu, Paul, 20th century French composer, **XII:** 78

Daser, Ludwig, 16th century German composer, **III:** 60

Dasque, Auguste, 19th century French composer, **IX:** 32

Dassonville, ?, 19th century French composer, **IX:** 32

Daubmann, Johann, 16th century publisher in Königsberg, **VI:** 69

Dauprat, Louis, 1781–1868, French hornist & composer, horn teacher at the Paris Conservatory, **IX:** 32; **X:** 24; **XI:** 164, 257, 286, 309; **XII:** 65

Dauxerre, 16th century French composer, **VI:** 49

Davenant, William, 1606–1668, English impresario, **III:** 179

Davenne, A., 19th century French composer, **IX:** 33

Davergne, A., 19th century French composer, **IX:** 33

David, 18th and 19th century publisher in Paris, **VIII:** 288; **IX:** 4, 11

David, Adolfo, 19th century Italian composer, *Ronda dei Pifferari,* **X:** 193

David, Carl Henrich, 1884–1951, Swiss composer, **XII:** 78, 131

David, Édouard, 19th century French composer, **IX:** 33

David, Felicien, 1810–1876, composer, **V:** 114 [judge of the 1867 world competition in Paris]; **IX:** 33

David, Ferdinand, 19th century German composer, **XI:** 132, 176

David, Jacques-Louis, 1748–1825, French painter, **IV:** 172ff, 178ff, 190ff

David, Johann Nepomuk, b. 1895, Austrian composer, **XII:** 78, 131

Davide da Bergamo, 1791–1863, pseudo. for Felice Moretti, Italian composer, **X:** 193

Davies, Henry Walford, 1869–1941, composer, **XII:** 78

Davis, Thomas, 18th century, English composer, **XI:** 19

Dawid, Josef, as 19th century arranger, **IX:** 130

Day, J., 16th century publisher in London, **VI:** 35

De Caix, d'Hervelois, Louis, 1680–1760, French, **XI:** 19

De Fesch, Willem, 1687–1761, Dutch composer, **XI:** 190

De Giorgi, Andrea, 1836–1900, Italian composer, **X:** 194

De Giovanni, Domenico, 19th century Italian composer for band, **X:** 197

De la Rue, 16th century composer, **VI:** 43

De Latre, Petit Jan, 1505–1569, composer, **VI:** 26, 107ff, 109, 114, 122ff

De Ler, Giovanni, leader of Torino town band in 1567, **II:** 197

De Maio, Gian Francesco, 18th century Italian, *Salve* for soprano and winds, **VIII:** 364

De Marinis, Clodomiro, 19th century Italian composer, *Sinfonia* for band, X: 198

De Michelis, Cesare, 1810–1867, Italian composer for band, **X:** 198

De Wailly, L., b. 1854, French composer, **IX:** 36

Deacon, Charles, 19th century English composer, **IX:** 270

Debali, Francisco José, 1791–1859 Hungarian, worked in Paraguay, **XII:** 55ff

Debrière ?, 19th century French composer, **IX:** 33

Debussy, Claude, 19th century French composer, **XII:** 197, 218

Declerck, 19th century French composer, **IX:** 2

Decombe, 18th century publisher in Paris, **VIII:** 7, 9, 268, 276

Decq, A., 19th century French composer, **IX:** 33

Dédé, Eugéne, 19th century French composer, **IX:** 33

Dedonati, Girolamo, 18th century Italian composer, **XI:** 190, 235

Deering, Richard, d. 1630, English composer of ensemble music, **VII:** 20, 23, 25, 26, 28, 42ff

Degen, Helmut, b. 1911, German composer, **XII:** 132

Degensee, Jonas, father of a Stadtpfeifer applicant in 1607, **III:** 159

Dehn, Johann Caspar, 17th century publisher in Zittau, **VII:** 119

Deiselbach, ?, 18th Century German, *Parthia* for Harmoniemusik, **VIII:** 309

Delabaut, Paul, 19th century French composer, **IX:** 33

Delaborde, ?, Ouverture de *Cinquantine*, arr. Fuchs for Harmoniemusik, **VIII:** 27

Delafont, 16th century French composer, **VI:** 45, 48ff

Delannoy, Marcel-François-Georges, b. 1898, French composer, **XII:** 132

Delarue, J., 19th century French composer, **IX:** 33

Delâtre, Lucien, 19th century French composer, **IX:** 33

Delattre, A., 19th century French composer, **IX:** 33

Delaunay, P.-D., 19th century French composer, **IX:** 34

Delaundis, Ad., 19th century French composer, **IX:** 34

Delaye, Georges, 19th century French composer, **IX:** 34

Delbove, ?, 19th century French composer, **IX:** 34

Delcambre, Pierre, faculty of the 1792 Paris Conservatoire, **IV:** 157

Delcambre, Thomas, 18th century French bassoon prof. at the 1792 Paris Conservatory, **IV:** 156; **XI:** 151

Delchavalerie, Henri, 19th century French composer, **IX:** 34

Delibes, Leo, 1836–1891, [judge of the 1867 world competition in Paris], **V:** 114

Della Maria, Pierre-Antoine Dominique, 1769–1800, operas arr. for Harmonie, **VIII:** 27 [*L'Oncle Valet, L'Opéra-comique, Le Prisonnier, vieux Chateau*]; unidentified works, 151, 274; **X:** 21 [*Der Gefangene*) arr. for Harmoniemusik]

Dellac, H., 19th century French composer, **IX:** 34

Delle Cese, Davide, 1856–1938, Italian composer for band, **X:** 197

Dello Joio, Norman, b. 1913, American composer, **XII:** 132

Delmas, Marc, 1885–1931, French composer, **XII:** 132

Delorme & Roger, 17th century publisher in Amsterdam, **XI:** 229

Delrieu, 20th century publisher in Nizza, **XII:** 164

Delsouc, F., 19th century French composer, **IX:** 34

Demachi, ?, 18th century Italian composer, **XI:** 191

Demance, 19th century French composer, **IX:** 34

Demanchi, Giuseppe, 19th century Italian composer, **XI:** 267

Demantius, Johannes, 1567–1643, German composer, **VI:** 66; **VII:** 153ff

Demaré, E., 19th century French composer, **IX:** 34

Demersseman, Jules, A. E.. 19th century French composer, **IX:** 34

DeMicco, Domenico, 18th century Italian composer, **XI:** 19, 105

Demoiver, ?, 18th century French flautist & composer, **XI:** 20

Demuth, Norman, b. 1938, English composer, **XII:** 79

Denner, Jacob, 18th century German woodwind maker, **III:** 213

Dentice, ?, Italian composer in 1616 canzoni collection, **VII:** 194

Dentice, Luigi, b. ca. 1510, Naples, composer, **VI:** 103

Déo, Louis, 19th century French composer, **IX:** 34

Deola, Paolo, 19th century Italian composer, **IX:** 117; **X:** 198 [church works with band]

Déplace, Claude, 19th century French composer, **IX:** 35

Deplaix, 19th century publisher in Paris, **XI:** 170

Deragini, ?, 18th century Italiam composer, **XI:** 191

Deransart, Édouard, 19th century French composer, **IX:** 35

Dertali, 17th century composer, **VII:** 149

Dervieux, ?, 19th century French composer, **IX:** 35

Desailly, L., 19th century French composer, **IX:** 35

Desblins, A., 19th century English composer, **IX:** 270

Descaudain, 16th century composer, **VI:** 118

Deschalumeaux, ?, 19th century composer arranged for band, **IX:** 197 [*Monsieur des Chalumeaux*) (ca. 1810) arr. Schmitt]

Descoins, ?, 19th century French composer, **IX:** 35

Descoteaux, flute player under Louis XIV, **III: 39**

Desderi, Ettore, b. 1892, Italian composer, **XII:** 132

Desehaye, 18th century composer, **XI:** 239

Deserbelles, Claude, 19th century French composer, **IX:** 35

Deshayes, Prosper-Diodier, d. 1815, composer of works arranged for Harmoniemusik, **VIII:** 29 [*Le faux serment, Zelia*]; unidentified works, 153, 274; **IX:** 35

DeSimoni, Pietro, 18th century (?), Italian composer, **XI:** 106

Desiro, ?, 19th century Italian composer, **IX:** 117

Desjardins, Jean Baptiste, oboist of the Les Grands Hautbois, **III:** 34; **VII:** 83

Desmarets, Henri, 1662–1741, French composer, **XI:** 20

Dessane, L. A., 19th century French composer, **IX:** 1, 2, 35

Dessauer, Joseph, 19th century Austrian composer, **XI:** 165

Destrube, ?, 19th century French composer, **IX:** 35

Desvignes, Pierre, late 19th century French composer, **IX:** 36

Dethick, ?, composer in early 17th century English fantasias collection, **VII:** 20

Dethou, Léon, 19th century French, *Treatise on Instrumentation*, **IX:** 36

Devasini, ?, 18th century Italian, *Sestetto*, for Harmoniemusik with flute, **VIII:** 364

Devasini, Giuseppe, 1822–1878, Italian composer, **IX:** 117; **X:** 198 [*Messe* for band]

Devienne, François, 1759–1803, composer, flute faculty of the 1792 Paris Conservatoire, **IV:** 156, 163, 168; **VIII:** [*Overture* and (2) works for voices, Harmonie]; **IX:** 113, 141; **XI:** 21, 22 [biographical note], 106, 132, 151, 165, 191, 217, 239, 243, 247, 251, 267, 274, 277, 280, 282, 298

Devienne, François, 1759–1803, as composer of works arranged for Harmoniemusik, **VIII:** 29 [*Les Visitandins, Le valet de deux maîtres*]; 35 [*L'Amour filial*]; , **XII:** 53 [*Les Visitandines,* arr. arranged for Harmoniemusik by Stumpf]

Dezède (Desaides), Nicolas, ca. 1740–1792, works arranged for Harmoniemusik, **VIII:** 28 [*Blaise et Babet, La fête de la Cinquantaine*]; 153, unidentified work

Diabelli, 19th century publisher in Vienna, **XI:** 98

Diabelli, Antonio, 1781–1858, Austrian composer, publisher, **VIII:** 30, 152 [works arranged for Harmoniemusik]; **IX:** 243, 244, 254; **X:** 45; **XI:** 304

Diane de Poitiers [dedication], **X:** 152

Dias, J.-B., 19th century French composer, **IX:** 36

Dibdin, Charles, 1745–1814, English, (12) *Marches* for Harmoniemusik, **VIII:** 254ff; **XI:** 22

Dickhut, ?, fl. 1800–1828, German composer, **IX:** 153

Diederichs, 18th century publisher in Amsterdam, **XI:** 84

Diehl, J., composer included in 19th century English band collections, **X:** 116, 117

Diemer, Louis Joseph, 1843–1919, French composer, **XII:** 132

Diepenbrock, Alphons, 1862–1921, French composer, **XII:** 133

Dieppo, ?, 19th century French composer, **IX:** 2

Dierolf, H., 19th century French composer, **IX:** 36

Diessineer (Diessener) Gerhard, 17th century German composer of instrumental suites, **VII:** 43, 154

Diethe, composer included in a 1874 English collection of band music, **X:** 113

Dietl, A.R., 20th century Austrian composer, **XII:** 79

Dietrich, Katharina, 16th – 17th century Nürnberg publisher, **VI:** 66

Dietrich, Sixt, 1492–1548, composer, **VI:** 62ff

Dietrichstein, Austrian Prince, as composer, **IV:** 41

Dietrichstein, Count as rider in a horse ballet in 1667, **III:** 62

Dietsch, Pierre, 1808–1865, French composer, **IX:** 36

Dietter, Christian Ludwig, 1757–1822, German composer, **XI:** 251, 268

Dietzl, Joseph, Jr, horn player at Esterházy in 1765, **IV:** 28

Dieupart, Charles, d. 1740, French composer, **XI:** 22

Diez, Johann, 1711–1793, German, *Lauda* for SATB, trumpets, **VIII:** 310

Dignam, Walter, 19th century American composer, **IX:** 137

Diodorus of Sicily, Etruscan, **I:** 49

Dioter, ?, 18th century composer, **XI:** 22

Diran, Adelaide, 19th century Italian composer for band, **X:** 198

Discher, J., 18th century Bohemian composer in Olmütz Harmoniemusik collection, **IV:** 22, fn. 9; **VIII:** 181 [(5) *Partias* for Harmoniemusik]

Distin, Henry, V: 82, 164 [on visiting Sax in 1844]

Distin, John, b. 1798, English brass player, **V:** 163

Distin, saxhornist, **V:** 203

Distler, Johann, 1760–1799, German composer, **XI:** 22

Dittersdorf, Karl Ditters von, 1739–1799, German composer at the court of Maria Theresia, **III:** 63; **IV:** 16, 22, fn. 10; **VIII:** 310ff [(67) *Partitas* for Harmoniemusik]; **XI:** 106, 257

Dittersdorf, Karl Ditters von, 1739–1799, operas arranged for Harmoniemusik, **VIII:** 30 [*Betrug durch Aberglauben, Der Doctor und Apotheker, Hironimus Knicker*]; unidentified work, 154

Dittrichstein, Graf Moritz, 1775–1864, *Minuetto* for Harmoniemusik, **VIII:** 181

Divoir, Victor, S., 19th century French composer, **IX:** 36

Dixon, William, b. 1760, English, Church music for voices and winds, **VIII:** 254; **XI:** 160

Dlabacz, Gottfried Johann, 1758–1820, Bohemian monk, **IV:** 37

Döbereiner, Christian, b. 1874, German composer, **XII:** 133

Dobihal, Josef, *Farso,* opera?, unknown arranger for Harmoniemusik. Dobihal was a clarinetist, military band conductor and mentioned in Beethoven's conversation book for 1813–1814, **VIII:** 31

Doblinger, 20th century publisher in Vienna, **XII:** 72, 118, 155

Dodwell, Samuel, 19th century English composer, **IX:** 270

Dodworth, Allen, 19th century American composer, **IX:** 137

Doering, ?, 19th century French composer, **IX:** 36

Doge of Venice [his wind band], 16th century, **II:** 134

Doinelle, A., 19th century French composer, **IX:** 36

Dolezálek, Jan, 1780–1858, Bohemian composer, **IX:** 210

Domenichini, Antonio, Italian oboist, composer, fl. ca. 1770, **X:** 36; **XI:** 22, 297

Domenichini, Carlo, 18th century (?), Italian composer, **XI:** 22

Domenico, Joan, 16th century composer, **VI:** 30

Domerque, Charles, 19th century French composer, **IX:** 36

Domerque, F., 19th century French composer, **IX:** 36

Dominick, M., 18th century French horn professor in the Paris Conservatory, **XI:** 165

Domnich, Henry, hornist, 1793 faculty of Paris Conservatoire, **IV: 162**

Don Lord Duarte, 17th century Spanish noble, **III:** 75

Donati, Ignazio, 1623, Italian composer for voices and winds, **VII:** 188ff; **XI:** 322

Donato, Baldassare, 1525–1603, Italian composer, **VI:** 65, 114

Donderer, Benedick, 19th century German composer, **IX:** 153

Donelli, ?, 18th century Italian composer, a composition for flute, **XI:** 22

Donelli, Benedetto, 19th century Italian composer for band, **X:** 199

Donizetti, Gaetano, 1797–1848, Italian composer, **III:** 103; **V:** 170, 180; **IX:** 117, 118; **X:** 199; 214 [dedication]; 215 [mss copy in Donizetti's hand of a work by Mayr]

Donizetti, Gaetano, 1797–1848, operas arranged for Harmoniemusik, **VIII:** 31 [*Anna Bolena, L'Elisiar d'Amore, Marino Faliero, Torquato Tasso*]; unidentified works, 151, 152ff

Donizetti, Gaetano, works arranged for band, **IX:** 43 [*L'Elisire d'Amore*]; 62 [*Lucrezia Borgia*]; 255 [*Belisar*, Esula di Rome, *Faust, La Favorita, Fernando e Bianca, dem Liebestrank, Linda di Chamonix, Lucia di Lammermoor, Lugretia, Lucrezia Borgia, Maria de Rudenza*]; unidentified works, 28, 174, 253; **X:** 137 [*I Martiri*, arr. Kappey];165 [unidentified arranger

of *Don Pasquale*]; 192 [*Lucia di Lammermoor* and *Poliuto*, arr. Petrelli]; 234 [*La Favorita*, arr. Ponchielli]; 235 [*Gemma di Vergy*, arr. Ponchielli]; 236 [*Don Sebastiano*, arr. Ponchielli]; 254 [*Lucrezia Borgia*, arr. Vessella]; **XI**: 49 [*Robert Devereus*, arr. Hünten, Franz]

Donizetti, Giuseppe, 1788–1856, band director and brother to the famous brother, **V**: 89, fn. 6; **IX**:118; **X**: 200

Donjon, Johannes, 19th century French composer, **IX**: 37

Donne, Francesco, 1599 publisher in Verona, **VI**: 93

Donninger, Ferdinand, 1716–1781, *Partita* in 10 movements, Harmoniemusik, **VIII**: 313

Donostia, P. Jose Antonio de, b. 1886, Spanish composer, **XII**: 132

Dopper, Cornelis, 1870–1939, Dutch composer, **XII**: 133

Doppler, ?, 19th century German composer, **X**: 97

Doppler, Franz, 1821–1883, Hungarian composer, **XI**: 22

Dorati, Bartolomeo, member of 16th century Lucca town band, **II**: 199

Dorati, Nicolao, 16th century trombonist and leader of the Lucca town band, **II**: 199

Dorbe, Hans, early 20th century German composer in Munich, **XII**: 79

Doremieulx, H. I. L., 18th century French flautist in Paris, **XI**: 23

Dörffeld, Anton, 19th century director of the Russian Kaiser's Guard Corps, **V**: 17 fn. 48, 85, 117; **IX**:141

Dorfner, Felise, 19th century Austrian composer, **IX**:210

Dorico, Valerio, 1558 publisher in Rome, **VI**: 96

Döring, Johann Friedrich, 1766–1840 *New Year's Song*, voices and brass, **VIII**: 313

Dorn, Joseph, 19th century Italian composer for band, **X**: 200

Dornaus, Jr., 1800–1828, German composer, **IX**:153

Dornaus, L., 18th century German horn player & composer, **XI**: 165

Dornaus, Philip, 18th century German horn player & composer, **XI**: 166

Dornel, Antoine, 1685–1765, French composer for Hautboisten, **VII**: 86; **XI**: 23, 228

Dornheckter, Robert, 1839–1890, German composer, **IX**: 153

Dornois, ?, 19th century French composer, **IX**: 37

Dosi, Edelberto, 19th century Italian composer for band, **X**: 200

Döthel, Nicolas, 1721–1810, German composer, **XI**: 23, 193, 268

Dotzauer, Giusto, 1807–1865, Italian composer, **XI**: 132

Dotzauer, I. F., 18th century (?) German composer, **XI**: 251

Dotzauer, Justus, 1783–1860, German composer, **XI**: 23

Douard, ?, 19th century composer for church music for choir and band, **V**: 215

Douard, A., 19th century French composer, conductor, 51e de Ligne, **IX**: 1, 2, 37

Doubravsky, Frantisck, 19th century Czech composer, **IX**: 211

Dourlen, Victor, 1780–1864, French composer, **XI**: 23

Dousa, Karl, 18th century, *Missa in honoren St. Venceslai* for voices and winds, **VIII**: 182

Dowland, John, 1563–1626, English of ensemble music, **VII**: 20, 24, 43, 180

Dozlowski, Józef, 1757–1831, Polish composer, **IX**: 130

Draeseke, Felix, 1835–1913, German composer, **XI**: 126

Drake, Sir Francis, 1540–1596, English admiral, **II:** 154

Dramar, unnamed work arranged for Harmoniemusik by Ruzni, **VIII:** 151

Drayton, Michael, 1563–1631, English poet, **II:** 38

Drechsler, Josef, 1782–1852, *Marcia Mor. di Nelson,* for Harmoniemusik, **VIII:** 182

Dreher, Jos, 19th century German composer, **IX:** 153

Dresden, Sem, b. 1881, Dutch composer, **XII:** 133

Dresen, Adam, 1620–1701, German composer of 4-part dances, **VII:** 155

Dressel, Erwin, b. 1909, German composer, **XII:** 133

Dressler, Gallus, 1533–1590, German composer, **VI:** 66

Dressler, Johann, 18th century German trombonist, **XI:** 176 [biographical note]

Dretzel, Valentin, German composer of 1620 canzona, ricercari, **VII:** 155

Dreux, Jacques-Philippe, fl. ca. 1730, French composer for Hautboisten, **VII:** 86

Drobisch, ?, 18th century German, (6) *Angloises* for Harmoniemusik, **VIII:** 313

Drobisch, Johannes Friedrich, 18th century German composer, **VII:** 114; **XI:** 24

Drobisch, Karl, 1803–1854, German composer, **IX:** 153

Drobney, bassoonist in original Vienna Harmoniemusik, **IV:** 35, fn. 77

Drosler, ?, (12) *Ländler* for Harmoniemusik, **VIII:** 182

Droste-Hülshoff de Vischering, Maximilian, 1764–1840, 18th century German, *Dances* and *Das Hallelujah* for voices and Harmoniemusik, **VIII:** 313; **XI:** 193, 217, 234, 268, 298

Drouet, Louis, 1792–1873, French flautist & composer, **XI:** 24 [biographical note], 193

Druckenmuller, Georg, late 17th century, sonatas for Hautboisten, **VII:** 114

Druot, ?, 18th century German, *Partita* for Harmoniemusik, **VIII:** 314

Druschetzky, Georg, 1745–1819, Hungarian composer of Harmoniemusik, **IV:** 17, 22 fn. 10 [Graf Pachta], 24, 31 ff, 41, 42 [Grassalkovics], 121; **V:** 101 [contemporary biographical note]; **VIII:** 182ff (102) *Partitas* for Harmoniemusik, plus music for voices and winds]; **XI:** 106, 147, 149, 296; **XII:** 10ff (70) Partitas for Harmoniemusik; 12 [list of compositions]

Druschetzky, Georg, 1745–1819, as arranger for Harmoniemusik, **VIII:** 6, 44, 45, 182, 206; **XII:** 46ff [as arranger, opera collections arranged for Harmoniemusik]; 49 [Mozart *Magic Flute,* arranged for Harmoniemusik]

Dryden, John, 1631–1700, English poet, **III:** 96

Du Caurroy, François, 1549–1609, French composer for Hautboisten, **VII:** 23, 93

Du Cousu, ?, d. 1658, French composer for Hautboisten, **VII:** 94, 167

Du Manoir, ?, composer in 1660 German collection of dance music, **VII:** 145

Duarte, Eleonora (?), English composer of 5-part Symphonias, **VII:** 43

Dubez, ?, 19th century Hungarian composer, **IX:** 211

Dubois, Charles, 19th century French composer, **IX:** 37

Dubois, François-Clément-Théodore, 1837–1924, French composer, **V:** 153; **IX:** 37; **XII:** 134, 194, 213

Dubourg, ?, 17th century composer, in *Musica bellicosa,* **VII:** 13

Dubreu, F., 19th century French composer, **IX:** 37

Dubreuil, E., 19th century French composer, **IX:** 37

Dubreuil, Pierre, member in 1777 of the Hautbois et Musettes du Poitou, **IV:** 64, fn. 5

Ducasse, Roge-Jean-Jules Aimable, b. 1873, French composer, **XII:** 134

Duchatel, Frans, engraving of Dutch trumpets and timpani in 1660, **III:** 153

Ducis, Benedictus, 1492–1544, German cleric and composer, **VI:** 27, 62, 65

Ducreux, ?, 18th century French composer, **XI:** 24, 193

Dudley, Lord Robert, 1531–1588, Earl of Leicester, **II:** 161ff

Duernoy, Frédéric, 1765–1838, *Pas de Manoeuvre* for band, **VIII:** 274

Dufant & Dubois, 18th and 19th century publisher in Paris, **VIII:** 11, 46, 76, 107, 154, 285; **IX:** 97, 106, 107, 220

Dufault, 19th century publisher in Paris, **XI:** 113, 168

Dufaut & Dubois, 19th century publisher in Paris, **XI:** 61, 135

Dufay, Guillaume, 1400–1474, **I:** 177, 178, 255; **VI:** viiiff, xi

Dufayel, ?, 19th century French composer, **IX:** 72

Duhamel, ?, 19th century French composer, **IX:** 38

Duhan, 18th century publisher in Paris, **XI:** 24, 50, 55, 113, 115, 137, 168, 244

Duhan, 19th century publisher in Paris, **VIII:** 46

Duhoslav, ?, 19th century composer in Vienna, **XI:** 289

Dukas, Paul, 1865–1935, French composer, **IX:** 38

Duke of Brunswick, visits Venice water pageant in 1685, **III:** 73

Duke of Infantado, 17th century Spanish noble, **III:** 75

Duke of Marlborough, VII: 157ff

Duke of Wellington, IX: 265

Duke of Württemberg, II: 235 [description of his band's performance], 230ff), **III:** 69

Dulon, Freidrich, 1769–1826, German composer, **XI:** 24, 193

Dumaine, A., 19th century French composer, **IX:** 38

Dumas, Alexandre, 19th century French composer, conductor Musique a bord du Montebello, **IX:** 2, 38

Dumonchau, Charles-François, 1775–1820, French composer, **XI:** 25, 166, 243, 251, 273

Dumonet, Henry, 1610–1684, French composer for Hautboisten, **VII:** 94

Duncan, Giacomo, 18th century (?) composer, **XI:** 25

Dunkler, ?, conductor of a Dutch band at the 1867 world competition, **V:** 117

Dunkler, Franc, 1816–1878, German composer, **IX:** 153

Dunkler, Franz, 1779–1861, Dutch composer for band, **IX:** 125

Dupart, Charles, 19th century French composer, **IX:** 38

Dupiré, A., 19th century French composer, **IX:** 38

Duport, Jean Louis, 1749–1819, in Paris, ballets arr. for Harmoniemusik, **V:** 218 [Zephir]; **VIII:** 32 [*Der blöde Ritter, Figaro, Zephir*]

Dupouy, A., 19th century French composer, **IX:** 39

Duprato, Jules, 19th century French composer, **IX:** 39

Dupré, Marcel, b. 1886, French composer, **XII:** 79

Duquat, ?, 19th century French composer, **IX:** 39

Durand, 19th century publisher in Paris, **IX:** 86, 96; **XI:** 35, 47, 80; **XII:** 64, 76, 112, 128, 150, 156

Dureau, Th., 19th century French composer, **IX:** 39

Dürer, Albrecht, 1471–1528, German artist, **II:** 170, 185; **V:** 132

Duret, composer, 1795 faculty of Paris Conseratoire, **IV:** 162, fn. 46

Düring, J. C. arr. Himmel *Fanchon* for Harmoniemusik, **VIII:** 48 [arr. Himmel *Fanchon* for Harmoniemusik]; **XI:** 304

Durrieu, Paul, 19th century French composer, **IX:** 39

Durrieu, R., 19th century French composer, **IX:** 39

Dusautoy, ?, 19th century French composer, **IX:** 39

Duscheck (Tuschek), ?, (6) *Parthias* for Harmoniemusik, **VIII:** 192

Dusek, Frantisek, 1731–1799, Bohemian composer in Graf Pachta Harmonie Coll., **IV:** 22, fn. 10; **VIII:** 188ff [(50) *Parthias* for Harmonie]

Dussap, Dey., 19th century French composer, **IX:** 39

Dussec, unnamed work arranged for Harmoniemusik by Rummel, **VIII:** 150ff

Dussek, Jan, 1760–1812, Bohemian composer, **V:** 97, **IX:** 178, 253; **XI:** 25

Dussek, Oliva, 1797–1847, Bohemian composer, **XI:** 25

Dust, Charles, 19th century English composer, **IX:** 270

Duttilieu, Pierre, 1754–1797, ballet, arr. for Harmoniemusik, **VIII:** 32ff

Duval, Jean-Baptiste, French Ambassador to Venice, 1607–1609, **III:** 219

Duvernoy, Charles, 18th century French clarinetist, **XI:** 132 [biographical note]

Duvernoy, Frédéric, 1765–1838, horn professor at the Paris Conservatory, **IV:** 156, 160; **XI:** 166

Dvorák, Antonín, 19th century Bohenian composer, **IX:** 211; **XII:** 213

Dwurzek, Josef, 19th century Czech composer, **IX:** 211

Dyke, Robert, 19th century English composer, **IX:** 270

E. S. T. M. Bn., anonymous 17th century composer, **VII:** 109ff

Earl of Hertford [visit by Elizabeth I], **II:** 53

Earl of Worcester, court of Elizabeth I, **II:** 42

East, Michael, d. after 1638, English composer of ensemble music, **VII:** 23, 25, 26, 44

Eastland, Edwin, 18th century English, (12) *Marches* for 2 flutes, bassoon, **VIII:** 255

Eaton, E. K., 19th century American composer, **IX:** 137

Eaton, William, 19th century English composer, **IX:** 271

Ebdon, Thomas, 1738–1811, English, *March,* 1795, **VIII:** 255

Ebell, H., 18th century German, *Partita* for Harmoniemusik, **VIII:** 314

Ebend, 19th century publisher in Paris, **VIII:** 3ff, 7ff, 10, 14ff, 21ff, 24, 26ff, 27ff, 29, 35ff, 40ff, 47, 49ff, 51ff, 53ff, 57ff, 60, 65ff, 79, 89, 93ff, 106ff, 108, 110ff, 112, 114, 124, 125ff, 132ff, 137, 147, 158, 276ff, 354; , **IX:** 7, 46, 59, 62, 109, 148, 155, 156, 158, 162, 163, 164, 168, 170, 178, 183, 188, 240ff, 246

Eberl, Anton, 1765–1807, German composer, **XI:** 107, 132, 249

Eberlin, Ernst, 19th century German composer, **XI:** 290

Ebers, Charles, 1770–1836, German composer, **IX:** 153

Eberwein, Christian, 1750–1810, German, (4) *Parthien*, Harmonie, flutes, **VIII:** 314; , **XI:** 25, 132, 278

Eberwein, Traugott, 1775–1831, German composer, **IX:** 153; **XI:** 278

Ebner, 19th century publisher in Stuttgart, **IX:** 154

Ebner, Wolfgang, 1612–1665, German composer and organist, St. Stefan, Vienna, from 1634, **III:** 215; **VII:** 2

Eckard, C., 19th century German composer, **IX:** 142

Eckardt, 17th century composer, **VII:** 120

Eckel, Mathias, d. 1538, German composer, **VI:** 27, 62ff

Eckert, ?, 19th century composer, **XI:** 132

Eckhardt, Josef, 19th century Austrian composer, **IX:** 211

Eckschlager, R., 19th century Austrian composer, **IX:** 211

Ed. Coll., 20th century publisher in Belgrad, **XII:** 184

Edelmann, Moritz, 17th century German composer, **VII:** 115

Eder, 18th and 19th century publisher in Vienna, **VIII:** 97, 202, 208ff; **IX:** 241, 246; **XII:** 35ff

Eder, Philipp, 19th century Austrian composer, **IX:** 211; **XII:** 59

Edition Française de Musique, 20th century publisher in Paris, **XII:** 180

Edition Modern, 20th century publisher in Munich, **XII:** 152

Editions Sociales Internationales, 20th century publisher in Paris, **XII:** 96

Edward I, 1272–1307, **I:** 187

Edward II, 1307–1327, **I:** 187

Edward III, 1327–1377, **I:** 79, 84, 189ff

Edward IV, I: 86, 197ff

Edward VI of England, 16th century, **II:** 32 [list of wind players for coronation], 29ff; **III:** 202

Edwards, 16th century composer in London, **VI:** 35

Effendi, Achmet, ambassador to Berlin, 18th century, **III:** 110

Effinger, Cecil, b. 1914, American composer, **XII:** 79

Egal, J., 19th century French composer, **IX:** 39

Egge, Klaus, b. 1906, German composer, **XII:** 134

Eggenberger, George, 19th century copyist at the Melk monastery, **XII:** 59

Egger, Franz, 19th century German arranger, **IX:** 255

Egk, Leopold, Bishop at Kromeriz, 1758–1760, **IV:** 21

Egwolf, Joseph, 19th century German composer, **IX:** 153

Ehmann, ?, 18th century German, *Marsch* for Harmoniemusik, **VIII:** 314

Ehrenberg, Karl Emil Theodor, b. 1878, German composer, **XII:** 134

Ehrenfried, ?, 18th century German flautist at Mainz, **XI:** 25

Ehrenfried, Henrico, as arranger for Harmoniemusik, **VIII:** 22, 40, 75, 105, 299

Eichhorn, A., 19th century German composer, **IX:** 154

Eichhorn, Adolarius, German composer, 1616 dances, **VII:** 155

Eichhorn, Johann, 18th century Swiss composer of Harmoniemusic with solo bassoon, **VIII:** 372

Eichner, Ernest, 1740–1777, German, (8) *Divertissement* for Harmoniemusik, **VIII:** 314ff; **XI:** 25, 132

Eidenbenz, ?, 18th century German composer, **XI:** 194

Eiffert, Philip, 18th century English composer, **XI:** 26

Eilenberg, ?, composer included in a 1885 English collection of band music, **X:** 116

Eilenberg, Richard, 19th century English composer, **IX:** 271

Eilhardt, Friedrich, 19th century German composer, **IX:** 154

Eisen, Franz, 18th century hornist in Milan, **IV:** 35

Eisen, Jakob, hornist in original Vienna Harmoniemusik, **IV:** 35, fn. 77

Eisenherdt, Mr., 19th century German band leader in England, **V:** 78

Eisenmann, Will, b. 1906, German/Swiss composer, **XII:** 135

Eisentraut, W., Baroque German composer of 5-part Galliarde, **VII:** 144, 155

Eisert, ?, clarinetist in the Prince Regent's band in London, **V:** 203

Eisler, Hanns, b. 1898, German composer, **XII:** 135

Eisner, Carl, 18th century German, *Sextett* for winds, **VIII:** 315

Eisner, Georg, horn player under Liechtenstein in Vienna, **IV:** 39

Eitzenberger, Joseph, 19th century Austrian composer, **IX:** 211

Elagabalus, Roman Emperor, 3rd century, performer on aulos & cornu, **I:** 65

Elding, Johann, b. Eisenach, Saxony, 1754–1786, German clarinetist & comp., **XI:** 132

Elector of Hesse (1830), **IX:** 189

Eler, André-Frédéric, 1764–1821, French/Austrian composer, **IV:** 206; **VIII:** 275 [original works for Harmoniemusik]; **X:** 21; **XI:** 26, 274, 299, 306, 309

Eley, Christopher Frederick, 1756–1832, English military composer, leader of the Duke of York's Band in London, **IV:** 108, 113ff; **V:** 201; **VIII:** 255ff [(32) *Marches* and *Military Pieces* for band]

Elgar, Edward, 1857–1937, English composer, **XII:** 80, 135

Elia, Giuseppe, 19th century Italian composer for band, **X:** 200

Elise von Bayern, 19th century princess, **IX:** 173

Elizabeth I, 1533–1603, **II:** 36ff, 47ff, 50 [visit to Norwich], 157, 226ff, **III:** 90, 202; **IV:** 12

Elizabeth, 1709–1762, Empress of Russia, **IV:** 75

Elizabeth, daughter to King James I of England, **III:** 69

Elizabeth, wife of Philip II of Spain (16th century), **II:** 73, 75ff

Ellerby, Martin, 20th century English composer, **XII:** 202

Elling, Catharinus, 1858–1942, Norway composer, **XII:** 135

Elliot, Stanislaus, 19th century English composer, **IX:** 271

Ellis, Samuel, b. 1776, English organist and flute professor, **XI:** 26

Elrington, William, 19th century English composer, **IX:** 271

Elsler, Johann Florian, Haydn's copyist at Esterházy, **IV:** 32

Elsler, Joseph, oboist in 1801 Harmoniemusik of Prince Esterházy, **IV:** 30ff

Elsner, Jozef, 1769–1854, Polish composer for band, **X:** 259

Elvigius, 17th century bassoonist in the Antwerp Cathedral, **III:** 199

Elwart, Antoine, 1808–1877, French composer, **IX:** 39

Emanuel, Vittorio, II, 1820–1878, 1st king of the united Italy, **V:** 90, 196; **X:** 166, 176, 183, 189, 193, 209, 218, 219, 231, 241, 247, 250, 252

Emberg, Jens Laursh, b. 1879, composer, **XII:** 135

Embury, ?, 19th century English composer, **IX:** 271

Emmerig, Joseph, 19th century German composer, **IX:** 154

Emmert, Adam, 19th century, Austrian composer, **IX:** 211; **XI:** 288

Emnerus, David, composer in 1622 German collection of dance music, **VII:** 145

Enckhausen, ?, fl. 1800–1828, German composer, **IX:** 154

Enderle, Wilhelm, 1722–1790, German composer, **XI:** 194, 268

Endres, Franz, 19th century German composer, **IX:** 154; **XI:** 321

Endter, 17th century publisher in Nürnberg, **VII:** 123, 151

Enesco, Georges, Romanian composer, **XII:** 192

Engelhardt, P., as 19th century arranger, **IX:** 142

Engelman, Christian, 17th century composer of English ensenble music, **VII:** 24

Engelmann, Georg, b. 1578, German composer of dances, **VII:** 155

Enke, H., as arranger of Mozart's, *Gran Partita*, K. 361, for 4-hand piano, **VIII:** 218

Enrique IV of Spain, 1425–1474, **I:** 221ff

Enzinger, Ludwig, 19th century German composer, **IX:** 154

Episcopius, Ludovicus, 1520–1595, **VI:** 107, 114

Eppinger, ?, 19th century Austrian civic militia composer, **V:** 126

Eppinger, ?, 19th century Austrian composer, **IX:** 211

Erard, 18th and 19th century publisher in Paris, **VIII:** 3, 26, 104, 124ff; **XI:** 28, 50, 99, 151, 273, 275

Erasmus, Desiderius, 1466–1536, scholar, **II:** 119

Eratosthenes, Etruscan historian, **I:** 51

Erb, Marie-Joseph, 1858–1944, French composer, **XII:** 136

Erbach, Christian, 1570–1635, German composer, **VI:** 57, 61; **VII:** 156

Erbach, Freidrich, 1680–1731, German composer, **XI:** 151, 194

Erban, Franz, 19th century German composer, **XI:** 290

Erban, Johann Quentels, 16th century publisher in Germany, **VI:** 67

Erben, 17th century publisher in Lübeck, **VII:** 112

Erben, Kellners, late 16th century publisher in Alten-Stettin, **VII:** 169

Erben, Revsner, 17th century publisher in Königsberg, **VII:** 135

Erbin, Francesco, 19th century Italian composer for band, **X:** 200

Ercilla, B. de, 19th century English composer, **IX:** 271

Ercole I, d'Este, 1471–1505, **I:** 230, 232; **II:** 125ff; **VI:** 80

Erdmuth Sophia, Duchess of Brandenburg, 17th century, **VII:** 151

Erdödy, Counts in Hungary, **IV:** 33

Ereditario of Florence, marriage in 1661, **III:** 71

Erffürt, 17th century publisher in Augsburg, **XI:** 254

Erickson, Frank, 20th century American composer, **XII:** 202

Erkel, Ferenc, 1810–1893, Austrian composer, **IX:** 212

Erlanger, Camille, 1863–1919, French composer, **XII:** 136

Erlebach, Philipp, 1657–1714, German composer Hautboisten music, **VII:** 156ff; **XI:** 254

Ermagora, Fabio, 19th century Italian composer, church works with winds, **X:** 201

Ermitasch, ?, *Parthia* for Harmoniemusik, **VIII:** 192

Ernest, Mr., as arranger for Harmoniemusik, **VIII:** 117ff

Ernesti, Titus, 19th century Austrian composer, **IX:** 212

Ernst, Edouard, 19th century French composer, **IX:** 39

Ernst, François, fl. 1786, German, *Harmoniemusik,* **VIII:** 315

Ernst, Franz, d. 1805?, *Tarrare,* opera, unknown arranger for Harmoniemusik, **VIII:** 33

Ernst, H. W. [dedication, *Elegie* by Röder], **XII:** 170

Ernst, Heinrich, 1814–1865, Austrian composer, **IX:** 212

Erpf, Hermann, b. 1891, German composer, **XII:** 80

Esch, Louis von, 18th century French composer, **VIII:** 275; **X:** 66; **XI:** 26

Eschig, M., 20th century publisher in Paris, **XII:** 144

Eschrich, hornist, 19th century court at Rudolstadt, **V:** 186, fn. 8

Eschstruth, Hans von, 1756–1796, German (12) *Marches* for Harmoniemusk, **VIII:** 315

Escobar, Andre de, 'Master of Shawms' in Portugal 1560–1580, **II:** 223

Escudié, H., 19th century French composer, **IX:** 40

Esmeister, 18th century Austrian composer, **IV:** 24; **VIII:** 192 [(3) *Partitas* for Harmoniemusik]

Espinosa, Manuel, Spanish, collection of band music, 1761, **VIII:** 370

Essex, Dr., 18th century (?) English composer, **XI:** 26, 194

Essex, Timothy, English composer, (4) *Marches* for band, ca. 1795, **VIII:** 256

Esterházy, Nicholas II, of Hungary, **IV:** 31ff

Esterházy, Nicolaus, 1714–1790, Prince Hungary, **IV:** 27ff

Esterházy, Paul Anton., 1711–1762, Prince of Hungary, **IV:** 27ff

Esterházy, Prince, 1762 church music, **IV:** 121

Esterl, ?, 19th century German composer, **IX:** 154

Estrée, Jean, d. 1576, royal oboist and publisher, **II:** 71; **VI:** 54ff

Etchepare, H., 19th century French composer, **IX:** 40

Eters, 19th century publisher in Leipzig, **IX:** 183

Ett, Casper, 19th century German composer, **IX:** 154

Ettinger, Markus Wolf, 1874–1951, German composer, **XII:** 136

Ettling, Emile, 19th century French composer, **IX:** 2, 40

Eugen zu Bentheim-Bentheim, Fürsten, **IX:** 161

Eugene, Prince of Savoy, 1663–1736, **III:** 63

Eurich, 19th century publisher in Linz, **IX:** 243

Euripides, ancient Greek playwright, **I:** 49; **XII:** 180

Eustache, Charles, 19th century French composer, **IX:** 40

Evans, Charles, 19th century English composer, **IX:** 271

Evelyn, John, 1620–1706, English historian, **III:** 93ff, 182, 184ff [use of timpani on the River Thames], 192 [musicians on slave ship], 205

Evertz, Theodor, mid-16th century Franco-Flemish composer, **VI:** 107, 114

Evette & Buffet, 20th century publishers in Paris, **XII:** 100

Evette & Schaeffer, 19th century publisher in Paris, **XI:** 136, 161, 177; **IX:** 34, 67; **XII:** 69, 136

Evraardus Venator, English trumpet & horn player, 1087–1100, **I:** 182

Eybert, ?, 19th century French composer, **IX:** 40

Eybler, Josef, 1765–1846, Austrian composer, **XI:** 26, 194, 321; **IX:** 212

Eyre, Joseph, 18th century English composer, **XI:** 194

Eysler, Edmond, 1874–1949, German composer, **XII:** 136

Eytelwein, 16th century German composer, **VI:** 62

Fabbrucci, Lorenzo, Italian composer ca. 1850, **V:** 89

Fabiani, Gaetano, 1841–1904, Italian composer for band, 201

Fabre, Casimir, 19th century French composer, **IX:** 40

Fabricius, Werner, 1633–1679, German composer of dances, **VII:** 156

Faccini, Augusto, 19th century Italian composer for band, **X:** 201

Faccio, Francesso, 1840–1891, Italian composer, overture for band, **X:** 201

Fach, Adolf, 20th century German composer, **XII:** 80

Fackler, M., 19th century, German composer, **IX:** 154

Fago, Nicola, 1672–1745, Italian composer, **XI:** 160

Fahrbach, ?, unidentified work arranged for band, **IX:** 186

Fahrbach, Anton, 19th century Austrian composer, **IX:** 212

Fahrbach, J., (1840) Austrian composer, **IX:** 212

Fahrbach, Philipp, Jr., 1843–1894, Austrian military band leader, **V:** 43, 177; **IX:** 212; **X:** 45, 116

Fahrbach, Philipp, Sr., 1815–1885, Austrian military band leader, **V:** 43, 45 fn. 28; **IX:** 196, 197, 212

Faignient, Noel, 1540–1598, Dutch composer, **VI:** 114

Faisst, Immanuel, 1823–1895, German composer, **IX:** 154; **X:** 97

Fajolle, A., 19th century French composer, **IX:** 40

Falla, Manuel de, 1876–1946, Spanish composer, **XII:** 80

Falter, 18th and 19th century publisher in Munich, **IX:** 183, 185, 186, 195; **XI:** 64, 97, 158

Faltis, Josef, 19th century Austrian composer, **IX:** 213

Fanciulli, Francesco, 19th century American composer, **IX:** 138

Fanshawe, Sir Henry, 17th century English nobleman, **VII:** 22

Fanst, Karl, 19th century Austrian composer, **IX:** 213

Fantini, Girolamo, 1600–1675, Italian author of trumpet treatise, **III:** 65, 71, 227; **VII:** 188

Fanucchi, Domenico, 19th century Italian composer, **XI:** 303; **IX:** 118

Fanzel, Josef, hornist in the 1910 Barrère Ensemble in NYC, **XII:** 214

Fardini, G., 19th century Italian composer for band, **X:** 201

Fare, Florence (pseud., A. W. Rawlings), 19th century English composer, **IX:** 271

Farigoul, J., 19th century French composer, **IX:** 41

Farina, Carlo, early 17th century German composer of dances, **VII:** 157, 199

Farmer, Henry, 1882–1965, military music historian, **IV:** 86, 106ff, 120

Farrell, James, 19th century English composer, **IX:** 271

Farrenc, 18th century publisher in Paris, **XI:** 24

Farrenc, Jacques Hyppolite, 1794–1865, French composer, **XI:** 27, 133, 194, 317

Farrenc, Jeanne-Louise, 1804–1875, composer, **IX:** 41

Fasch, Johann Friedrich, 1688–1758, German composer, **III:** 17; **VII:** 115ff; **X:** 6; **XI:** 27, 107, 151, 228, 233, 235, 239, 241, 268, 276, 301

Fasch, Johann, German Baroque composer, **XII:** 202

Fasch, Karl, 1736–1800 German composer, **XI:** 274, 278

Fasquel, ?, 19th century French composer, **IX:** 41

Fassio, Giovanni, 19th century Italian composer for band, **X:** 202

Fattorini, ?, 19th century Italian composer, **X:** 202

Fattorini, Gabriele, fl. 1598–1609, Italian composer, **III:** 14

Fauchet, Paul, 20th century French composer, **XII:** 202

Fauconier, B. C., 19th century Belgium composer, **IX:** 259

Faulwetter, ?, composer included in 19th century English collection of band music, **X:** 115

Faure, Gabriel, 1845–1924, French composer, **XI:** 27; **XII:** 212, 218

Faurel, ?, 19th century French composer, **IX:** 41

Faust, ?, composer included in 19th century English band collections, **X:** 113ff

Faust, C., 19th century English composer, **IX:** 271

Faveretto, Bartolomeo, trombonist employed in church in Padua, 16th century, **II:** 243

Favre, E., 19th century French composer, **IX:** 41

Favre, Joanny, 19th century French composer, **IX:** 41

Favre-Danne, E., 19th century French composer, **IX:** 41

Fawcett, John, 1789–1867, English composer, **XI:** 194

Fayrfax, 16th century English composer, **VI:** 35

Feautrier, E., 19th century French composer, **IX:** 41

Feautrier, L., 19th century French composer, **IX:** 41

Febore, Gustave, 19th century French composer, 42

Fèbus, Gaston, 1331–1391 nobleman, **VI:** 3

Febvre, F., 19th century composer, **IX:** 154

Fechner, A. M., 19th century English composer, **IX:** 271

Fedeli, Pietro, b. 1785, 19th century Italian composer for band, **X:** 202

Federici, Francesco, d. 1830, composer of *Zaira,* opera, arr. for Harmonie, **VIII:** 33

Fedou, A., 19th century French composer, **IX:** 42

Feldmayer, Georg, 1756–1818, German, Harmoniemusik composer for the Wallerstein court, **IV:** 56; **VIII:** 315ff, 336 [(24) *Partitas,* for Harmoniemusik]; **X:** 24

Feldmayer, Georg, 1756–1818, as arranger of Mozart's *Die Zauberflöte,* opera, for Harmoniemusik, **VIII:** 81

Fendt, A., 19th century Austrian composer, **IX:** 213

Fentum, 18th century publisher in London, **VIII:** 264

Fentum, 19th century publisher in Paris, **XI:** 205

Fentum, J., 18th and 19th century Publisher in London, **XI:** 15, 69, 76, 77, 117, 192, 199, 205, 208, 214, 224, 259, 267

Fentus, 19th publisher in London, **XI:** 48, 203

Feo, Francesco, 1691–1761, Italian composer of church music, voices & winds, **X:** 13

Ferand, Henri, 19th century French composer, **IX:** 42

Feraud, 18th century French political figure, **VIII:** 284, 289

Feray, Abbé, fl. 1792, French composer, **IV:** 202; **VIII:** 275 [music for chorus and Harmoniemusik]

Ferber, Augustin, 16th century publisher in Griefswald, **VI:** 72

Ferdinand I, Emperor, **II:** 102

Ferdinand II of Insbruck, reigned 1564–1595, **II:** 101ff [instrument collection]

Ferdinand II, Emperor, 1578–1637, **III:** 66 [edict of 1623 regarding royal trumpets], 110

Ferdinand III, Emperor, 1608–1657, **III:** 61ff, 66 [edict of 1653 regarding royal trumpets]; **VII:** 2 [as composer]

Ferdinand, Duke of Bavaria, 16th century, **II:** 130

Ferdinandes, III, 1608–1657, emperor, **XI:** [as composer] 268, 285

Ferdinando II of Florence in 1661, **III:** 71

Fergus, John, English composer, *Grand March,* 1794, for Harmoniemusik, **VIII:** 256

Fergusio, Giovanni, II: 235 [discussion of 16th century German multi-choral music]

Ferguson, Howard, b. 1908, English composer, **XII:** 80, 136

Ferioli, 17th century publisher in Milano, **VII:** 196

Ferlendis, Giuseppe, 1755–1802, Italian oboist & composer, **XI:** 107, 126, 194

Fernandez, Oscar Lorenze, 1897–1948, Brazilian composer, **XII:** 137

Fernando V, 1474–1516 and **Dona Isabel,** 1474–1504, **I:** 223ff

Fernier, Anton, 1758–1760, court clarinet player in Olmütz, **IV:** 21

Ferrabosco, Alfonso, composer in 1621 ensemble collections, **VII:** 24, 180

Ferrabosco, Alfonso, Jr., 1575–1628, Italian composer of wind music, **III:** 84, 94; **VI:** 36; **VII:** 13, 15, 20, 22, 23, 25, 26, 44ff

Ferrabosco, Sen., 17th century composer of wind music, **VII:** 20, 22, 23, 25, 26

Ferradini, Mario, 19th century Italian composer for band, **X:** 202

Ferrandini, Giovanni, 1710–1791, Italian flautist & composer, **XI:** 27

Ferrante, Pasqual, 19th century Italian composer, *Sinfonio* for band, **X:** 202

Ferranti, L., 19th century French composer, **IX:** 42

Ferrari, Carlo, 1710–1789, Italian composer, **XI:** 27, 195

Ferrari, Comenico, 18th century Italian composer, **XI:** 187

Ferrari, Giacomo, 1759–1842, *La Villenella rapita,* arranged for Harmoniemusik, **VIII:** 33

Ferraud, French Revolution politician, **X:** 22

Ferretti, composer in 1600 dance collection published in Heidelberg, **VII:** 180

Ferri, Angelo, 19th century Italian composer, **IX:** 118

Ferro, Antonio, 1649, Italian composer for wind sonatas, **VII:** 188

Ferro, Vincenzo, 16th century composer, **VI:** 30

Ferroud, Piere Octave, 1900–1936, French composer, **XII:** 137

Fesca, Alexander, 1820–1849, German composer, **IX:** 154

Fesca, Friedrich, 1789–1826, German composer, **XI:** 27

Fesch, Willem, 1687–1757, Dutch composer, **XI:** 27, 195, 251

Fessy, Alexandre, 1804–1856, French composer, **V:** 69 fn 20, 70, 73; **IX:** 42

Festa, Constantio, 1490–1545, Franco-Flemish composer, **VI:** 27, 38, 44, 48

Festival Artistique, 19th century publisher in Paris, **IX:** 5

Fétis, François Joseph, 1784–1871, Belgium, composer and writer, **IV:** 78

Fétis, François, 1784–1871, Belgium composer, historian, **IX:** 259; **XI:** 27

Fetras, Oscar, 19th century English composer, **IX:** 271

Fevin, Antonius, 1470–1512, Franco-Flemish composer, **VI:** 27, 63

Feyerabend, Sigmund, 16th century Frankfurt publisher, **VI:** 72, 75

Fezzardi, Giovanni, 19th century Italian composer for band, **X:** 203

Fiala, Alois, 19th century Austrian composer, **IX:** 213

Fiala, Anton, 19th century Austrian composer, **IX:** 213, 255

Fiala, Josef, 1754–1816, Bohemian Harmonie composer and oboist at Donaueschingen, **IV:** 24, 41, 58; **VIII:** 317ff [(29) *Divertimenti* for Harmoniemusik; **XI:** 107, 133, 195, 240, 257, 299

Fibiger, Jan, 19th century Austrian composer, **IX:** 213

Fichu, J., 19th century French composer, **IX:** 43

Fick, 17th century composer of Hautboisten music, **III:** 19

Fick, Peter, d. 1743, German composer for Hautboisten, **VII:** 116

Fiedler, ?, fl. 1800–1828, German composer, **IX:** 155

Fiehrer, ?, 19th century English composer, **IX:** 272

Field, Alfred, 19th century English composer, **IX:** 272

Field, John, 1782–1837, English celebrated pianist, student of Clementi, **XI:** 27

Filardi, Gregori, 19th century Italian composer for band, **X:** 203

Filiberti, ?, 19th century French composer, **IX:** 43

Filippa, Giuseppe, 1836–1905, Italian composer for band, **X:** 203

Filippa, Vittorio, 19th century Italian composer for band, **X:** 203

Filser, 20th century publisher in Augsburg, **XII:** 119

Filtz, Anton, 1730–1760, German composer, **XI:** 28, 195

Finali, ?, 19th century Italian composer, concerto for clarinet with band, **X:** 204

Finck, Heinrich, 1444–1527, Franco-Flemish composer, **VI:** 11, 60, 62ff

Finck, Hermann, German artist, **II:** 206

Finger, Gottfried, 1660–1723, German composer for Hautboisten, **III:** 17; **VII:** 116, 156; **XI:** 28, 74, 195, 268, 315

Finke, Fidelio, b. 1891, German composer, **XII:** 80

Finkelmann, Michael, 20th century American oboist, definitive authority on the English horn, **XII:** 189, 197, 211

Fioravanti, Valentino, 1764–1837, works arranged for Harmoniemusik, **VIII:** 33, 34

Fiorillo, Federigo, 1755–1823, Italian composer, **XI:** 28, 195, 256, 299

Fiorillo, Ignazio, 1715–1787, *Il Venditore d'aceto,* arr. for Harmonie, **VIII:** 34

Fiquet, Gabriel, 19th century French composer, **IX:** 43

Fiquet, Montididier, 19th century French composer, **IX:** 43

Fischer, ?, 19th century arranger, **IX:** 113

Fischer, ?, arr. Grétry, *Raul der Blaubart,* **XII:** 49

Fischer, ?, as 19th century arranger, **IX:** 113

Fischer, ?, *Todten Marsch* in E minor for Harmoniemusik, **VIII:** 193

Fischer, ?, *Vincent,* opera, arranged by Triebensee for Harmoniemusik, **VIII:** 34

Fischer, 18th century English oboist, **X:** 30ff

Fischer, 19th century publisher in Frankfurt, **IX:** 157

Fischer, Anton, as arr. of Grétry's, *Raoul Barbe Bleue*, opera, for Harmoniemusik, **VIII:** 40

Fischer, C, German composer, early 19th century, **V:** 148

Fischer, C., 20th century publisher in New York, **XII:** 149

Fischer, C., fl. 1800–1828, German composer, **IX:** 155

Fischer, Emile, 19th century French composer, **IX:** 43

Fischer, G., 19th century French composer, arranger, **IX:** 34, 43

Fischer, Heinrich Wilhelm, 19th century German composer, **VIII:** 319; **IX:** 155

Fischer, Henri, XI: 269 [dedication by composer Gaspard Kummer]

Fischer, Hermann, 19th century German composer, **IX:** 155

Fischer, J. G. C., 1800–1828, German composer, **IX:** 155

Fischer, J., German composer (5) *Partitas* for Harmoniemusik, **VIII:** 319ff

Fischer, Johann Caspar, c. 1660–1746, German composer of suites, **VII:** 116, 158

Fischer, Johann Christian, 1733–1800, composer for Frederick Wilhelm II, **IV:** 90; **VIII:** 319 [*Triumphmarsch* for Harmoniemusik]

Fischer, Johann III, Baroque German composer for Hautboisten, **VII:** 116, 157

Fischer, Johann, 1733–1800, oboist under George III, **XI:** 29, 103, 104, 107, 108 [biographical note], 196, 229

Fischer, Thomas, 18th century (?) composer, **XI:** 233

Fischer, Thomas, *Il Couraggio* for Harmoniemusik (soli oboe, Eng. hn), **VIII:** 193

Fischlin, E., 19th century French composer, **IX:** 43

Fish, W., b. 1775, English composer, **XI:** 108

Fisher, ?, English oboist at Vauxhall in 1785, **IV:** 131, note on pgs. 132–133

Fisher, John Abraham, 1744–1806, English violinist & composer, **XI:** 108, 195

Fitzpatrick, Capt. Joseph, Isle of Wight Volunteers, **VIII:** 264

Fiumi, Francesco, 19th century Italian composer, church works with band, **X:** 204

Flachs, as arranger of Weber's *Der Freischütz*, opera, for Harmoniemusik, **VIII:** 132; **XII:** 54

Flack, Casper, 18th century English composer of military divertimenti, **IV:** 114; **VIII:** 256 [(36) *Military Divertimenti*, 1793, for Harmoniemusik]

Flad, Anton, 19th century German oboist, **IX:** 191

Flament, Edouard, 1880–1958, French composer, **XI:** 321, 322; **XII:** 80, 137, 194

Flaska, Joseph, 1706–1772, *Musique d'harmonie* and *Marches* for Harmonie, **VIII:** 275

Flath, P., 18th century French flautist in Paris & composer, **XI:** 29, 156

Flèche, F., 19th century French composer, **IX:** 44

Fleming, Hans von, treatise on military music of 1726, **III:** 128ff

Flemming, Wilhelm, 18th century, Polish, *Partie*, for Harmoniemusik, **VIII:** 369

Fletcher, Grant, 20th century American composer, **XII:** 202

Fleury, B., 19th century French composer, **IX:** 44

Flippa, Giuseppe, 19th century Italian composer, **XII:** 202

Flittner, clarinetist, 19th century court at Rudolstadt, **V:** 186, fn. 8

Flori, ?, 19th century French composer, **IX:** 44

Florio, Pietro, d. 1795, German flutist & composer for flute at Dresden, **XI:** 29, 191

Florius, 16th century composer, **VI:** 107

Florschutz, Eucharius, b. 1757, German composer, **IX:** 155

Flotow, Friedrich von, 1812–1883, **V:** 112

Flotow, *Marta,* arranged for band by Petrali, **X:** 229

Flurschütz, Caspar, 17th century composer, **VII:** 144

Foare, Charles, 19th century French composer, **IX:** 44

Fodor, ?, 18th century composer, compositions for flute, **XI:** 29

Foerster, 17th century German composer, **III:** 18

Foerster, Christoph, 1693–1745, German composer for Hautboisten, **VII:** 116

Foerster, Emmanuel, 1748–1823 composer in Vienna, **XI:** 233

Foerster, Joseph Bohuslav, 1859–1951, Czech composer, **XII:** 139

Foetisch, 19th century publisher in Lausanne, **XI:** 174

Fogenauer, Franz, 1758–1760, court clarinet player in Olmütz, **IV:** 21

Foignet, Charles, 1750–1823, *Le mont Alphéa,* opera, arranged for Harmonie, **VIII:** 34

Foinelli, ?, 18th century (?) Italian composer, **XI:** 156

Fondard, J. T., 19th century French composer, **IX:** 44

Fontaine, Pierre, 1380–1450, French composer, **VI:** viii

Fontanelli, O., 19th century Italian composer for band, **X:** 205

Fontbonne, Leon, principal flute, Garde Républicaine Band, **IX:** 91

Fontebasso, Pietro, 19th century Italian composer, **IX:** 118

Fontenelle, Emile, 19th century French composer, **IX:** 44

Forberg, 19th century publisher in Leipzig, **IX:** 148, 154

Forbes, Alexander of Aberdeenshire, 1611 wind band collection, **VII:** 22

Forchheim, 17th century German composer, **III:** 215

Forchheim, Johann Wilhelm, 1634–1682, German composer of dances, **VII:** 117, 158

Ford, Ernest, 1858–1919, English composer for band, **X:** 119

Ford, Thomas, ca. 1580–1648, English composer of ensemble music, **VII:** 50ff

Forkel, Johann, 1749–1818, German composer, **XI:** 29

Förkelrath, Kaspar, German composer of music for voices and winds, **VII:** 158

Formichi, Pietro, 19th century civic band conductor in Siena, **V:** 157

Formschneider, H., 16th century publisher in Nürnberg, **VI:** 61

Fornasini, Nicola, 1803–1861, Italian composer, *Sinfonia* for band, **X:** 205

Foroni, Jacopo, 1825–1858, Italian composer, *Sinfonia* for band, **X:** 205

Forster, 18th century publisher in London, **XI:** 9, 104

Förster, 19th century publisher in Breslau, **IX:** 179

Förster, Christoph, 1693–1745, German composer of Hautboisten music, **X:** 7

Förster, Emanuel, 1748–1823, Austrian composer, **XI:** 29, 108

Forster, Georg, 1515–1568, German composer, **VI:** 62ff

Förster, Josef, 1838–1817, German composer, **XI:** 290

Förster, Kaspar, 1616–1673, German composer, **III:** 18

Forstmeyer, Ehrenfried, 1730–1787, (4) *Partitas* for Harmoniemusik, **VIII**: 320

Fortia de Piles, Alphonse, 1758–1826, French composer, **XI**: 151, 229

Förtsch, Johann Philipp, 1652–1732, German composer of dances, **VII**: 158

Fortunato, Ferdenado, 19th century (?) Italian composer, **XI**: 108

Foster, D., 19th century English composer, **IX**: 272

Fouant, Jolibois, 19th century French composer, **IX**: 44

Fougas, ?, 18th century French bassoon professor in Paris, **XI**: 151

Fouque, Octave, 19th century French composer, **IX**: 44

Fournier, C., 19th century French composer, **IX**: 44

Fournier, Giuseppe, Classical Period composer, **XII**: 34

Fournier, Giuseppe, 19th century Italian composer, **XI**: 307

Foy, James, 18th century English composer, **XI**: 275

Framery, unnamed work arranged by Beinet for Harmoniemusik, **VIII**: 153

Francaix, Jean, 20th century French composer, **XII**: 202

Francella, Albert, 19th century flautist in London, **XII**: 216

Francesca da Rimini, X: 220

Franceschini, Ernesto, b. 1837, 19th century Italian composer for band, **X**: 205

Francesco da Milano, 1497–1543, lutanist, 16th century, **II**: 10; **IV**: 11

Francesco de' Medici, 16th century, **II**: 130ff

Francesco Sforza, Duke of Milan, 15th century, **I**: 205

Francesco, Giovannni, famous trombonist of Siena, **II**: 135

Franchetti, Alberto, 1860–1942, Ital. comp., *Impressione sinfonica* for band, **X**: 205

Franchois, Johannes, fl. ca. 1410–1430, composer, **VI**: ix

Franciosio, ?, leader of a children's band in Florence in 1586, **II**: 199

Francis II of France, 16th century, **II**: 73

Francis, Duke of Brabant, visits Antwerp in 1581, **II**: 170

Francisco de Sandoval y Rois, 17th century Spanish noble, **III**: 76

Franck, César, 1822–1890, French composer, **XII**: 191 [*Panis Angelicus*, arranged by Strasser]; 194, 202, 219

Franck, Melchior, 1573–1639, German composer, **III**: 215; **VII**: 117, 144, 158ff

François I, King of France, 1494–1547, **II**: 23, 62ff, 64 [list of players in the shawm and sackbut ensemble], 124, 181, 217ff, **III**: 35; **IV**: 6; **VI**: 37; **VII**: 81 [as composer]; **IX**: 74

François, ?, 19th century French composer, **IX**: 44

François, Emile, 19th century French composer, **IX**: 44

François, L., 19th century French composer, **IX**: 44

Frank, Ernst, 1847–1889, German composer, **IX**: 155

Franke, F. C., 19th century German composer, **IX**: 155

Franke, Theodor, 19th century English composer, **IX**: 272

Franklin, Benjamin, 1706–1790, American politician, **IV**: 140 fn. 5, 173

Franklin, C., composer included in a 1890 English collection of band music, **X**: 116

Franz I, 1768–1835, Emperor, visits Wallerstein court in 1764, **IV**: 55

Franz Josef, 19th century Austrian emperor, **V:** 51; **IX:** 80, 209, 211, 226, 240; **X:** 109 [dedication]

Franz, Étienne, 18th century (?) composer, **XI:** 29, 156

Franz, Johann, 1758–1760, court horn player in Olmütz, **IV:** 21

Franz, Karl, hornist in Harmoniemusik of Cardinal Batthyány, **IV:** 33, fn. 71

Fränzel (Frantzl) 19th century German composer, **IX:** 155

Fränzl, Ignaz, 1736–1811, German, *Partia* for Harmoniemusik, 320

Franzoni, Amante, 1575–1630, Ital. composer church music with winds, **III:** 14, 220; **VII:** 188

Frattesi, Constantino, 19th century Italian composer, **X:** 205

Fraulich, Joseph, 19th century Austrian composer, **IX:** 214

Frayling, ?, 19th century English composer for band, **X:** 119

Fré-d'rick, L., 19th century French composer, **IX:** 45

Frédéric Guillaume de Prusse, 19th century, **IX:** 171

Frédéric of Hesse, 19th century, **IX:** 170

Frederick II ('the Great'), 1712–1786 of Prussia, **III:** 6, 126, 130; , **IV:** 6, 62, 85ff; **V:** 9, 18, 26; **VIII:** 301, 320 [(3) *Marches* for band], 324; **IX:** 141 [as composer], 143; **XI:** 30, 75 [as composer]

Frederick II, 1194–1250, **I:** 263ff

Frederick III, Emperor, 15th century, **I:** 151, 165, 186, 269

Frederick Wilhelm I 1744–1797, **IV:** 85, 90; **V:** 16 [founds Prussian mil. music school in 1792]

Frederick Wilhelm III, reigning 1797–1840, in Prussia, **V:** 109, 135, 159

Frederick William I, 1713–1740, 'the Soldier-King,' **III:** 60, 70, 110, 122, 124, 126ff

Frederick William II, 1786–1797, **V:** 9, fn 1

Frederick, Duke of Württemberg, **II:** 226

Frederik II, 1559–1588, of Denmark, **VI:** 28ff

Fredhe, ?, 19th century English composer, **IX:** 272; **X:** 119

Freeman, 18th century publisher in London, **XI:** 7

Freeman, Thomas Augustine, 18th century English composer, **VIII:** 266

Freillon-Poncein, Jean-Pierre, oboist for Louis XIV, composer, **VII:** 87

Frère, 18th and 19th century publisher in Paris, **VIII:** 4, 276; **IX:** 11; **XI:** 12, 239

Freschi, Giovanni, 1640–1690, composer of the opera *Berenice* in 1680, **III:** 74

Frescobaldi, Girolamo, 1583–1643, Italian composer, **III:** 220; **VII:** 199ff, 208

Frese, C., 19th century German composer, **IX:** 155

Freudenrich, Erich, 17th century German composer, **VII:** 144, 161

Freundthalier, ?, (4) *Divertimenti* for Harmoniemusik, **VIII:** 193

Frewin, Edward, 19th century English composer, **IX:** 272

Frey, 19th century publisher in Paris, **VIII:** 16, 20, 49ff, 53, 56ff; **IX:** 48, 60, 109; **XI:** 136, 164, 257, 278

Frey, Emil, 1889–1946, Swiss composer, **XII:** 139

Fribourg, Henri de, early 15th century composer, **VI:** ix

Fricke, C., 19th century English composer, **IX:** 272; **X:** 119

Fricke, Elias, 18th century German editor, *Collection of Dances* for Harmonie, **VIII:** 320

Frid, Géza, b. 1904, Hungarian composer, **XII:** 81

Friderich, Johann, 1601 German composer of a instrumental fugue, **VII:** 161

Friderici, Daniel, 1633 German composer of music for voices and winds, **VII:** 161

Fried, Gotther, 19th century Austrian composer, **IX:** 214

Friedem, ?, 18th century French, (2) *Sextets,* for Harmoniemusik, **VIII:** 275

Friedemann, F., 19th century German composer, **IX:** 155

Friedheim, ?, 19th century French composer, **IX:** 45

Friedl, Carl, 19th century German composer, **XI:** 176

Friedrich August I, V: 193

Friedrich August von Sachsen, King, **IX:** 168

Friedrich Augustus II, 1696–1763, Elector of Saxony, **III:** 163

Friedrich der Niederlande (and Prinzessin Louise, 1828), **IX:** 184

Friedrich Franz I, Grossherzog, **IX:** 145

Friedrich Franz III, IX: 160

Friedrich Franz, 1756–1837, Duke of Mecklenburg-Schwerin, **IV:** 59

Friedrich Heinrich, Duke of Sachsen-Zeitz, b. 1668, **III:** 58

Friedrich I of Saxony, 1503–1554, **VI:** 57

Friedrich I, 1688–1713, his military music, **III:** 125ff

Friedrich II, King, 19th century German, **IX:** 148, 155 [as composer], 159

Friedrich III, 1688–1713, of Berlin, **III:** 65

Friedrich Leopold v. Anhalt-Dessau, IX: 188

Friedrich of Mechlenburg-Schwerin, V: 185

Friedrich Wilhelm I of Germany, early 18th century, **III:** 8

Friedrich Wilhelm III, 1770–1840, king in Berlin, **IV:** 60; **V:** 15ff, 18, 25ff, 191; **IX:** 155 [as composer], 235

Friedrich Wilhelm IV, German, **V:** 34; **IX:** 154, 156 [as composer], 195

Friedrich Wilhelm von Prussia (1870), **IX:** 151; 173 [dedication

Friedrich Wilhelm, Elector, 1640–1688, 'the Great Elector,' **III:** 123ff

Friedrich, Duke of Bavaria, **II:** 133

Frier, ?, 19th century French composer, **IX:** 45

Friesse, 19th century publisher in Dresden, **IX:** 183

Frion, Eugène, 19th century French composer, **IX:** 45

Frischenschlager, Friedrich, b. 1885, Austrian composer, **XII:** 81

Frisnais, ?, 19th century French composer, conductor, 34e de Ligne, **IX:** 1, 45

Frissoni, Italian composer in 1626 collection of canzoni, **VII:** 205

Fritsch, Balthasar, 1606 German composer of dances, **VII:** 161, 180

Fritsch, E., 19th century French composer, **IX:** 45

Fritz, Ernst Paul, 19th century, (?), German composer, **XI:** 282

Fritz, Kasper, 1716–1783, Swiss composer, **XI:** 30

Fritzsch, 19th century publisher in Leipzig, **XI:** 114

Froberger, Basilius, Kapellmeister at Württemberg in 1621, **III:** 211

Fröhlich, ?, 19th century German composer, **IX:** 156

Fröhlich, ?, 18th century Swiss, *Märche* for Harmoniemusik, **VIII:** 373

Fröhlich, 19th century publisher in Berlin, **V:** 34

Fröhlich, Franz, 1780–1862, German composer, **XI:** 232

Frohmann, C., 19th century Austrian composer, **IX:** 214

Froidebise, Pierre-Jean-Marie, b. 1914, French composer, **XII:** 139

Froidmont, Libert, d. 1653, Th.D at the University of Louvain, **III:** 199

Froissart, Jean, 1337–1405, French historian, **I:** 122, 178, 189; **VI:** 4

Fromentin, L., 19th century French composer, **IX:** 45

Frommel, Gerhard, b. 1906, German composer, **XII:** 81

Fromm-Michael, Ilse, b. 1888, German composer, **XII:** 139

Fromont, Célestin, 19th century French composer, **IX:** 45

Fromschneider, Hieronymus, 16th century German publisher, **VI:** 62

Fronsperger, Lienhart, author of a 1555 manual for the field trumpeter, **II:** 111

Frontini, Martino, 1827–1909, Italian composer, works for band, **X:** 206

Frontzel, ?, 18th century, German, *Parthia* for Harmoniemusik, **VIII:** 320

Frosali, Giovanni, 1827–1909, Italian composer, *Sinfonia* for band, **X:** 206

Frosch, Johann, 16th century German composer, **VI:** 62ff

Frugatta, Giuseppe, 1860–1933, Italian composer, **XI:** 133, 249

Frühling, Carl, 1868–1937, Austrian composer, **XI:** 30, 133, 157, 268

Fuchs, ?, 18th century composer, compositions for flute, **XI:** 30

Fuchs, Georg Frederick (also known as Giovanni), 1752–1821, French, clarinet faculty of the 1792 Paris Conservatoire, Paris **IV:** 71ff, 156; **VIII:** 216ff, 275 [original works for Harmoniemusik]and as arranger for Harmoniemusik, **VIII:** 9, 11, 13, 18ff, 21, 23ff, 27, 29, 34, 39, 53, 55, 57ff, 61, 64ff, 75, 77ff, 79, 89, 91, 93, 100ff, 106, 108ff, 110ff, 122ff, 126, 129ff, 153, 155, 158ff, 240; **XI:** 133, 166, 232, 309

Fuchs, Julius 19th century German composer, **IX:** 156

Fuchswild, Johann, 16th century German composer, **VI:** 62

Fucik, Julius, b. 1872–1916, Czech composer, Austrian military band leader, **V:** 43ff, 55; **IX:** 214; **XI:** 280

Fuetsch, Joachim, 1766–1852, Austrian composer, **XI:** 257

Fugger, John Jacob, 16th century diplomat and businessman, **VI:** 10

Fugger, R., the elder, owner of 50 ensemble works published in 1523, **VI:** 106

Fugger, Raimund of Augsburg, merchant, supporter of music, 16th century, **II:** 144

Führer, Robert, 19th century Austrian composer, **IX:** 214; **XI:** 176

Fuhrmann, 17th century publisher in Nürnberg, **VII:** 160, 165, 170, 181

Fuhrmann, Georg, 1615 German composer of dances, **VII:** 162

Fulda, Adam von, 1444–1505, German composer, **II:** 230 [on conducting in Torgau]; **VI:** 61

Füllsack, Zacharias, 17th century publisher in Hamburg, **VI:** 37; **VII:** 60, 69, 166

Fumagalli, Disma, 1826–1893, Italian composer, Milano faculty, **X:** 206

Fumagalli, Polibo, 1830–1901, Italian composer, **X:** 206;

Gabetti, Giuseppe, 1796–1862, composer and famous band conductor in Piedmont, **V:** 77; **IX:** 253

Gabriel, ?, 19th century French composer, **IX:** 45

Gabrieli, Andrea, 1532–1585, Italian composer, **II:** 133, 245; **VI:** 84ff, 96, 101; **VII:** 180

Gabrieli, Giovanni, 1554–1612, composer, **II:** 134, 235ff, 245ff, 253, **III:** 13, 14, 66, 219, 220; **VI:** 86, 96, 103; **VII:** 143, 144, 196, 208

Gabrielli, Domenico, 1659–1690, Italian composer, **XI:** 160

Gabrielli, Graf Nicolaus, 1814–91, German composer, **IX:** 156

Gabrielsky, Jean, 19th century composer in Vienna, **XI:** 295

Gabrielsky, W., 19th century Viennese, **XI:** 30 [biographical note], 197

Gache, F., 19th century French composer, **IX:** 45

Gadenne, Henri, 19th century French composer, **IX:** 45

Gaelle, Meingosus, 1752–1816, German composer, **XI:** 30

Gaffet, E., 19th century French composer, **IX:** 45

Gagne, fils., 19th century French composer, **IX:** 45

Gagnebin, Henri, 1886–?, French composer, **XI:** 31, 108, 133, 151, 160, 176, 275, 311

Gaillaguet, E., 19th century French composer, **IX:** 46

Gaillard, C., 19th century French composer, **IX:** 46

Gaillard, Marius-François, b. 1900, French composer, **XII:** 139

Gaittet, J. B., 19th century French composer, **IX:** 46

Gál, Hans, b. 1890, Austrian composer, **XII:** 82

Galeazzo Maria Sforza, I: 233

Galindo, Blas, b. 1910, Mexican composer, **XII:** 82

Gallatee, period of Louis XIV collection, **VII:** 83

Gallenberg, Conte di, [collection], **X:** 186

Gallenberg, Robert, 1783–1839, composer of works arranged for Harmoniemusik, **VIII:** 34 [*Alfred der Grosse*]; 35 [*Jeanne d'Arc, Ottavio Pinelli*]

Gallenberg, Wenzel, von, *Alfred der Grosse,* arr. Hieronymus Payer, for band, **XII:** 49

Gallet, André, faculty of the 1792 Paris Conservatoire, **IV:** 156

Galli, Amintore, 1845–1919, Italian composer, **IX:** 118; **X:** 206

Galli, Antonio, d. 1565, Italian composer, **VI:** 107, 109, 123

Galliard, Johann Ernst, 1687–1749, composer of a work for 24 bassoons, **III:** 179; **VII:** 15; **XI:** 31, 151

Gallignani, G., 18th century Italian, *Suonatina* for Harmoniemusik, flute, **VIII:** 365

Gallo (1762), German composer, **III:** 129

Gallo, ?, German composer for Hautboisten, *Parade Sinfonien,* **VII:** 117

Gallo, Domenico, 1730–1768, Italian composer, *Magnificat* with band, **X:** 206

Gallo, Vincenzo, 19th century Italian composer, *Sinfonia* for band, **X:** 207; **XII:** 202

Gallois-Montburn, Raymond, b. 1918, French composer, **XII:** 139

Gallus, Jakobus, Slovenian composer, **II:** 232; **VI:** 108, 116, 118ff

Gambaro, ?, 18th century Italian, *Harmonie* for Harmoniemusik, **VIII:** 366

Gambaro, 19th century publisher in Paris, **VIII:** 8, 47, 110ff; **IX:** 2, 5, 12, 19, 31, 46, 54, 70, 164; **XI:** 193

Gambaro, as arranger for Harmoniemusik, **VIII:** 13, 47, 67, 93, 107, 109ff, 121

Gambaro, Giovanni, 19th century Italian composer, **X:** 207

Gambaro, V., 18th century French, (4) Suites, *Overture* for band, **VIII:** 278

Gambaro, Vincenzo, 19th century German composer, **XI: 299**

Gamberale, F., 19th century Italian composer for band, **X:** 207

Ganassi, Silvestro di, b. 1492, member of the Doge of Venice wind band, **II:** 134; **VI:** 88 author of treatise on improvisation

Ganassi, Sylvestro, member of the Doge of Venice wind band, 16th century, **II:** 134

Gand, jeune, 19th century French composer, **IX:** 46

Gandini, A., 18th century Italian, *Tantum Ergo* for tenor and winds, **VIII:** 365

Gandini, Antonio, late 18th century Italian arranger, **X:** 37

Gandner, Victor, 19th century French composer, **IX:** 1, 2, 46

Ganne, Louis, 19th century French composer, **IX:** 47

Gänsbacher, Johann Baptist, 1778–1844, Austrian composer, arranger, **V:** 126; **IX:** 214, 257; **XI:** 31, 133, 249

Gantz, J., 19th century French composer, **IX:** 47

Gantzland, Christian, 1711, *Dissertation on the Rights of the Trumpeter*, **VII:** 117

Garaudé, Alexis, 1779–1852, French composer, **XI:** 3, 133, 166

Garciau, Ernest, 19th century French composer, **IX:** 47

Gardane, Antonio, 16th century publisher in Venice, **VI:** 45, 48ff, 63, 83, 85ff, 89, 92, 94ff, 96ff, 99ff, 102, 104, 121; **VII:** [17th century] 194ff, 202ff, 207, 187, 188ff, 196, 205

Gardano/Magni, 17th century publisher in Venice, **VII:** 191

Gardel, composer of unnamed work arranged by Ozi for Harmoniemusik, **VIII:** 153

Gardner, John Linton, b. 1917, English composer, **XII:** 139

Gardom, 18th century publisher in London, **XI:** 222

Gargano et Nucci, 17th century publisher in Napoli, **VII:** 205

Gargiulo, ?, 19th century Italian composer for band, **X:** 207

Garibaldi, Giuseppe, 1807–1882, Italian politician, **IX:** 10 [dedication]; **X:** 182, 222, 236; **XII:** 204

Gariel, arr., 19th century French arranger, conductor, 2e Carabiniers, **IX:** 2

Gariel, J. A. V., 19th century French composer, **IX:** 47

Garnier, Felix, 19th century French composer, **IX:** 47

Garnier, Joseph-François, 1755–1825, professor of oboe to Louis XVI, faculty of the 1792 Paris Conservatoire, **IV:** 156; **XI:** 108

Garnier, le jeune, 18th century French flautist in the Paris Opera and professor of flute, **XI:** 31

Garnier, M., 18th century publisher in Paris, **XI:** 188

Garot, Pierre, 19th century French composer, **IX:** 47

Garrouste, J., 19th century French composer, **IX:** 47

Garzaroli, ?, 18th century (?), composer, **XI:** 31

Gascon, Adam, 17th century Dutch composer, 4-part sonata, **VII:** 214

Gasparini, Giovanni, 1661–1727, Italian composer, **XI:** 31

Gasparini, Giovanni, 19th century Italian composer, **IX:** 118

Gasser, Alexandre, 19th century French composer, **IX:** 47

Gasser, Victor, 19th century French composer, **IX:** 47

Gassmann, Florian, 1729–1774, in Olmütz Harmoniemusik collection, **IV:** 22, fn. 9; **VIII:** 193ff [(10) original *Partitas* for Harmoniemusik]; **XI:** 31, 109, 133

Gassner, G., 19th century English composer, **IX:** 272

Gastoldi, Giovanni, Italian composer, **VII:** 180, 196, 201ff

Gaston, *Randgesang,* a wind work performed in a Weber opera, **VIII:** 195

Gatayes, Guillaume, 1774–1846, French composer, **XI:** 33

Gattermann, Hubert, 19th century French composer, **IX:** 47

Gattermann, Philippe, 19th century French composer, **IX:** 48

Gattermann, Prosper, 19th century French composer, **IX:** 48

Gatti, Domenico, 1816–1891, civic band composer and conductor in Naples, **V:** 157; **X:** 207

Gatti, Luigi, 19th century Italian composer, **XI:** 258

Gaubert, Eugène, 19th century professor at the Conservatoire de Lille, **IX:** 110

Gaudefroy, E., 19th century French composer, **IX:** 48

Gautier, Jean Mathurin, member in 1768–77 of the Les Grands Hautbois, **IV:** 64, fn. 4

Gautier, Léon, 19th century French composer, **IX:** 48

Gautier, Pierre, 1643–1697, French composer, **XI:** 33, 229

Gautrol, 19th century publisher in Paris, **IX:** 145

Gavaert, F. A., 18th century composer, **XI:** 59

Gavaldá, José, 1818–1890, Spanish composer, **IX:** 131

Gaveaux Frere, 19th century publisher in Paris, **VIII:** 17, 19ff, 36, 269, 276

Gaveaux, 19th century publisher in Paris, **IX:** 15, 59

Gaveaux, G., 19th century publisher in Paris, **IX:** 48

Gaveaux, Pierre, 1761–1825, as composer of works arranged for Harmoniemusik, **VIII:** 35 [*L'Amour filial, Le diable en vacances, Le petit Matelot*]; 36 [*Le Diable Auteur, Le traité nul, Monsieur Deschalumeaux, Sophie et Moncars*]

Gaveaux, Pierre, 1761–1825, as composer of a work arranged for band, **IX:** 113

Gaveaux, S., 19th century publisher in Paris, **IX:** 48

Gaveaux, S., 19th century publisher in Paris, **VIII:** 36

Gayer, Johann, 1746–1811, Bohemian composer, **XI:** 33, 110, 152, 166, 243

Gazella, ?, composer in an 1615 Italian collection, **VII:** 198

Gazzaniga, Giuseppe, 1743–1818, Italian, *Quoniam* for Bass and seven winds, **VIII:** 365

Gebauer, ?, 18th century four brothers with this name were French composers, **XI:** 197

Gebauer, ?, 18th century French composer, **XI:** 243

Gebauer, Etienne, as arranger of Spontini, *La Vestale,* opera, for Harmoniemusik, **VIII:** 125

Gebauer, F. R., as arranger of a Haydn Symphony for Harmoniemusik, **VIII:** 47

Gébauer, François René, 1773–1844, bassoon, 1793 faculty of Paris Conservatoire, original compositions for Harmoniemusik, **IV:** 162; **VIII:** 279ff; **IX:** 48; **X:** 67; **XI:** 33, 152, 166, 297, 317

Gebauer, Josef, 1763–1812, French composer, **XI:** 33, 251, 252

Gebauer, Josef, 1763–1812, French composer, as arranger of Mozart, *Cosi fan tutte,* opera, for Harmoniemusik, **VIII:** 77

Gebauer, M. J., as arranger for Harmoniemusik, **VIII:** 11, 13, 25ff, 28, 36, 45ff

Gebauer, Michel, oboe faculty of the 1792 Paris Conservatoire, **IV:** 157

Gebaur, Franz, 1784–1822, German composer, **IX:** 156

Gebel, ?, (2) Harmonie, Op.11 for Harmoniemusik, **VIII:** 194

Gebel, ?, fl. 1800–1828, Austrian composer, **IX:** 214

Gebel, A. François, fl. ca. 1834, composer, **IX:** 48

Gebel, A. Franz, 1787–1843, German composer, **XII:** 34

Gebhard, Ludwig, b. 1907, German composer, **XII:** 82

Geerhart, 16th century composer, **VI:** 107, 120

Gehot, Joseph, Belgium composer (24) *Military Pieces* for Harmoniemusik, **VIII:** 248

Gehring, Johann, d. 1787, German bassoonist, **XI:** 152 [biographical note]

Geiser, Walther, b. 1897, German composer, **XII:** 140

Geisler, Victor, 19th century Austrian composer, **IX:** 214

Geissel, ?, composer included in a 1885 English collection of band music, **X:** 116

Gélin, Charles, 19th century French composer, **IX:** 48

Gelinek, Joseph, 1758–1825, Czech composer, **XI:** 33

Gellert, ?, 19th century Austrian composer, **IX:** 214

Geminiani, ?, 17th century composer, in *Musica bellicosa,* **VII:** 13

Geminiani, Francesco, 1679–1762, Italian composer, **XI:** 33, 197

Genard, ?, 19th century French composer, **IX:** 48

Gendre, Le, 16th century composer, **VI:** 39

General Bertrand, IX: 144

Général Lafayette, IX: 183 [dedication]

General Walter, IX: 235

Generali, Pietro, 1773–1832, Italian composer, **IX:** 118

Genero, Scipione Vargnanosuo, 1599 publisher in Verona, **VI:** 93

Genin, T., 19th century French composer, **IX:** 48

Genlis, Madame de, 1746–1830, critic of French etiquette, **IV:** 170 [on Gossec], 174

Gensmer, Harald, b. 1909, German composer, **XII:** 140

Gentil, Victor, 19th century French composer, **IX:** 49

Gentsch, E., 19th century German composer, **IX:** 156

George I, 1714–1727, King of England, **III:** 99

George IV, 1762–1830, King of England, **V:** 161, 201ff, 204

Georges, Jules, 19th century French composer, **IX:** 49

Geraert, 16th century composer, **VI:** 108ff

Gerard, James, 18th century English composer, **XI:** 197

Gérard, Marcelin, 19th century French composer, **IX:** 49

Gerardus (Gerardus Mes), mid-16th century Franco-Flemish composer, **VI:** 107, 119ff

Gerber, Ernst Ludwig, 1746–1819, publisher of an encyclopedia of music, **IV:** 56; **V:** 101, 185 [article in 1809 in *Allgemenen Musikalischen Zeitung* on Harmoniemusik]

Gerber, Matthias, clarinet faculty of the 1792 Paris Conservatoire, **IV:** 156

Gerhard, 17th century publisher in Nürnberg, **VII:** 133

Gerhard, Roberto, b. 1896, Spanish composer, **XII:** 82, 140

Gérin, Louis, 19th century French composer, **IX:** 49

Gerke, Auguste, 19th century French composer, **IX:** 49, 156

Gerl (Görl), Franz Xaver, 1764–1827, *Der dumme Gärtner aus dem Gebirge,* **VIII:** 36

Gerlach, Dieterich, 16th century publisher in Nürnberg, **VI:** 66, 69, 72, 74ff

Gerlach, Katharina, 1580 Nürnberg publisher, **VI:** 66, 68, 70, 73

Germain, Emile, 19th century French composer, **IX:** 49

German, Edward, 1862–1936, German composer, **XII:** 82

Gernsheim, Friedrich, 1839–1916, German composer, **XI:** 33

Gero, Jhan, fl. 1540–1555, Franco-Flemish composer, **VI:** 63

Gerold, ?, composer included in a 1871 English collection of band music, **X:** 113

Gerstenbüttel, Joachim, 1650–1721, German composer, **VII:** 117

Gerster, Ottmar, b. 1897, German composer, **XII:** 140

Gervaise, Claude, fl. 1540–1560, French composer, **II:** 70; **VI:** 46ff, 50ff

Gesius, Bartholomaeus, 1555–1621, 1615 German composer of dances, **VII:** 162

Gesualdo, Carlo, 1561–1613, Italian composer, **VI:** 104

Gesus, R., 19th century French composer, **IX:** 49

Getzmann, Wolfgang, 17th century German composer, **VII:** 162

Geucke, composer in 1604 dance collection published in Kassel, **VII:** 181

Geveaux, French composer, **IV:** 163

Gevhart, François, 1828–1908, French composer, **XI:** 282

Geyaert, 19th century publisher at Gent, **XI:** 279

Ghedini, Giorgio Fedeice, b. 1892, Italian composer, **XII:** 140

Gheerkin (Gheerkin de Hondt), d. 1547, Dutch composer, **VI:** 108

Gherardeschi, Gherardo, 19th century Italian composer for band, **X:** 208

Gherardeschi, Guiseppe, 1759–1815, Italian, 3 *Quintetti, Miserere,* for winds, **VIII:** 365

Gherardeschi, Luigi, 1791–1871, 19th century Italian composer for band, **X:** 208

Gherardi, Gherardo, late 18th century Italian composer, **X:** 37

Ghillini di Asuni, ?, 18th century composer, **XI:** 197, 236

Ghiselin, Jean, late 15th – early 16th century Franco-Flemish composer, **VI:** 17, 120

Ghisi, Federico, b. 1901, Italian composer, **XII:** 82

Ghiti, G., 19th century Italian composer for band, **X:** 208

Ghizeghim, Hayne van, 1445–1497, Franco-Flemish composer, **VI:** 31

Ghro, ?, composer in a 1620 Frankfurt collection, **VII:** 172

Gianella, Louis, 1778–1817, *Acis et Galathée*, ballet, arr. for Harmoniemusik, **VIII:** 36

Gianella, Luci, 18th century (?) composer, **XI:** 197

Gianella, Luigi, 19th century French flutist & composer, **VIII:** 100 [as arranger of Paisiello's, *Nina*, opera, for Harmoniemusik]; **XI:** 34

Giannotti, Pietro, d. 1765, Italian composer, **XI:** 34

Gianotti, Giacomo, fl. 1584, composer, **VI:** 106

Giardini, Felice, 1716–1796, Italian composer, **XI:** 34

Giarnovick, unnamed work arranged by Beinet for Harmoniemusik, **VIII:** 153

Gibbons, Christopher, 1615–1676, English composer of ensemble music, **VII:** 51

Gibbons, Orlando, 1583–1625, English composer, **VII:** 20, 22, 25, 51ff

Gibbons, Richard, mid-17th century, English composer of ensemble music, **VII:** 52

Gibbs, John, early 17th century English composer of ensemble music, **VII:** 52

Gibert, ?, 19th century arranger, **IX:** 113

Gibert, Antoine, 19th century French composer, **IX:** 49

Gideon, military leader, Old Testament, **I:** 23

Gieseking, Walter, b. 1895, famous French/German pianist, composer, **XII:** 141

Gigl, Georg, 19th century German composer, **XI:** 321

Gilg, Franz, 19th century German composer, **XI:** 134

Gilg., Frz, 19th century German composer, **IX:** 204

Gill, Georg, early 17th century of English ensemble music, **VII:** 53

Gillard, F., 19th century French composer, **IX:** 50

Gilles de Zamore, 12th century theorist, **I:** 95

Gilles, Jean, 1668–1705, French composer for Hautboisten, **VII:** 87

Gillet, F., 19th century French composer, **IX:** 50

Gillo, Giovanni, 1618, Italian composer of church concerti, **VII:** 202

Gillotot, François, 17th century, oboe student, **III:** 34

Gilmer, Emile, conductor 1912 London Civil Band, **XII:** 217

Gilmore, Patrick, 19th century American composer for band, **IX:** 138

Gilson, Paul, 1865–1942, Belgium composer, **IX:** 259

Ginastera, Alberto, b. 1916, Brazilian composer, **XII:** 141

Ginguene, 18th century French poet, **IV:** 209

Gintscher, Anton, 1779 account of music in the Melk monastery, **IV:** 121

Giordani, Tommaso, 1730–1806, Italian composer, **XI:** 34, 197

Giorgi, Carlo, 19th century Italian composer for band, **X:** 208

Giorza, Paolo, 1832–1914, Italian composer for band, **X:** 208

Giorza, Paul, 19th century Italian composer, **IX:** 118

Giranek, Anton, 1712–1760, Bohemian composer, **XI:** 110

Girard, ?, 19th century French composer, **V:** 75

Girard, L., 19th century French composer, **IX:** 50

Giraud, Adolphe, 19th century French composer, **IX:** 50

Girerd, Edouard, ?, 19th century French composer, **IX:** 50

Girolet, ?, 19th century French composer, **IX:** 50

Giroult, composer of unnamed work arranged by Ozi for Harmoniemusik, 153

Girschner, Christian, 1794–1860, German composer, **XI:** 134

Gistou, Nicolas, d. 1609, Copenhagen, composer 5-part dances, **VII:** 11, 166

Gitter, Joseph, 18th century German composer, **XI:** 35

Giudici e Strada, 19th century publisher in Torino, **XI:** 159

Giudici, Eugenio, b. 1874, Italian composer for band, **X:** 208

Giuliani, Giovanni, 18th century Italian composer, **XI:** 35

Givord, ?, 19th century French composer, **IX:** 50

Glachant, Antoine, 1770–1851, French composer, **XI:** 198

Gladman, ?, composer included in a 1883 English collection of band music, **X:** 115

Glanner, Caspar, 16th century German composer, **VI:** 66

Glanville-Hicks, b. 1912, Peggy, Australian composer, **XII:** 141

Gleissner, F., as 18th century arranger, **VIII:** 218 [Mozart's *Gran Partita*, K. 361, for 9 winds, string quartet]; **X:** 18

Gleissner, Franz, 1759–1818, German, original works for Harmoniemusik, **VIII:** 320ff; **XI:** 35, 198, 258, 290; **XII:** 34

Gleize, F., 19th century French composer, **IX:** 50

Glenn, Karl, Past President, MENC, **XII:** 207

Glete, Johann, 17th century German composer, **XI:** 254

Glinka, Mikhail, 1804–1857, **V:** 117, 121; **XII:** 204

Gloger, ?, 18th century German, *Exercises* for fifes and percussion, **VIII:** 321

Gloger, 19th century German composer, **IX:** 141

Glöggel, 19th century publisher in Vienna, **IX:** 242, 244; **XI:** 310

Glorio, G., 18th century publisher in London, **XI:** 15

Glover, Charles, 19th century English composer, **IX:** 272

Gluck, Christoph Willibald, 1714–1787, works arranged for Harmoniemusik, **VIII:** 37 [*Alceste, Iphigénie en Aulide, La Rencontre imprevus*]; 38 [*Armide, das kleine Wasser, Iphigénie en Tauride, Mochomet*]

Gluck, Christoph, 1714–1787, German composer, **V:** 35 [arr. by Wieprecht], 73, 132 ; **IX:** 141, 248; **XI:** 35, 229

Gnecco, Francesco, b. 1769, Italian composer, **XI:** 134

Gnisson, Emile, 19th century French composer, **IX:** 48

Godard, Amédée, 19th century French composer, **IX:** 50

Godard, Benjamin, 1849–1895, French composer, **XI:** 35, 110; **XII:** 197

Godard, Charles, 19th century Austrian composer, **IX:** 214

Godard, Robert, 16th century French organist and composer, **VI:** 44ff, 49, 109ff

Godart, 16th century composer, **VI:** 109, 114, 119

Godefroid, 19th century French composer, **IX:** 2

Goderick, Hans, church bassoonist in Alost, 1603–1605, **III:** 199

Godfrey, Adolphus Frederick, 1837–1882, English composer, **V:** 81, fn 14; **IX:** 272

Godfrey, Arthur, 19th century English composer, **IX:** 273

Godfrey, C., composer included in a 1874 English collection of band music, **X:** 113

Godfrey, Charles, English band leader, 1790–1863, **V:** 81, fn 14

Godfrey, Charles, Jr., English band leader, 1839–1919, **V:** 81, fn 14; **IX:** 273

Godfrey, Charles, Sr., 19th century English composer, **IX:** 273

Godfrey, Daniel, English band leader, 1831–1903, **V:** 81 fn 14, 84

Godfrey, Sr. Daniel, 19th century English composer, **IX:** 273

Godfrey, W., English composer, *The Thrush,* ca. 1785, band, solo piccolo, **VIII:** 256

Goepfert, 19th century German composer, **IX:** 180

Goepfert, Carl, b. 1768, German clarinetist, **XI:** 134 [biographical note]

Goepffert, ?, harpist for La Pouplinière, 1763, **IV:** 68, fn. 26

Goethe, German poet, **IX:** 227

Goetzel, François, 18th century flautist in court of the Elector of Saxony in Dresden in 1756, **XI:** 35, 198

Goguelat, E., 19th century French composer, conductor, 56e de Ligne, **IX:** 1

Golabek, ?, *Partita* for Harmoniemusik, **VIII:** 194

Golabek, Jakub, 1739–1789, Polish, *Partita* for Harmoniemusik, **VIII:** 369

Golar, ?, ca. 1600, composer of English ensemble music, **VII:** 53

Golde, J., fl. 1813–1815, German composer, **IX:** 156

Goldmark, Carl, 1830–1915, Austrian/Hungarian composer, **IX:** 215; **XI:** 309

Goleminov, Marin, b. 1908, composer, **XII:** 141

Golin, Guilielmo, mid-16th century composer, **VI:** 92

Göller, ? 18th century German, *Partita* for Harmoniemusik, **VIII:** 321

Goller, Vinzenz, 1873–1953, Austrian composer, **XII:** 82

Gombart, 18th and 19th century publisher in Augsburg, **VIII:** 79, 207, 333; **IX:** 177, 181, 188; **XI:** 196, 224, 226, 232, 275

Gombert, Nicolas, 1495–1560, Franco-Flemish composer, **VI:** 27, 38ff, 45, 63, 84, 109ff, 114, 118ff, 122

Gomez, Carlos, 19th century composer, arranged for band, **IX:** 255

Gonkeritz, 17th century publisher in Dresden, **VII:** 157

Gonzaga, Viccenzo, coronation in 1587, **II:** 133

Goodale, Ezekiel, 19th century American composer, **IX:** 138

Goosens, Eugene, b. 1893, English composer, **XII:** 83, 141, 197

Göpfert, Carl, fl. 1800–1828, German composer, arranger for Harmoniemusik, **VIII:** 7, 17, 81, 82ff; **IX:** 156; **XII:** 53 [as arranger of Steibelt *Combat Naval,* for small band]

Gor, Alph., 19th century French composer, **IX:** 72

Gorb, Adam, 20th century English composer, **XII:** 202

Gorlier, Simon, fl. 1550–1580, French composer & a treatise on flute, **XI:** 35

Gorman, 17th century publisher in Wittenberg, **VII:** 168

Gorner, Johann, 1702–1762, German composer, **III:** 160

Goschelock, J. [see Kozeluch]

Gossec, François Joseph, 1734–1829, French composer, **IV:** 66ff, 68ff, 146ff [*Te Deum*], 149ff, 151 [*March lugubre*], 156, 159ff, 164ff, 175ff, 184ff, 186, 188ff, 191, 197, 204ff, 209, 211; **VIII:** 280ff [(38) original works for band or Harmoniemusik]; **VIII:** 292 [as arranger of Rouget de Lisle's, *Marche des Marseillois* for band]

Gossec, François, 18th century French composer, **XII:** 202

Gossec, Mme, clavecinist for La Pouplinière, 1763, **IV:** 68, fn. 26

Gossec, works arranged for Harmoniemusik, **VIII:** 39, 151

Gössel, 17th century publisher in Hamburg and Hildesheim, **VII:** 148

Gostiau, G., 19th century French composer, **IX:** 50

Gotherot, G., 19th century French composer, **IX:** 50

Gotkovsky, Ida, 20th century French composer, **XII:** 202

Göttling, ?, 18th century German, (6) Harmoniemusik works, **VIII:** 321

Gottsched, Johann, 1700–1766, German composer, **XI:** 160

Gotz, 18th century publisher in Mannheim, **XI:** 15, 84

Götz, 18th century publisher in Munich, **VIII:** 320

Götz, Francesco, 19th century Austrian composer, **IX:** 215

Götz, François, 19th century French composer, **XI:** 35

Goudeaul, 16th century composer, **VI:** 45, 49

Goueytes, R., 19th century French composer, arranger, **IX:** 51

Gouirand, Joseph, 19th century French composer, **IX:** 51

Gould, Morton, 20th century American composer, **XII:** 203

Goulding, 18th century publisher in London, **VIII:** 262, 265; **XI:** 21, 35, 44, 46, 139, 220

Goulding, Phipps & D'Almainc, 18th century publishers in London, **VIII:** 258

Gouly, ?, 19th century French composer, **IX:** 51

Goumas, 19th century publisher in Paris, **IX:** 6

Gounod, Charles, 1818–1893, French composer, **V:** 112, 147 fn. 2, 153, 156; **IX:** 51; **X:** 6; **XII:** 212, 213, 218, 219, 194

Gounod, Charles, 1818–1893, as composer of works arranged for band, **IX:** 255, **X:** 234 [*Faust,* arr. Ponchielli]; 254 [*Faust,* arr. Vessella]

Gouvy, Louis Theodore, 1819–1898, German composer, **V:** 153; **IX:** 156

Gow, Mr., 19th century English band leader, **X:** 117

Gow, Nathaniel, 1763–1831, English band composer, **VIII:** 257

Goyer, ?, 19th century French composer, **IX:** 51

Grabbe, Johan, composer in 1621 publication of English ens. music, **VII:** 23, 24, 163

Grabner, Hermann, b. 1886, German composer, **XII:** 83

Graf von Sparr (17th century), **III:** 124

Graf, Christian Ernst, 1726–1804, German composer, **XI:** 36

Graf, Friedrich Harmann, 1727–1795, German flautist, composer, **XI:** 36, 240

Graf, Johann, 1669–1734, 'Hoboistenmeister' in Bamberg, **III:** 130

Gräfe, Johann Friedrich, 1711–1787, German composer, *March*, **VIII:** 340

Grafe, Postrath, Baroque German composer for Hautboisten, **III:** 131; **VII:** 117

Graff, ?, 18th century German composer, **XI:** 198

Graff, 18th century composer, **XI:** 295

Graff, C. E., 18th century German, *Die Schlacht bei Austerlitz*, for band, **VIII:** 321

Graff, Johann, 1711–1787, German flautist, composer, **XI:** 36

Graffeuil, Charles, 19th century French composer, **IX:** 51

Grainger, Percy, b. 1882, Australian composer, **XII:** 84, 203

Grammont, French ambassador visiting Saxony in 1606, **III:** 61

Grancini, Michel'angelo, 1622, Italian composer of church concerti, **VII:** 201

Grand magazin de musique, publisher in Amsterdam, **VIII:** 220

Grandi, Alessandro, 1586–1630, Italian composer, **III:** 215; **VII:** 144, 188

Grandi, Ottavio, fl. 1610–1630, Italian composer of sonatas with organ, **VII:** 202

Grangé, Léon, 19th century French composer, **IX:** 51

Grange, Théodore, 19th century French composer, **IX:** 51

Granman, ?, 18th century (?) German composer, **XI:** 37

Grano, Giovanni, 18th century Italian composer, **XI:** 37, 110

Granom, Lewis, 18th century English composer, **XI:** 37, 198

Gras, D.-L., 19th century French composer, **IX:** 51

Grass, 19th century publisher in Breslau, **IX:** 144

Grassalkovics, Anton, d. 1794, Prince of Pressburg, **IV:** 31, 42

Grasso, F. P., 19th century Italian composer, **X:** 209

Graun, ?, 18th century (?) German composer, **XI:** 37

Graun, August Friedrich, 1698–1765, German composer, **XI:** 38, 125, 152, 198, 229

Graun, Carl Heinrich, 1703–1759, German composer, **XI:** 38, 166, 199, 279

Graun, Johann, 1703–1771, German composer, **XI:** 125

Graun, Johann, Baroque German composer for Hautboisten, **VII:** 117

Graun, Karl Heinrich, 1703–1759, German composer for Hautboisten, **III:** 19, 131, 169; **VII:** 118

Graupner, Christoph, 1683–1760, German Hautboisten composer, **III:** 17, 213; **VII:** 118ff; **X:** 7; **XI:** 38, 111, 125, 234, 236, 238, 237, 258

Graven (or Grave, or Graun, Karl), 1703–1759, German composer, **XII:** 2

Graves, W. T., 19th century English composer, **IX:** 274

Grawert, E., 19th century German composer, **IX:** 157

Gray, 20th century publisher in New York, **XII:** 79

Grazioli, Giovanni, 1746–1820, Italian, *Credo* for voices and 6 winds, **VIII:** 365

Grazzini, Reginaldo, 1848–1906, Italian composer for band, **X:** 209

Greber, Jakob, Baroque German composer, **XI:** 38

Greeting, Thomas, d. 1682, English composer, **XI:** 38

Grefinger, Wolfgang, 1480–1525, German composer, **VI:** 61ff

Greggiati, Giuseppe, 1793–1866, Italian clarinetist, composer, **X:** 17, 171, 209

Grégoire, as arranger for Harmoniemusik, **VIII:** 107ff, 110ff.

Gregora, Franz, 1819–1887, Czech composer, **XI:** 38, 290

Gregori, Alberto, considered best trombonist in 17th century Italy, **III:** 193

Gregori, Giovanni, late Baroque Italian composer, **III:** 16

Grell, Eduard, 1800–1886, composer for voices and band, **V:** 132; **IX:** 157

Grenser, ?, 19th century composer, **XI:** 134

Grenser, Johann, 1758–1887, German/Swedish professor of oboe to the King of Sweden in 1783, **VIII:** 321ff [(7) *Partitas* for Harmoniemusik]; **XI:** 39

Grenser, Karl Augustin III, 1794–1864, **XI:** 39, 199

Grep, ?, composer in a 1609 Hamburg collection, **VII:** 166

Grétry, André, 1741–1813, Belgium/French composer, **V:** 182; **IX:** 197

Grétry, André, 1741–1813, as composer of works arranged for Harmoniemusik, **VIII:** 39 [*La Caravane du Caire, Silvain, Zémire et Azor*]; 40 [*Panurge dans l'Isle des Lanternes, Raoul Barbe Bleue, Richard Coeur-de-Lion]; unidentified works, 41, 153, 154;* **XII:** 40, 49 [*Raul der Blaubart,* opera, arranged by Fischer, ? for Harmoniemusik]; 50 [movements from *Panurge,* arranged by Étienne Ozi for Harmoniemusik]; 51 [unidentified work arranged by Ozi]

Grétry, André, 1741–1813, as composer of works arranged for band, **IX:** 180, 245

Gretsch, Johann Konrad, 1710–1778, German (2) *Partitas* for Harmoniemusik, **VIII:** 322; **XI:** 111

Greventhal, Christian, composer in 1622 German collection, **VII:** 145

Grieg, Edvard, 1843–1907, Norway composer, **IX:** 127

Griesbach, Charles, 18th century English comp., (24) *Military Divertimenti,* for Harmonie, **VIII:** 257; **XI:** 199

Griesbach, William, 19th century English composer, **XI:** 39, 111

Griessbacher, 'great clarinetist,' in Harmoniemusik of Prince Grassalkovics, **IV:** 41

Griessbacher, Jacob, bassoonist in 1780 for Count Palm in Vienna, **IV:** 42

Griessbacher, Reimund, Director of the Harmoniemusik for Prince Grassalkowitz in Vienna in 1796, **VIII:** 195

Griffes, Charles, 1884–1920, American composer, **XII:** 84

Grignis, M., 17th century person, **VII:** 81

Grillet, 19th century arranger, **IX:** 113

Grillet, Laurent, 19th century French composer, **IX:** 52

Grillo, composer in 1608 Venetia canzoni collection, **VII:** 208

Grimm, ?, (ca. 1810), German composer, **IX:** 157

Grimm, Anton, 19th century composer in Vienna, **IX:** 215; **XI:** 301

Grimm, Julius, 1827–1903, German composer, **IX:** 157

Groenemann, Johann, 18th century German composer, **XI:** 199

Groh, A., 19th century Austrian composer, **IX:** 215

Groh, Johann, 1603 German composer of dances, **VII:** 142, 162

Groh, Josef, 19th century Austrian composer, **IX:** 215

Gross, ? German, ca. 1770, *Echo* for Harmoniemusik with solo oboe, **VIII:** 322

Gross, G., 19th century French composer, **IX:** 52

Gross, Peter, 1616 German composer of dances, **VII:** 163

Grosseteste of Lincoln, Robert, 1175–1253, **I:** 99, 107

Grossin, Estienne, fl. 1418–1421, French composer, **VI:** iv, ix

Grossmann, ?, 18th century German composer, **XI:** 244

Grossse, Samuel, 1757–1789, German composer, **XI:** 111

Grot, ?, *Parthia* for Harmoniemusik, **VIII:** 195

Grote, A. R. 19th century German composer, **IX:** 157

Grove, Stefans, b. 1922, German composer, **XII:** 84, 142

Grovlez, ?, 19th century French arranger, **XII:** 193

Gruber, 17th century publisher in Guben, **VII:** 127

Gruber, Felix, 19th century Austrian composer, **IX:** 215

Gruber, Franz, 1787–1863 Austrian composer, **XI:** 258

Gruber, Georg, 1729–1796, German composer, **XI:** 39

Gruber, Johann, 19th century Austrian composer, **IX:** 215; **XI:** 322

Gruber, Josef, 19th century Austrian composer, **IX:** 215

Grund, Eduard, 1802–1871, German composer, **IX:** 157; **XI:** 39, 166, 302

Gruner, 17th century publisher in Coburg, **VII:** 160

Gruner, Nathaniel, 1732–1792, German, music for chorus and Harmoniemusik, **VIII:** 322

Grunewald, Jean-Jacques, b. 1911, French composer, **XII:** 84, 142

Grutsch, Franz, 19th century Austrian (?) composer, **XI:** 282

Gualdo da Vandero, Giovanni, 18th century Italian composer, **XI:** 199

Guami, Giosoffo, 1540–1611, Lucca, composer, **II:** 245; **VI:** 82ff, 91, 104

Guami, Giuseppe, 1612, Italian composer of ensemble music, **VII:** 22, 202ff, 208

Guarneri, Andrea, 19th century civic band conductor in Milan, **V:** 156; **X:** 209

Gudea of Sumeria, King of Sumeria, 2,600 BC, **I:** 10

Gudon, General, VIII: 182

Guédron, Pierre, period Louis XIII, French composer for Hautboisten, **VII:** 94

Guera, 18th century publisher in Lyon, **XI:** 211

Guering, ?, 19th century arranger, **X:** 38

Guerings, ?, 19th century Austrian composer, **IX:** 215

Guéroult, Th., 19th century French composer, **IX:** 52

Guerra, E., 19th century German composer, **IX:** 157

Guerrero, Spanish composer, music copied for use in New World, **II:** 221

Guerriee, Rocco, flutist in the 1910 Barrère Ensemble in NYC, **XII:** 214

Guerrini, Guido, b. 1890, Italian composer, **XII:** 142

Guès, A., 19th century French composer, **IX:** 1, 52

Guespereau, ?, 19th century French composer, **IX:** 52

Guest, George, 1771–1831, English composer, **IX:** 274

Guévin, Arthur, 19th century French composer, **IX:** 52

Gugel, H., 18th century horn player and composer, **XI:** 167 [biographical note]

Guglielmi, Pietro, 1728–1788, operas arranged for Harmoniemusik, **VIII:** 41, 42

Guglielmo II, S. M. of Rome [dedication], **X:** 253

Guglielmo, Pietro, 1728–1804, Italian composer, **XII:** 34

Guida, Agostino, Banda del L. di Linea, **IX:** 122

Guidé, Guillaume, 19th century Belgium oboist, **XII:** 216

Guidi, 19th century publisher in Firenze, **IX:** 171

Guidi, Lorenzo, 19th century Italian composer, **X:** 209

Guidobaldi I, Duke of Urbino, trumpet choir in church, **II:** 241

Guignard, Claude, 18th century French author of a military treatise, **III:** 141

Guilbert, ?, 19th century French composer, **IX:** 52

Guiliani, unnamed work arranged for Harmoniemusik, **VIII:** 152

Guille, J., 19th century French composer, **IX:** 52

Guillemant, Benoit, 18th century French composer, **XI:** 39, 199, 252

Guillement, G., 19th century French composer, **IX:** 52

Guillet, Charles, early 17th century Dutch composer of 4-part Fantaisies, **VII:** 214

Guilmant, Felix, 1837–1911, German composer, **XI:** 39

Guimbal, A., 19th century French composer, **IX:** 53

Guion, Edmond, 19th century French composer, **IX:** 53

Gulda, Friedrich, Austrian, 20th century composer, **XII:** 203

Gumbert, Friedrich, 1841–1906, German composer of a work for band, **X:** 97

Gunderman, 17th century publisher in Hamburg, **VII:** 176

Gung'l, Jozsef, 1810–1889, Austrian/Hungarian composer, **V:** 43; **IX:** 215; **X:** 45, 113ff

Gunn, John, 1765–1824, English composer, treatises on flute playing, **XI:** 39

Günther & Böhme, 18th century publishers in Hamburg, **VIII:** 360

Günther, Carl, 18th century, (32) *Marches* for the German army, **VIII:** 322

Günther, Karl, early 19th century German composer, **IX:** 157

Güntzel, 17th century publisher in Oels [Poland], **VII:** 167

Gurtner, ?, 19th century French composer, conductor, Musique 4e de Ligne, **IX:** 53

Gurtner, Jean, 19th century French composer, **IX:** 1, 274

Gussago (Gussaghi), Cesario, (1608), Italian composer, **III:** 194; **VII:** 203

Gutenberg, IX: 186, 234

Guth, 17th century publisher in Berlin, **VII:** 150

Guthmann, François, trumpet faculty of the 1792 Paris Conservatoire, **IV:** 156

Gutiérrez de Padilla, Juan, 1590–1664, instrument maker in Mexico, **III:** 221

Guttenberg, 1398–1468, **V:**132

Guy, ?, composer in James I band library, 1603–1665, **VII:** 13

Guyon, Jean, 16th century composer, **VI:** 38, 49ff

Guyot, Jean, 1512–1588, Dutch composer, **VI:** 120, 122

Guzinger, Johann, 17th century German composer for voices and winds, **VII:** 118

Gwin, Matthew, professor of music at Oxford in 1582, **II:** 39

Gwnneth, 16th century composer, **VI:** 35

Gyrowetz, Adalbert, 1763–1850, Austrian composer, **IV:** 17; **VIII** 195ff [(36) original compositions for Harmoniemusik]; **IX:** 249; **XI:** 39, 149, 302

Gyrowetz (Girovetz, Jirovec), Adalbert, 1763–1850, his works arr. for Harmoniemusik,
  VIII: 42 [*Agnes Sorel*]; 43 [*Der Augenarzt, Die Hochzeit der Thetis und des Peleus, Die Pagen
  des Herzoge von Vendome, Federica ed Adolfo*]; 44 [*Die beiden Eremiten, Die Zwey Tanten,
  Miriam*]; 154 [*Der Zauberschlaf*]; **XII:** 50 [*Die Hochzeit der Thetis*, arranged by Sedlak for
  Harmoniemusik, *Agnes Sorel*, unidentified arranger for Harmoniemusik]
Gyrowetz, Adalbert, 1763–1850, as composer of a work arranged for band, **X:** 37 [*Die beiden
  Eremiten*, arranged for band by Gandini]
Gyrowetz, Naturna, 18th century composer, **XI:** 40

Haas, Joseph, 1879–1960, German composer, **XII:** 85

Haba, Alois, b. 1893, Czech composer, **XII:** 142

Haba, Karl, b. 1898, Czech composer, **XII:** 142

Haberer, ?, 19th century conductor in Sackingen, Germany, **V:** 129

Habert, Johannes, 1833–1896, German composer, **IX:** 157

Habert, M., arr., Grétry, *Richard Coeur-de-Lion*, opera, for Harmoniemusik, **VIII:** 40

Habicht, V., composer included in a 1876 English collection of band music, **X:** 114

Hacker, Benedikt, 1769–1829, German composer, **IX:** 157

Hacquart, Carolus, 1649–1730 Dutch composer of sonatas, **VII:** 213, 214

Haddock, George, b. 1860, English composer for band, **X:** 119

Haensel, Pietro, 19th century composer, **XI:** 134

Haering, Joseph, 18th century Swiss, (60) works for winds, **VIII:** 373

Hafemeister, Richard, 19th century French composer, **IX:** 53

Haffner, 18th century publisher in Nürnberg, **XI:** 50

Hagen, ?, 18th century composer, **XI:** 200

Hagius, Conrad, 1616 German composer of dances, **VII:** 144, 163

Hagmann, ?, 1800–1828, German composer, **IX:** 157

Hahocker, Johann, 19th century (?) composer, **XI:** 40

Haidner, bassoonist, 19th century court of Mechlenburg-Schwerin, **V:** 185, fn. 4

Haigh, T., (student of Haydn) pianist & composer, **XI:** 40

Hailland, 16th century composer, **VI:** 107

Hainaut, A., 19th century French composer, **IX:** 53

Haindl, Franz, 1727–1812, German (?) composer, **XI:** 40

Haindl, Josef, 19th century German composer, **XI:** 167

Haine, ?, composer included in a 1878 English collection of band music, **X:** 115

Hainl, George of Lyon, **V:** 146 [letter from Berlioz.

Hairaud, Hte., 19th century French composer, **IX:** 53

Hájek, Josef, 19th century Hungarian composer, **IX:** 216

Hake, John, fl. before 1548, English composer, **VI:** 35

Haken, Hans, 1654 German composer of dances, **VII:** 164

Halbmayer, 17th century publisher in Nürnberg, **VII:** 182

Halévy, Jacques François Fromental, 1799–1862, French composer, **V:** 62ff, 73, 121; **IX:** 54; **XII:** 60, 203, 218

Halffter Escriche, Ernesto, b. 1905, Spanish composer, **XII:** 85

Hall, Richard, 19th century founder of a brass band contest in Hull, **V:** 167

Hallager, A., 19th century, German composer, **IX:** 157

Haller, Michael, 19th century Austrian composer, **IX:** 216

Hallervord, 17th century publisher in Rostock, **VII:** 161

Hallmayr, Victtorin, 19th century Austrian band composer, **V:** 157; **IX:** 216

Hamal, Henri, 1747–1823, French composer, **XI:** 111

Hamelle, 19th century publisher in Paris, **IX:** 57; **XI:** 110

Hamilton, 18th century publisher in London, **XI:** 40

Hamilton, Maximilian, 1761–1776, Bishop of Olomouc at Kromeriz, **IV:** 22

Hamm, ?, composer included in 19th century English band collections, **X:** 113

Hamm, Johann Valentin, 1811–1875, German composer, **IX:** 158

Hammer, 19th century publisher in Vienna, **IX:** 253

Hammer, August, 19th century German composer, Principal Oboe 'chez le 7 Reg. s. Hollande,' **IX:** 158

Hammer, Carl, German, ca. 1800, *Partita* for Harmoniemusik, **VIII:** 323

Hammer, Richard, 2nd half, 19th century composer, **XII:** 60

Hammerl, as arranger of Mozart operas for Harmoniemusik, **VIII:** 73, 78ff

Hammerl, clarinetist, 19th century court of Mechlenburg-Schwerin, **V:** 185, fn. 4

Hammerl, Cornelius, 1769–1839, German composer, **IX:** 158

Hammerschmidt, Andreas, 1611–1675, German composer, **III:** 16; **VII:** 119ff, 164ff

Hanache, 16th century composer, **VI:** 120

Hand, Hermann, Viennese horn player, in New York in 1905, **XII:** 212

Handel, Georg Friedrich, 1685–1759, German composer, 1685–1759, **III:** 8, 11, 18, 99ff. 106. 178; **V:** 26, 35 [arrangements by Wieprecht], 73, 99, 168, 170ff, 202; **VII:** [as composer of wind ensemble music] 16ff, 104, 121; **VIII:** 44 [*Saül*, arranged for Harmoniemusik]; **XI:** 40, 111, 200, 236, 276 323 [*Alexander's Feast*, unknown arr. for 5 brass]; **IX:** 113 [unidentified work arranged for band]; **XII:** 214, 215

Handke, Mauritius, 18th century composer in a Partita collection, **VIII:** 163

Handl, J., arranger, Salieri, *Palmira, Regina di Persia*, opera, for Harmoniemusik, **VIII:** 118

Handl, Johann, 19th century Austrian composer, **IX:** 216

Hänisch, Johann, 1601 collector of Polish dances, **VII:** 143, 163

Hanisch, Joseph, 1812–1892, German composer, **XI:** 176, 311

Hanke, Karl, 1750–1803, German composer, **XI:** 111, 160, 167, 258

Hannibal, Carthaginian general, 247–183 BC, **I:** 38, 57

Hanot, François, 1697–1770, French composer, **XI:** 41

Hans Neuschel, 16th century instrument maker in Nürnberg, **II:** 120

Hanschke, ?, *Partia* for Harmoniemusik, **VIII:** 196

Hänsel, Peter, 1770–1831, German composer, **XI:** 41

Hansen, 20th century publisher in Kopenhagen, **XII:** 93

Hansen, J. P., composer included in a 1883 English collection of band music, **X:** 115

Hansen, Jules, 20th century French composer, **XII:** 85

Hanslick, Eduard, 1825–1904, Viennese critic, **V:** 99, 103, 114ff, 118, 149

Hanssens, Charles-Louis, 1802–1871, century Belgium composer, **IX:** 259; **XI:** 41, 134

Hantzsch, Andreas, 16th century publisher in Mühlhausen, **VI:** 65

Hantzsch, Georg, 16th century publisher in Mühlhausen, **VI:** 65

Hanus, Jan, b. 1915, Czech composer, **XII:** 85

Hanzel, A., fl. 1800–1828, German composer, **IX:** 158

Harbordt, Gottfried, 1768–1837, German flutist and composer for the Russian court and a member of the Royal Academy of Music in Paris, **VIII:** 323 [*Trauer Marsch*, for Harmoniemusik]; **XI:** 41, 200

Harchadelt, 16th century composer, **VI:** 44ff

Harding, composer in James I band library, **VII:** 13

Hardouin, Gabriel, trumpet faculty of the 1792 Paris Conservatoire, **IV:** 157

Hardy, 18th century publisher in London, **XI:** 213, 237

Hardy, Alexandre, bassoon, 1793 faculty of Paris Conservatoire, **IV:** 162

Hare, 18th century publisher in London, **XI:** 6, 103

Hare, Edwin, 19th century English composer, **IX:** 274

Harelbecanus, Sigerus, 16th century composer, **VI:** 67

Hargrave, Henry, 18th century English, (5) *Concerti*, bassoon ensemble, **VIII:** 257; **XI:** 152

Haring, Alfred, 19th century French composer, **IX:** 54

Harington, John Sir, 17th century English noble, **III:** 82

Harison, 18th century publisher in London, **XI:** 16, 17

Harke, Friedrich, 18th century composer (6) *Märchen* for Harmoniemusik, **VIII:** 197

Harmat, Arthur, b. 1885, Hungarian composer, **XII:** 143

Harnisch, Johann, bassoonist, in Prince Liechtenstein Harmonie, **IV:** 39

Harnisch, Otto, 16th century composer, **VI:** 67

Harper, ?, 19th century English composer, **IX:** 275

Harrach, 18th century Graf von Hungary, supported Harmoniemusik, **IV:** 34

Harrer, Johann, 1703–1755, German Baroque composer, **XI:** 111, 200

Harris, Franklin, 1856–1931, English composer for band, **X:** 120

Harris, Roy, b. 1898, American composer, **XII:** 85, 143

Harrison & Co, 18th century publisher in London, **XI:** 6

Harsányi, Tibor, 1898–1954, Hungarian composer, **XII:** 143

Hart & Fellows, 19th century publisher in London, **XI:** 160

Hartman, 19th century publisher in Paris, **XI:** 307

Hartmann, ?, 18th century English, *A Set of Military Pieces*, **VIII:** 257

Hartmann, 17th century publisher in Frankfurt, **VII:** 169

Hartmann, 19th century publisher in Paris, **IX:** 26

Hartmann, Albert, 1860–1952, English composer of many works for band, **X:** 120

Hartmann, C., 18th century German flautist & composer, **XI:** 41 [biographical note], 200

Hartmann, Emil, 1836–1898, Danish composer, **IX:** 261

Hartmann, Ernst, brother to John Hartmann, 19th century English composer, **X:** 121

Hartmann, Johann, 1805–1900, Danish composer, **IX:** 261

Hartmann, John, 1830–1897, Prussian composer, numerous works for band, **X:** 122

Hartmann, R. E., 20th century German composer, **XII:** 87

Hartner, H., 19th century English composer for band, **X:** 125

Hartner, H., 19th century English composer, **IX:** 275

Hartung, hornist in the Duke of Sondershausen Harmoniemusik, **V:** 185, fn. 2

Hartwig, 1762 German composer for Hautboisten, **VII:** 120

Harzebski, Adam, 1627 Polish composer of canzoni and concerti, **VII:** 218

Hase (Hasz), Georg, 1602–1610 German composer of dances, **VII:** 164

Haslinger, ?, fl. 1800–1828, 19th century Austrian composer, **IX:** 216

Haslinger, 19th century publisher in Vienna, **VIII:** 6ff, 8, 32, 51, 59, 102, 113, 125, 127, 136, 157; **IX:** 48, 211, 214, 216, 221, 227, 240, 243, 244, 245, 246, 254; **XI:** 169

Haslinger, J., 19th century French composer, **IX:** 54

Haslinger, L.-J., 19th century French composer, **IX:** 54

Hasse, ?, 18th century German, *Marches* for military band, **VIII:** 323

Hasse, A. G., 19th century German composer, **IX:** 158

Hasse, Johann (Giovanni), 1699–1783, German composer, **III:** 18, 215; **VII:** 120ff; **X:** 24

Hasse, Johann Adolf, 1699–1783, German composer, **XI:** 42, 200, 276

Hasse, Karl, b. 1883, German composer, **XII:** 86

Hasse, Nikolous, 1617–1672, dance music for winds, **VII:** 120

Hassler, Hans Leo, 1562–1612, German composer, **II:** 236, **III:** 169; **VII:** 120, 145, 164, 180; **XII:** 130 [transcription by Collier]

Hassloch, Carl, 1769–1829, German composer, **IX:** 158

Hattasch (Hatas), Dismas Jan, 1724–1777, (9) *Parthias* for Harmoniemusik, **VIII:** 205ff

Hauck, 17th century publisher in Coburg, **VII:** 159

Haudebert, Lucien, b. 1877, French composer, **XII:** 143

Hauff (Hanff), Wilhelm, German, ca. 1776, (6) *Sextuers* for winds, **VIII:** 323

Haug, Hans, b. 1900, German composer, **XII:** 143

Haunreiter, Peter, 19th century, German composer, **IX:** 158

Haupt, ?, 18th century French author (with Punto), method for horn, **XI:** 167

Hauptmann, Moritz, 1792–1868, German composer, **IX:** 158; **XI:** 42, 311

Hauricq, 16th century composer, **VI:** 123

Hause, Carl, 19th century German composer, **IX:** 158

Häusler, Ernst, 1760–1837, German composer of church music with winds, **IV:** 124; **VIII:** 323 [original *Notturni* and church music with Harmoniemusik]; **XI:** 258, 263, 288, 305, 310; **XII:** 35

Hausmann, Valentin, 1570–1614, German composer, **VI:** 67; **VII:** 144, 165, 172, 180

Hausser, Josef, 19th century Austrian composer, **IX:** 54, 216

Hausswald, Gunter, b. 1908, German composer, **XII:** 143

Havel, ?, 19th century Austrian composer, arranger, **IX:** 216, 222ff

Havel, as arranger for Harmoniemusik, **VIII:** 16, 141, 150

Havericq, Damien, fl. 1538–1556, composer, **VI:** 119

Hawkes, W., 19th century English composer, **IX:** 275

Hawkes, William, 1830–1900, English composer; numerous works for band, **X:** 126

Hawks, David, 1791–1860, English composer (as a child) for band, **X:** 129

Haydenreich, Giuseppe, as arranger, **VIII:** 80, 83 [Mozart]; **XII:** 51 [Müller's *Das Nere Sonntagskind*]

Haydn, Johann Michael, 1737–1806, **IV:** 124; **VIII:** 47 [*Sinfonia par Hayden*, arranged for Harmoniemusik]; **IX:** 236; **XI:** 219, 283, 290, 298

Haydn, Josef, 1732–1809, Austrian composer, **III:** 21; **IV:** 22 fn. 9, 25ff, 27ff, 32, 35, 52ff, 73, 113, 129ff; **V:** 107, 114, 170ff, 187, 201ff; **VIII:** 197ff, 202 [(56) original works for Harmonie and band]; **X:** 17; **XI:** 43, 111, 167, 201, 236, 258, 268, 271, [unidentified theme, arr. Triebensee], XI: 296

Haydn, Josef, 1732–1809, as composer of music arranged for Harmoniemusik, **VIII:** 44 [*Die Schöpfung* Oratorio (complete!); 45 [Symphony, I, 51, Symphony, I, 55, Symphony I, 70, *The Seasons* Oratorio *(complete!)*]; 46 [*Symphony* ('Oxford'), *Symphony* (I, 75), '*Andante mit den Paukenschlag,*' '*Presto*']; 47 [*Symphony in Eb*] unidentified works arr. for Harmoniemusik, 46, 47, 153, 155, 222ff, 330; **XII:** 35, 48 [*Andante and (2) Variations*, arr. Druschetzky for Harmoniemusik]; 50 [string quartets arranged for Harmoniemusik by Nicolas Schmitt, b. 1779]; 52 [*Symphony* Hob. I, 51, arranged for Harmoniemusik by Soller]; 201, 203, 214, 215

Haydn, Josef, 1732–1809, as composer of works arranged for band, **VIII:** 46 [Symphonies I, 85; I, 91 and I, 102, arranged by Bochsa]; **IX:** 9 [the *Creation*]; 113 ['*Surprise,*' '*la Reine,*' *Militaire*' symphonies and from *Die Schöpfung* [10 movements]; 180 [*Symphonies*, Hob. I, 93, 94, 99, 101, 103, 104;]; unidentified works, 158, 236, 250, 253; **XI:** 271 [unidentified theme, arr. Triebensee]

Heberle, Antonio, 18th century (?) Italian composer, **XI:** 43

Heckel, 18th century publisher in Mannheim, **VIII:** 359

Hecker, Johann, 19th century English composer for band, **X:** 129, 130

Hegel, Georg, 1770–1831, German philosopher, **V:** 132

Heidenreich, 19th century Austrian composer, **VIII:** 218 [as arranger of Mozart *Gran Partita* for 8 winds]; **IX:** 216

Heiller, Anton, b. 1923, Austrian composer, **XII:** 87

Heimichen, ?, Baroque composer, **XII:** 3

Heine, ?, 19th century composer, **V:** 212

Heine, Gotthelf (1805), German composer, member of the court ensemble in Ludwigslust, **IX:** 159

Heine, Samuel Friedrich, 1764–1821, German composer, **IX:** 159; **IX:** 43, 112, 135, 152, 201, 240

Heings, Michael, 17th century Hamburg publisher, **VII:** 23

Heinichen, Johann David, 1683–1729, German composer, **X:** 7; **XI:** 125

Heinrich of Brunswick, VI: 57

Heinrich, Anthony, 1781–1861, American composer, **IX:** 138

Heinrich, Anton, 1781–1861, German composer, **XI:** 160

Heinrich, Baroque German composer, **III:** 131

Heinrich, Carl, 19th century Austrian composer, **IX:** 216

Heinrich, Carl, trumpeter in the 1910 Barrère Ensemble in NYC, **XII:** 214

Heinrich, Johann Gottfried, 18th century (?), German composer, **XI:** 112

Heinrich, Joseph, as arranger of an unidentified opera for Harmoniemusik, **VIII:** 158

Heinrich, Nicolaus, 17th century publisher in Munich, **VII:** 113

Heinrich, Prinz, Baroque German composer for Hautboisten, **VII:** 121

Heinrichshofen, 19th century publisher in Berlin, **IX:** 192

Heinrici, Georg, clarinetist in the Duke of Sondershausen Harmonie, **V:** 185, fn. 2

Heinrici, trombonist for 19th century Duke of Sondershausen, **V:** 185, fn. 2

Heinsdorf, ?, composer included in a 1873 English collection of band music, **X:** 113

Heinsdorff, ?, 19th century English composer, **IX:** 275

Heinsdorff, G., 19th century German composer, **X:** 97

Heintze, Georg, 1849–1895, German composer, **XI:** 177

Heitz, Allexis, 19th century French composer, **IX:** 54

Hejtmanek, ?, 19th century Austrian composer, **IX:** 216

Helenia, Hanns, b. 1890, German composer, **XII:** 89

Heller, bassoonist, 19th century court of Mechlenburg-Schwerin, **V:** 185, fn. 4

Hellinck, Joannes (also known as Lupi, Lupus), 1493–1541, Flemish composer, **VI:** 27, 63, 114, 120

Hellmuth, ?, 19th century French composer, **IX:** 54

Hemet, E., 19th century French composer, **IX:** 1, 54

Hemmerlé, ?, 19th century French composer of band works, **V:** 151

Hemmerlé, Charles, 19th century French composer, **IX:** 54

Hemmerlé, J., 19th century French composer, **IX:** 55

Henchenne, Laurent, 19th century Belgium composer, **IX:** 259

Hendel, ?, German Baroque composer of Hautboisten, **X:** 7

Hendel, 18th century publisher in Halle, **VIII:** 301

Henkel, Michael, b. 1780, German organist at Fulda & composer, **XI:** 43

Henkemanns, Hans, b. 1913, German composer, **XII:** 143

Henn, 19th century publisher in Paris, **XI:** 108

Henneberg, Carl Albert Wilhelm Richard, 1853–1925, Swedish composer, **XII:** 87

Henneberg, J., 19th century German composer, **XI:** 303

Henneberg, Johann, 1768–1822, Austrian composer, **IX:** 216

Henneberg, Richard, 1853–1925, Swedish composer, **IX:** 133

Hennessy, Swan, 1866–1929, French composer, **XII:** 144

Hennig, ?, 18th century, German, (3) *Marsche for military Harmoniemusik*, **VIII:** 324

Hennig, J. C., 18th century German flautist & composer, **XI:** 44

Hennig, Karl, 1819–1873, German composer, **IX:** 159

Hennig, T., 19th century German composer, civic music director in Gustrow, **IX:** 159

Henning, Carl Wilhelm, 1784–1867, German composer, **XI:** 201

Henning, Carl, civic music director in Zeitz, Germany in 1858, **V:** 17

Henny, H., 19th century French composer, **IX:** 56

Henrich IV, of Russia, composer, **IX:** 135

Henriques, Fini Valdimar, 1867–1940, Danish composer, **XII:** 144

Henry I, 1100–1135, **I:** 183

Henry II of France, reigning 1547–1559, **II**: 72

Henry III of England, 1216–1272, **I**: 131, 186

Henry III, 1551–1589, King of France, **II**: 80ff, **III**: 25, 35; **VI**: 37, 55; **VII**: 93, 81

Henry IV of England, 1399–1413, **I**: 194 [list of players in fn. Nr. 63]

Henry IV, 1553–1610, King of France, ensemble collection, **II**: 83ff ; **VI**: 37; **VII**: 81, 93

Henry of England, Prince of Wales (1610), **III**: 82

Henry V of England, 1413–1422, **I**: 195ff

Henry VI, 1422–1471, **I**: 196

Henry VII of England, 1485–1509, **I**: 201ff [with list of players]; **II**: 8

Henry VIII of England, 1491–1547, **II**: 6, 9, 15ff [court wind players names], 23 [foreign wind players in his court], 28ff [names of players for funeral], 66ff, 148, **III**: 90; **VI**: 31 [works associated with]

Henry, 19th century publisher in Paris, **IX**: 113

Henry, Louis, 1768–1855, French (?) composer, **XI**: 135, 244

Hentz, 18th and 19th century publisher in Paris, **VIII**: 276; **IX**: 12

Hentzschel, ?, 1649 canzon, German composer, **VII**: 121

Hentzschel, Caspar, on trumpet performance practice, 1620, **III**: 69

Henze, Hans Werner, b. 1926, German composer, **XII**: 87, 144

Hepworth George, 19th century German composer, **IX**: 159

Heradorus of Megara, ancient Greek trumpet player, **I**: 32

Hérard, Camille, 19th century French composer, **IX**: 56

Herbeck, Johann, 1831–1877, German composer, **V**: 133; **IX**: 217

Herberigs, Robert, b. 1886, Belgian composer, **XII**: 87, 144

Hérbert, Charles, 19th century French composer, **IX**: 56

Herbert, Victor, 1859–1924, American composer and band leader, **IX**: 138; **XII**: 201

Herbst, Johann, 1588–1666 German composer of canzons, sonatas, **VII**: 165, 172

Herbuté, E.-N., 19th century French composer, **IX**: 56

Herchenröder, ?, 19th century German composer of works for band, **X**: 97

Herfurth, R., 19th century German composer, **IX**: 159

Herfurth, W., 19th century German composer, **X**: 98

Hering, Michael, 17th century publisher in Hamburg, **VII**: 72, 150, 175

Herman, Alphonse, 19th century French composer of works for band, **X**: 67

Hermann, C., composer included in a 1880 English collection of band music, **X**: 115

Hermann, Monk of Salzburg, 1350–1410, **I**: 100; **VI**: 4

Hermstedt, Friedrich, bassoon in the Sondershausen Harmonie, **V**: 185, fn. 2

Hermstedt, Johann Simon, 1778–1846, clarinetist, **V**: 23, 185

Herodotus, Roman historian, 5th century BC, **I**: 10, 17

Herold, A., 19th century German composer, **IX**: 159

Hérold, Louis Joseph Ferdinand, 1791–1833, as composer of works arranged for Harmoniemusik, **VIII**: 47 [*La Clochette, Le dernier jour de Missolonghi, Zampa*]; 48 [*Zweikampf oder Schreiber Wiese bey Paris*]

Herold, Louis Joseph Ferdinand, 1791–1833, as composer of works arranged for band, **IX:** 255 [unidentified work arr. for band]; **X:** 105 [unidentified work arranged for band by Lindpainter]

Herold, Nicolas, 1721–1790, German composer, **XI:** 152, 284

Herrfurth, M., 19th century composer, **XII:** 60

Herrmann, ?, 19th century German composer, **X:** 98

Herrmann, 19th century bass hornist for Duke of Sondershausen, **V:** 185, fn. 2

Herrmann, Gottfried, 1808–1878, German composer, **XI:** 112, 135, 161, 167

Herrmann, Hugo, b. 1896, German composer, **XII:** 87, 145

Herschel, Friedrich William, 1738–1822, famous 19th century English oboist and astronomer as bandmaster, **IV:** 112; **V:** 201, fn. 4; **VIII:** 257 [(3) original works for Harmoniemusik]; **IX:** 278 [as composer]

Hertel, Johann W., 1727–1789, German composer, **III:** 18, 131; **VII:** 121ff; **VIII:** 324 [(6) original *Märche* for band; **XI:** 44, 112, 152, 161, 310

Hertel, Johann Wilhelm , 1727–1789, German composer, **XII:** 3

Hertel, Peter, 1817–1899 German composer of works for band, **X:** 98

Hertl, ?, 19th century German composer, **X:** 98

Herulo, ?, 16th century Italian composer, **II:** 236

Hervaux, Charles, horn faculty of the 1792 Paris Conservatoire, **IV:** 156

Hervé, ?, 19th century English composer for band, **X:** 131

Herweg, Georg, 19th century German composer, **IX:** 159

Herwich (Herwig), Chr., Baroque German composer of dances, **VII:** 166

Herwich, Christian, 1605–1663, German composer, **VI:** 78

Herzebsky, Adamo, 17th century composer, **VII:** 144

Herzeele, F., late 19th century Belgium composer, works for band, **X:** 61

Herzog von Gotha [dedication], **IX:** 191

Herzog, Auguste, 19th century French composer, **IX:** 56

Herzogenberg, Heinrich, 1843–1900, German composer, **IX:** 217; **XI:** 242, 303

Herzogin Amalia, 19th century, **IX:** 145

Hesdin, 16th century composer, **VI:** 44

Heseltine, Philip, 1894–1930, English composer, **XII:** 145

Hess, Ernst, b. 1912, German composer, **XII:** 145

Hess, Willy, b. 1906, German composer, **XII:** 146

Hesse, Ernst Christian, 1676–1762, German composer, **XI:** 44

Hessen, Paul and Bartholomeus, 16th century composers, **VI:** 69

Hestier, Nicolas, in charge of civic music in Tours, 1508, **II:** 179

Hetz, Adam, 1626 German composer of dances, **VII:** 166

Heugel, 19th century publisher in Paris, **IX:** 37, 85

Heugel, Johannes, 1500–1585, German composer, **VI:** 39, 44, 63, 76ff

Heuschkel, Johann, fl. 1800–1828, German composer, **IX:** 159

Heuval, W., 19th century English composer for band, **X:** 131

Hewet, Robert, leader of York town band in 1567, **II:** 152

Hewitt, C. W., 19th century English composer for band, 131

Hewitt, James, 1770–1827, English militia band leader to traveled to America, **IV:** 106, fn. 4; **VIII:** 257, (4) Quick Marches for Harmoniemusik

Heyde, Jörgen, trumpeter for Albert of Prussia, 16th century, **II:** 110

Heyer, H., hornist in the 1910 Barrère Ensemble in NYC, **XII:** 214

Heylanus, 16th century composer, **VI:** 108

Heyn, Catharina, 19th century German composer, **IX:** 159

Heyne, Frederich, 18th century German composer, **XI:** 201 [biographical note]

Heyse, A. G., late 18th century German harpist & composer at Halle, **XI:** 44

Hicks, Alfred, 1898–1976, American composer, **XII:** 197

Hidas, Frigyes, 20th century Hungarian composer, **XII:** 203

Hiebesch, Johann, 1766–1820, German composer, **VIII:** 80 [as arranger of Mozart, *Die Zauberflöte*, opera, for Harmonie]; **IX: 159; X:** 24

Hilber, Johann Baptist, b. 1891, Swiss composer, **XII:** 88

Hildebrand, 17th century publisher, **VII:** 69

Hilge, W. G., 19th century German composer, **X:** 98

Hill, Alfred, b. 1870, American composer, **XII:** 146

Hill, Edward Burlingame, b. 1872, composer, **XII:** 146

Hill, Frederic, English composer, (4) Marches ca. 1780, for Harmoniemusik, **VIII:** 258; **X:** 28

Hill, John, 1724–1797, English, *Hill's Church music, with symphonies,* **VIII:** 258

Hilldebrand, Christian, ca. 1570–1649, German composer of dances, **VII:** 60, 166ff

Hillemacher, Paul, 1852–1933, French composer, **XI:** 44, 161

Hiller, Ferdinand, 1811–1885, German composer, **IX:** 159

Hiller, Johann, 1728–1804, German, *Hymn* for voices and brass, 1790, **VIII:** 324

Hilscher, 18th century publisher in Dresden, **XI:** 86, 100

Himmel, Frederick Heinrich, 1765–1814, German composer, KM, king of Prussia, **VIII:** 324 [original *Marches, Trauer-Cantate* for Harmonie]; **XI:** 44, 258

Himmel, Friedrich, as composer of a work arranged for Harmoniemusik, **VIII:** 48 [*Fanchon, das Leiermädchen,* arranged by Düring]

Himmelstosse, oboist in the Duke of Sondershausen Harmonie, **V:** 185, fn. 2

Hinchliff, W. S., 19th century English composer, **IX:** 275

Hindemeith, Paul, 1895–1963, German composer, **XII:** 89, 203

Hindsley, Mark, University of Ilinois, as arranger, **XII:** 204

Hingeston, John, d. 1683, composer of English ensemble music, **VII:** 53

Hinkel, ?, as 19th century arranger, **IX:** 198

Hintze, Jacob, 1622–1661, German composer, **III:** 215

Hintze, Jacob, 1695, German composer for tower music, **VII:** 121

Hippolochus, Macedonian writer, 3rd century BC, **I:** 42

Hirich, ?, 18th century composer, **XI:** 112

Hirtel, Jacob, oboist in 1801 Harmoniemusik of Prince Esterházy, **IV:** 31, fn. 57

Hirtius, 1st century BC Roman historian, **I:** 56

Hirtl, H., 18th century (?) German composer, **XI:** 167

Hitchcock, E. A., General, American military band collection ca. 1825, **IX:** 138

Hitz, Franz, 1828–1891, composer in Paris, **IX:** 56; **X:** 67

Hitzemann, H., 19th century French composer, **IX:** 56

Hladky, ?, as 19th century arranger, **IX:** 256, 257

Hlobil, Emil, b. 1901, Czech composer, **XII: 88,** 146

Hnojil, J., 19th century Hungarian composer, **IX:** 217

Hoberecht, J. L., *A Grand Military Piece,* ca. 1799 for Harmoniemusik, **VIII:** 258

Hobrecht, early 19th century English composer, **V:** 201

Hoby, C., 19th century English composer, **IX:** 275

Hoby, John, 1869–1938, English composer for band, **IX:** 275; **X:** 116, 131

Hoch, ?, 19th century Austrian composer, **IX:** 217

Hoche, General Lazare, 1768–1797, France, **IV:** 213ff; **VIII:** 273, 290, 367; **XII:** 77 [dedication]

Hochreiter, Emil, 1871–1938, German composer, **XII:** 146

Hochstein, 20th century publisher in Heidelberg, **XI:** 259; **XII:** 88, 96, 104

Hôdieir, Romain, 19th century French composer, **IX:** 56

Hoeberechts, John, 1760–1820, English composer for band, **X:** 29; **XI:** 44

Hoelzlin, Joseph, 1603, German composer of 4-part secular songs for ens., **VII:** 166

Hoezl (Hoelzl) Ludwig, 17th century German composer, **VII:** 166

Hofer, Frédéric, 19th century French composer, **IX:** 56

Hoffding, Niels Finn, b. 1899, Danish composer, **XII:** 146

Hoffer, Andrea, Baroque composer, **VII:** 2

Höffer, Paul, 1895–1949, German composer, **XII:** 89, 147

Hoffkuntz, ?, composer in a 1616 Nürnberg collection, **VII:** 163

Hoffman, 1762, German composer for Hautboisten, **VII:** 122

Hoffman, Giovanni, 18th century German composer, **XI:** 167

Hoffman, Leopold, 1738–1793, Austrian composer, **XI:** 45, 201, 219

Hoffmann, 19th century publisher in Prague, **IX:** 215

Hoffmann, C. L., 19th century English composer for band, **X:** 131

Hoffmann, Ernst, 1776–1822, German composer, important literary person, **IX:** 160

Hoffmann, Karl, 18th century (?) composer, **XI:** 233

Hoffmann, Philipp Carl, 1769–1842, German composer, **XI:** 45

Hoffmeister & Kühnel, 19th century publishers in Leipzig, **IX:** 166

Hoffmeister, ?, 18th century German composer, **XI:** 202, 229, 272, 277, 298, 303

Hoffmeister, ?, as arranger for Harmoniemusik, **VIII:** 159

Hoffmeister, 1754–1812, composer in Olmütz Harmoniemusik collection, **IV:** 22, fn. 9

Hoffmeister, 19th century publisher in Vienna, **VIII:** 101, 107, 130

Hoffmeister, 19th century publisher in Vienna, **XI:** 67

Hoffmeister, 19thcentury publisher at Leipzig, **XI:** 67, 49, 64, 120, 148, 287, 318

Hoffmeister, Franz, 1754–1812, German, **VIII:** 325ff [(50) *Parthias* for Harmoniemusik]; **X:** 25; **XI:** 45, 112, 135, 152, 167, 201, 234, 244, 258, 279

Hoffmeister, Franz Anton, as composer of a work arranged for Harmoniemusik, **VIII:** 48 [*Der Konigssohn*]

Hoffmeister, J. F., late 18th century, English treatise on flute playing, **XI:** 46

Hofhaimer, Paul, 1459–1537, Austrian composer, **VI:** 23, 61ff

Hofmann, 17th century publisher in Darmstadt, **VII:** 171ff

Hofmann, Heinrich, 1842–1902, German composer, **IX:** 160, **X:** 98

Hofmann, Josef, 1876–1957, English composer for band, **X:** 132

Hofmann, Richard, 1831–1909, English composer for band, **X:** 132

Hofmeister, 19th century publisher in Leipzig, **VIII:** 59, 92ff, 94, 132, 137, 140, 143, 302, 334; **IX:** 148, 153, 168, 172, 173, 187

Hofmeister, Friedrich, 18th and 19th century publisher in Leipzig, **VIII:** 302

Hofmeister, Heinrich, German treatise on flute playing, **XI:** 46

Hoftheater, 19th century publisher in Vienna, **IX:** 253

Höhe, 18th century publisher in Braunschweig, **XI:** 99

Hohner, 20th century publisher in Trossingen, **XII: 145**

Hol, Richard, b. 1825, Dutch composer, **IX:** 125

Holbein, Hans, German artist, 16th century, **II:** 208ff

Holborne, Antony, d. 1606, composer for wind consorts, **II:** 58; **VI:** 33ff, 36ff; **VII:** 25, 53; **X:** 1

Holbrooke, Joseph, 1878–1958, English, called the 'cockney Wagner,' **XII:** 194

Holden, A., Jr., 19th century English composer, **IX:** 275

Holden, Smollet, 19th century, Irish, *A Collection of Quick & Slow Marches,* **VIII:** 258

Holfritz, Hans, b. 1902, Swiss composer, **XII:** 147

Hollande, J., 16th century composer, **VI:** 118, 120, 122

Hollander, Christian, 1510–1569, Dutch composer, **VI:** 27, 69, 120

Hollander, Jean, 16th century French composer, **VI:** 107ff

Hollandre, Jean, 1785–1837, French composer, **IX:** 56

Holler, Augustin, 1745–1814, German, (2) *Parthias* and *Dances* for band, **VIII:** 328

Höller, Karl, b. 1907, German composer, **XII:** 147

Hollmayer, Anton, hornist and leader, Prince Liechtenstein Harmonie, **IV:** 39

Holmboe, Vagn, b. 1909, Danish composer, **XII:** 147

Holmes, Augusta, 1847–1903, French composer, **XI:** 47, 136

Holmes, Edward, 1792–1859, [1829 account of travels in Germany], **IV:** 39 [personal description of Triebensee]; **V:** 104ff, 133, 180, 186ff, 191, 213

Holmes, Valentine, 18th century English composer, **XI:** 259

Holst, Gustav, 1874–1934, English composer, **XII:** 89, 203, 209

Holstein-Gottorp, Lt. General and Prince von, 18th century, **IV:** 88

Holwein, 17th century publisher in Wolfenbüttel, **VII:** 136, 180

Holzbauer, Ignaz, 1711–1784, German composer, **IV:** 120, fn. 8; **VIII:** 329, *Divertimento* for bassoons & horns; **XI:** 47, 203, 273

Holzbogn, Giovanni, 18th century German composer, **XI:** 153

Holzinger, ?, 18th century German, *Missa* for voices and winds, **VIII:** 329

Holzinger, ?, early 19th century composer, **XII:** 35

Homer, 9th to 12th century BC, poet, **I:** 29, 30

Homilius, Gottfried, 1714–1785, German composer, **XI:** 113

Honauer, Leonz, fl. 1760–1778 in Paris, (3) *Suites* for Harmoniemusik, piano, **VIII:** 284

Honig, ?, as 19th century arranger, **IX:** 227

Hoof, Jef Van, b. 1886, Belgian composer, **XII:** 90

Hook, James, English composer, organist at Vauxhall in 1785, **IV:** 131, note on pgs. 132–133; **XI:** 47, 269

Hookhan & Carpenter, 18th century publisher in London, **VIII:** 253ff

Hopkins, Anthony, b. 1921, composer, **XII:** 147

Hopkins, J., 19th century English composer for band, **X:** 132

Höppler, ?, 19th century Austrian composer, **IX:** 217

Horace, Étienne, d. 1799, faculty of the 1792 Paris Conservatoire, **IV:** 157

Horix, ?, *Marche,* 1798, for band, **VIII:** 285

Horman, William, 16th century English historian, **II:** 264 [on trumpet vs clarion]

Hörmann, Johann, hornist in 1801 of Imperial Harmoniemusik, **IV:** 35, fn. 77

Horn, August, 19th century German composer of a work voices & brass, **X:** 99

Horn, Johann Kaspar, ca. 1630–1685, German comp. for Hautboisten, **III:** 215; **VII:** 122

Horn, Johann, composer in Dresden in 1681, **III:** 215;

Horn, Karl Friedrich, 1762–1830, German composer, **XI:** 47

Horn, Karl, 1762–1830, German composer, **IX:** 160

Horsley, Charles, 1822–1876, English composer, **XI:** 47

Hortense, Reine, 1783–1837, Queen of Holland, as composer, **IX:** 56

Horton, Florence, 19th century English composer for band, **X:** 132

Hoschna, Jacob Phil., *Parthia* in F for Harmoniemusik, **VIII:** 204

Hosek, Miroslav, 18th century (?) composer, **VII:** 192

Hoste, L., 19th century French composer, **IX:** 56

Hostie, ?, 18th century French clarinetist, **XI:** 136 [biographical note]

Hostie, Jean-Marie, d. 1794, faculty of the 1792 Paris Conservatoire, **IV:** 157

Hotis, Jan, 19th century Austrian composer, **IX:** 217

Hotteterre, ?, member in 1768 of the Les Grands Hautbois, **IV:** 64, fn. 4

Hotteterre, Jacques, d. 1761, French flautist, treatise on flute playing, **XI:** 47 [biographical note]

Hotteterre, Jean, d. 1720, Paris instrument maker, **III:** 39

Hotteterre, Louis, ca. 1708, French composer for Hautboisten, **VII:** 87

Hotteterre, Martin, French composer for Hautboisten, **VII:** 87

Hottisch, ?, 19th century Austrian composer, **IX:** 217

Hourenaeghel, L., 19th century French composer, **IX:** 56

Houziaux, H., 19th century French composer, **IX:** 57

Hoven, J. (pseudonym for von Püttlingen), arr., *Johanna d'Arc,* for Harmonie, **VIII:** 130

Hovhaness, Alan, 20th century Armenian composer, **XII:** 203

Howard, Howard, former Principal Horn, Metropolitan Opera, **XII:** 207

Howard, Lord, 17th century English noble, **III:** 88

Howe, Elias, Jr., 19th century American composer, **IX:** 138

Howells, Herbert, b. 1892, English composer, **XII:** 90

Howet, composer in 1600 dance collection published in Heidelberg, **VII:** 180

Hradecky, ?, 19th century Hungarian composer, **IX:** 217

Hradezky, Joseph, substitute member of Imperial Harmoniemusik, **IV:** 36

Hranailovich, F. X., 19th century (?) composer, 47

Hubans, Charles, 19th century French composer, **IX:** 57

Hubeau, Jean, b. 1917, French composer, **XII:** 148

Huber, Emile, 19th century French composer, **IX:** 57

Huber, Hans, 1852–1921, Swiss composer, **XII:** 148

Huber, Jakub, 18th century Bohemian composer, **IV:** 123; **VIII:** 204, (2) *Messa choralis* for SATB and winds

Huber-Anderach, Theodor, b. 1885, German composer, **XII:** 91, 148

Hübschmann, J., ca. 1803–1816, German composer, **IX:** 160

Hüe, Georges, 1858–1948, 19th century French composer, **IX:** 57

Hug, 20th century publisher in Zurich, **XII:** 148, 172

Hugo, Victor, 19th century French writer, **XII:** 61

Hugot, Antoine, d. 1803, flute faculty of the 1792 Paris Conservatoire, **IV:** 156; **XI:** 48, 203

Hugot, F. G., 19th century French flautist, **XI:** 48 [biographical note], 203

Hugues, Luigi, 1836–1913, Italian composer for band, **X:** 209

Hühne, 19th century trumpeter for Duke of Sondershausen, **V:** 185, fn. 2

Hulbe, Franze, 1867–1876, as arranger, **IX:** 254

Humberti, composer in 1600 dance collection published in Heidelberg, **VII:** 180

Hume, James, 1864–1932, English composer for band, **X:** 132

Hummel, works arr. for Harmoniemusik, **VIII:** 49, 52

Hummel, 18th century publisher in Amsterdam, **XI:** 15, 28, 55, 76 205, 216, 225, 271

Hummel, 18th century publisher in Berlin, **VIII:** 117, 159, 196, 220, 291, 306, 334, 369; **XI:** 9, 15, 36, 89, 155, 192, 201, 227, 231, 273

Hummel, 19th century publisher in Berlin and Amsterdam, **VIII:** 33, 323

Hummel, 19th century publisher in Den Haag, Amsterdam, **VIII:** 59, 352, 361; **XI:** 212

Hummel, 19th century publisher in London, **XI:** 82

Hummel, Ferdinand, 1855–1928, German composer, **XI:** 49, 168, 259

Hummel, Johann Nepomuk, 1778–1837, Austrian composer, **VIII:** 325 [(2) military *Marsches* for Harmonie]; **IX:** 217; **X:** 45 [works for band]; **XI:** 48, 113, 136, 153, 161, 247, 279, 309

Hummel, Johann Nepomuk, 1778–1837, as composer of works arr. for Harmoniemusik, **VIII:** 49 [*Helena und Paris*, ballet?, arranged by Triebensee for Harmoniemusik]; 152 [unidentified work arranged by Sedlak for Harmoniemusik]; **XII:** 50 [*Helene e Paris*, ballet, arranged for Harmoniemusik by Sedlak]; 203

Hummel, Joseph Friedrich, 20th century Austrian composer, **XII:** 91

Hummel, Joseph, 1841–1919, German composer, **IX:** 218; **XI:** 136, 153

Hummel, Karl, military *Marsch*, ca. 1770, **VIII:** 258

Hummel, works arranged for band, **IX:** 143, 180, 189, 197

Hummell, Charles, 18th century English composer for band, **X:** 29; **XI:** 49

Humpert, Hans, 1901–1943, German composer, **XII:** 91

Humphrey, ?, 19th century French arranger, **XII:** 194

Hunt, Richard, d. 1683, English composer, **XI:** 49

Hunten, 19th century French composer, **V:** 73

Hünten, Franz, 1793–1878, German composer, **XI:** 49

Hunter, ?, 19th century English composer for band, **X:** 133

Hupauf, Johann, 19th century German composer, **XI:** 289

Hupfeld, Bernard, 1717–1796, **XI:** 49

Huré, Jean, 1877–1930, French composer, **XII:** 148, 194

Hurlstone, William, 1876–1906 English composer, **XI:** 248, 274, 298

Hurnik, Ilja, b. 1922, Czech composer, **XII:** 148

Husa, Karel, 20th century Czech composer, **XII:** 203

Hustel, 20th century publisher in Paris, **XII:** 128

Hut, Abraham, Stadtpfeifer in Zwickau in 1569 (his contract), **II:** 191

Hutcheson, Jere, 20th century American composer, **XII: 203**

Hutschenrieyter, Sr., as arr. of Beethoven *Symphony Nr. 1* for Harmoniemusik, **VIII:** 7

Hutschenruyter, Wouter, 1859–1943, Dutch composer, founder of the band of the Rotterdam Municipal Guard, **IX:** 125

Huwet, ?, composer in a 1616 Nürnberg collection, **VII:** 163

Huyts, C., 19th century French composer, **IX:** 57

Hyde, James, reorganization of English trumpet signals, **IV:** 112, fn. 35; **X:** 29 [(1799), composer for cavalry trumpets]

Hymnes de la Revolution Franaise, 18th century publisher in Paris, **VIII:** 269

Hyrtner, Giovanni, 19th century (?) composer, **XI:** 259

Iacchini, Giuseppe, Baroque Italian composer, **XI:** 255

Iansen, Giovanni, Italian composer, **XI:** 49

Ibotte, ?, 19th century German composer, **XI:** 252

Ignazio, ? oboist for La Pouplinière, 1763, **IV:** 68, fn. 26

Imbault, 18th and 19th century publisher in Paris, **VIII:** 9ff, 13ff, 18ff, 33, 41ff, 56ff, 60ff, 65, 81, 89, 92ff, 100ff, 103, 106, 117, 123, 153ff, 157, 159ff, 196, , 230, 269ff, 287, 290, 292ff; **IX:** 15; **XI:** 20, 31, 50, 103,105, 130, 165, 191, 192, 198, 203

Imbault, J.J., 17th century French publisher, **IV:** 71

Impallomeni, Gaetano, 1841–1908, Italian composer for band, **X:** 209

Imprimerie chimique, 19th century publisher in Vienna, **XI:** 41

Imprimerie du Conservatoire, 18th century publisher in Paris, **VIII:** 274

Imprimerie mus., 19th century publisher in Paris, **IX:** 7

Ines de la Cruz, Juana, 17th century Spainish poet, **III:** 221

Inge, William Phillips, 18th century officer in the British military, **VIII:** 257

Ingegnieri, Marc'Antonio, 1535–1592, Italian composer, **VI:** 97

Ingenhoven, Jan, 1876–1951, Dutch composer, **XII:** 148

Inglis, Alexander, 1845–1929, English composer for band, **X:** 133

Inglis, Col., 18th century officer in the British military, **VIII:** 251

Inico, Carlo, 1863–1947, Italian composer for band, **X:** 210

Innocenzo X, 1574–1655, Pope, trumpets in 1644, **III:** 72

Innocenzo XI, 1611–1689, Pope, trumpets in 1676, **III:** 73

Innocenzo XII, 1615–1799, Pope, trumpets in 1689, **III:** 73

Ippisch, Franz, b. 1883, German composer, **XII:** 91, 149

Ippolitow Iwanow, Michail Michailowirsch, 1859–1935, Russian composer, **XII:** 91, 149

Ireland, John, b. 1879, English composer, **XII:** 91

Isaac, Heinrich, 1450–1517, Franco-Flemish composer, **VI:** 11, 61, 62ff, 65, 106; **XII:** 182 [arranged by Strasser]

Isabella d'Este and Mantua, I: 231, 239; **II:** 133ff; **VI:** 15, 80

Isabella of Savoy, III: 193

Isabella, Archduchess visits Brussels in 1615, **III:** 187

ISCM, 20th century publisher in Amsterdam, **XII:** 74

Isenmann, Carl, 19th century German composer of a chorus with brass, **X:** 99

Isouard, Niccoló, 1775–1818, works arranged for Harmoniemusik, **VIII:** 50 [*L'Intrigue aux Fenêtres, Le Médecin Turc, Les Confidences, Michel-Ange, Un Jour á Paris*]; 51 [*Cendrillon, (Aschenbrödel), Le Billet de Loterie*]; 52 [*Jeannot et Colin, Joconde, Le Magicien sans Magie, Le Prince de Catane, Lully et Quinault*]; 53 [*Aladin, Josepf und der Kleinen Dieblin, L'impromptu de campagne, Léonce*]

Isouard, Nicolas, 1775–1818, Maltese composer, **IX:** 197

Isouard, work arranged for band, **IX:** 180 [*Aschenbrodel*]

Istres, H., 19th century French composer, **IX:** 57

Ithier, Louis, 19th century French composer, **IX:** 57

Ito, Yasuhide, 20th century Japanese composer, **XII:** 203
Ivanschiz, Amandus, 18th century Slovenian composer, **XI:** 49, 203
Iversen, 18th century publisher in Lübeck, **VIII:** 320
Ives, Charles, 1874–1954, American composer, **XII:** 92
Ives, Simon, 1600–1662, composer of English ensemble music, **VII:** 22, 25, 53ff

J. S. (Schechinger?), 16th century composer, **VI:** 62

Jaarzebski, Adam, 1590–1649 Polish composer for winds and keyboard, **VII:** 217

Jacchini, Giuseppe, d. 1727, Italian composer, **XI:** 161, 255

Jachino, Carlo, b. 1887, Italian composer, **XII:** 149

Jackson, Enderby, founds 1860 national brass band contest, **V:** 169ff

Jacob, ?, 19th century French composer, **IX:** 57

Jacob, 16th century composer, **VI:** 107, 109

Jacob, E., 19th century French composer, **IX:** 57

Jacob, Jules, 19th century French composer, **IX:** 57

Jacobi, Christian, 18th century director of Prussian army music school, **IV:** 90

Jacobi, F., 19th century (?) German composer, **XI:** 153

Jacobi, Georg, 1840–1906, German composer, **X:** 99, 113

Jacobi, Michael, 1618–1663, German composer, **XI:** 255

Jacotin (Godebrye), d. 1529, Flemish composer, **VI:** 38, 40, 49ff

Jacotin, L., 19th century French composer, **IX:** 58

Jacque, E., 19th century French composer, **IX:** 58

Jacquemet, L., 19th century French composer, **IX:** 58

Jacquet of Mantua, 1483–1559, French composer, **VI:** 63

Jacquet, Charles, 19th century French composer, **IX:** 58

Jadassohn, Saloman, 1831–1902, German composer, **IX:** 160; **XI:** 50

Jadin, ?, 19th century French composer, **IX:** 1

Jadin, Françoise, member in 1777 of the Les Grands Hautbois, **IV:** 64, fn. 4

Jadin, Hyacinthe, 1769–1800,French Revolution composer, **IV:** 162 fn. 46, 202, 206; **VIII:** 285; **XI:** 50; **XII:** 203

Jadin, Louis Emmanuel, 1768–1853, French Revolution composer, faculty of Paris Conservatoire, **IV:** 162 fn. 46, 162 fn. 46, 176, 204; **VIII:** 285ff; **XI:** 50, 113, 136, 168

Jaeger, Will., 19th century German composer, **IX:** 160

Jaeggi, Oswald, b. 1913, German composer, **XII:** 92

Jahn, August, 18th century German, *Military signals* for pfieffen & clarini, **VIII:** 329

Jähn, editor, *Weber Verzeichnis,* **IX:** 190

Jahn, H., an actor, supported a Harmoniemusik in Vienna, **IV:** 41

Jahn, Otto, 1813–1869, German musicologist, **VIII:** 218

Jaime II, 1291–1327, **I:** 219

Jam, ?, 19th century (?) composer, **XI:** 259

James I, King of England from 1603–1625, **III:** 77ff, 181, 201

James II, 1633–1701, King of England, **III:** 96

James, Philip, b. 1890, American composer, **XII:** 92, 149

Janaitzsch, ?, 18th century composer, **XI:** 203

Jancières, V., 19th century French composer, **IX:** 58

Jancourt, E., 19th century French composer, **IX:** 58

Janequin, Clément, 1485–1558, French composer, II: 12, 177; VI: 27, 38, 45, 49ff, 63, 85, 107ff, 120, 122ff

Janet et C., 19th century publisher in Paris, VIII: 18ff, 27, 56ff, 59, 65, 79, 89, 91, 93ff, 110, 123, 126, 130, 158, 160, 196, 276ff, 285; IX: 2, 11, 22, 25, 31, 59, 62, 73, 90, 101, 107

Janike, ?, composer included in a 1881 English collection of band music, X: 115

Janin-Jaubert, ?, 19th century French composer, IX: 58

Janitsch, Johann Gosslich, 18th century German composer, XI: 50, 113

Janitzsch, 18th century composer, XI: 229

Jannopulos, Anastas, (1847), Greek composer, IX: 160

Jansa, Leopold, 1795–1875, Bohemian composer, XI: 50

Jantian, 16th century composer, VI: 45

Janvier, L., 19th century French composer, IX: 58

Járdányi, Pál, b. 1920, Hungarian composer, XII: 149

Jaubert, J., 19th century French composer, IX: 58

Jauffret, ?., 19th century French composer, IX: 58

Jaussaud, C., 19th century French composer, IX: 58

Javault, ?, fl. 1800–1828, French composer, IX: 59

Javault, as arranger of Cherubini, Les deux Journées, opera, for Harmoniemusik, VIII: 17

Javelot, Jules, 19th century French composer, IX: 59

Jeandel, F., 19th century French composer, IX: 59

Jeanjean, Camille, 19th century French composer, IX: 59

Jeannin, ?, 19th century French composer, IX: 59

Jedlüczka, 19th century Austrian composer, IX: 218

Jefferson, Thomas, tries to hire Harmoniemusik for his estate, IV: 6

Jefferson, William, 19th century English composer for band, X: 135

Jeffries, Matthew, composer in 1600 collection of ensemble music, VII: 20

Jehan Van Vincle, performer in court of Charles V, II: 90

Jelich, Vincenz, early 17th century German composer for canzona, VII: 122

Jell, J., 19th century Austrian composer, IX: 218

Jenette, Adolf, 19th century German composer, IX: 160

Jenkins, John, 1592–1678, composer of English ensemble music, VII: 25, 54ff, 73

Jenny Lind, 19th century singer, IX: 65

Jenny, Albert, 1912–1992, organist, XII: 92, 149

Jenson, Adolf, 1837–1879, German composer, XI: 259

Jenson, Niels Peter, 1802–1846, Danish composer, XI: 51, 203

Jeppesen, Knud, b. 1892, German, Palestrina scholar, composer, XII: 149

Jeremias, Otakar, b. 1892, Czech composer, XII: 93

Jerger, Wilhelm, b. 1902, German composer, XII: 150

Jerome, Claude, faculty of the 1792 Paris Conservatoire, IV: 157

Jersild, Jorgen, b. 1913, Danish composer, XII: 93

Jeschko, L., composer included in a 1880 English collection of band music, X: 115

Jetschmann, ?, 18th century German, *Parade Marsch & Fast Marsch*, **VIII:** 329

Jhan ('Maistre'), 1485–1838, French composer, **VI:** 63

Jirak, Karle Boleslav, b. 1891, Czech composer, **XII:** 150

Joachim II of Brandenburg, 16th century, **II:** 107

Joachim, 19th century publisher at Leipzig, **XI:** 226

Joachim, Johann, early 19th century Austrian, works for Harmoniemusik, **X:** 46

Joan of Arc, I: 214; **IX:** 30, 51; **XII:** 61

Jobin, E., 19th century French composer, **IX:** 59

Jochum, Otto, 19th century German composer, **IX:** 160

Jochum, Otto, b. 1898, German composer, **XII:** 93, 150

Jocolot (Jocolor), Claudius, 1622, German composer of dances, **VII:** 167

Joerg, N., fl, 1800–1828, German composer, **IX:** 160

Johann Albrecht of Mecklenburg-Schwerin, 19th century, **IX:** 144

Johann David Wunderer, German historian, 16th century, **II:** 11

Johann Friedrich, Duke at Württemberg, 1608–1628, **III:** 211

Johann Georg I of Saxony, Elector in 1606, **III:** 61

Johann Georg I, Duke of Saxony, **VII:** 142

Johann von Sachsen, German duke 16th century, **II:** 6

Johann von Sachsen-Halle, visits Leipzig in 1671, **III:** 69

Johann, Duke of Mecklenburg, 16th century, **II:** 113

John de Hertford, 13th century Abbot of St. Albans, **I:** 99

John II of France, 1350–1364, **I:** 209

John the Fearless, Duke of Burgundy, **I:** 244

John the Steadfast, later Elector of Saxony, 16th century, **II:** 229

John, Cardinal of Lorraine, Paris, 1498–1550, **II:** 217

Johnsen, Heinrich, 1717–1779, **XI:** 252

Johnson, ?, ca. 1600, composer of English ensemble music, **VII:** 20, 60

Johnson, 18th century publisher in Edinburgh, **XI:** 181

Johnson, 18th century publisher in London and Edinburgh, **VIII:** 262, 265

Johnson, 18th century publisher in London, **XI:** 8, 10, 34, 62, 63, 81, 82, 89, 119, 154, 184, 197

Johnson, Edward, 17th century English composer, **VII:** 24, 60

Johnson, J., 18th century publisher in London, **XI:** 17, 164

Johnson, Robert, 17th century composer, **VII:** 13, 24

Johnston, Longman, Lukey, 18th century publisher in London, **XI:** 34

Joinville, 13th century historian, **I:** 72, 183, 207ff

Jokl, Josef, 19th century composer, **XII:** 60

Jolivet, 18th century publisher in Paris, **XI:** 15

Jolivet, André, b. 1905, French composer, **XII:** 93, 150

Jolivet, Jules, 19th century French composer, **IX:** 59

Jommelli, Nicolò, 1714–1774, Italian composer, **IV:** 124; **VII:** 189, marches for Hautboisten; **VIII:** 366, church music, marches for winds; **XI:** 203

Jommi, Alfonso, 19th century Italian composer of a *Sinfonia* for band, **X**: 210
Jonas, Émile, 1827–1905, French composer, professor, Conservatoire Impérial, **IX**: 1, 59
Jonckers, Goessen, 1500–1555, Belgium composer, **VI**: 122
Jones, 16th century composer, **VI**: 35
Jones, Charles, b. 1910, American composer, **XII**: 150
Jones, Daniel, b. 1912, Welsh composer, **XII**: 93
Jones, J. G., 19th century English composer, **IX**: 276; **X**: 135
Jones, J. G., editor of a 19th century English band journal, **V**: 82
Jones, James, 1861–1946, English composer of many works for band, **X**: 135ff
Jones, Sidney, 19th century English composer, **IX**: 276
Jones, W. Grant, 19th century English composer for band, **X**: 136
Jongen, Joseph, 1873–1953, Belgian composer, **XII**: 94
Jonnet, Henry, 19th century French composer, **IX**: 59
Jonson, Ben, 1572–1637, masque composer, **III**: 78, 84ff
Joos Zoetens of Ghent, 1493 teacher, **I**: 138
Jordain, 16th century composer, **VI**: 107
Jordan, Thomas, English Baroque descriptions of pageants, **X**: 11
Jorelle, J., 19th century French composer, **IX**: 59
Jörg Eyselin, wind player at Memmingen in 1501, **II**: 191
Jörg, Nicolas, as arranger for Harmoniemusik, **VIII**: 27, 159ff
Joseph II, 1741–1790, Kaiser, forms Harmoniemusik in 1782, **IV**: **4, 77**
Joseph, 1776–1847, Archduke, Viceroy of Hungary, visits Eisenstadt in 1796, **IV**: 33
Joseph, 19th century Archduke Palatine of Hungary, **X**: 47
Josepha von Menz, of Wasserburg, **IX**: 145
Josneau, August, 19th century French composer, conductor Musique du 1er de Ligne, **IX**: 1, 59
Josquin des Prez, 16th century Italian composer, **II**: 61, 177; **VI**: 17, 26, 63, 107, 119ff
Joubert, General, of France, **IV**: 213
Joubert, John, b. 1927, South African composer, **XII**: 94
Jourdan, Barthélemy, 1769–1799, General, Battle of Fleurus, **IV**: 195
Jouve, ?, fl. ca. 1800–1828, French composer, **IX**: 60
Jouve, 19th century publisher in Paris, **XI**: 166
Jouve, early 19th century composer, **V**: 201
Jouve, J., 19th century English composer, **IX**: 276
Jouve, Joseph, 18th century English composer for band, **X**: 31
Joyce, F., 19th century English composer for band, **X**: 136
Juan I of Spain, 1350–1396, **I**: 79, 220 [with names of players]
Juana of Spain, 16th century, **II**: 87
Jubal, musician named in Genesis 4:21, **I**: 23
Julien, ?, 19th century French composer, **IX**: 60
Julius II, Pope, 1443–1513, **II**: 119
Jullien, ?, 19th century English composer, **IX**: 276

July, Fortune, 19th century French composer, **IX:** 60

Jungbauer, Coelestin, 17th century German composer for winds, **III:** 215; **VII:** 122

Junger, Oskar, military band arranger, 19th century, **V:** 123

Junghaus, 19th century oboist, court at Rudolstadt, **V:** 186, fn. 8

Junker, Carl, 1748–1797, German writer on Maximilian's Harmonie in Bonn, **IV:** 63ff

Junod, Laurent, 19th century French composer, **IX:** 60

Juon, Paul, 1872–1940, Russian composer, **XII:** 151

Jurgenson, 20th century publisher in Moskau, **XII:** 91

Jusdorff, ?, 18th century German flautist at Göttingen, **XI:** 51

K & S, 19th century publisher in Leipzig, **XI**: 170

K & S, 20th century publisher in Leipzig, **XII**: 87, 89

K. K. Hof Theatermusik Verlag, 19th century publisher in Vienna, **VIII**: 62, 107

K. K. Priv. Chem. Druckerie, 19th century publisher in Vienna, **VIII**: 51, 73, 137; **XII**: 41

Kaa, Franz, 18th century Swiss, *Motetto* for chorus, Harmoniemusik, fls, **VIII**: 373

Kabelác, Miloslav, b. 1908, Czech composer, **XII**: 94

Kadosa, Pál, b. 1903, Hungarian composer, **XII**: 151

Kaeberlie, ?, 18th century celebrated oboist at Beuthen on the Oder in 1740, **XI**: 113

Kaernpfert, Max, 1871–1941, German composer, **X**: 99

Kaffka, Wilhelm, 1751–1806, German, *Divertimento* for Harmonie (& violas?), **VIII**: 329

Kahnt, 19th and 20th century publisher in Leipzig, **VIII**: 200; **XII**: 84

Kaiser, Johann, 19th century (?) composer, **XI**: 51

Kakosky, ?, 19th century French composer, **IX**: 60

Kalckstein, 18th century German military leader, **VIII**: 334

Kalick, ?, 18th century German composer in Vienna, **XI**: 51, 269

Kalick, early 18th century composer of wind Sinfonie, **VII**: 3

Kalkbrenner, Friedrich, 1785–1849, German composer, **V**: 20ff; 34; **VIII**: 150ff, 152 [unnamed works arranged for Harmoniemusik]; **IX**: 178; **XI**: 51, 168, 303

Kallenberg, ?, 1867–1944, German composer, **XII**: 94

Kalliwoda, Johann, 1801–1866, Bohemian/German composer, **V**: 212; **IX**: 160; **XI**: 51, 114, 136, 153, 168, 259

Kallstenius, Edvin, b. 1881, Swedish composer, **XII**: 94, 151

Kallusch, W., 19th century Slovakian composer, **XI**: 136

Kaminski, Heinrich, 1886–1946, German composer, **XII**: 95

Kammel, ?, (2) *Serenata* for Harmoniemusik, **VIII**: 205

Kammel, A., 1730–1788, Czech composer, **XI**: 51

Kammerlander, Carl, 19th century German composer, **XI**: 290

Kanka, Johann, 1772–1865, German composer, **IX**: 160

Kanne, ?, *Orpheus*, opera, arranged by Triebensee for Harmoniemusik, **VIII**: 53

Kanne, ?, (1810) Austrian composer, **IX**: 218

Kansak, J., composer included in a 1887 English collection of band music, **X**: 116

Kappey, J. A., editor of a 19th century English military journal, **V**: 81; **VII**: 108

Kappey, Jacob, 1825–1907, English composer of works for band, **IX**: 276; **X**: 114ff, 137ff

Kaps, Karl, 19th century English composer for band, **X**: 139

Kapsberger, Johann, composer of dances published in Italy, **VII**: 203ff

Kara Mustafa Pasha, 17th century attack on Vienna, **III**: 106

Karajan, Herbert von, 20th century Austrian conductor, **XII**: 203

Karajew, Kara Abdulfas, b. 1918, Russian, composer, **XII**: 95

Kardos, Dezider, b. 1914, Slovak composer, **XII**: 151

Karg-Elert, Sigfrid, 1877–1933, German composer, **XII**: 151

Karl I, of Graz, **II**: 100

Karl II, Archduke in Graz, 16th century, **II:** 101

Karl VI, 1711–1740 of Austria, regarding the winds in his court, **III:** 63

Karl von Mecklenburg-Strelitz, Duke, 19th century, **V:** 16

Karlowicz, Misczyslaw, 1876–1909, Polish composer, **IX:** 130

Karren, Leon, 19th century French composer, conductor, Musique a la Division de Brest, **IX:** 60

Kaschte, Franz, as 19th century arranger, **IX:** 256, 257

Kasparek, 20th century publisher in Munich, **XII:** 162

Kastner, Jean, 1810–1867, French writer on various wind instruments, **X:** 67

Kastner, Jean-Georges, 1810–1867, French composer and military historian, **I:** 9, 115, **III:** 134ff; **IV:** 100ff, 103; **V:** 12ff 28, 30, 38, 42, 44, 47ff, 62ff, 85, 105 [as composer], 114; **IX:** 60

Kathaliery, ?, 19th century Austrian composer, **IX:** 218

Katschthaler, Philipp, 19th century Austrian composer, **IX:** 218

Kattner, Otto, 19th century German composer, **IX:** 160

Katzer, Ignace, b. 1785, French composer of works Harmoniemusik, **IX:** 61

Katzer, Ignaz (1820), German composer, **IX:** 161

Kauer, Ferdinand, 1751–1831, Moravian/Austrian composer, **IV:** 33, fn. 68; **XI:** 52, 114, 136, 153, 161, 217, 252, 259, 286

Kauer, Ferdinand, 1751–1831, works arranged for Harmoniemusik, **VIII:** 54, 151, 205ff

Kauffman, Paul, 16th century Nürnberg publisher, **VI:** 66, 68, 74, 79, 86

Kauffmann, ?, 19th century French composer, **IX:** 61

Kauffmann, 17th century publisher in Nürnberg and Jena, **VII:** 154ff, 159, 162, 164ff, 175, 178ff, 180

Kauffmann, Leo, 1901–1944, German composer, **XII:** 95, 152

Kaufmann, Armin, b. 1902, Romanian composer, **XII:** 95

Kaulich, Josef, 19th century Austrian composer, **IX:** 218

Kauntze George, English, *The Downfall of Paris March*, ca. 1800, 4 winds and pf, **VIII:** 258

Kauzner, bassoonist in original Vienna Harmoniemusik, **IV:** 35, fn. 77

Kayser, Leif, b. 1919, Danish composer, **XII:** 95, 152

Kayser, Phillipp, 1755–1823, German composer, **XI:** 259

Kechtler, ?, arranger for Harmonie, 1834 collection in Stuttgart, **X:** 95

Kegel, A. H., Baroque composer, **XII:** 3

Keil, Johann, 18th century German, *Parthia* for Harmonimusik, **VIII:** 329

Keiper, 17th century German composer, **III:** 215

Keiper, Johann, 1683, Baroque German composer for voices and winds, **VII:** 122

Keiser, Reinhard, 1674–1739, German composer, **III:** 8 [in Württemberg in 1720]; **XII:** 2

Kelderfer, Viktor, b. 1873, Austrian composer, **XII: 95**

Kélér, Béla, 1820–1882, Hungarian composer, **IX:** 218; **X:** 46; **XI:** 161

Keller, 17th century German composer, **III:** 17

Keller, C., 19th century Austrian composer, **XI:** 52

Keller, Gottfried, d. 1704 in London, German composer Hautboisten, **VII:** 123; **XII:** 3

Keller, Wilhelm, b. 1920, German composer, **XII:** 152

Kellie, Edward, Master of the Chapel Royal in Scotland in 1632, **III:** 201

Kellnern, Andree, 16th century publisher in Erben, **VI:** 71

Kelly, 19th century publisher in London, **XI:** 28

Kelsen, ?, 19th century French composer, conductor Musique de l'Ecole d'Artillerie de Bourges, **IX:** 61

Kempf, ?, composer included in a 1881 English collection of band music, **X:** 115

Kempter, ?, 19th century composer of a Mass for band and choir, **V:** 211

Kempter, Friedrich, b. 1810, German composer, **IX:** 161

Kempter, Karl, 1819–1871, German composer, **IX:** 161

Kenessey, Jenö, b. 1906, Hungarian composer, **XII:** 152

Kenn, Joseph, horn faculty of the 1792 Paris Conservatoire, performer at the Paris Opera, **IV:** 156; **XI:** 168

Kerl, Johann Kaspar, 1625–1693, composer, **VII:** 7, 167

Kern, Max, 19th century German composer, **IX:** 161

Kerner, A. and I., inventors of 1806 trumpet valve, **V:** 4

Kerntl, C. F., 18th century composer, **XI:** 204

Kerstein, ?, 18th century composer in London, **XI:** 232; **XI:** 204

Kertzinger, Pater August, late 17th century, German composer, **VII:** 7

Kessel, Johann, 1672, German composer of dances, a canzon, Sonatas, **VII:** 167

Kessels, Joseph, 19th century German composer, **IX:** 161

Keutzenhoff, Johannes, German composer ca. 1550, **VI:** 60

Kewitsch, Th., 19th century German composer, **IX:** 161

Key, T., 18th publisher in London, **VIII:** 251

Keyser, ?, fl. 1800–1828, French composer, **IX:** 61

Keyser, M., Baroque composer, **XII:** 3

Khayll, Aloys, 1791–1868, German composer, **XI:** 52

Khym, ?, 18th century composer, **XI:** 244

Kiefert, Carl, 1855–1937, German composer, **X:** 99

Kilian, 16th century composer, **VI:** 64

Kilner, W. A., composer included in a 1883 English collection of band music, **X:** 115

Kinast, G. A., as 19th century arranger, **IX:** 255, 256, 257

Kinckom, Anthony van, member of the Mechelen town band, 16th century, **II:** 168

Kindermann, Johann, 1616–1655, German composer, **III:** 17, 169; **VII:** 123ff

King of Bavaria (1870), **IX:** 160

King of Hannover, as 19th century composer, **IX:** 192

King, Matthew, 1733–1823, (4) military marchs, for Harmoniemusik, **VIII:** 259ff

King, Robert, Baroque English composer, **XI:** 204

Kinsky, Comte, 19th century Vienna, **XI:** 244 [dedication to]

Kinsky, Josef, Prince of Bohemia, b. 1781, opera arranged for Harmoniemusik, **VIII:** 54

Kinzi, Heinrich, as arranger, with biographical note, **XII:** 51

Kircher, author of *Mussurgia universalis*, publisher **VII:** 94, 167

Kirchner, Johann, 1765–1831, (4) *Cantatas* for voices and winds, **VIII:** 329

Kirchner, Wolfgang, 16th century publisher in Nürnberg, **VI:** 66

Kirnberger, Johann Philipp, German, 1721–1783, **XI:** 52; **XII:** 49 [*Miserere a quatre Voce, et Organo,* arranged for SATB, organ and Harmoniemusik by Druschetzky]

Kirsten, 18th century Bohemian composer, **IV:** 24; **VIII:** 205, (2) *Partitas* for Harmoniemusik

Kistler, Cyrill, 1848–1907, German composer, **IX:** 161

Kistner & Siegel, 18th century publisher in Lippstadt, **XI:** 32

Kistner, ?, composer included in a 1876 English collection of band music, 114

Kistner, 19th and 20th century publisher in Leipzig, **IX:** 156, 162; **X:** 103; **XI:** 168, 176, 250, 300, 317, 318; **XII:** 174

Kittl, Jan Bedrich, 1809–1868, 19th century Czech composer, **IX:** 218

Kittl, Johann, 1806–1868, German composer, **XI:** 317

Klami, Uuno, b. 1900, Finnish composer, **XII:** 96

Klaus, Josef, 19th century Austrian composer, **IX:** 218

Klebe, Giselher, b. 1925, German composer, **XII:** 153

Kleczinsky, Jan, d. 1828, Polish composer, **IX:** 130

Klee, L., 19th century German composer, **IX:** 161

Kleiber, Leonhard, b. 1863, German composer, **IX:** 161

Klein, Bernhard, 1793–1832?, German composer, **IX:** 161; **X:** 95

Klein, Georg, clarinetist in Vienna, **IV:** 35 fn. 77, 39

Klein, Jacob, late Baroque composer, **XI:** 114

Kleinheinz, Franz, 1765–1832, German composer, **IX:** 161; **XI:** 136

Kleinknecht, Jakob, 1722–1794, German composer, **XI:** 52, 204, 229

Kleinknecht, Johann Wolfgang, 1715–1786, composer, **XI:** 252

Kleitz, ?, fl. 1800–1828, French composer, **IX:** 61

Klemcke, Louis, 19th century composer, **XI:** 114

Kliebenschadl, Josef, 18th century (?) Austrian (?) composer, **XI:** 260

Kling, Henri (Hippolyte), 1842–1918, French composer, **IX:** 61; **X:** 68; **XII:** 60, 203

Klingenbrunner, G., 19th century Germany composer, **XI:** 52

Klinkicht, 19th century publisher in Meissen, **IX:** 159

Kllyn, ?, member of the 1775 Harmoniemusik of the Prince of Monaco, **IV:** 69

Klöffler, G. F., 18th century (?) composer, **XI:** 205

Klöffler, Johann, d. 1792, German composer, **XI:** 52, 205

Klopow, 19th century German composer, **IX:** 141

Klopstock, 18th century German poet, **XII:** 164

Klosé, F. J., 19th century French composer, **XI:** 53

Klosé, Hiacynthe, 1808–1880, French composer, arranger and educator, **V:** 62, 73; **IX:** 62, 113; **X:** 69; **XII:** 60

Klosmann, 17th century publisher in Leipzig, **VII:** 145, 175

Klughardt, August, 1847–1902, German composer, **IX:** 161; **XI:** 114

Kluhs, Th., 19th century German composer, **X:** 99

Klussmann, Henry, 19th century English composer for band, **X:** 139

Knab, Armin, 1881–1951, German composer, **XII:** 87

Knaust, 17th century publisher in Danzig, **VII:** 152

Knezek, Vaclav, 1745–1806 (2) *Partitas* for Harmoniemusik, **VIII:** 205

Kniess, Fr., b. ca. 1800, German composer, **IX:** 161

Knipfer, F., 19th century German composer, **IX:** 161

Knoblauch, Johann, hornist in 1761 for Prince Esterházy, **IV:** 27

Knobloch, ?, 19th century German composer, **X:** 99

Knoep, Lüder, d. before 1667, German composer for Hautboisten, **VII:** 124, 167

Knofl, G., 19th century Austrian composer, **IX:** 219

Knorr, Barone, 18th century (?), German composer, **XI:** 204, 320

Knorr, Bernhard, Freiherr von, 18th century, Vienna, *Quintet* for winds, **VIII:** 205

Knorr, Ernst-Lothar von, b. 1896, German composer, **XII:** 153

Knorr, Iwan, 1853–1916, German composer, **XI:** 53

Knorr, Nicolaus, 16th century publisher in Nürnberg, **VI:** 70

Knüpfer, Sebastian, 1633–1676, German composer of Intrada, Sonata, **VII:** 167

Koch, ?, composer included in a 1876 English collection of band music, **X:** 114

Koch, 19th century contrabassoonist, court at Rudolstadt, **V:** 186, fn. 8

Koch, A., 19th century German composer, **IX:** 161

Koch, Heinrich, 1749–1816, *Chorale book* for Harmoniemusik, *Marches,* **VIII:** 330

Köchel, Ludwig, 1800–1877, botanist, amateur musicologist, **III:** 62; **VIII:** 217

Köcken, ?, 19th century (?) German composer, **XI:** 252

Koczwara, Franz, 18th century composer, **XI:** 53

Kodrin, ?, 19th century Austrian composer, **IX:** 219

Kodrin, ?, 19th century composer, **XI:** 137

Koechlin Charles, 1867–1950, French composer, **XII:** 96, 153, 203

Koehler, Benjamin, b. 1777, French composer, **IX:** 62

Koenemann, ?, composer included in a 1871 English collection of band music, **X:** 113

Koenig, H. L., 19th century English composer, **IX:** 276

Koenig, Herman, 1827–1898, 19th century English composer for band, **X:** 139

Koffler, Jozef, 1896–1943, Polish composer, **XII:** 97

Kohault, Josef, 18th century (?) Czech composer, **XI:** 53

Köhler, ?, 17th century publisher in Leipzig, **VII:** 150

Köhler, ?, 18th century German composer, **XI:** 205

Kohler, 19th century publisher in London, **XI:** 245

Kohler, David, late 17th century, German composer of sonatas, suites, **VII:** 168

Köhler, Ernst, 19th century German composer, **IX:** 162

Köhler, Gottlieb, 1765–1833, German (3) *Parthien* for Harmoniemusik, **VIII:** 331

Kohler, John, 18th century English militia band leader, **IV:** 112

Kohn, Andreas, 19th century German composer, **X:** 95

Kohon, Benjamin, bassoonist in the 1910 Barrère Ensemble in NYC, **XII:** 214

Kókai, Rezzö, b. 1906, Hungarian composer, **XII:** 153

Kölb, ?, 19th century, Austrian composer, **IX:** 219

Kolb, Stefan, b. 1743, German, (9) *Partitas* for Harmoniemusik, **VIII:** 330

Kolbe, Oscar, arr., Leidersdorf, *Fest Overture* (1837) arr. for Harmoniemusik, **VIII:** 56

Kolbetz, M., 'a Wien,' late Baroque composer, **VII:** 3

Kollmann, 19th century publisher in Leipzig, **IX:** 188

Kollmann, August, 1756–1829, 18th century, composer, **VIII:** 259

Kollmann, Augustus Frederic, 18th century English music theorist, **IV:** 114

Kolovrátek, Tomás, 19th century Czech composer, **IX:** 219

Kolsdirfu, Matej Mencl, early 17th century composer, **VII:** 3

Komma, Karl Michael, b. 1913, Czech composer, **XII:** 97, 153

Komzák, Karl, 1850–1905, Bohemian composer and Austrian military band leader, **V:** 43; **IX:** 219; **X:** 47, 95; **XII:** 219

König, Johann Mattheus, 18th century (?), German composer, **XI:** 53

König, M., 18th century German, (7) *Marches* for Harmoniemusik, **VIII:** 331

Konink, Servaas, d. 1717, Dutch composer, **XI:** 53, 229

Konjus, Georgij Eduardowitsch, 1862–1933, Russian composer, **XII:** 97

Kopff, ?, 19th century French composer, **IX:** 62

Koppel, Herman David, b. 1908, Danish composer, **XII:** 153

Kopprasch, Wilhelm, 1750–1832, German composer for brass instruments, **VIII:** 331ff; **XI:** 153

Korn dem altern, 18th century publisher in Breslau, **XI:** 76

Körner, 19th century publisher in Erfurt, **XI:** 261

Körner, Gotthilf Wilhelm, 18th century Austrian (?) composer, **XI:** 53

Körner, Johann, 18th century German flautist at the court at Cassel, **XI:** 53

Körnlein, Justus, d. 1866, German composer, **IX:** 162, 198

Kósa, György, b. 1897, Hungarian composer, **XII:** 97, **153**

Koschowitz, Josef, 19th century composer, **VIII:** 206 [(6) *Hongroises* arr. Druschetzky for Harmoniemusik]; **XI:** 137 [biographical note]

Kosleck, ?, 19th century German composer, **IX:** 162

Koslowsky, 19th century composer, **IX:** 141

Koslowsky, J., 'amateur,' arr. Boieldieu, *Ma Tante Aurore,* opera for Harmonie, **VIII:** 11

Kösporer, Johann, 19th century German composer, **IX:** 162

Kospoth, Otto, 1753–1817, (2) *Parthias* for Harmoniemusik, **VIII:** 331; **XI:** 54, 114, 321

Kottaun, Celian, 19th century English composer for band, **X:** 140

Kotterz, ?, *Parthia* for Harmoniemusik, 206ff

Koubek, ?, 19th century Austrian composer, **IX:** 219

Kouloff, 18th century member of Russian horn band, **IV:** 81

Kovacs, Josef, 19th century Austrian composer, **IX:** 219

Kovarovic, Karl, 1862–1920, Czech composer, **XII:** 154

Kowalowsky, Johann, 18th century (?) Austrian composer, **XI:** 168

Kozeluch, Jan Antonin, 1738–1814, Austrian composer, **VIII:** 206 [*Cassation* for Harmoniemusik]; **XI:** 114, 137, 153, 234, 301

Kozeluch, Leopold, 1747–1818, Bohemian composer, **IV:** 22, fn. 9 [in Olmütz Harmoniemusik collection]; **V:** 201; **VIII:** 206ff, (17) *Partitas*, (2) *Marche* for Harmoniemusik

Kozeluch, Leopold, as composer of works arranged for Harmoniemusik, **VIII:** 54; **XII:** 45 [unidentifed march arranged by an unidentified arranger]

Kracher, Jose, 1752–1827, German composer, **XI:** 260

Kraft, Karl Joseph, b. 1903, German composer, **XII:** 98, 154

Kraknest, Herrmann, 19th century German composer, **IX:** 162

Kral, ?, composer included in a 1887 English collection of band music, **X:** 116

Kral, Johann, 19th century Austrian composer, **IX:** 219

Kramer, Christian, leader of the Prince Regent's band in London, **V:** 107, 202ff

Krasa, ?, 19th century Austrian composer, **VIII:** 208 [two partitas for Harmoniemusik]; **IX:** 219

Krasinsky, ? (pseudo. Ernst Muller), 18th century composer, **XI:** 54, 205

Kraus, Hermann, 20th century German composer, **XII:** 98

Kraus, Joseph, 19th century German composer, **IX:** 162

Krause, 1762, German composer for Hautboisten, **VII:** 124

Krause, J. H., 19th century composer, **XI:** 168; **IX:** 162

Krauss, Joseph, 1756–1792, German composer, **XI:** 54

Krebs, Johann Lewis, d. 1780, German organist, student of Bach, & composer, **XI:** 54

Krebs, Johann Tobias, 1690–1762, student of Bach and court organist to the Duke of Saxe-Weimar, **XI:** 54, 114

Krechtler, arranger of Mozart, *La Clemenza di Tito*, opera, for Harmoniemusik, **VIII:** 78

Krein, Alexander Abemowitsch, 1883–1951, composer, **XII:** 154

Krein, Michel, 19th century French composer, **IX:** 62

Kreith, arranger of Paisiello, *Il Re Teodoro in Venezia*, opera, for Harmoniemusik, **VIII:** 97

Kreith, Karl, 1746–1803, Austrian flutist and composer in Graf Pachta Harmonie Coll., **IV:** 22, fn. 10; **VIII:** 208ff, (32) *Partitas*, (23) *Marches* for Harmoniemusik; **X:** 17; **XI:** 54, 137, 205, 300; **XII:** 35 [15 works for Harmoniemusik]

Kreith, Robert, 18th century (?), instruction book on flute playing, **XI:** 52

Kreitner, 18th century publisher in Worms, **VIII:** 359

Krejcí, Isa, b. 1904, Czech composer, **XII:** 154

Kremberg, Jacob, 1658–1718, Polish composer for flutes, **VII:** 124; **XI:** 206, 269

Kremenliev, Boris Angeloff, b. 1911, Bulgarian composer, **XII:** 98, 155

Krempel, Charles, 19th century French composer, **IX:** 62

Krempel, Em., 19th century French composer, conductor, Musique au 54e de Ligne, **IX:** 62

Krenn, Franz, 1839–1890, 19th century Austrian composer, **IX:** 219; **XI:** 55, 168 206, 311, 317, 137, 206

Kress, Johann, d. 1730, German composer, **XI:** 55

Kresser, ?, 19th century French composer of a trumpet method, **X:** 69

Kretschmer, Edmund, 1830–1908, German composer, XI: 55, 317

Kreusser, Georg, 1743–1810, German composer, XI: 55, 206

Kreutzer, Conradin, 1780–1849, German composer, XI: 169, 232, 244, 248, 275

Kreutzer, IX: 180 [*Lodoiska*]; 198, 219, 364

Kreutzer, Konradin, 1780–1849, German composer, IX: 162

Kreutzer, Rodolphe, 1766–1831, his operas arranged for Harmoniemusik, VIII: 55 [*Antonius und Cleopatra, Lodoïska, Paul et Virginia*]; unidentified works, 150, 153

Kreutzer, Rolophe, 1766–1831, German, XII: 61

Kreutzer, Rudolphe, 1766–1831, violinist, 1793 faculty of Paris Conservatoire, IV: 162; VIII: 286 [as composer for band]

Kricka, Jaroslav, b. 1882, composer, XII: 155

Krickel, ?, IX: 219

Krieger, Johann Philipp, 1649–1725, composer of mil. concert music, III: 129, 215; IV: 90; VII: 124, 156, 168

Kriesstein, M., 1540 German publisher in Augsburg, VI: 63, 76

Krimpel, ?, 19th century French composer, IX: 63

Kroh, ?, 19th century Austrian composer, IX: 219

Krokowitsch, as 19th century arranger, IX: 197

Krombbhorn, Tobias, 1586–1617, German composer of dance music, VII: 168

Krommer, Franz, 1759–1831, Bohemian-Austrian court composer in Vienna, IV: 19; V: 148, 183, 218; VIII: 54 [as arranger of Kozeluch, ballet, for Harmoniemusik]; 56 [*Symphony*, arr. by Triebensee for Harmoniemusik]; IX: 220ff [original compositions]; , X: 47ff, 95; XII: 37 [5 partitas and 6 marches]; 45 [unidentified march arranged by an unidentified arranger]

Kröner, Michael, 16th century publisher in Ülzen, VI: 75; XI: 55, 114, 137, 230, 244

Kronsteiner, Hermann, b. 1914, German composer, XII: 98, 155

Krosch, Johann, composer in 1621 German publication of English music, VII: 24

Krottendörffer, Josef, 18th century German composer, XI: 291

Krufft, Nikolaus, 1779–1818, 19th century composer, XI: 138, 153, 169, 269

Krug, Diederich, 1821–1880, German composer, IX: 162

Krüger, 17th century German composer, III: 17

Kubicek, V., 19th century Czech composer, IX: 225, 253

Kucharz, Johann Baptist, 1751–1829, *Partitas* for Harmoniemusik, VIII 210

Kuecken, F. W., 19th century English composer, IX: 276; X: 100

Küffner, as arranger for Harmoniemusik, VIII: 110, 132

Küffner, Johann, 1727–1786, German composer, XI: 115, 138, 244

Küffner, Joseph, 1776–1856, German composer, arranger, V: 39, 73 fn. 24; IX: 162ff, 196; X: 100

Kugelmann, Johann, 1495–1542, German trumpeter, composer, II: 110; VI: 76

Kugelmann, Paul, composer, 16th century, II: 110; VI: 69, 77

Kugler, Lorenz, 19th century (?) German composer, XI: 56

Kuhlau, Friedrich, 1786–1832, German/Danish composer, XI: 56, 206

Kühn, ?, Classical Period composer, XII: 39

Kuhn, F., 19th century French composer, **IX:** 63

Kuhnau, Johann Christoph, 1735–1805, Bach's predecessor in Leipzig, **IV:** 3; **VIII:** 331 [*TeDeum* with brass instruments]; **XII:** 39

Kuhnau, Johann, 1660–1722, critical of Leipzig Stadtpfeifers, **III:** 162, 166, 170

Kühnel, 18th century publisher in Leipzig, **XII:** 35, 54

Kühnel, 19th century publisher in Leipzig, **VIII:** 130, 202ff, 220, 324; **XI:** 148, 258, 259

Kühner, ?, 19th century composer, **IX:** 276

Kuhner, ?, composer included in 19th century English band collections, **X:** 113, 115

Kühner, Wilhelm, b. 1851, German composer of works for band, **X:** 100ff

Kummer, ?, 18th century German bassoonist, **XI:** 154 [biographical note]

Kummer, Gaspard, 19th century (?) composer, **XI:** 269

Kün, composer in 1600 dance collection published in Heidelberg, **VII:** 180

Kundigraber, Hermann, 1879–1944, German composer, **XII:** 99, 155

Kunerth, J. Leopold, 19th century Austrian composer, Stadt Kremierer Turnermeister, **IX:** 225

Kunerth, Johann, 19th century German composer, **IX:** 164

Kunheim, W. L., 19th century German composer, **IX:** 164

Kunst- und Industrie-Compotior, 18th century publisher in Vienna, **VIII:** 173; **XI:** 72, 98, 269

Kunstanstalt, 19th century publisher in Innsbruck, **IX:** 214

Kuntze, Carl, 19th century German composer, **IX:** 164

Kuntzen, Adolph, 1720–1781, German (7) *Marches* for Harmoniemusik, **VIII:** 331

Kunz, Ernst, b. 1891, German composer, **XII:** 155

Kunz, Konrad, 1812–1875, German composer, **IX:** 164

Kunze, Carl, 18th century German professor of music at Heilbronn, **XI:** 56, 169

Kunzen, Adolph, 1720–1781, German composer, **XI:** 56, 115

Kunzen, Friedrich, 1761–1817, *Chorale*, voice and Harmoniemusik, **VIII:** 332

Kunzen, Friedrich, *Das Fest der Winzer*, opera, arranged by Simoni for Harmonie, **VIII:** 56

Kunzer, ?, 18th century German, (6) *German Dances*, for Harmoniemusik, **VIII:** 332

Kupler, ?, 19th century German composer, **IX:** 165

Kurpinski, Karol, 1785–1857, Polish composer, **XI:** 138, 161, 169, 217

Kürzinger, Paul, ca. 1755–1820, *Robert und Caliste*, arr. Süssmayr for Harmonie, **VIII:** 56

Kurzweil, Franz, 18th century German, (7) *Parthia* for Harmoniemusik, **VIII:** 332ff; **XI:** 248

Kussy, Franz, 19th century Austrian composer, **IX:** 226

Kuula, Toivo, 1883–1918, Finnish composer, **XII:** 99

Kvapil, Jaroslav, 1892–1958, Czech composer, **XII:** 155

Kwiatkowski, ?, 19th century Austrian composer, **IX:** 226

Kyle, Alexander, 19th century American composer, **IX:** 138

l'Imprimerie du Cons. de Musique, 19th century publisher in Paris, **XI:** 131, 299

l'Orphéon, 19th century publisher in Paris, **XII:** 60

La Barre, Michel, 1675–1743, French composer, flutist and government official in 1730, **III:** 38; **XI:** 206

La Bretesche, J., 19th century French composer, **IX:** 64

La Chevardière, 18th and 19th century publisher in Paris, **VII:** 86; **VIII:** 70, 102, 160

La Mailliere, M. de, 18th century French composer, **XI:** 206

La Rue, Pierre de, 1452–1518, Franco-French composer, **VI:** 49, 63

Labarbiera, Baldassare, 19th century (?) Italian composer, **XI:** 260

Labit, Henri, 19th century French composer, conductor, Musique au 84e de Ligne; Directeur de l'Ecole Nationale de Musique de Valenciennes, **IX:** 63

Labitsky, Josef, 1802–1881, German composer of works for band, **X:** 102

Labitzki, ?, 19th century French composer, **IX:** 63

Labitzky, A., composer included in a 1870 English collection of band music, **X:** 113

Labitzky, Josef, 1802–1881, Czech composer, **XI:** 138, 244

Lábler, Frantiscek, 19th century Austrian composer, **IX:** 226

Labole, P.-N., 19th century French composer, **IX:** 63

Laborde, E., 19th century French composer, **IX:** 64

Laborde, Jean-Benjamin, 1734–1794, music historian, **IV:** 99

Laborde, Léon, 19th century French composer, **IX:** 64

Labric, J. B., 19th century French composer, conductor, Musique du 23e de Ligne, **IX:** 1, 64

Lacaire, Thé., 19th century French composer, **IX:** 64

Lach, Robert, 1874–1958, Austrian, **XII:** 99

Lacher, 19th century French arranger, conductor, 9e Cuirassiere a Andrinople, **IX:** 2, 64

Lachner, Franz, 1803–1890, German composer, **IX:** 165; **X:** 103; **XI:** 250, 309, 318; **XII:** 195

Lachner, Franz, as composer of a work arranged for Harmoniemusik, **VIII:** 151 [unidentified work arranged by Poisel]

Lachner, Vinzenz, 1811–1893, German composer of a march for band, **X:** 103

Lachner, work arranged for band, **IX:** 174

Lachnith, Ludwig, 1746–1820, German composer, **VIII:** 93 [as arranger of Paer, *Agnesse di Fitz-Henry*, opera, for Harmoniemusik]; **XI:** 169

Lackner, Ignaz, 18th century Austrian composer, **XI:** 169

Lacombe, Louis, 1818–1884, French composer, **IX:** 64

LaCroix, Eugene, 19th century, French composer, **XII:** 192

Lacy, Raphino, 1797–1867, Spanish violinist & composer, **XI:** 57

Ladmirault, Paul, 1877–1944, French composer, **XII:** 155

Laet, J., publisher in Antwerpen, 1556, **VI:** 123

Lafayette, General, 1757–1834, France, **IV:** 141ff, 171

Lafeur, 19th century publisher in Paris, **XII:** 62, 64

Laffe, 20th century publisher in Paris, **XII:** 78

Lafille, Charles, 19th century French composer, **IX:** 64

Lafitte, Jacques, 19th century French composer, **IX:** 64

Laforest, Thiard, 19th century Austrian composer, **IX:** 226

Lagard, A., 19th century French composer, **IX:** 64

Lagny, A., 19th century French composer, **IX:** 64

Lahmer, Ruel, b. 1912, American, **XII:** 99, 156

Laigre, Paul, 19th century French composer, **IX:** 65

Laimable, ?, 19th century French composer, **X:** 69

Lair, Alfred, as 19th century arranger, **IX:** 28

Lajarte, Théodore, 1826–1890, French composer, arranger, **IX:** 65, 113; **X:** 69

Lajtha, László, b. 1892, Hungarian composer, **XII:** 156, 157

Lalande, Michel-Richard, 1657, 1726, French composer for Hautboisten, **VII:** 83ff, 88ff, 95

Lalo, Édouard, 1823–1892, French, **XII:** 198

Laloire, Marie, faculty of the 1792 Paris Conservatoire, **IV:** 157

Lamalle, Pierre (1672), composer, **III:** 199

Lambel, Wenzel, 19th century Czech (?) composer, **XI:** 311

Lamberg, 17th century publisher in Leipzig, **VII:** 154, 172

Lambert, Auguste, 19th century French composer, **IX:** 65

Lambert, E., 19th century French composer, **IX:** 65

Lambert, Johann, 18th century writer on theory of the flute, **XI:** 57 [biographical note]

Lamberti, Louis, b. 1769, *Pièces en harmonie,* **VIII:** 286

Lamberto, 16th century composer, **VI:** 30

Lamiable, 19th century French composer, **IX:** 1, 2

Lamote de Grignon, b. 1899, Ricardo, Spanish composer, **XII:** 99

Lamotte, ?, Émile, 19th century French composer, **V:** 75

Lamotte, Antony, 19th century French composer, **IX:** 65

Lamotte, Nicolas, 19th century French composer of works for band, **X:** 70

Lampe, Walther, b. 1872, German composer, **IX:** 165; **XII:** 100

Lamperini, ?, 19th century Italian composer, **IX:** 118

Lampugnani, Giovanni, 1706–1784, Italian composer, **XI:** 206

Lamy, Fernand, b. 1881, French composer, **XII:** 156

Lancen, Serge, 20th century French composer, **XII:** 203

Landa, W., 19th century Austrian composer, arranger and Kapellmeister, Kaiser Franz Josef Infantrie Regiment N.1, **IX:** 226, 257; **XII:** 61

Landi, Antonio, playwright, 16th century, **II:** 129

Landowska, Wanda, b. 1879, Polish composer, **XII:** 100

Landowski, Marcel, b. 1915, French composer, **XII:** 156

Landré, Guillaume, b. 1905, Dutch composer, **XII:** 156

Landsberg, Ludwig, 1807–1858, German composer of a cantata with winds, **X:** 103

Lang, Friderich, paid to restore Nürnberg crumhorns in 1620, **III:** 161

Lang, Johann, 1724–1800, Bohemian/German composer, **XI:** 57

Langa, Pascal, 19th century French composer, **IX:** 66

Lange, Gustav, 1830–1889, German composer of works for band, **IX:** 165, 276; **X:** 104

Langen, Paul, 17th century Hamburg publisher, **VII:** 23

Langenaw, Leonhard von, 16th century German composer, **VI:** 62ff

Langius, Balthasar, 1605, German composer of lieder for insts, **VII:** 168

Langius, Gregor, 16th century composer, **VI:** 70

Langlais, Jean, b. 1907, French composer, **XII:** 100, 156

Langland, William, English poet, 14th century, **I:** 191

Langlane, Geo., 19th century French composer, **IX:** 65

Langlé, Honoré François, 1741–1807, (6) *Sinfonie* and a *Hymn* for Harmonie, **VIII:** 286

Langlois, 19th century publisher in Paris, **VIII:** 14, 65ff

Langlois, Jules, 19th century French composer, **IX:** 66

Lanier, Andrea, musician of Charles I, **III:** 90

Lanier, Nicholas, Jr., 1588–1666, English composer of ens. music for cornets, **III:** 95; **VII:** 18

Lanner, composer in a collection of Harmoniemusik by an unknown arranger, **VIII:** 152

Lanner, Josef, 1801–1843, Austrian composer, **V:** 112, 136, 177; **IX:** 226; **X:** 51

Lanner, work arranged for band, **IX:** 186

Lanz, Engelbert, 19th century Austrian composer, **IX:** 226

Lapara, ?, 19th century French composer, **IX:** 66

Lapicida, Erasmus, fl. 1510–1521, Franco-Flemish composer, **VI:** 61ff

Lapini, 19th century publisher in Firenze, **X:** 178, 183, 197, 203

Lapis, Santo, 18th century Italian composer, **XI:** 207

Laporte, Raymond, 19th century French composer, **IX:** 66

Lappi, Pietro of Brescia, Italian composer, **III:** 220; **VII:** 204, 208

Larchier, Joannes, 16th century composer, **VI:** 27, 61ff, 107, 119ff,

Lardenois, Arthur, 19th century French composer, **IX:** 66

Lardeur, Henri, 19th century French composer, conductor, Musique a l'École d'Artilerie de Versailles, **IX:** 66

Larmanjat, Jacques, 1878–1952, French composer, **XII:** 156

Laroche, Pierre, 19th century English composer for band, **X:** 140

Larriu, A., 19th century French composer, **IX:** 66

Larsen, Libby, 20th century American composer, **XII:** 203

Larsson, Lars-Erik, b. 1908, Swedish composer, **XII:** 157

Lasalle, E., 19th century German composer, **IX:** 165

Lasek, ?, 19th century German civic militia composer, **V:** 125; **IX:** 166

Lasso, Orlando, 1532–1594, composer, **II:** 97, 231; **VI:** 27, 30, 65, 77ff, 85, 109, 118; **VII:** 180

Lasso, Rudolphum [son of Orlando], **VI:** 65

Lastra, Erich Eder de, fl. 1970s, Austrian composer, **XII:** 100

Lasueur, *Paul et Virginia,* opera, arranged for Harmonie, **VIII:** 58

Latann, C., 19th century German composer, **IX:** 336

Latii, Joanne, 16th century composer, Antwerp, **VI:** 124

Latilla, Gaetano, 1711–1788 Italian composer, **XI:** 57

Latins, Arnoldus de, early Renaissance composer, **VI:** ix

Latour, Henri, 19th century French composer of works for band, **X:** 70

Latour, T., 1766–1837, composer, **XI:** 57

Lattenberg, Felix, 19th century Austrian composer, **IX:** 226

Latti, ?, 18th century composer, **XI:** 154

Laube, Antonin, 1718–1784, composer in Graf Pachta Harmonie Coll., **IV:** 22, fn. 10; **VIII:** 211ff, (12) *Partitas* and a *Te Deum* for Harmoniemusik; **XI:** 126, 154, 322

Lauder, composer in 1604 Scottish ensemble collection, **VII:** 22

Lauffenberg, Heinrich, 1390–1460, German composer, **VI:** ix

Laurendeau, L. P., 19th century American composer for band, **X:** 265

Laurent, E., 19th century French composer, **IX:** 66

Laurent, H., 19th century English composer, **IX:** 276; **X:** 140

Lautier, F., 19th century French composer, **IX:** 66

Lauzun, F., 19th century French composer, **IX:** 66

Lavasseur, Henry, cellist, 1793 faculty of Paris Conservatoire, **IV:** 162

Lave, 18th century publisher in London, **XI:** 195

Lavenu, L., 19th century publisher in London, **XI:** 18

Lavoye, ?, mid 17th century, French composer for Hautboisten, **VII:** 95

Lawes, William, d. 1645, composer of English ensemble music, **VII:** 60

Layer, Antoine, clarinet faculty of the 1792 Paris Conservatoire, **IV:** 157

Layolle, Francesco de, 1492–1540, Florentine composer, **VI:** 97

Lazansky, Count, replaces trumpets with horns in 1732 in Manetin, **IV:** 4

Lazarus, Daniel, b. 1898, French composer, **XII:** 157

Lazennec, I., 19th century French composer, **IX:** 67

Lazowski, Claude, subject of a Revolutionary Festival in Paris, **IV:** 180

Lazzari, Sylvio, 1857–1944, Italian composer, **V:** 153; **IX:** 67; **XII:** 100

Le Blanc Duvernoy, Paul, 19th century French composer, **IX:** 67

Le Boulch, Jules, 19th century French composer, **IX:** 67

Le Bref, A., 19th century French composer, **IX** 67

Le Breton, H., 19th century French composer, **IX:** 67

Le Cene, 18th century publisher in Amsterdam, **XI:** 82

Le Chant du Monde, 20th century publisher in Paris, **XII:** 105

Le Chevalier, Amadée, 1654–1720, French composer, **XI:** 57

Le Clerc, 18th century publisher in Paris, **XI:** 42, 34, 201, 251

Le Clerc, flutist for La Pouplinière, 1763, **IV:** 68 fn. 26

Le Cocq, 16th century composer, **VI:** 107, 108, 118ff

Le Duc Successeur, Mr. Chevardiere, 18th century publisher in Paris, **XI:** 12

Le Duc, 18th century publisher in Paris, **VIII:** 153, 159; **XI:** 14, 106, 192

Le Febure, 16th century composer, **VI:** 65

Le Gendre, Arnauld, clarinet faculty of the 1792 Paris Conservatoire, **IV:** 157

Le Heurteur, fl. 1530–1545, French composer, **VI:** 49, 50, 92

Le Jeune, Claude, 1530–1600, Franco-Flemish composer, **VI:** 107, 108

Le Jeune, Henry, *Phantasie*, 1636, French composer for Hautboisten, **VII:** 87

Le Maistre, Mattheus, 16th century composer in Munich, **VI:** 72

Le Menu et Boyer, 18th century publisher in Paris, **XI:** 79

Le Menu, 18th century publisher in Paris, **VIII:** 291

Le Moyne, 16th century composer, **VI:** 43

Le Peletier, 18th century French politician, **IV:** 178

Le Roy, Adrian, 1520–1598, French composer, **VI:** 120, 122, 123

Le Roy, Ballard & Patisson, 16th century publishers in Paris, **VI:** 55

Le Sueur, Jean-François, work arranged for band, **IX:** 113 [*Paul et Virginie*]

Le Thière, Charles, late 19th century French composer of works for band, **X:** 70ff

Leach, Thomas (1801), English composer for band, **X:** 32

Lebeau, 19th century publisher in Paris, **IX:** 51

Lebigre, Auguste, 19th century French composer, **IX:** 67

Leblan, E., 19th century French composer, **IX:** 67

Leblanc, L., 19th century French composer, **IX:** 67

Lebon, in a 1616 Nürnberg collection, **VII:** 163

Lebrun, 16th century German composer, 63

Lebrun, Jean, 1759–1809, French composer, **XI:** 169

Lebrun, Ludwig, 1752–1790, German composer, **XI:** 57, 115, 138, 207

Lechleitner, ?, 19th century French composer, conductor, Musique 14me d'Artillerie, **IX:** 67

Lechner, ?, in 1600 dance collection published in Heidelberg, **VII:** 144, 180

Lechner, Leonhard, 1553–1606, Austrian composer, **VI:** 65, 70, 78

Lecoeur, E., 19th century French composer, **IX:** 67

Lecomte, A., 19th century French composer, **IX:** 67

Lecomte, Pierre, conductor of the Douai civic band in 1827, **V:** 148

Lecourt, Louis XI period collection, **VII:** 83

Leduc, 18th and 19th century publisher in Paris, **VIII:** 36, 273, 276ff, 285

Leduc, 19th century publisher in Paris, **IX:** 1, 3, 37, 44, 48, 57, 68, 86; **XI:** 31, 44, 61, 151, 164, 176; **XII:** 64, 77, 150, 156, 157, 168, 182

Lee, J. S., 19th century English composer for band, **X:** 141

Lee, J., 18th century publishers in Dublin, **XI:** 208

Lee, Walter, 19th century English composer for band, **X:** 141

Leeds, 20th century publisher in New York, **XII:** 92

Leetherland, composer in early 17th century English ensemble music, **VII:** 20

Lefabre, A., 19th century French composer, **IX:** 68

Lefebvre, Charles, 1843–1917, French composer, **IX:** 68

Lefebvre, Fortuné, 19th century French composer, **IX:** 68

Lefévre, Jean Xavier, 1763–1829, French, first clarinet in the Paris Opera and composer, **IV:** 160, 163ff, 206, 202: **VIII:** 287, (17) works for the French Revolution; **X:** 21; **XI:** 138, 280

Lefèvre, Jean, Burgundian historian, 15th century, **I:** 248

Lefèvre, Louis, 1751–1828, clarinetist, on faculty of the 1792 Paris Conserv., **IV**: 156

Lefèvre, Xavier, 1763–1829, French composer, **XI**: 248; **XII**: 203

Leffloth, Johann, b. 1705, German composer, **XI**: 57

Lefranc, ?, 1837–1871, director of civic band school in Douai, **V**: 148

Lefrancois, F., 19th century French composer, **IX**: 68

Legat de Furcy, Antoine, b. 1740, French composer, **XI**: 207

Legendre, Jules, 19th century French composer, **IX**: 68

Legier, John Bernard, 18th century English, (13) *Sets of Military Pieces,* **VIII**: 259

Legley, Victor, b. 1915, Belgian composer, **XII**: 157

Legrand, as arranger for Harmoniemusik, **VIII**: 76, 106, 108, 110

Legrand, German composer 1834 Hoftheater collection in Stuttgart, **X**: 95

Legrand, historian, Army of the Rhein, 18th century, **VIII**: 274

LeGrand, William, late 18th century, vast collection of Harmonie music, **V**: 186; **IX**: 336ff

Lehman, Frederick, 18th century German, (6) *Marches* for winds, **VIII**: 332

Lehmann, Friedrich, 19th century German composer, **IX**: 166

Lehmann, R., as 19th century arranger, **IX**: 196

Lehne, 19th century publisher in Hannover, **IX**: 178

Lehnhardt, Gustav, 19th century German composer of a work for band, **X**: 104

Lehnhardt, Julius, 19th century German composer of works for band, **X**: 104

Leibl, Karl, 1784–1870, German composer, **V**: 133; **IX**: 166

Leibowitz, René, b. 1913, French composer, **XII**: 157

Leicester, Earl of, II: 45

Leidersdorf, Franz, 19th century Austrian composer, **IX**: 226

Leidersdorf, Franz, *Fest Overture* arranged by Oscar Kolbe for Harmoniemusik, **VIII**: 56

Leidesdorf, 19th century publisher in Vienna, **XI**: 269

Leidesdorf, Maximilian, 1787–1840, German composer, **XI**: 58, 170

Leigh, Walter, 1905–1942, English composer, **XII**: 157

Leister, Franz, 19th century (?) German composer, **XI**: 58

Lekeu, Giullaume, 1870–1894, Belgium composer, **IX**: 259

Leleu, Jeanne, b. 1898, French composer, **XII**: 100, 195

Lelong, ?, 19th century French composer, **IX**: 68

Lemaigre, A.-T., 19th century French composer, **IX**: 68

Lemaire, J., 16th century composer, **VI**: 38

Lemalle, J., 19th century French composer, **IX**: 68

Lemarié, A., 19th century French composer, **IX**: 68

Lemière de Corvey, Jean, 1770–1832, French composer, **IX**: 68

Lemin, 16th century composer, **VI**: 62, 63

Lemle, Sebastian, early 17th century, German composer, **VII**: 125

Lemoine, 18th 19th and 20th century publisher in Paris, **VIII**: 275ff; **IX**: 22, 51, 75, 80; **XII**: 128, 155, 183

Lemoine, H., 19th century publisher in Paris, **VIII**: 27ff

Lemoyne, Jean Baptiste, 1751–1796, opera arranged for Harmoniemusik, **VIII:** 56; **XI:** 58

Lendvay, Gabriel, clarinetist in 1801 Harmoniemusik of Prince Esterházy, **IV:** 31, fn. 57

Lenepvue, Charles, French, 1840–1910, **XII:** 61

Lennert, V., 19th century German composer, **IX:** 166

Lentz, Frédéric, 19th century French composer, **IX:** 68

Lenzi, Carlo, 1735–1805, Italian composer, **X:** 38

Leo X, pope, 1475–1521, **II:** 92, 119ff; **VI:** 79

Leo, Leonardo, 1694–1744, Italian composer, **XI:** 207, 233

Leoncavallo, 19th century Italian composer, **IX:** 198; **X:** 254 [*Pagliacchi,* arranged for band by Vessella]

Leone XIII [dedication], **X:** 59, 241

Leonhardt, Andreas, 1800–1866, composer and leading figure in Austrian mil. music, **V:** 50; **IX:** 226; **X:** 52

Leopold I of Belgium, 19th century, **IX:** 260

Leopold I, Emperor 1658–1705 and composer, **III:** 61ff, 152; **VII:** 3 [as composer]

Leopold II, 1747–1792, coronation in Pressburg in 1790, **IV:** 31

Leopold, Archduke of Austria, ca. 1638, **VII:** 186

Leopoldo II, Grand Duke, 1797–1870, sponsors band in Napoli, **V:** 195

Lépagnole, L., 19th century French composer, **IX:** 68

Leplat, E., 19th century French composer, **IX:** 68

Leprevost, Alexandre, 19th century French organist, **XII:** 61

Leroux, Charles, 19th century French composer, **IX:** 69

Leroux, Felix, 19th century French composer, conductor, Musique l'École d'Artillerie de Vincennes, **IX:** 69

Leroux, Gabriél, solfeggio faculty of the 1792 Paris Conservatoire, **IV:** 156

Leroy, 19th century publisher in Lyon, **IX:** 1

Leroy, Henry Léon, clarinetist in Paris and then in the 1910 Barrère Ensemble in NYC, **XII:** 212, 214

Lescornet, 16th century Franco-French composer, **VI:** 119

Leslie, Steward, 19th century English composer, **IX:** 276

Lessel, Franciszek, 1780–1835, Polish composer, **IX:** 130

Lessel, François, 1780–1835, Polish composer, **XI:** 58

Lessing, German poet, IX: 150

Lesuer, Jean François, 1760–1837, French composer, Paris Conservatoire faculty, **IV:** 162, 164, 216; **V:** 197 [wind composer for Napoleon]; **VIII:** 287ff [(8) Revolutionary *Hymns* for band]

Lesueur, Jean François, his operas arranged for Harmoniemusik, **VIII:** 57ff

Lesueur, L., 19th century French composer, **IX:** 69

Leto, Antonio, 19th century Italian composer for band, **X:** 210

Lettorio, Marino, 18th century composer in Paris, **XI:** 236

Leuckart, 19th century German publisher in Breslau, **V:** 34; **VIII:** 177; **IX:** 148

Leuckart, 19th and 20th century publisher in Leipzig, **IX:** 175, 217; **XII:** 165

Leuis, ?, 18th century (?) composer, **XI:** 58

Leunis, Jan, copyist or composer for the Bruges town band, 16th century, **II:** 167

Leutner, 19th century band composer working in England, **V:** 82

Lévêque, Emile, 19th century French composer, **IX:** 69

Lévêque, L., 19th century French composer, **IX:** 69

Levy, Ernst, b. 1895, German composer, **XII:** 100

Levy, J., 19th century English composer for band, **X:** 141

Lewis, Giovanni, 18th century (?) Italian (?) composer, **XI:** 207

Leye, L., 19th century German composer, **X:** 104

Leyroy, 19th century publisher in Lyon, **XII:** 70

Lhotka, Fran, b. 1883, Czech composer, **XII:** 157

Liadov, ?, 1855–1914, Russian composer, **IX:** 135

Liber, Joseph, 1732–1809, *Divertimento*, Harnmonie with 2 violas (?), **VIII:** 332

Liberati, 20th century band conductor, **XII:** 201

Libero Castro, Henricus de, 1390–1460, Spanish composer, **VI:** x

Liberti, Hendrik, 1600–1661, Antwerp, composer of instrumental dances, **VII:** 214

Librarie centrale, 19th century publisher in Paris, **XII:** 66

Lichtenthal, Peter, 1780–1853, German composer, **XI:** 58

Lichtlein, Wilhelm, 16th century German composer, **VI:** 61

Lickl, F. Georg, 1769–1843, Hungarian composer, **XI:** 58, 283, 303, 318

Lickl, Johann, 1769–1843, Austrian composer, **IX:** 227; **XII:** 39

Lidarti, Cristiano, 1730–1793, Austrian composer, **XI:** 58, 207

Liddell, John, 19th century English composer, **IX:** 276; **X:** 142

Lidel, ?, 18th century composer, **XI:** 58

Lidmanzky, Franz, 19th century composer in Austria, **XI:** 305

Liebermann, Rolf, b. 1910, Swiss composer, **XII:** 158

Liebeskind, Johann, German author, treatise on the German flute, **XI:** 59

Liebig, ?, 19th century German composer of works for band, **X:** 104

Liechtenstein, Johann, 1700–1771, Austrian Prince in Vienna, **IV:** 18, 38, 95

Liechtenstein, Prince in Vienna, 1759–1805, **V:** 177ff; **IX:** 249

Liechtenstein-Casstelcorn, 1664–1695, Archbishop at Kromeriz, **IV:** 21

Lier, Betus Van, b. 1906, composer, **XII:** 158

Liess, ?, as 19th century arranger, **IX:** 143

Lieu-Pang, Emperor of China, 2nd century BC, **I:** 9

Ligner, F., 19th century French composer, **IX:** 69; **X:** 73

Lilman, V., 19th century French composer, **IX:** 70

Limnander, ?, 19th century French composer, **IX:** 70

Lincke, P., 19th century English composer, **IX:** 276

Lind, Jenny [dedication], **X:** 63

Lindner, Fr., 19th century German composer, **XI:** 318

Lindner, Friedrich, fl. 1750–1789 at the Berlin court, German composer, **VI**: 70; **XI**: 318

Lindner, H., fl. 1800–1828, 19th century German composer, **IX**: 166, 180

Lindner, Henri, 19th century French composer, **IX**: 70

Lindpainter, Peter, 1791–1856, 19th century German composer, **V**: 105; **IX**: 166; **X**: 105; **XI**: 139, 318

Lindpainter, Peter, 1791–1856, works arranged for Harmoniemusik or band, **VIII**: 58; **IX**: 196

Linek, J. I., 1725–1791, Bohemian composer, **VII**: 3

Linek, Jiri, *Fanfare*, 1785, 4 trumpets and timpani, **VIII**: 212

Linek, Yiri, 19th century Czech composer, **IX**: 227

Ling, William, 18th century English composer, **XI**: 207

Linglin, ?, 19th century French composer, **IX**: 70

Linicke, Johann, fl. ca. 1680, German composer for Hautboisten, **X**: 7

Linike, Johann Georg, early 18th century, German composer, **VII**: 125; **XII**: 3

Link, Joseph, 1783–1837, 19th century German composer, **IX**: 166

Linley, 18th century publisher in London, **XI**: 29, 40

Linley, Francis, 18th century, English composer, **XI**: 59

Linn, Robert, 20th century American composer, **XII**: **203**

Lionardo, Simone di, famous trumpeter in Florence, 17th century, **III**: 71

Lipawsky, ?, 19th century composer, unidentified march arranged by an unidentified arranger, **XII**: 45

Lipawsky, Giuseppe, 19th century Italian composer, **IX**: 118

Lipparino, Guglielmo, fl. 1600–1637, Bologna, Italian composer of canzoni, **VII**: 204

Lisle, Rouget de, 1760–1836, French composer, **IV**: 211

Liszt, Franz, 1811–1886, Hungarian composer, pianist, **V**: 22, 122, 213; **IX**: 227; **XII**: 201, 218, 219

Lithographisches Institut, 19th century publisher in Vienna, **VIII**: 132

Liverani, ?, 18th century (?) composer, **XI**: 245

Liverati, Giovanni, 1772–?, *David, oder Goliaths Tod*, oratorio, arr. for Harmonie, **VIII**: 58

Livorka, ?, 19th century Austrian composer, **IX**: 228

Livy, 1st century BC Roman historian, **I**: 52, 57, 59, 60

Llaue, 19th century publisher in Berlin, **IX**: 173

Lobe, J. C., 19th century German composer, **IX**: 198

Lobkowitz, Franz Joseph, Prince, 1772–1816, in Vienna, **IV**: 42

Locatelli, Pietro, 1695–1764, Italian composer, **XI**: 59

Locke, Matthew, 1621–1677, English composer, **III**: 94, 204; **VII**: 18ff, 61

Lockelvitz, P., 1702, German composer for voice and winds, **VII**: 125

Loeb, Wilhelm, 19th century German composer, **X**: 95

Loeffler, Charles M., **XII**: 215

Loeillet, Jean, d. 1728, Flemish, composer, **XI**: 59 [biographical note], 115; **XI**: 60, 116, 208, 230

Loetz, Paul de, 19th century English composer, **IX:** 277

Loewe, Johann, 1796–1869, German composer, **IX:** 166

Loewe, Johann, b. 1766, German, *Notturno* for Harmonie and 2 Eng. hns, **VIII:** 333

Löfler, Herr., dedication on a 19th century German march in Italy, **X:** 163

Logier, 19th century publisher in Berlin, **V:** 34; **VIII:** 314

Logier, Jean, 1780–1846, French composer, **IX:** 70

Logier, Johann, inventor of the chiroplast, as leader of militia band, **IV:** 112

Lohr, Michael, 1629, German composer for voices or instruments, **VII:** 168ff

Loibl, Benedikt, 1766–1833 German, OSB, *Parthia* for Harmoniemusik, **VIII:** 333

Lointier, Eugene, 19th century French composer, **IX:** 70

Lomazzo, Filippo, 1699–1613, Milano publisher of canzoni, **VII:** 198, 204ff

Longman & Broderip, 18th century publisher in London, **VIII:** 250ff, 255ff, 302; **XI:** 4, 8, 18, 19ff, 29, 34, 44, 71, 87, 103, 104, 107, 127, 129, 186, 191, 197, 209, 212, 213, 226, 228, 229

Longman Lukey & Co., 18th century publishers in London, **X:** 33; **XI:** 5, 19, 90, 195, 204, 208, 209, 226

Longman, Lukey & Broderip, 18th century publisher in London, **XI:** 19, 208, 209

Longy, Georges, Principal oboe, Boston Symphony, **XII:** 182ff, 193, 201

Lorentz, (13) *Parthias* for Harmoniemusik, **VIII:** 212ff

Lorenz (Lorentz), 18th century composer in Graf Pachta Harmonie Coll., **IV:** 22, fn. 10

Lorenzini, Raimondo, 1730–1806, 6 *Nocturnes* for Harmoniemusik, serpent, **VIII:** 366

Lorenziti, Bernardo, 18th century in Paris, *Canon ou divertissement* for 4 winds, **VIII:** 288

Lorenzo de' Medici 'Il Magnifico' of Florence, **I:** 241, **II:** 120

Lorenzo de' Medici, 16th century, not the 'Il magnifico,' **II:** 127

Lorenzoini, Antonio, 18th century Italian composer, **XI:** 60

Lorraine, Duke of, as rider in a horse ballet in 1667, **III:** 62

Lortzing, Gustav Albert, 1801–1851, German composer of an overture for band, **IX:** 166, 277; **X:** 106

Lortzing, Gustav Albert, 1801–1851, as composer of a work arranged for Harmoniemusik, **VIII:** 59 [*Czaar und Zimmermann*]

Lose, 19th century publisher in Kopenhagen, **XI:** 203

Lots, Theodor, clarinetist and leader of the Harmonie of Cardinal Batthyány, **IV:** 33

Lotter, early 18th century publisher in Augsburg, **VII:** 173

Lotti, Antonio, 1667–1740, Italian composer of Hautboisten, **X:** 13; **XI:** 125

Lottich, Jacob, poet in 1679 on Stadtpfeifer duties, **III:** 164

Lottum, 18th century German Count, **VIII:** 301

Loubet, A., 19th century French composer, **IX:** 70

Louel, Jean, b. 1914, Belgian composer, **XII:** 101

Louis de Rouvroy, Duke Saint-Simon, 1675–1755, diplomat, diarist, **III:** 27

Louis de Szechny, Count, of Hungray, **VIII:** 188

Louis IX, 'St. Louis,' 1226–1270, **I:** 145, 207

Louis XI, 1461–1483, **I:** 215; **IX:** 86

Louis XII, 1498–1515, II: 61ff, 197

Louis XIII, 1601–1643, King of France, III: 25ff, 90; VI: 37; VII: 81, 93; IX: 14; XII: 203

Louis XIV, 1638–1715, the 'Sun God,' King of France, III: 5, 7, 10, 27ff, 35 [*Les Grands Hautbois*], 37 [*Musettes et Hautbois du Poitou*], 39 [*Les Cromornes*], 40 [*Les Fifres et Tambours* and *Les Trompettes*], 41 [*Les Mousquetaires*], 45, 75, 136ff, 217; IV: 6, 63; VII: 83

Louis XV, 1710–1774, King of France, III: 47ff; IV: 101, 183; VIII: 281

Louis XVI, 1710–1774, King of France, IV: 138ff, 144, 148, 169, 180ff, 200; V: 22, 143

Louis XVIII of France, VIII: 279; IX: 48

Louis, ?, 19th century French composer, IX: 1, 70

Louis, ?, hornist and string bass for La Pouplinière, 1763, IV: 68, fn. 26

Louis, Émile, 19th century French composer, X: 73

Louise of Mecklenburg-Strelitz, 1776–1810, V: 9, fn 2

Louise, Queen of Prussia (1876), IX: 151

Louner, 19th century publisher in Paris, XI: 123,

Loustallot, G., 19th century French composer, IX: 1, 70

Louys, Jean (Jhan de Loys), 16th century Flemish composer, VI: 107, 108

Löw, Jos., 19th century German composer, IX: 166

Löwe, Johann Jacob, 1628–1703, German composer of dance music, VII: 168

Lozes, L., 19th century French composer, IX: 71

Lübeck, Hendrich, trumpeter and scribe, 16th century, II: 110

Lubert, ?, composer included in a 1874 English collection of band music, X: 114

Lubuissière, 17th century oboist and leader of Berlin court Hautboisten, III: 58

Lucas, Charles, 1808–1869, English composer, IX: 277

Lucca, 19th century publisher in Milano, XI: 117, 224, 298

Lucca, Francesco [dedication by Ponchielli], X: 234

Lucchini, P., 19th century Italian composer, X: 210

Luce, ?, 19th century French composer, IX: 1

Luce, E., 19th century French composer, IX: 71

Luce, L., 19th century French composer, IX: 1, 71

Lucii (Lucium, Lucius), Jacobi, 16th century publisher in Helmstdt, VI: 61, 67, 72

Lucino, 17th century Italian composer, III: 220

Luckhardt, 19th century German publisher, XI: 33, 55

Ludislaus, King of Hungary, 15th century, I: 214

Ludolf von Sachsen, Dominican monk, 14th century, I: 166

Ludovico Sforza, I: 235ff

Ludwig Friedrich, 1667–1718, Prince at Rudolstadt, supports for military music, IV: 59; V: 186

Ludwig I, IX: 145, 174, 178, 186

Ludwig II of Bavaria, V: 194

Ludwig III, Duke of Württemburg, reigning 1568–1593, II: 110, 193

Ludwig IX, of Hessen-Darmstadt, 1719–1790, composer of military marches, **IV:** 91ff; **VIII:** 333, (54) *Märsche* for band; **IX:** 143 [as composer]

Ludwig, composer included in a 1871 English collection of band music, **X:** 113

Ludwig, Eberhard, 'Herzog v. Wurtt.,' 17th century, **VII:** 138

Ludwig, F., 19th century German composer, **IX:** 167

Luetkemann (Lutkeman), Paul, 1597, German composer of dance music, **VII:** 169

Luigi Ferdinando Marsigli, 17th century Italian military leader, **III:** 107

Luigini, ?, 19th century Italian composer for bassoon and band, **X:** 210

Luigini, Joseph, 19th century French composer, **IX:** 71

Luigini, Laurent, 19th century French composer, **IX:** 71

Luitpold v. Bayern, 19th century, **IX:** 161

Lukas, Zdenek, 20th century Hungarian composer, **XII:** 203

Lull, Ramon, 1232–1315, Spanish philosopher, **I:** 221

Lully, Jean Baptiste, 1632–1687, French composer, **III:** 46ff, 144; **VII:** 14, 88ff, 91; **XII:** 1

Lumbye, Hans, 1810–1874, Danish composer, works for band, **X:** 63

Lundershause, 19th century oboist in the Duke of Sondershausen Harmonie, **V:** 185, fn. 2

Lupacchino, Bernardino, 1500–1555 Italian composer, **VI:** 30

Lupi, Johannes (Jean), 1506–1539, Franco-Flemish composer, **VI:** 27, 38, 39, 45, 49, 50, 63, 107, 108, 118, 119

Lupo, Thomas, 17th century composer, **VII:** 13, 20, 22, 23, 25, 26, 27, 61ff, 72

Luschwitz, ?, composer included in a 1890 English collection of band music, **X:** 116

Luschwitz, H., 19th century English composer, **IX:** 277

Luscomb, Fred, 19th century American composer for band, **X:** 265

Luther, Martin [19th century Luther Festival], **X:** 131

Luther, Martin, II: 92, 229, 232; **VI:** 73, 78; **VII:** 114

Luther, Martin, XII: 44

Lutkeman, Paul, 16th century composer, Wismar, **VI:** 71

Lutter, ?, *Parthia,* for Harmoniemusik, **VIII:** 212

Lutyens, Elisabeth, b. 1909, English composer, **XII:** 101

Lutz, Meyer, 19th century English composer, **IX:** 277

Luzaschi, composer in 1608 Venetia canzoni collection, **VII:** 208

Luzio, 17th century publisher in Helmstedt, **VII:** 170

Luzzaschi, Luzzascho, 1545–1607, Italian composer, **VI:** 97

Lwoff, Alexis Theodore, Russian composer of 1835 *Fantaisia militaire,* **V:** 86

Lyche, 20th century publisher in Kopenhagen, **XII:** 164

Lygate, John, 1370–1451, poet, **I:** 160

Lyttich, Johannes, 1609, German composer of dance music, **VII:** 169ff

Maanen, J. C., 19th century composer, **IX:** 277

Maanen, J., van, 19th century Dutch composer for band, **X:** 142

Maasz, Gerhard, b. 1906, German composer, **XII:** 158

Mabellini, ?, chairs Italian military band study in 1848, **V:** 89

Mabellini, Teodulo, 1817–1897, Italian composer, **IX:** 118; **X:** 210; **XI:** 301

Mabille, H., 19th century French composer, **IX:** 71

Mabire, E., 19th century French composer, **IX:** 71

MacDowell, Edward, 1860–1908, American, **XII:** 198

Machiavelli, Italian politician, writer, 1469–1527, **I:** 34, 45 [fn Nr. 63];

Machinger, 16th century German composer, **VI:** 62

Machtle, Adolf, 19th century German composer, **X:** 95

Machy, Thomas de, member in 1777 of the Hautbois et Musettes du Poitou, **IV:** 64, fn. 5

Mackenzie, Alexander, 1847–1935, English composer, **IX:** 277

Mackintosh, Robert, 1745–1807, Scottish, *Edinburgh March*, for Harmonie, **VIII:** 259

Maconchy, Elizabeth, b. 1907, English composer, **XII:** 158

Macque, Jean, 1555–1613 Dutch composer of ensemble music, **VII:** 213

Madame D., *Airs pour le clavecin*, unknown arranger for Harmoniemusik, **VIII:** 157

Madetoja, Leevi, 1887–1947, Finnish composer, **XII:** 101

Maelzel, V: 97ff

Maes, Paul, member of the Oudenaarde town band, 16th century, **II:** 169

Magaldi, Vito, 19th century Italian composer, **X:** 211

Magasin de l'imprimere chimique, 19th century publisher in Vienna, **XI:** 307, 318; **IX:** 227, 243; **XII:** 34, 37ff, 39

Magasin de musique, 18th and 19th century publisher in Paris, **VIII:** 49ff, 65, 269ff, 276ff; **XI:** 33, 150, 192

Magasin della Caes. Real priv., 19th century publisher in Vienna, **IX:** 227; **XII:** 40, 43

Magazino di Musica, 19th century publisher in Bronsvico, **XI:** 54

Magdelain, 16th century French composer, **VI:** 43, 49

Magini, Francesco, 18th century composer and leader of wind ensemble at Conservatory at Rome, **III:** 194; **VII:** 189

Magnan, G., 19th century French composer, **IX:** 71

Magnan, Louis, 19th century French composer, **IX:** 71

Magnard, Lucian Alberic, 1865–1914, French composer, **IX:** 71; **XII:** 158

Magni, 17th century publisher in Venetia, **VII:** 185ff, 189ff, 194, 198ff, 205ff

Magrini, Antonio, 19th century Italian composer for Harmoniemusik, **X:** 211

Maguet, H., 19th century French composer, **IX:** 71

Mahault, Antoine, 18th century Dutch/German composer, **XI:** 60 [biographical note]

Mahler, Gustav, 19th century composer, **XII:** 203, 210

Mahmut II, Sultan, **III:** 103

Mahon, John, 1749–1834 English, (2) *Marches*, ca. 1797, **VIII:** 259; **XI:** 139, 245

Mahr, Signr. German Baroque composer, **XII:** 3

Mahu, Stephen, 1480–1541, Austrian composer, **VI:** 62, 63, 64

Maier, L, German, fl. 1782, (2) *Parthias* for Harmoniemusik, **VIII:** 333

Maillard, ?, 19th century English composer for band, **X:** 142

Maillard, Jean, fl. 1538–1572, French composer, **VI:** 44, 48, 123

Maillart, L. A., 19th century composer, **IX:** 277

Maille, 16th century composer, **VI:** 45

Maillochaud, J. B., 19th century French composer, **IX:** 71

Mailly, A., 19th century French composer, **IX:** 72

Maimo, ?, conductor of Spanish band in the 1867 world competition in Paris, **V:** 115

Main, ?, 18th century German, *Sextour* for Harmoniemusik, **VIII:** 333

Mainberger, ?, Kapellmeister in Nürnberg in 1804, **V:** 113

Mainerio, Giorgio, 1530–1582, Italian composer, **VI:** 90

Mainzer, ?, 18th century German clarinetist & composer, court of the Margrave of Schwendt, **XI:** 60

Mairetet, E., 19th century French composer, **IX:** 72

Makoweczky, ?, 18th century hornist, **XI:** 170 [bibiographical note]

Malchow, F., 19th century German composer, **IX:** 167

Male, Zeghere van, 1504–1601, Bruges merchant, owner of ensemble works, **VI:** 106

Malerbi, Giuseppe, 1771–1849, Italian composer for band, teacher of Rossini, **X:** 211

Malézieux, L., 19th century French composer, **IX:** 72

Malherbe, Edmond, 1870–1963, French composer, **XII:** 101, 192

Malherbe, l'ainé, *Trois marches* arranged for Harmonie, **VIII:** 59

Malipiero, Gian Francesco, 1882–1914, Italian composer, **XII:** 158

Malipiero, Riccado, b. 1914, Italian composer, **XII:** 159

Mallorie, composer in 1600 English collection of ensemble music, **VII:** 20

Malsch, oboist in band of George IV, **V:** 203, fn. 10

Maltoni, Dominico, 1866–1937, Italian composer for band, **X:** 211

Malvezzi, Christofano, 1547–1599, Italian composer, **VI:** 82, 98

Malzat, Ignaz, 1757–1804, Austrin composer, **VIII:** 212 [(6) *Parthias* for Harmoniemusik]; **XI:** 6, 116, 126, 154, 236, 240, 277

Mameli, Goffredo, [dedication by Vessella], **X:** 252

Manchicourt, Pierre, 1510–1564, Franco-Flemish composer, **VI:** 27, 38, 49ff, 107ff, 118ff

Mancinelli, Domenico, 1775–1802, Italian composer, **XI:** 60, 208

Mancini, A., ?, 19th century French composer, **IX:** 72

Mancini, Francesco, 1672–1737, Italian composer, **XI:** 61

Mancinus, Thomas, 1550–1612, German composer, **VI:** 72

Mandanici, Placido, 1798–1852, Italian composer, **IX:** 119

Manente, Giuseppe, 1867–1941, Italian composer for band, **X:** 212

Manente, Liborio, 19th century Italian composer for band, **X:** 212

Manesson-Mallet, Alain, 1630–1706, French treatise on the military, **III:** 140

Manfredi, Giuseppe, 19th century civic band director in Rome, **V:** 155

Manfredini, Francesco, 1684–1762, Italian composer, **III:** 14

Manfredini, Francesco, 1688–1748, Italian composer, **XI:** 161

Manfrin, Giuseppe, 19th century Italian composer, **IX:** 118

Mangeant, ?, 19th century French composer, **IX:** 72

Mangold, Wilhelm, 1796–1875, Ger. composer, **IX:** 167

Manina, Fortunato, 19th century Italian composer, **IX:** 119

Mankell, 18th century composer in a Dutch collection of marches, **VIII:** 360

Mankels, ?, fl. 1800–1828, German composer, **IX:** 167

Mansion, Horace, 19th century French composer, **IX:** 73

Mansion, P., 19th century French composer, **IX:** 73

Manzoni, Alessandro, [dedication], **X:** 236

Marasco, Giuseppe, 1860–1930, Italian composer, **X:** 212

Marat, French politician, **IV:** 199, 203

Marcello di Capua, 1730–1799, *Furberia et Pontiglio*, arranged for Harmoniemusik, **VIII:** 59

Marcello, Alessandro, 1684–1750, Italian composer, **XI:** 116, 236

Marcello, Benedetto, 1686–1739, Italian composer, **XI:** 61

Marcelo, Alessandro, 1684–1750, Italian composer, **XII:** 3

Marchal, ?, 19th century French composer, **IX:** 73

Marchal, P. A., 18th century German composer in Paris, **XI:** 61

Marchand, 18th century publisher in Paris, **XI:** 90

Marchant, Stanley, 1883–1949, English, **XII:** 101

Marchesi, Pompeo, sculpturer [dedication], **X:** 199

Marchesi, Tommaso, 1773–1852, Italian composer, **IX:** 119

Marchetti, Luigi, b. 1848, 19th century Italian composer for band, **X:** 212

Marchetto of Padua, 14th century Italian theorist, **I:** 227

Marciliac, Pierre, trombonist, 1793 faculty of Paris Conservatoire, **IV:** 162

Marcillac, 19th century publisher in Genève, **VIII:** 147

Marcipor, slave aulos player, 2nd – 3rd century BC, **I:** 64

Marcus, ?, 15th century composer in Florence, **VI:** 12

Marcus, P., 19th century French composer, **IX:** 73

Marechal, Henri, 1842–1924, French composer, **XI:** 170

Marenzio, composer in 1600 dance collection published in Heidelberg, **VII:** 25, 180

Marescalchi, Luigi, 18th century (?) Italian composer, **XI:** 209

Maresch, Johann (Jan Mares), 1719–1794) early leader of Russian horn band, **IV:** 75ff

Margaret of Austria, 1480–1530, Regent of the Low Countries, **II:** 165, 167, 215

Margueritat, 19th century publisher in Paris, **IX:** 5

Maria Anna, daughter of Philip III of Spain, **III:** 61

Maria Antonietta [19th century dedication], **X:** 201, 202

Maria Theresia, Empress, 1717–1780, regarding her court winds in 1741, **III:** 63, 214

Maria-Amelia, Queen of France, 1818–1857, **V:** 145

Mariani, Giuseppe, 19th century Italian composer for band, **X:** 212

Maric, Ljubica, b. 1909, Yugoslavian composer, XII: 159

Marie Antoinette, V: 143

Marie Antoinette, wife to Louis XVI of France, IV: 139

Marie de Prusse, Princess, 19th century, IX: 170

Marie Esterházy, Prinzessin, *Ländler,* arr. by Triebensee for Harmoniemusik, VIII: 59

Marie Leszcynska of Poland, wife to Louis XV, III: 54

Marie of Bayern (1842), IX: 186

Marie von Hessen, 19th century Prinzessin, X: 110

Marie, 19th century composer for church music for choir and band, V: 215

Marie, E., 19th century French composer, IX: 73ff; X: 73ff

Marie-Louise d'Orléans, Queen of Belgium, IX: 259

Marie-Thérèse, b. 1638, queen consort of France, III: 46

Marin, E., 19th century French composer, IX: 74

Marini, Biagio, 1587–1663, Venice, Italian composer for wind church works, III: 194, 219ff; VII: 189, 205

Marino, Alessandro, 16th century composer, VI: 98

Marinuzzi, Gino, b. 1882, Italian composer, XII: 159

Marion, Claude, 19th century French composer, IX: 74

Marisck, Martin-Pierre-Joseph, 1848–1924, French composer, XII: 159

Markham, Gervase, 1568–1634, author of military treatise, III: 146ff

Marle, Nicolas de, 16th century composer, VI: 49

Marliani, M. A., 19th century English composer, IX: 277

Marolles, Michel, de, 1600–1681, French writer, III: 192

Maron, A., 19th century French composer, IX: 74

Maros, Rudolf, b. 1917, Hungarian composer, XII: 159

Marpurg, Friedrich, 1718–1795, III: 207, 211

Marquis of Buckingham, early 17th century English noble, III: 87

Marra, Vincenzo, 19th century Italian conductor, composer, IX:119

Marro, Tommaso, 19th century Italian composer Harmoniemusik, X: 213

Marsal, E., 19th century French composer, IX: 74

Marsand, Luigi, 19th century Italian composer, X: 213

Marsano, Luigi, 1769–1841, Italian composer, IX: 119

Marschalk, ?, 19th century composer, IX: 74, 143

Marschner, arranged for band, IX: 255

Marschner, Heinrich, 1795–1861, *Der Templer und die Jüdin,* arr. for Harmonie, VIII: 59

Marsick, Armand-Louis-Joseph, 1877–1959, French composer, XII: 159

Marteau, Henri, 1874–1934, French composer, IX: 167; XII: 101

Martelli, Bartolomeo, 19th century Italian composer, X: 213

Marti, Esteban, 19th century Italian composer, pupil of Massenet, X: 213

Martial, 1st century Roman poet, I: 61

Martin de La Moutte, L., 19th century French composer, IX: 75

Martin le Franc, 15th century French poet, **I**: 178

Martin y Solar ('Marini'), Vicente, 1754–1806, composer in Vienna, **IV**: 16, 41

Martin y Soler, Vicente, 1754–1806, works arranged for Harmoniemusik, **VIII**: 59 [*Una Cosa rara*]; 61 [*L'Abore di Diana, La scola de'maritati*]; 62 [*Die geberserte Eigensinnige, Andramaca*]

Martin, ?, 18th century composer, **XI**: 284 [work arranged]

Martin, Camille, 19th century French composer, **IX**: 74

Martin, ?, *Capricciosa* (opera), arranged for Harmoniemusik by Stumpf, **XII**: 53

Martin, Frank, b. 1890 Swiss composer, **XII**: 102, 159

Martin, H., 19th century English composer and bandmaster, **X**: 143

Martin, L., 19th century French composer, **IX**: 75

Martin, T., 19th century English composer for band, **X**: 143

Martin, The., 19th century French composer, **IX**: 74

Martinelli, Pietro, 19th century Italian composer for band, **X**: 213

Martini il Tedesco [née Johann Schwartzendorf], 1741–1816, composer, **IV**: 212

Martini, Jean Paul, 1741–1816, works arranged for Harmoniemusik, **VIII**: 62, 153, 154, 301

Martini, Johann (Martini el Tedesco), 1741–1816 (2) Revolutionary *Hymns*, **VIII**: 288

Martini, P. Giambattista, 18th century Italian composer, **XI**: 308

Martini, Padre, 18th century Italian composer, **XII**: 175

Martinides, Carlo, 1731–1794, German, *Parthia* for Harmoniemusik, **VIII**: 333

Martinn, Jacques, 1775–1836, French composer, **XI**: 61, 209

Martinu, Bohuslav, 1890–1959, Czech composer, **XII**: 102, 160

Martucci, Giuseppe, 1856–1909, Italian composer for winds, **X**: 213

Marty, Georges, 1860–1908, French composer, **XI**: 139

Marulli, Angelo, 19th century Italian composer, **IX**: 119

Marx, director of Prussian army music school, **IV**: 90

Marx, Karl, b. 1897, German composer, **XII**: 102, 160

Mary Lenom, widow of Clement Lenom of the Longy Club, **XII**: 193

Mary Tudor, Queen of England, 16th century, **II**: 33ff, 35 [list of wind player names in her court]

Mary, Queen of Scots, 16th century, **II**: 21, 73

Marzo, Simone, 19th century Italian composer, **X**: 213

Mascagni, 20th century French composer, **X**: 255 [*I Rantzau* and *Isabeau,* arranged for band by Vessella]; **XII**: 203

Maschek, Albin, 1804–1878, Czech composer, **IX**: 228

Maschek, Paul, Czech composer, 1761–1826, **V**: 102, 187; **VIII**: 142, as arranger of Weigl, *Die Tänzerin,* ballet, for Harmoniemusik; **IX**: 228ff; **XII**: 203

Maschek, Vincenc, 1755–1831, Bohenian composer, **IV**: 19, 22 fn. 10, 24; **V**: 201, 213; **IX**: 229ff; **XII**: 40

Maschera, ?, composer in 1608 Venetia canzoni collection, **VII**: 208

Maschera, Fiorenzo, 1540–1584, Italian (Brescia) composer, **VI**: 82, 98

Maslanka, David, 20th century, American composer, **XII**: 203

Mason, ?, composer in 17th century English pavan and galliard collection, **VII:** 20

Mason, Lowell, 1792–1872, American educator, on bands in Germany, **V:** 107

Masotti, 17th century publisher in Rome, **VII:** 200

Massa, Pietro, 18th century (?) Italian composer, **XI:** 209

Massaino, Tiburtio, 1550–1608, Italian composer, **II:** 245, **III:** 220; **VII:** 208

Massak, Franz, 19th century Austrian composer, arranger, **IX:** 233, 254

Massard, R., 19th century French composer, **IX:** 75

Massat, F., 19th century French composer, **IX:** 75

Massenet, 19th century French composer, **V:** 150; **XII:** 212, 218

Massenet, composer of works arranged for band, **X:** 255 [*Il Re di Lahore* and *Il Cid*, arranged for band by Vessella]

Masson du Breuil, ?, 19th century French composer, **IX:** 75

Massonneau. Louis, 1766–1848, German composer, **XI:** 116, 154, 170, 209, 240

Mastio, E., 19th century French composer, **IX:** 75

Masutto, Renzo, b. 1858, 19th century Italian composer for band, **X:** 214

Matacena, Sebastiano, 19th century Italian composer for band, **X:** 214

Matador, Jose, 19th century Spanish composer for band, **X:** 261

Matauschek, ?, 19th century Viennese abbé & composer, **XI:** 61

Matha, ?, 19th century French composer, **IX:** 75

Mathes (Matthes), Carl, Baroque oboist in court of Margrave of Brandenburg-Schwedt, **XI:** 116

Mathias, 16th century German composer, **VI:** 63, 64

Mathieu, Jean, serpent faculty of the 1792 Paris Conservatoire, **IV:** 156

Matiegka, W., (12) *Aufzüge* for brass ensemble and timpani, **VIII:** 213ff

Matous, ?, 19th century Austrian composer, **IX:** 233

Matouschek, performed Beethoven *Quintet* with Beethoven in 1798, **IV:** 32, fn. 67

Mattei, Stanislao, 1750–1825, Italian composer, **XI:** 61, 154; **XII:** 40

Mattel, Padre Stanislao, 19th century Italian composer, **XI:** 260

Matthäi, 17th century publisher in Freiberg, **VII:** 111

Mattheson, Johann, 1681–1764, German composer, writer on performance practice, **III:** 7, 59, 207; **VII:** 125; **XI:** 62, 209, 269; **XII:** 4

Matthias, Archduke, visits Brussels in 1578, **II:** 172

Matthison-Hansen, Hans, 1807–1890, German composer, **XI:** 170

Matthysz, 17th century publisher in Amsterdam, **VII:** 213

Mattiozzi, Pietro, 19th century civic band conductor in Florence, **V:** 157

Mattiozzi, Rodolfo, 1832–1875, Italian composer, **X:** 214

Mattiozzi, Rudolphe, 19th century German composer, **IX:** 167

Mauchen, W., 19th century French composer, **IX:** 75

Maurer, Ludwig, 1789–1878, German composer, **IX:** 168; **XI:** 139

Maurer, Ludwig, 1789–1878, works arranged for Harmoniemusik, **VIII:** 62, 152, 333

Mauser, ?, 18th century German, (2) *Parthia* for Harmoniemusik, **VIII:** 334

Maw, Nicholas, 20th century, American composer, **XII:** 203

Maximilian Franz, 1756–1801, the Elector of Bonn, **IV:** 51ff

Maximilian I of Bavaria, 17th century, **III:** 4

Maximilian I, 1459–1519, Emperor of the Holy Roman Empire, 16th century, **I:** 237, 258, 266, 269, 271ff; **II:** 18, 87, 191, 229; **VI:** 11

Maximilian I, IX: 187

Maximilian II, 1680–1726, [his military band], **III:** 125

Maximilian II, Emperor, reigning 1564–1576, **II:** 103

Maximilian II, IX: 187

Maximilian Josef, 19th century King of Bavaria, **V:** 12

Maximilian of Mexico, emperor [dedication], **X:** 53

Maximilian V, 19th century, **XI:** 310

Maximilian, Abt of Scheyern, **VII:** 131

Maximus, Valerius, 1st century AD Roman historian, **I:** 62

Mayer, ?, 19th century German composer, **IX:** 168

Mayer, 18th century composer in Olmütz Harmoniemusik collection, **IV:** 22, fn. 9

Mayer, Ambros, 18th century Swiss, *Stationes* for voices and Harmoniemusik, **VIII:** 373

Mayer, C. H., as arranger of Lindpainter, *Joko,* ballet for Harmoniemusik, **VIII:** 58

Maÿer, Franz, (5) *Parthias* for Harmoniemusik, **VIII:** 213

Mayer, I. M., 18th century German composer, **XI:** 209

Mayer, Rupert, 1646–1712, German composer of an instrumental *Lamento,* **VII:** 170

Mayeur, L., 19th century French composer, **IX:** 75

Mayone, Ascanio, 1603, Italian composer of canzoni, partitas, toccatas, **VII:** 205

Mayr, Johann Simon, 1763–1845, works arranged for Harmoniemusik, **VIII:** 62 [*Lodoiska*]; 63 [*Adelasia e Aleramo, Alonso e Cora, Ginevra di Scozia*]; 64 [*Ercole, Solitari*]; 150, works arranged by Triebensee for Harmoniemusik

Mayr, Johannes, 1763–1845, German composer, numerous works for band, **X:** 214ff; **XI:** 275

Mayr, Placidus, OSB, 18th century Swiss, Harmoniemusik, **VIII:** 373

Mayr, Simone, 1763–1845, Italian composer, **IX:** 119

Mayseder, unnamed work arranged by Starke for Harmoniemusik, **VIII:** 152

Mazzi, Luigi, 16th century Ferrara composer, **VI:** 91; **VII:** 205

Mazzinghi, Felice, 18th century Italian composer, **XI:** 62

Mazzinghi, Joseph, 1765–1844, Italian composer, **IX:** 277; **XI:** 116, 287

Mazzorin, ?, 18th century Italian, *Tantum Ergo* for voices and winds, **VIII:** 366

Mazzorin, Michele, 19th century Italian composer, **IX:** 119; **X:** 218 [church work for voices & winds]

McCoy, David, 20th century American composer, **XII:** 204

McEwen, John Blackwood, 1868–1948, Scottish composer, **XII:** 158

McGibbon, William, 1690–1756, Scottish composer, **XI:** 62, 210

McLean, J. M., English, (4) *Marches,* 1795, for Harmoniemusik, **VIII:** 260

McPhee, Colin, b. 1901, American composer, **XII:** 102, 161

Meares, 18th century publisher in London, **XI:** 92

Mechetti, 19th century publisher in Paris, **IX:** 85

Mechetti, 19th century publisher in Vienna, **VIII:** 35, 43, 149; **IX:** 240

Mecir, Frantisek, 18th century composer in Graf Pachta Harmonie Coll., **IV:** 22, fn. 10

Mecklenburg-Schwerin, duke of, **IV:** 57

Medau, 19th century publisher in Prag, **IX:** 245

Meder, Johann, 18th century German, (6) *Marches* for Harmoniemusik, **VIII:** 334

Mederitsch, Johann, 1752–1835, German composer, **VIII:** 213 [*Chor der Tempelherrn,* for SATB, winds]; **XI:** 62

Medici, Giuliano de, ca. 1492–1494, Florence, **VI:** 16

Mees, Joseph, 1777–1858, Belgium composer, **IX:** 260

Meester, Louis de, b. 1904, Belgian composer, **XII:** 161

Méhul, Étienne Nicolas, 1763–1817, French composer, **IV:** 162ff, 188, 196ff, 200ff, 204, 207ff, 211ff; **V:** 35 [arrangements by Wieprecht], 57, 197, 203; **VIII:** 288ff, original *Overture* for band, 7 works for voices and band; **X:** 21 [works for chorus & band]; **XII:** 204

Méhul, Etienne Nicolas, 1763–1817, as composer of operas arranged for Harmoniemusik, **VIII:** 64 [*Adrien, Cora, Euphrosine, Le jeune Henry*]; 65 [*Ariodant, L'Irato, Le Trésor suppose*]; 66 [*Joseph, Les deux Aveugles de Toledo*]; 67 [*Bion, Der Bauer, La Journée aux Aventures, Stratonice*]; 68 [*Der Temperamente*]; unidentified works, 153, 285

Méhul, Etienne, 18th century, French composer of a work arranged for band, **IX:** 180 (*La jeune Henri*]

Meier, ?, 19th century German composer, **IX:** 168

Meifred, Joseph, 1791–1867, German composer, **XI:** 170, 260

Meiland, Jakob, 1542–1577, German composer, **VI:** 72

Meilers, Wilfrid, b. 1914, English composer, **XII:** 160

Meinhardt, F., 19th century German composer, **IX:** 168

Meisaler, J., 19th century English composer, **IX:** 277

Meissler, Joseph, b. 1851, pseud. for Wm. M. Hutchinson, English composer, **X:** 143

Meissner, F. W., 19th century German composer, **IX:** 168, 180

Meissner, Filippo, 19th century composer, **XI:** 139

Meissonnier, 19th century publisher in Paris, **IX:** 41

Meister, G., 19th century French composer, **IX:** 75

Mejo, Guillaume, 19th century French composer of a *Variations* for band, **X:** 75; **XII:** 204

Mejo, W, 19th century German composer, **IX:** 168

Melartia, Erkki, 1857–1937, Finnish composer, **XII:** 161

Meldaert, Leonardo, 1550–1600, composer, **VI:** 65

Mele, Giovanni, b. 1701, Italian composer, **XI:** 62

Melegari, Andrea, 18th century (?) Italian composer, **XI:** 210

Mellers, Wilfrid, b. 1914, English composer, **XII:** 102

Meloni, Annibale, 1601, Italian composer of ensemble concerti, **VII:** 205

Melusin, Rudolf, 19th century Austrian composer, **IX:** 233

Melville, Sir James, courtier, hears Elizabeth I play keyboard, II: 36

Menander, Roman poet, 342–291 BC, I: 42

Mencken, H. L., 20th century American critic, XII: 199

Mendelssohn, Arnold, 1855–1933, German composer, IX: 168; XI: 116

Mendelssohn, Felix, 1809–1847, German composer, V: 5, 22, 35 [Wieprecht arr.], 81, 105, 114, 132ff, 150, 170, 174, 185, 190, 193; VIII: 68, *Overture zum Sommernachtstram*, arranged by C. H. Meyer for Harmoniemusik; IX: 168; XI: 116; XII: 204, 213, 198

Mendelssohn, Felix, 1809–1847, works arranged for band, IX: 198, 213

Mendieta, Geronimo de, author of study on music in New World church, II: 222

Menesini, Bartolomeo, 18th century (?) composer, XI: 62

Mengal, Martin, 1784–1851, German composer, XI: 170, 260, 279, 315

Mengel (Menzel) Georgio, ca. 1700, Weimar composer of 12-part sonata, VII: 170

Menghetti, Giuseppe, 1784–1806, Italian composer, *Tre Sinfonie* for band, X: 218

Mennesson, A., 19th century French composer, IX: 76

Mérat, Léon, 19th century French composer, IX: 76

Mercadane, Saverio, 1795–1870, Italian composer, IX: 119; X: 218

Mercadante, Saverio, 1795–1870, works arranged for Harmoniemusik, VIII: 68 [*Elisa e Claudio, Il Posto abbandonato*]; 69 [*Anacreonte in Samo, Donna Caritea*]; unidentified work, 150

Mercadantes, ?, chairs Italian military band study in 1865, V: 89

Mercier, Roger, 19th century French composer, IX: 76

Mercier, V., 19th century French composer, IX: 76

Mercker, Matthias, fl. 1600–1622, cornet player, composer of dance music, VII: 144, 166, 170

Mercy, Louis, d. 1751, French composer, XI: 62, 154

Mereaux, Jean, 1767–1838, French composer, XI: 62

Meric, Jean, clarinet faculty of the 1792 Paris Conservatoire, IV: 156

Mérigeault, Désireé, 19th century French composer, IX: 76

Merikanto, Frans Oskar, 1868–1924, Finnish composer, XII: 103, 161

Mering, ?, *Parthia* in C, for Harmoniemusik, VIII: 213

Mersenne, Marin, 1588–1648, French philosopher, composer, I: 287; II: 253, 262ff, III: 6ff, 9, 37, 133ff, 226; VII: 87, 93; XI: 269, 295

Mertens, Hardy, 20th century Dutch composer, XII: 204

Merula, Tarquinio, 1595–1655, Italian composer, III: 220

Merulo, Claudio, 1533–1604, Italian composer, II: 245; VI: 82, 91, 99; VII: 205ff, 208; X: 1

Merz, C., 19th century composer, IX: 142

Merz, Karl, 1836–1890, German composer, IX: 169

Merzdorf, A., 19th century German composer, X: 106

Meser, ?, 19th century publisher in Dresden, IX: 158

Mesnard, Auguste, French bassoonist, in New York in 1905, XII: 212

Messiaen, 20th century French composer, XII: 204

Messner, Joseph, b. 1893, Austrian composer, XII: 103

Methfessel, Albert, 1785–1869, German composer, X: 106

Métra, Olivier, 1830–1889, French composer, **IX:** 76; **X:** 75

Mettenleiter, Johann, 1812–1858, German composer, **IX:** 169

Metz, Theodore, 19th century American composer for band, **X:** 265

Metzdorff, F. G., 19th century German composer, **IX:** 169

Metzdorff, Richard, 19th century German composer, **IX:** 170

Metzger, Ambrosius, 1612, German composer of songs for voices or insts., **VII:** 170

Metzger, Georg, d. 1794, German flautist & composer, **XI:** 63, 210

Metzger, K., 18th century (?) German composer, **XI:** 63

Metzner Leblanc, 19th century publisher in Angers, **IX:** 13

Metzsch, Woff, trumpeter of Albert of Prussia, 16th century, **II:** 110

Meucci, Giuseppe, 18th century Swiss, *Messa* for male voices and winds, cello, **VIII:** 374

Meulemans, Arthur, b. 1884, Belgium composer, **XII:** 161

Meunier, Armand, 19th century French composer, **IX:** 76

Meurer, Maurice, 19th century French composer, **IX:** 76

Meurgey, L., 19th century French composer, conductor, Musique, 2e Reg. de Zouaues; Chavlier de la Legion d'Honneur, **IX:** 76

Meyer, ?, 19th century French composer, **IX:** 77

Meyer, ?, *Theresa et Claudio,* opera?, arranged by Richter for Harmoniemusik, **VIII:** 69

Meyer, 19th century publisher in Braunschweig, **XI:** 139

Meyer, C. H., as arranger for Harmoniemusik, **VIII:** 68

Meyer, Carl, b. 1772, 19th century German composer, **IX:** 170

Meyer, J., 19th century French composer, **IX:** 77

Meyer, leader of civic band in Dresden ('brother of the celebrated composer'), **V:** 187

Meyer, oboist, 19th century court at Rudolstadt, **V:** 186, fn. 8

Meyerbeer, Giacomo, 1791–1864, Italian composer in Berlin, **V:** 5, 22, 26, 28, 35, 73, 82, 86, 115, 120, 122, 148, 156, 190, 191, 205; **IX:** 170; **X:** 106; **XII:** 61ff, 204

Meyerbeer, Giacomo, 1791–1864, as composer of operas arranged for Harmoniemusik, **VIII:** 69 [*Il Crociato in Egitto, Les Hugeunots, Margherita d'Anjou, Robert-le-Diable*]; unidentified work, 151

Meyerbeer, Giacomo, 1791–1864, as composer of operas arranged for band, **X:** 105 [unidentified work arranged by Lindpainter]; 169 [Dinorah, unidentified arranger]; 232 [*Roberto il Diavolo,* arr. Ponchielli]; 235 [*Dinorah,* arr. Ponchielli]; 242 [Robert Le Diable, arr. Rosi]; 255 [*L'Africana, Il Perdono di Ploermal,* and *Gli Vgonotti,* arr. Vessella]; 107 [works arranged by Wieprecht]; **IX:** 130 [*Die Hügenotten & Robert der Teufel*]; 256 [*Huguenotten, Die Kreuzfahrt in Egypten*]; unidentified works, 166, 198

Meyn, 19th century publisher in Hambourg, **XII:** 45

Miaskovsky, Nikolai, 20th century Russian composer, **XII:** 204

Mica, Jan, 1746–1811, Moravian composer, **XI:** 63, 116, 230

Michael, ?, 18th century composer, **XI:** 210

Michael, David, 19th century American composer, **IX:** 138

Michael, Samuel, 1627, German composer of dance music, **VII:** 171

Michaëli, Jean, 19th century French composer, **IX:** 77

Michaelis, ?, 19th century English composer, **IX:** 277

Michalicka, ?, 19th century Austrian composer, **IX:** 233

Michel, ?, 19th century French composer, **IX:** 77

Michel, F., works arranged by Pleyel, for chamber winds, **VIII:** 103

Michel, Josef (pseud. for Michel Yost), 1754–1786, Fr. clarinetist & composer, **XI:** 139, 245

Michelangelo, 1475–1564, **II:** 121

Michiels, ?, late 19th century French composer, **X: 75**

Michl, Johann, bassoonist in 1801 Harmoniemusik of Prince Esterházy, **IV:** 31, fn. 57

Michl, Joseph, 1745–1815, German composer, **VIII:** 214 [*Polonaise* and church music for voices and winds]; **XI:** 154

Michon, (Mlle), French composer for Hautboisten, **VII:** 91

Mico, Richard, early 17th century English composer, **VII:** 27, 67ff

Micrio, Salvatore, 19th century Italian composer for band, **X:** 218

Miedt, Johann Christoph, 1698, 6-part *Passigaglia* for church, **VII:** 171

Migette, E., 19th century composer, **V:** 215; **IX:** 77

Miglio, Pietro, 19th century Italian composer for band, **X:** 218

Migliorini, ?, 19th century Italian composer for band, **X:** 219

Mignon, L., 19th century French composer, **IX:** 77

Migot, Georges, b. 1891, French composer, **XII:** 102 [biographical note], 160

Miguel, 19th century composer published in England, **IX:** 263

Miksichowsky, Antoni, Classical Period composer, **XII:** 40

Milan, Cornel de, 16th century composer, **VI:** 27, 108

Milanscoff, Arman, 19th century French composer, **IX:** 77

Milde, 19th century publisher in Kopenhagen, **XI:** 51

Milhaud, Darius, 20th century French composer, **XII:** 204

Mililotti, Giuseppe, 1828–1883, civic band conductor in Rome, **V:** 157; **X:** 219

Millars, Francis, 19th century English composer of works for band, **X:** 144ff

Miller, ?, 19th century French composer, **IX:** 77

Miller, ?, composer included in a 1881 English collection of band music, **X:** 115

Miller, Edward, 1735–1807, English composer, **XI:** 63

Miller, F. J., 18th century German composer, **XI:** 63

Miller, George John, Jr., 1853–1928, English composer for band, **X:** 146

Miller, George, 1826–1886, English composer for band, **X:** 146

Miller, M., 18th century, English, (12) *Military Marches*, for Harmoniemusik, **VIII:** 260

Millerau, 19th century publisher in Paris, **XI:** 122

Millescampa, Jules, 19th century French composer, **IX:** 77ff

Millet, 16th century composer, **VI:** 122

Millet, E., 19th century French composer, **IX:** 78

Milleville, Ferrarese, 1617, Italian composer of concerti, canzoni, sinfonia, **VII:** 206

Milliard, 16th century composer, **VI:** 49

Milling, ?, (2) *Parthias* for Harmoniemusik, **VIII**: 214

Milling, 18th century composer in Olmütz Harmoniemusik collection, **IV**: 22, fn. 9

Millingre, ?, 19th century French composer, **VIII**: 289 [*Suite pour la Harmonie*, 1794]; **IX**: 77,

Millon, E., 19th century French composer, **IX**: 78

Millot, Marius, 19th century French composer, **IX**: 78

Miltitz, ?, fl. 1800–1828, German composer, **IX**: 171

Milton, John, 1563–1647, composer of English ensemble music, **VII**: 69ff

Mimart, Auguste, 19th century French composer, arranger, **IX**: 78

Minasi, Antonio, d. 1870, Italian composer for band, **X**: 147

Mingozzi, Giuseppe, 19th century Italian composer, conductor National Guard Band of Rome, **X**: 219

Minguet e Irol, Pablo, d. 1801, Spanish author of a treatise on flute, **XI**: 63

Minichini, 20th century Italian band conductor, **XII**: 201

Minoja, Ambrogio, b. 1752, French, *March* and *Funeral symphony*, for band, **VIII**: 290

Miolan, Felix, oboe faculty of the 1792 Paris Conservatoire, **IV**: **157**

Mirabeau, 18th century French politician, **IV**: 168ff, 173, 203

Mirambeau, E., 19th century French composer, **IX**: 78

Mirouze, Marcel, 20th century French composer, **XII**: 103

Mischel, ?, 18th century composer, **XI**: 210

Mischke, L., 19th century German composer, **IX**: 171

Misik, Frantisek, 18th century Bohemian composer, **IV**: 22 fn. 10, 23; **VIII**: 214ff, (19) *Partitas* for Harmoniemusik

Missud, Jean, American military band collection ca. 1840, **IX**: 138

Mitchell, J., 19th century English composer for band, **X**: 148

Mitscha, François Adam, 1746–1811, French, *Pièces d'harmonie*, **VIII**: 290

Mittantier, 16th century composer, **VI**: 44, 49, 50

Mizler von Kolof, Lorenz, 1711–1778, **XI**: 63

Mme Duhan, 18th century publisher in Paris, **VIII**: 216ff

Modena, Francesco, 18th century publisher in Venice, **XI**: 60

Modena, Julio da, 1498–1561, composer, **II**: 244; **VI**: 92

Moderne, J., 16th century publisher in Lyon, **VI**: 46

Moellendort, General, **VIII**: 297ff, 301

Moeshinger, Albert, b. 1897, Swiss composer, **XII**: 161

Mohammed II, 1451–1481, **III**: 106

Mohaupt, Richard, 1904–1957, German composer, **XII**: 102

Mohler, Philipp, b. 1908, German composer, **XII**: 104, 161

Mohn, Jean-Baptiste-Victor, 19th century French composer, **XII**: 103

Mohr, Andreas, 19th century German composer, **IX**: 172

Mohr, Hermann, 1830–1896, German composer of works for band, **X**: 107

Mohr, Jean-Baptiste-Victor, 1823–1891, French composer and band leader, **V**: 81 fn 15; **IX**: 78; **XII**: 62ff

Mohr, Wilhelm, b. 1904, German composer, **XII:** 162

Molet, 16th century composer, **VI:** 123

Moliere ('de la Musique du Roy'), French composer for Hautboisten, **VII:** 91

Moliére (Jean-Baptiste Poquelin), 1622–1673, French playwright, **III:** 47; **IV:** 66

Molique, Wilhelm, 1802–1869, German composer, **XI:** 63

Moliter, S., 19th century composer at the Melk monastery, **XII:** 62

Molitor, Ingeninus, 1668, German composer of canzoni, **VII:** 171

Molke, Graf von, *Grossen Kurfuraten Reitermarsch* for band, **VIII:** 334

Möllendorf, early 19th century German composer, **V:** 26

Möller (Mollerus), Johann, 1610, German composer of dance music, **VII:** 171ff

Möller, author of a military treatise in 1672, **III:** 73

Möller, M., 19th century German composer, **IX:** 172

Mollo, 19th century publisher at Vienna, **XI:** 287

Mollo, T., [Artaria], 18th century publisher in Vienna, **VIII:** 209, 219

Molloy, J. L., 19th century English composer, **IX:** 277

Molnár, Antal, b. 1890, Hungarian composer, **XII:** 162

Molter, Johann, 1696–1765, German composer, **III:** 13ff, 17ff; **VII:** 125ff; **X:** 8; **XI:** 63, 117, 140, 154, 162, 170, 233

Momigny, 19th century publisher in Paris, **IX:** 112

Momigny, Lysias, 19th century Belgian composer, organiste de la Cathédrale d'Angouleme, **V:** 215; **IX:** 2, 79; **XII:** 63

Monbarin, E., 19th century French composer, **IX:** 79

Moncel, A., 19th century French composer, **IX:** 79

Monchii, 17th century Italian publisher, **VII:** 185

Monckton, Robert, 1726–1782, English, (2) *Minuets*, for Harmoniemusik, **VIII:** 260

Mondrik, ?, 18th century composer in Paris, **XI:** 64

Mondrone, Pasqual, 19th century Italian composer, *Capriccio sinfonico* for band, **X:** 219

Moneta, Giuseppe, 1754–1806, Italian composer, **X:** 38

Money, William, 19th century English composer for band, **X:** 148

Monge, Fernandez, 19th century French composer, **IX:**79

Monicard, G., 19th century French composer, **IX:** 79

Monier, F., 19th century French composer, **IX:** 79

Monina, Fortunato, 19th century Italian composer, **X:** 219

Moniuszko, Stanislaw, 1819–1872, *Halka*, opera, unknown arranger for Harmonie, **VIII:** 70

Monn, Georg, 1717–1750, German composer, **XI:** 64

Monn, Giovanni, *Musica turchese,* 1799, for small band, **VIII:** 215

Monnereau, J., 19th century French composer, **IX:** 79

Monnikendam, Marius, b. 1896, Dutch composer, **XII:** 104, 162

Mons, Thomas, ca. 1600, composer of English ensemble music, **VII:** 69

Monsigny, Pierre, 1729–1817, works arranged for Harmoniemusik, **VIII:** 70, 153, 154

Montalent, R., 19th century French composer, **IX:** 79

Montanari, Angelo, 19th century Italian composer for band, **X**: 219

Monte, Filippo de, 1521–1603, Flemish composer, **VI**: 84, 109

Monte, M. d'alto, composer in 1600 collection published in Heidelberg, **VII**: 180

Monte, P., composer in 1600 dance collection published in Heidelberg, **VII**: 180

Montebagnoli, Sante, 19th century Italian composer for Harmonie, **X**: 219

Montéclair, Michel, 1667–1737, French composer, **XI**: 64, 210

Monteilli, ?, 18th century Italian composer, **XI**: 232

Montesquieu, 1689–1755, French philosopher, **IV**: 168

Monteux, Pierre, 1875–1964, French conductor and composer, **XII**: 195

Monteverde, Claudio, 1567–1643, Italian composer for voices and winds, **III**: 74; **VII**: 206

Montferini, ?, 18th century Italian, (6) *Partien*, 1782, for Harmoniemusik, **VIII**: 366

Montgomery, William, 1811–1886, English composer for band, **X**: 148

Montorlo, Antonio, 18th century Italian, *Che Fernando* for 2 soprani, Harmoniemusik, **VIII**: 366

Monzani and Hill, 19th century publisher in London, **XI**: 44

Monzani, 18th and 19th century publisher in London, **XI**: 10, 76, 184, 210

Monzani, 18th century publisher in London, **VIII**: 261

Monzani, Tebaldo, 1762–1839, Instruction manuals for the flute, **XI**: 64

Moore, Douglas, b. 1893, American composer, **XII**: 162

Moore, Warwick, composer in a 1891 English collection of band music, **X**: 117

Moore, William, 19th century English composer for band, **X**: 148

Moornay, A., 19th century French composer, **IX**: 79

Moralt, Adam, 1741–1811, German composer, **XI**: 64

Morand, G., 19th century French composer, **IX**: 79

Morandi, Giovanni, 1777–1856, Italian composer, **IX**: 120

Moravetz, ?, *Parthia*, 1799, for Harmoniemusik, **VIII**: 216

Morawetz, Giovanni, 18th century composer in Vienna, **XI**: 230, 297

Moreau, Charles, 19th century French composer, **IX**: 80

Moreau, Léon, 1784–1841, French, **XII**: 195

Moreau, Simon, fl. 1553–1558, Franco-Flemish composer, **VI**: 123

Morel, Jean de, 1511–1581, French composer, **VI**: 44, 49, 108, 120

Morelli, A., 19th century English composer for band, **X**: 148

Morelly, L., 19th century German composer of works for band, **X**: 108

Morequx, ?, 19th century (?) French composer, **XI**: 162

Morera, Enrique, 1865–1942, Spanish composer, **XII**: 104

Moret, Victor, 19th century French composer, **IX**: 80

Moretti, Felice, 1791–1863 [see Davide da Bergamo], **X**: 193

Moretti, Niccolo, 19th century Italian composer, **IX**: 120

Morgan, ?, 17th century English composer, **XI**: 211

Morgan, T., 19th century English composer for band, **X**: 149

Morgerotti, Carlo, 18th century Italian composer, **XI**: 211

Morhange, Charles [see Alkan], **XII:** 193

Morhange, Emile, 19th century French composer, **IX:** 80

Morigi, Angelo, 18th century (?) Italian composer, **XI:** 240

Morillon, F., 19th century French composer, **IX:** 80

Morin, Jean-Baptiste, 1677–1754, French composer, **XI:** 255

Moritz of Saxony, Elector, **II:** 106 [instrument collection], 229

Moritz, Duke of Dresden, reigning 1541–1553, **II:** 113

Moritz, Edvard, b. 1891, German composer, **XII:** 162

Moritz, J. G., co-inventor of the tuba, **V:** 25

Moritz, Landgrave of Hessen-Kassel, 1572–1632, composer for wind consorts, **II:** 105ff; **VII:** 127, 143, 144, 181

Morlacchi, Francesco, 1784–1841, Italian composer for band, **X:** 220

Morlacchi, Francesco, 1784–1841, composer of works arranged for band, **VIII:** 70 [*Tebaldo e Isolina*, opera arr for Harmonie]; **X:** 255 [*Francesca da Rimini*, arranged for band by Vessella]

Morles, Cristóbal de, 1500–1553, Spanish composer, **VI:** 63

Morley, Thomas, 1557–1602, English composer, **II:** 151

Morley, Thomas, 1557–1603, composer of English ensemble music, **VII:** 11, 25, 69

Mornable, Antoine de, b. ca. 1512, composer, **VI:** 49

Morris, composer in repertoire of band of George IV, **V:** 201

Morris, Joseph, 18th century composer, **VIII:** 201, 222

Morris, Samuel, 19th century American composer for band, **X:** 265

Morse, Samuel, 19th century American composer, **IX:** 139

Mortaro, Antionio, fl. 1587–1610, Italian composer, **III:** 220; **VII:** 206

Morten, F., 19th century English composer, **IX:** 277

Mortier, 18th century publisher in Amsterdam, **VII:** 86

Mortiz, 18th century German prince, **VIII:** 297

Morton, Edward, 19th century American composer for band, **X:** 266

Morzin, Ferdinand Maximilian, 1693–1763, employer of Haydn, **IV:** 25ff

Moscheles, Ignaz (Ignazio), 1794–1870, German composer, **XI:** 64, 140, 170, 250, 287

Moscheles, J., 18th century German composer, **XI:** 155, 260

Moscheni, Francesco, 16th century publisher in Milano, **VI:** 99

Mosel, Giovanni, 18th century first violinist at Florence & composer, **XI:** 64

Mosel, M., 19th century composer in Vienna, **XI:** 308

Mosell, Egisto, 19th century Italian military band conductor, **V:** 89

Möser, ?, *Die Berg-Schotten*, arranged by Triebensee for Harmoniemusik, **VIII:** 70, 72

Moser, Franz, 1880–1930, 19th century Austrian composer, **IX:** 233; **XI:** 276, 297, 303, 323

Moser, Franz, 1880–1942, Austrian composer, **XII:** 104, 162

Moser, Rudolf, b. 1892, German composer, **XII:** 105

Mösner, ?, 19th century French composer, **IX:** 80

Mosonyi, Mihaly, 1815–1870, Hungarian composer, **XI:** 64

Mosto, composer in 1600 dance collection published in Heidelberg, **VII:** 180

Moths, ?, 19th century English composer, **IX:** 277

Mougeot, C., 19th century French composer, **IX:** 80

Mouquet, Jules, b. 1860–1946, French, **IX:** 80; **XII:** 195

Mourque, F., 19th century French composer, **IX:** 80

Moussard, A., 19th century French composer, **IX:** 80

Mouton, Jean, 1459–1522, French composer, **VI:** 27, 63, 118, 119

Moya, Christophorus, 1580 artist, **II:** 208

Moyzes, Mikulás, 1872–1944, Slovakian composer, **XII:** 105, 163

Mozart, Carl Thomas, 1784–1858, Austrian composer, **XI:** 287

Mozart, Constanza, IV: 14, 48ff

Mozart, Leopold, IX: 256

Mozart, Wolfgang Amadeus, 1756–1791, Austrian composer, **III:** 8, 103; **IV:** 8, 10ff, 15 [arranging his *Die Entführung aus dem Serail* for winds], 16ff, 38 [on the job offer from Liechtenstein], 41, 44ff, 53, 79; **V:** 23, 36 [arrangements by Wieprecht], 81, 103, 105ff, 12, 114, 133ff, 153, 168, 174, 179, 186ff, 201ff, 217; **VIII:** 216ff, (28) original, spurious works, arrangements for Harmoniemusik; **IX:** 64, 66 [work based on an unidentified theme], 117, 170; 284 [*Zauberflöte*, unknown arr. for 3 basset horns], 304 [unidentified opera movement, arr. Düring, J. C.]; 245

Mozart, Wolfgang, 1756 1791, as composer of operas arranged for Harmoniemusik, **VIII:** 70 [*Idomeneo*, also page 30]; 71 [*Der Schauspieldirektor, Die Entführung aus dem Serail*]; 72 [*Le Nozze di Figaro,* also page 30]; 73 [*Don Giovanni*]; 76 [*Cosi fan tutte*]; 77 [*La Clemenza di Tito,* also page 83]; 79 [*Die Zauberflöte*]; unidentified works, 82, 150, 151, 152, 154; **XII:** 40, 43, 49 [*Magic Flute* arr. Druschetzky for Harmoniemusik]; 53 [unidentified works arranged for Harmoniemusik by Stumpf]; 63 [*Magic flute*] arranged by Amand Polster]; 204, 213, 214, 215, 216, 221

Mozart, Wolfgang, 1756–1791, as composer of instrumental works arranged for Harmoniemusik, **VIII:** 82, 83 [3 Quartets], 84 [Sonate, K, 300/331, Symphony, K. 425, Symphony, K. 543]; unidentified instrumental works, 82, 83, 70, 201, 222, 266; **X:** 17

Mozart, Wolfgang, as composer of works arranged for band, **IX:**113 [*Ave verum*]; 177 [*Zauberflöte*]; 179 [*Clemenza di Tito*], 180 [*Don Juan*]; 181 [*Zauberflüte*]; 198 [*Don Juan, Idomeneo, Clemenza di Tito, Zauberflöte*]; 256 [*Don Juan, Symphony, K. 319, Symphony, K. 162b, Symphony, K. 161a*]; unidentified works arranged for band, 55, 141, 246, 249; **X:** 33 [anonymous march on a theme from *Marriage of Figaro*]; 95 [unidentified work in 1834 Hoftheater collection in Stuttgart]

Mozart, Wolfgang, as composer of a work arranged for orchestra, **X:** 18 [*Gran Partita*, K. 361, arranged for orchestra by F. Gleissner]

Mr. Charles, a Frenchman performing in London in the 1740s, **IV:** 105, fn. 2

Mrkvicka, Josef, Hungarian composer, **IX:** 233

Muck, Beda, 19th century Austrian composer, **IX:** 233

Mueller, ?, 18th century composer, **XI:** 211

Muffat, composer in Erlebach, mss collection of Hautboisten music, **VII:** 156

Muffat, Georg, 1653–1704, German composer, **III:** 17, 19

Mühling, ?, fl. 1800–1828, German composer, **IX:** 172

Mühling, Heinrich, 1786–1847, German composer, **XI:** 65, 211

Mulder, ?, 19th century French composer, **IX:** 81

Müllen, van der, 16th century composer, **VI:** 107

Müller, ?, 18th century composer in Vienna, **XI:** 288; **XI:** 65

Müller, ?, 19th century Austrian composer, **IX:** 233

Müller, ?, 19th century French composer, **IX:** 81

Müller, 16th century German composer, **VI:** 63

Müller, 17th century publisher in Jena, **VII:** 117

Müller, 17th century publisher in Magdeburg, **VII:** 136

Muller, 18th century publisher in Leipzig, **VIII:** 324

Müller, 19th century work arranged for band, **IX:** 199

Müller, 20th century publisher at Heidelberg, **XII:** 111, 125, 168

Müller, Adolph, Jr., 19th century German composer, **XI:** 65, 261

Müller, August Eberhard, 1767–1817, German composer, **VIII:** 334 [*Cantatine zu Familienfesten*, voices, Harmonie]; **XI:** 65, 211

Müller, August, 1767–1817, *Cantatine zu Familienfesten*, voices, Harmonie, **VIII: 334**

Müller, C. F., fl. 1800–1828, German composer, **IX:** 172

Müller, Christian, fl. 1800–1828, German composer, **IX:** 172

Müller, clarinetist, 19th century court at Rudolstadt, **V:** 186, fn. 8

Muller, Ernst (pseud. is Krasinksy), composer, **XI:** 54

Müller, F. D., 19th century German composer, **IX:** 172

Müller, F., 18th century German composer, **XI:** 66

Müller, Franz, bassoonist in the Joseph Schwarzenberg Harmonie, **IV:** 41, fn. 104

Müller, Frederic, 1786–1871, German composer, **IX:** 172

Muller, Georges, 1805–1898, German composer, **XII:** 63

Müller, Iwan, 1786–1854, German clarinetist & composer, **XI:** 140, 245

Müller, J., 19th century French composer, **IX:** 81

Müller, Johann Michael, 1683–1736, German composer for Hautboisten, **VII:** 127; **XI:** 141

Müller, Johann, German composer of music for Hautboisten in 1709, **III:** 9

Müller, P., 19th century German composer, **XI:** 318

Müller, Paul, b. 1898, German composer, **XII:** 163

Müller, *Tiroller Vastell*, 6 movements arranged for Harmonie, **VIII:** 86

Müller, W., 18th century German composer, **XI:** 242

Müller, W., 19th century work arranged for band, **IX:** 256

Müller, Walter, b. 1899, Czech composer, **XII:** 105

Müller, Wenzel, 1767–1835, Bohemian composer of works arranged for Harmoniemusik, **VIII:** 84 [*Das Sonnenfest der Braminen*]; 85 [*Betrüg durch Abergländen, Kaspar der Fagottist*]; 86 [*Die Jungfrauen, Die Schwestern von Prag*]; 87 [*Der Alte Uiberall u. N, Pizzichi*]; unidentified works, 224; **XII:** 46 [7 movements from unnamed work, arranged by Druschetzky]; 47

[*Kaspar der Fagottist*, 15 movements arr. Druschetzky for Harmoniemusik]; 48 [movements from *Kaspar der Fagottist*, arranged by Druschetzky for Harmoniemusik]; 51 [*Das Neue Sonntagskind*, arranged by Giuseppe Haydenreich, for Harmoniemusik]

Mülling, ?, *Parthia* in B♭ for Harmoniemusik, **VIII:** 224

Mullot, E., 19th century French composer, **IX:** 81ff

Munch, Charles, 19th century French composer, **XII:** 63, 204

Münchs, 19th century French composer, **IX:** 1, 70

Münchs, A., fl. 1800–1828, German composer, **IX:** 172

Münchs, Conrad, 19th century French composer, **IX:** 82

Mundy, William, 17th century English composer, **VII:** 22, 23, 25, 70

Muñez, Melleda, Jose, b. 1905, composer, **XII:** 164

Murat IV, Sultan, reign: 1623–1640, **III:** 108

Musard, ?, 19th century English composer for band, **X:** 149

Musgrave, Frank, 1833–1888, English composer for band, **X:** 149

Musik-Comptoir, 19th century publisher in Leipzig, **IX:** 188

Mussard, 18th century publisher in Paris, **XI:** 14

Muth, A., 19th century English composer, **IX:** 277

Muth, August, 19th century German composer, **X:** 108, 117

Müthel, Johann, 1728–1836, German composer, **XI:** 66, 252

Mutij, Heirs of, 17th century publisher in Rome, **VII:** 207

Mutor, Giuseppe, 19th century Italian composer for band, **X:** 220

Myslivecek, Josef, 1737–1781, Bohemian composer, **VIII:** 224ff [(3) *Partitas* for Harmoniemusik; **XI:** 233, 272

Naderman, 18th and 19th century publisher in Paris, **XI:** 20, 50, 108, 166, 205, 207

Naderman, F. J., b. 1780, celebrated harpist player in Prague, **XI:** 171

Nadermann, 18th century publisher of military music in Paris, **IV:** 71

Nadermann, 19th century publisher in Paris, **VIII:** 13ff, 26ff, 28, 34, 39, 57ff, 60, 100, 102, 122, 126, 147ff, 158ff, 244, 276ff

Nagel, Hans, 16th century trombonist and spy, **II:** 166, 167, 215

Nagel, hornist in 1780 for Count Palm in Vienna, **IV:** 42

Nägeli, 19th century publisher in Zürich, **VIII:** 50; **XI:** 217

Nageli, Hans, 1773–1836, German composer, **XI:** 66

Naghele, Hans, performer in court of Charles V, **II:** 90

Nagiller, Mathäus, 19th century Austrian composer, **IX:** 233

Naich, 16th century German composer, **VI:** 63

Naigueli, Jean George, 19th century publisher at Zuric, **XII:** 10

Nanisch, Franz, 18th century celebrated oboist, **XI:** 117 [biographical note]

Nanke, Sr., 19th century Austrian composer, **IX:** 234

Napi, Emanuele, 1767–1836, Italian composer, **X:** 38

Napier, London, 18th century publisher in London, **XI:** 7, 34, 74, 86, 98, 99, 221, 225

Napier, William, 18th century publisher in London, **VIII:** 248, 251

Napoleon III, XII: 69

Napoleon, I, 1769–1821, **IV:** 103, 138, 212ff, 216; **V:** 34, 57ff, 60, 77ff, 102, 113, 119, 138, 143, 182, 187, 195, 197ff; **VIII:** 183, 276, 290, 298; **IX:** 187, 228ff, 239, 263; **XII:** 60, 63, 203

Napoleon, III, of France, **V:** 334, 119; **IX:** 11, 56, 79; **X:** 226, 242

Napoli, Giovanni, 19th century Italian composer for band, **X:** 220

Napolitano, Pasquale, 19th century Italian composer for band, **X:** 220

Napp, Cyril, 1792–1867, leader of monastery Harmoniemusik, **V:** 217ff

Napravnik, ?, 19th century composer, **IX:** 277

Nardini, Pietro, 1722–1793, Italian composer, **XI** 66, 211

Nasolini, Sebastiano, 1768–1806, *Sesostri*, unknown arranger for Harmonie, **VIII:** 87

Natale, Luigi, 19th century Italian composer for band, **X:** 220

Nau, Francesco, 19th century Italian composer for Harmoniemusik, **X:** 220

Nau, Stephanus, ca. 1650, German composer of dances, **VII:** 172

Naudin, T., 19th century French composer, **IX:** 82

Naudot, ?, late Baroque French flautist at Paris & composer, **XI:** 67

Naudot, Jacques, d. 1762, Paris, French composer for Hautboisten, **VII:** 91

Naue, J. F., 19th century German composer, **V:** 212; **IX:** 142, 173

Naumann, Johann Gottlieb, 1741–1801, German composer for Frederick Wilhelm II, **IV:** 90; **VIII:** 334, (8) *Marches*, music for voices and band; **XII:** 47

Naumann, Johann Gottlieb, 1741–1801, as composer of works arranged for Harmoniemusik, **VIII:** 87

Nava, Gaetano, 1802–1875, Italian composer, **IX:** 120

Navieres, Charles de, 16th century court poet in Paris, **II:** 78

Navratil, Fran., 19th century Austrian composer, **IX:** 234

Navratil, Franz, 18th century Austrian in Olmütz Harmoniemusik coll., **IV:** 22, fn. 9

Naylor, Craig, 20th century American composer, **XII:** 204

Naylor, Edward, 1867–1934, English composer for band, **X:** 150

Nebuchadnezzar, Old Testament king, **I:** 19

Necchi, Francesco, 18th century Swiss, church music for voices and winds, **VIII:** 374

Necchi, Francesco, 19th century Italian composer, **X:** 220; **XI:** 117, 278

Necke, Herman, 19th century German composer, **IX:** 173

Neckham, Alexander, 13th century English Abbot, **I:** 116

Neel, 17th century publisher in London, **XI:** 49

Negri, Giacomo, 19th century Italian flautist & composer, **XI:** 211

Nehl, ?, composer included in a 1885 English collection of band music, **X:** 116

Nehr, Emile, 19th century French composer, **IX:** 82; **X:** 75

Neilson, Laurence, 18th century English composer **XI:** 212

Neithardt, as arranger for Harmoniemusik, **VIII:** 69, 133

Neithardt, August, 1793–1861, German composer, arranger, conductor, Kaiser Franz Grenadier Regiment, Berlin, **V:** 19ff, 105; **IX:** 142, 173

Nelson, Jacob, English timpanist at Vauxhall in 1785, **IV:** 131, note on pgs. 132–133

Neri, ?, 19th century *Fantasia on Otello* (Verdi), **X:** 221

Neri, Giuseppe, 19th century Italian composer for band, **X:** 221

Neri, Massimiliano, 1651, Italian composer for wind ensemble sonatas, **VII:** 190

Nerito, composer in 1600 dance collection published in Heidelberg, **VII:** 180

Nero, Roman Emperor, 1st century, performer as singer and bagpipe player, **I:** 65

Netrefa, Cölestin, 19th century Viennese trumpet professor, **V:** 52

Neubauer, early 19th century composer, **V:** 201

Neubauer, Franz, 1760–1795, Bohemian composer, KM for Princess of Schaumburg at Buckeburg, **XI:** 67 [biographical note], 183

Neubauer, Johann, 1649, German composer of dances, **VII:** 172

Neubauer, Johann, 18th century German composer, **XI:** 67, 141, 245

Neuber, publisher of 1549 in Nürnberg, **VI:** 62

Neubuer, ?, 18th century German composer, **XI:** 171

Neubuer, Franz Christoph, 1760–1795, (23) *Partitas* for Harmoniemusik, **VIII:** 224ff

Neufchâteau, François de, 18th century French politician, **IV:** 198

Neuhauser, ?, *Marcia Turcica,* 1797, for small band, **VIII:** 225

Neukäufler, F., ca. 1780–1843, German composer, **IX:** 173

Neukomm, Sigismund, 1778–1858, Austrian composer for choir and winds, **V:** 212; **IX:** 180, 234ff; **X:** 52

Neumann, ?, 19th century English composer, **IX:** 278

Neumann, Anton, 1740–1776, Kapellmeister at Kromeriz, **IV:** 22; **VIII:** 225, (7) original *Partitas* for Harmoniemusik

Neumann, Edmund, b. 1819, English composer for band, **X:** 150

Neumann, Frantisek, 1874–1929, Czech composer, **XII:** 105

Neumann, G., 18th century Dutch composer, **XI:** 67

Neumann, H., 19th century German composer, **IX:** 173

Neusser, ?, 18th century composer, **XI:** 67

Neutzerling, ?, composer included in a 1878 English collection of band music, **X:** 114

Nevaux, Henri, late 19th century French composer, **X:** 76

Nevi, Pio, orchestrater, 19th century, Italian, **X:** 193

Nevue, Alban, 19th century French composer, **IX:** 82

Newton, Ernest, 19th century English composer for band, **X:** 150

Nicaise, E., 19th century French composer, **IX:** 82

Niccolini, Bernardino, ca. 1465 his wedding music, **VI:** 14

Niccolini, Giuseppe, 1763–1842, works arranged for Harmoniemusik, **VIII:** 87, 88

Niccolò III of Ferrara, 1393–1441, **I:** 229

Nichelmann, Christoph, 1717–1762, German composer, **XI:** 212

Nicholaus, Kaiser of Russia, **V:** 26ff

Nicholls, George, 18th century English composer, **XI:** 212

Nicholson, Charles, 1795–1837, eminent English flautist & composer, **XI:** 67

Nickl, performed Beethoven Quintet with Beethoven in 1798, **IV:** 32, fn. 67

Nicola, Georg, 19th century Austrian composer, **IX:** 238

Nicolai, composer in Erlebach, mss collection of Hautboisten music, **VII:** 156

Nicolai, Friedrich, 1733–1811, German writer, **IV:** 97

Nicolai, Johann Gottlieb, 18th century German composer, **XI:** 68

Nicolai, Johann, 1629–1685, German composer, **XI:** 272

Nicolai, oboist, 19th century court of Mechlenburg-Schwerin, **V:** 185, fn. 4

Nicolai, Willem, 1829–1896, Dutch composer, **IX:** 125

Nicolas, ?, 19th century French composer, 82

Nicolas, Grand Duc de Russia, 19th century, **IX:** 217

Nicolas, M. L., 19th century conductor of the Trélonnaise civic band in France, **V:** 151

Nicolaus, Grossfürsten, 19th century composer, **IX:** 141

Nicolini, Giuseppe, 1762–1842, Italian composer, **V:** 148; **IX:** 166, 196 [arranged for band]; **X:** 221; **XI:** 288

Nicolo, ?, 19th century composer, **IX:** 141

Nicolo, *Du Médicin Turc,* arranged by Amand Vanderhagen, for small band, **XII:** 51

Nicosias, Charles, 19th century French composer, **IX:** 82

Nicou, G., 19th century French composer, **IX:** 82

Niedermayr, 17th century publisher in Regensburg, **VII:** 122

Niedermeyer, 19th century German composer, **IX:** 149

Niedt, Friedrich Erhardt, d. 1717, German composer, **XII:** 4

Niedt, Friedrich, 1674–1708, German composer for Hautboisten, **VII:** 127

Nielsen, Carl August, 1865–1931, Danish composer, **XII:** 164, 204

Niemann, Gallus, 17th century publisher in Leipzig, **VII:** 114ff

Niessel, Hte., 19th century student, Gymnase Musical Militaire, **IX:** 1

Nigg, Serge, b. 1924, French composer, **XII:** 105, 164

Nikl, Mathias, 18th century hornist in Esterházy and Vienna, **IV:** 36

Nini, Alessandro, 1805–1880, Italian composer, **X:** 221

Nipel, Francesco, 19th century Italian composer for band, **X:** 221

Nisle, Johann, b. 1780, German hornist & composer, **XI:** 171

Nitzchke, C., 19th century German composer, **IX:** 173

Niverd, Lucien, b. 1879, French composer, **XII:** 164

Niverd, M., 19th century French composer, **IX:** 82

Niverd, R., 19th century French composer, **IX:** 82

Niverd, V., 19th century French composer, **IX:** 83

Nivers, Guillaume, 1617–1714, French composer of fugues for Hautboisten, **VII:** 95

Nobili, Silvio, 19th century Italian composer for band, **X:** 221

Nocentini, Domenico, 1848–1924, Italian composer, **X:** 221

Nocentino, Domenico, 1848–1924, Italian composer, **IX:** 120

Noël Le Mire, A., 19th century French composer, **IX:** 83

Noël, 20th century publisher in Paris, **XII:** 148, 170

Noferi, Giovanni, 18th century Italian composer, **XI:** 212

Nopitsch, Christoph, 1758–1824, German composer, **VIII:** 334 [*Ariette,* 1790, voices and winds]; **XI:** 141

Norroy, H., 19th century French composer, **IX:** 83

North, Roger, 1651–1734, English biographer, **II:** 227, 262

Northbrooke, John Rev., 16th century, **II:** 163

Nosek, Wenzel, 19th century Austrian composer, **X:** 52

Nosvadba, J., 1824–1876, German composer, arranger, **IX:** 173, 198

Nott, W., 17th century London publisher, **VII:** 13

Noury, ?, 1835–1837, director of civic band school in Douai, **V:** 148

Nouvelle France chorale, 19th century publisher in Paris, **IX:** 6

Novácek, Rudolf, 1860–1929, Austrian composer, **IX:** 239

Novaro, Michele, 1818–1885, Italian composer, **X:** 222

Novello, 19th century publisher in London, **XI:** 305

Novello, Vincent, 1781–1861, travels in Germany, **V:** 42, 106, 133, 210, 216

Novorks, Leopold, 19th century composer, **XI:** 141

Novotni, ?, 19th century Austrian composer, **IX:** 239

Nowatny, as arranger for Harmoniemusik, **VIII:** 72ff, 74

Nowotny, A., 1845–1847, as arranger, **IX:** 256

Nudera, Vojtech, *Parthia* for Harmoniemusik, **VIII:** 226

Nudra, J., 19th century Austrian composer, **IX:** 239

Nuffel, Julius, 1883–1953, German composer, **XII:** 106

Nürnbergische Schembartbuch, lost music for Stadtpfeifers, **VII:** 107

Nutti, Attilio, 19th century Italian composer for band, **X:** 222

Nutti, Dante, 19th century Italian composer for band, **X:** 222

Oberndöffer, David, d. 1654, German composer of dances, **VII:** 172

Obersteiner, Johann, 19th century Austrian composer, **IX:** 239

Oberthür, Carl, 1819–1895, German composer, **X:** 108

Oboussier, Robert, 1900–1957, German composer, **XII:** 164

Obrecht, Jacob, 1457–1505, Dutch composer, choir master in Antwerp, 1509, **II:** 214; **VI:** 8, 106, 107, 108

Ochernal, ?, 19th century German composer, **IX:** 174

Ochs, Siegfried, 1858–1929, German composer of variations for band, **X:** 108; **XII:** 204

Odontium (Odontius), Matthaem, 1612, German composer, **VII:** 172

Oelschlegl, Alfred, 19th century English composer, **IX:** 278

Oertel, 19th century publisher in Berlin, **IX:** 192

Oertel, 19th century publisher in Hannover, **VIII:** 70; **IX:** 158, 161, 166, 172, 173, 175, 181, 182, 183; **X:** 108

Oestreich, Carl, 19th century German composer, **XI:** 68, 141, 171, 177, 255, 260, 283, 286, 288, 309, 316

Offenbach, 19th century French composer, **IX:** 19

Ogilby, John, observer of coronation of Charles II, **III:** 92

Ohr, Philipp von, 16th century German composer, **VI:** 75

Ohr, von, 17th century publisher in Hamburg, **VII:** 166

Okeover (Okar), John, d. 1664, composer of English ensemble music, **VII:** 20, 25, 70

Oldenburg, P. G., 19th century English composer, **IX:** 278

Olegio, Giovanni, 1608 Italian composer of 14-part canzona, **VII:** 209

Oliva, Franz, bassoonist in the Joseph Schwarzenberg Harmonie, **IV:** 41, fn. 104

Oliver, J. A., 18th century French composer (14) *divertissements militaires*, 1792, **VIII:** 260

Olivieri, Alessio, 19th century Italian composer for band, **X:** 222

Olsen, Carl Gustav, b. 1903, Danish composer, **XII:** 64

Olsen, Ole, 1850–1927, Norway composer, **IX:** 127

Omar Pacha, Sultan of Turkey, **X:** 263

Omega Music Edition, 20th century publisher in New York, **XII:** 180

Omer Fort, ?, 19th century French composer, conductor Musique au 7e Hussards, **IX:** 83

Onslow, Georges, 1784–1853, Anglo/French composer, **V:** 63; **IX:** 83; **XI:** 300, 318; **XII:** 195

Orafi, Pietro, fl. 1640–1652, Italian composer of concerti da chiesa, canzona, **VII:** 206

Ordonez, Carlo, 1734–1786, *Octet* for Harmonie and *Partitta Turc* for small band, **VIII:** 226

Orelly, J. de, 19th century French composer, **IX:** 83

Orgalesi, Tomaso, 19th century Italian composer for band, **X:** 222

Orlandi, ?, 19th century Italian composer for band, **X:** 222

Ormandy, Eugene, 20th century violinist and conductor, **XII:** 201

Orologio, Alessandre, 16th century Italian composer, **VI:** 61; **VII:** 163

Orrego-Salas, Juan, 20th century Chilian composer, **XII:** 204

Orsi, d', ?, 19th century Italian composer for band, **X:** 222

Oser, ?, composer included in a 1881 English collection of band music, **X:** 115

Osi, 19th century publisher in Paris, **XI:** 298

Oslislo, composer included in a 1889 English collection of band music, **X:** 116

Osswald, A., 19th century Austrian composer, arranger, **IX:** 239, 256

Osswald, as arranger for Harmoniemusik, **VIII:** 74, 80, 109, 157

Osterc, Slavko, 1895–1941, Slovakian composer, **XII:** 164

Österreich Bendesverlag, 20th century publisher in Vienna, **XII:** 95

Ostlere, May, 19th century English composer for band, **X:** 150

Ostreich, Carl, 19th century, German composer, **IX:** 174

Oswald, J., 18th and 19th century publisher in London, **XI:** 5, 18, 23,77, 193, 197, 201, 218, 219

Oswald, James, 1711–1768, English, **VIII:** 260 [(57) military marches, ca. 1765]; **XI:** 68

Othegraven, August von, 1864–1946, German composer, **XII:** 165

Othmayr, Casper, 1515–1553, German composer, **VI:** 60, 63, 64

Otterloo, Willem van, b. 1907, Dutch composer, **XII:** 106

Ottheinrich of Heidelbert, Elector, 16th century, **II:** 229

Öttingen-Wallerstein, Kraft Ernst von, Prince, 1748–1802, his court music, **IV:** 54

Ottl, Josef, 19th century Austrian (?) composer, **XI:** 141

Otto I, King of Greece, **IX:** 160, 186

Otto, Georg, 16th century teacher of Heinrich Schütz, **VI:** 73

Otto, Valerius, 1611, German composer of dances, **VII:** 3, 172

Ouvrard, René, 17th century French writer, **XII:** 1

Ovid, 1st century BC Roman poet, **I:** 59, 60, 61

Oxford University Press, 20th century publisher in London, **XII:** 139

Ozi, Étienne, 1754–1813, French bassoonists on faculty of the 1792 Paris Conservatoire, **IV:** 156, 160; **VIII:** 290ff, (35) original works for Harmoniemusik]; **XI:** 155 [biographical note], 248, 252

Ozi, as arranger for Harmoniemusik, **VIII:** 29, 65, 153, 159; **XII:** 50 [Panurge, by Grétry]; 51 [unidentified works by Sacchini and Champein]

Pacak, Frantisek, 19th century Austrian composer, **IX:** 239

Pachelbel, ?, composer in Erlebach, mss collection of Hautboisten music, **VII:** 156

Pachta, ?, *Sinfonia,* ca. 1780 for Harmoniemusik, **VIII:** 335

Pachta, Ernst Karl, Count, 1718–1803 of Citoliby, hires Wendt, **IV:** 37

Pachta, Johann Joseph Philipp, b. 1756, Graf of Prague, supported wind band, **IV:** 22ff

Pachty, Jana, Prag, (35) *Partitas* from the estate of Jana Pachty, for Harmonie, **VIII:** 167ff

Pacini, 19th century publisher in Paris, **VIII:** 15, 28, 29; **IX:** 21, 22, 46, 82, 89, 94, 105, 149

Pacini, G., arranged for band, **IX:** 166, 256

Pacini, Giovanni, 1796–1867, Italian composer, **IX:** 120 ; **X:** 223; **XI:** 68, 117, 141, 162, 172, 177, 256, 308

Pacini, Giovanni, 1796–1867, **VIII:** 88, 150 [works arranged for Harmoniemusik]

Padny, Josef, bassoonist in Harmoniemusik of Cardinal Batthyány, **IV:** 33, fn. 71

Padovano, Annibale, 1527–1575, Venetian composer, **II:** 246; **VI:** 85, 99

Padovano, Radino, 1607, Italian composer of canzoni, ricerars, **VII:** 207

Paer, Ferdinand, 1771–1816, French composer, **IX:** 83; **X:** 223

Paer, Ferdinando, 1771–1839, as composer of works arranged for Harmoniemmusik, **VIII:** 89 [*L'Intrigo amoroso, Il Principe di Taranto, La Virtù al Cimento*]; 90 [*Camilla, Il Morto vivo*]; 91 [*Achille*]; 92 [*Sargino, Una in bene et en male*]; 93 [*Agnesse di Fitz-Henry, Numa Pompillo*]; 94 [*Cantate per Il Natale, Der lustige Schuster, Die Wanderuten Komedianten, Le Maître de Chapelle, Oratorio del Passione, Tarsino*]; unidentified works, 94, 95, 152; **XII:** 51 [*Sargines,* unidentified arranger for Harmoniemusik, *Griselda,* arranged for Harmoniemusik by C. Ahl]; 53 [, *la Camilla* (opera) arr. Stumpf]; 54 [*Il morto vivo* (opera), arranged for Harmoniemusik by Stumpf]

Paer, Ferdinando, 1771–1839, as composer of works arranged for band, **IX:** 180 [*Angnese*]; 199 [*Der Lustige Schuster, Achilles, Sargino, Angnese*]; 256 [*Alexander von Indien*]; unidentified works arranged for band, 122, 141, 256

Paganelli, Carlo, work dedicated to in Milano in 1814, **X:** 242

Paganelli, Giovanni, 19th century Italian composer for band, **X:** 223

Pagani, Matteo, painter of Doge's Procession c. 1520 in Venice, **II:** 134

Paganini, 19th century composer, **IX:** 149; **X:** 245 [funeral march for]

Paganini, Ercole, 1770–1825, Italian composer, a work for Harmoniemusik, **X:** 223

Pagés, Paul, 19th century French composer, **IX:** 84

Pagni, 18th century publisher in Firenze, **XI:** 35

Pagnier, 16th century composer, **VI:** 43

Pagniez, Jacques, solfeggio faculty of the 1792 Paris Conservatoire, **IV:** 156

Pahissa, Jaime, b. 1880 Spanish composer, **XII:** 165

Paillard, Jean, horn faculty of the 1792 Paris Conservatoire, **IV:** 157

Paimparé, ?, 19th century French composer, **IX:** 84

Paiola, Antonio, 19th century, Italian orchestrater, **X:** 226

Paisa, ?, member of the 1775 Harmoniemusik of the Prince of Monaco, **IV:** 69

Paisible, James, late Baroque English composer, **III:** 98; **XI:** 212

Paisiello, Giovanni, 1740–1816, wind composer for Napoleon, **IV**: 22 fn. 9, 16; **V**: 197; **VIII**: 367, (16) original *Divertimenti*, 3 *Marches*, for Harmoniemusik; **IX**: 122, 246

Paisiello, Giovanni, 1740–1816, composer of works arranged for Harmoniemusik, **VIII**: 95 [*La Frascatana, Le finte Contessa*]; 96 [*Gli Astrologi immaginari, La finta Amante, La Nitteti, Le due Contesse*]; 97 [*Il Barbiere di Siviglia, Il Re Teodoro in Venezia, La Passione di Gesù Cristo, La Serva Padrona*]; 98 [*L'Olimpiade, La Gare generosa*]; 99 [*L'Amor contrastato* (known as *La Molinara*]; 100 [*Didone abbandonata, La Cantadina di Spinto, Nina* (also pages 154, 278), *Noces de Dorine, Proserpine*]; unidentified works 61, 101, 153; **XII**: 51 [unidentified opera arranged by unidentified arranger for Harmoniemusik, 52 [*Il Re Theodoro in Venezia*, arranged by Guering for Harmoniemusik]

Paisiello, Giovanni, 1740–1816, composer of works arranged for band, **X**: 38 [*Le Re Teodore*, arranged by Guering]; 175 [unidentified work arr. by Petronio Avoni]

Pajon, Henry Martial, member in 1768–77 of the Les Grands Hautbois, **IV**: 64, fn. 4

Palausi, ?, 19th century French composer, **IX**: 84

Palazzi, Ercolo, 19th century Italian composer (arr.?) for Harmoniemusik, **X**: 224

Palester, Roman, b. 1907, Polish composer, **XII**: 106

Paliard, Leon, 19th century French composer, **IX**: 84

Palladino, Giuseppe, 18th century Italian composer, **XI**: 212; **XII**: 41

Pallavincino, composer in 1613–1619 Tregian ensemble collection, **VII**: 23

Palm, Karl von, Count in Vienna, maintained Harmoniemusik in 1780, **IV**: 42

Palma, Silvestro, 1762–1834, works arranged for Harmoniemusik, **VIII**: 11, 101, 155

Palmer, Robert, b. 1915, American composer, **XII**: 165

Palmerini, Luigi, 1768–1842, Italian composer, church work with winds, **X**: 224

Palmieri, Giuseppe, 19th century Italian composer for band, **X**: 224

Paluselli, Stefan, 1748–1805, church music for voices and winds, *Partiten*, **VIII**: 367

Paminger, Leonard, 1495–1567, German composer, **VI**: 63, 64

Pangaldi, ?, 19th century Italian composer for band, **X**: 224

Panizza, Giacomo, 19th century Austrian composer, **IX**: 239

Panizza, Giovanni, *Sextet* for Harmoniemusik and flute, **VIII**: 226

Pannocchia, U., 19th century Italian composer for band, **X**: 224

Panoff, Peter, early 20th century German historian, **IV**: 107

Panoitschka, ?, 18th century German, *Parthia* for Harmoniemusik, **VIII**: 355

Panseron, ?, 19th century composer, **IX**: 149

Pansi, ?, 19th century Italian composer, *Messa* with small band, **X**: 224

Pantaleo, Luigi, 19th century Italian composer for band, **X**: 224

Panuccio, Domenico, 19th century Italian composer for band, **X**: 224

Panufnik, Tomasz, 1876–1951, Polish composer, **XII**: 165

Paocher, François, faculty of the 1792 Paris Conservatoire, **IV**: 157

Paoletti, 19th century publisher in Firenze, **IX**: 118

Papandopulo, Boris, b. 1906, Croatian composer, **XII**: 106, 165

Pâque, M. J. L. Désiré, 1867–1939, French composer, **XII**: 165

Parabsco, Girolamo, 1524–1577, Italian composer, **VI:** 94

Paradis, Maria Theresia, 1759–1824, for whom Mozart composed K. 456, **IV:** 47

Paravicini, ?, 19th century Italian composer for band, **X:** 225

Parcham, Andreas, d. 1730, Dutch (?)composer, **XI:** 68, 212

Parès, Gabriel, 19th century French composer, conductor, Musique de la Garde Républicaine, **IX:** 84; **X:** 76

Paris, Hte., 19th century French composer, **IX:** 84

Pariser, E., 19th century French composer, **IX:** 85

Parisi, Filippo, 19th century Italian composer, **X:** 225

Parisi, Vittorio, 19th century Italian composer for band, **X:** 225

Paris-Kerjullou, Charles, 19th century French composer, **IX:** 84

Parízek, Alexius, 19th century Czech composer, **IX:** 239

Parke, John, 1745–1829, 19th century English composer, **XI:** 117, 212

Parke, W. T., oboist, autobiography of 1783–1785, **IV:** 107ff, 134

Parke, William, 18th century English composer, **XI:** 69, 213

Parker, Henry, 1842–1917, English composer for band, **X:** 150

Parlow, A., composer included in a 1880 English collection, **X:** 115

Parlow, Albert, 1824–1888, Austrian composer, **IX:** 239; **X:** 53

Parma Raffaele, 19th century Italian composer, **XI:** 117

Parmegiani, Gaetano, 19th century Italian composer, *Sinfonia* for band, **X:** 225

Parmenio, 400–330 BC, Macedonian general, **I:** 11

Parrott, Ian, b. 1916, English composer, **XII:** 166

Parry, C. H., 1848–1918, 19th century English composer, **IX:** 278

Parry, John, 1776–1851, 19th century English composer, **IX:** 278; **XI:** 69, 213

Parsons, Robert, 1535–1572, English composer, **VI:** 32, 35

Parsons, Robert, 17th century English composer, **VII:** 18, 20, 22, 23, 25

Parzízek, Alexis, b. 1748, Polish, *Nocturne* for winds, **VIII:** 369

Pascal, ?, 19th century, French composer, **XII:** 196

Pasini, Timoteo, d. 1889, Italian composer, church works with band, **X:** 225

Pasque, 17th century publisher in Erfurt, **VII:** 112

Passereau, Pierre, 1509–1547, composer, **VI:** 39, 40

Paston, Edward, 1550–1630, English nobleman, sponsor of wind music, **VII:** 21ff

Paston, Johan, 1520–1576, Dutch composer, **VI:** 27

Paterson, ?, composer included in a 1888 English collection of band music, **X:** 116

Pathe-Marconi, 20th century publishers in Paris, **XII:** 94

Pathie, Rogier, French composer, **VI:** 108, 109, 110, 114, 118, 122

Patiomkin, Prince, of 18th century Russia, **IV:** 78

Patoni, Giovanni, 18th century Italian composer, **XI:** 213

Patrie, J., 19th century French composer, **IX:** 85

Pattarina, Maria, early 17th century, Italian composer 3-part Canzone, **VII:** 190

Paul III, Pope, 1468–1549, **II:** 123ff

Paulis, Johann, as arranger, Director, Military Music Club of Prague, **IX:** 255, 256

Paulmann, S. A., 19th century Austrian composer, **IX:** 240

Paulus, ?, conductor of the French *Garde Républicaine* band in 1867, **V:** 117

Pautrat, Pierre, 19th century French composer, **IX:** 85

Pavesi, Stefano, 1779–1850, *Ser Mercantonio*, arr. Sedlak for Harmoniemusik, **VIII:** 101

Pavlis, ?, composer included in a 1880 English collection of band music, **X:** 115

Pawlikowski, Franz, 19th century Austrian composer, **IX:** 240

Paxton, Stephen, 18th century English composer, **XI:** 155

Payen, Nicolas, 1512–1559, Franco-French composer, **VI:** 118

Payer, ?, 19th century (?) composer, **XI:** 248

Payer, Hieronymus, 19th century Austrian composer, **IX:** 174, 240; **XII:** 52

Payer, Hieronymus, as arranger of Gallenberg *Alfred der Grosse*, for band, **XII:** 49

Payer, Jerome, 1787–1845, French composer, **IX:** 85

Payer, unnamed work arranged by Sedlak for Harmoniemusik, **VIII:** 150

Pazdírek, 20th century publisher in Brünn, **XII:** 173

Peacham, Henry, author of treatise on manners in 1622, **III:** 89

Peacock, Stephen, 16th century Lord Mayor, London, **II:** 26

Pearsall, Robert, 1795–1856, Swiss composer, **IX:** 174

Peasible, ?, 17th century composer, published in London, **VII:** 14

Pechacek, Frantisek, 1763–1816, Czech (?) composer, **XI:** 141

Pechacek, Franz, 1793–1840, Czeck composer, **IX:** 240

Pechatschek, Franz, 1795–1840, Austrian, **XII:** 41

Pedro III, 1276–1285, **I:** 219

Pedrotti, Carlo, 1817–1892, Italian composer, *Fiorini Sinfonica* for band, **X:** 226

Peerson, (Pierson), Martin, d. 1650, composer of English ensemble music, **VII:** 20, 22, 70ff

Peeters, Emil, b. 1893, Dutch composer, **XII:** 166

Peeters, Flor, b. 1903, Belgian composer, **XII:** 166

Peetrino, Jacobo, composer, ca. 1583, **VI:** 124

Peile, F. O., 19th century English composer for band, **X:** 151

Peirot, J., 19th century French composer, **IX:** 85

Pejrinovsky, Martin, 19th century Austrian composer, **IX:** 240

Pelegrini, Vincenzo, Italian composer in 1617 collection of canzoni, **VII:** 204

Peletier, Jacques, 1517–1582, French composer, **VI:** 45, 63, 92

Pelkam, Segar van, leader of the London Waits, 16th century, **II:** 152

Pellarin, Giuseppe, 1815–1865, Venetian composer, **IX:** 120; **X:** 226 [church works with band]

Pellegrini, Giulo, 1800–1858, Italian composer for band, **X:** 226

Pembroke, Earl of, II: 46

Penderecki, Krzysztof, 20th century Polish composer, **XII:** 204

Pennauer, 19th century publisher in Vienna, **IX:** 165

Pensel, unnamed work arranged by Sedlak for Harmoniemusik, **VIII:** 150

Pentland, Barbara, b. 1912, Canadian composer, **XII:** 106

Peplow, ?, 19th century English composer, **IX:** 278

Pepping, Ernst, b. 1901, German composer, **XII:** 106, 166

Pepusch, Gottfried, 1692–1736 German oboist & composer, founder of Prussian army music school (1724), **III:** 8, 58ff, 128; **IV:** 90

Pepusch, Johann Christoph, 1667–1752, German composer of Hautboisten music, **III:** 58; **VII:** 18; **XI:** 19, 69, 162, 233

Pepys Samuel, 1633–1703, England diarist, **III:** 95, 109, 183

Peraut, ?, 18th century French composer, **XI:** 213

Percival, John, English, *Bristol Volunteer March*, 1799, for Harmoniemusik, **VIII:** 261

Pererl, Paul, composer in 1622 German collection of dance music, **VII:** 145

Pérez, Casas, 1873–1956, Spanish composer, **XII:** 107

Perez, Davide, 1711–1778, Italian composer, **XI:** 155

Peri, 17th century Italian composer, **III:** 74

Peri, Jacopo, 1561–1633, Sinfonia for 3 flutes in Euridice, **VII:** 190, 197

Pericles, Athens general, 495–429 BC, **I:** 40

Perilhou, Armand, d. 1936, French composer, **IX:** 85

Perin, L., 19th century French composer, **IX:** 85

Perlat, Lucien, 19th century French composer, **IX:** 85

Perolini, Eugenio, 1829–1907, Italian composer, **X:** 226

Peroni, Alessandro, 1874–1964, 19th century Italian composer for band, **X:** 227

Perosi, Lorenzo, 1872–1956, Italian composer, **XII:** 166

Perosi, Lorenzo, b. 1872, Italian composer, church works for band, **X:** 227

Perotta, G., 19th century Italian composer, *Emilia. Sinfonia* for band, **X:** 227

Perotti, ?, 19th century Italian composer for band, **X:** 227

Perron, Ed., 19th century composer, **V:** 215; **IX:** 85

Persaeus, Greek historian, 3rd century AD, **I:** 43

Perschl, as copyist, for Sedlak's Harmoniemusik arrangements, **VIII:** 5, 8, 9, 31, 34, 69, 104

Persuis, Louis, 1769–1819, his operas arranged for Harmoniemusik, **VIII:** 102 [*Estelle, Nina*]; 154 [*Der Zauberschlaf*]; **XII:** 52 [*Nina*, ballet, arranged for Harmoniemusik by Sedlak]

Pertl, Vincez, 19th century Austrian composer, **IX:** 240; **X:** 116

Pesch, ?, 19th century (?) composer, **XI:** 69

Pesch, 16th century German composer, **VI:** 64

Peschin, Gregor, 1500–1547, Slovak composer, **VI:** 62, 63

Pessard, E., 19th century French composer, **XII:** 213

Pessard, Emile, 1843–1917, French composer, **V:** 153; **IX:** 85; **X:** 76

Pessière, Émile, 19th century French composer, **IX:** 85

Peter the Great, 1682–1725, reorganizes Russian military music, **III:** 155

Peter, Christoph, 1626–1669, German composer for voices and winds, **III:** 215; **VII:** 127

Péter, Sylvestre, 19th century French composer, **IX:** 86

Peters, 19th and 20th century publisher in Leipzig, **VIII:** 6, 59, 83ff, 123ff, 130ff, 218; **IX:** 153, 170, 171, 184; **XII:** 147, 167

Peters' American *Saxhorn Journal*, ca. 1859, **IX:** 286

Petersen P., 18th century flautist & composer at Hamburg, **XI:** 69 [biographical note]

Petit, A., 19th century publisher in Paris, **VIII:** 4, 10, 19, 35, 67, 94, 107, 132; **IX:** 59, 97, 106, 109

Petit, Alexandre, 19th century French composer, **IX:** 86

Petit, Fernand, 19th century French composer, **IX:** 86

Petit, I., 19th century French composer, **IX:** 86

Petit, Oscar, 19th century French composer, **IX:** 86

Petrali, Giuliano, 19th century Italian composer, **IX:** 120

Petrali, Vincenzo, 1832–1889, 19th century Italian composer, works for band, **X:** 227

Petreius, Johann, 16th century publisher in Nürnberg, **VI:** 24, 62

Petrella, Errico, 1813–1877, Italian composer for band, **X:** 229

Petricek, ?, 19th century composer, **XI:** 141

Petridis, Petro, b. 1892, Greek composer, **XII:** 107

Petrucci, Ottaviano, 1501 Venice publisher of *Odhecaton*, **VI:** 16ff

Petrucci, Pietroiacomo, 1577 publisher in Perugia, **VI:** 98

Petrzelka, Vilém, b. 1889, Moravian composer, **XII:** 166

Petyrek, Felix, b. 1892, Austrian composer, **XII:** 107

Peu d'Argent, Martin, 16th century composer, **VI:** 84, 108

Peuerl, Paul, 1611, German composer of dances, **VII:** 172

Pez (Petz), Johann, 1664–1716, German composer, **VII:** 128, 156; **XI:** 69, 213, 237

Pezel, Johann, 1639–1694, German composer for civic music, **III:** 17, 165ff; **VII:** 128ff

Pezival, Caspar, bassoonist in 1801 Harmoniemusik of Prince Esterházy, **IV:** 31, fn. 57

Pezold, Christian, 1677–1733, German composer, **XI:** 69, 117, 172

Pezzini, ? 19th century civic band conductor in Rome in 1882, **V:** 158

Pezzoli, Antonio, 1842–1908, Italian composer for band, **X:** 230

Pezzoli, Giovanni, 1870–1934, Italian composer, church works with band, **X:** 230

Pezzoli, Giuseppe, 1831–1908, Italian composer, church works with band, **X:** 230

Pfaffe, Carl, Stadtpfeifer applicant in 1745, **III:** 160

Pfeffel, ?, 19th century German composer, **IX:** 174

Pfeffel, Johann Andrea, engraving of military band in Vienna in 1712, **III:** 125

Pfeffinger, Philip, 1765–1821, German composer, **XI:** 172

Pfeiffer, Francoise, 18th century composer, **XII:** 41

Pfeiffer, Franz Anton, 1754–1787, German composer, **XI:** 117, 155 [biographical note], 237, 240

Pfeiffer, Georges Jean, 1835–1908, German composer, **XI:** 177

Pfeiffer, Giovanni, 1697–1761, German composer for voices and winds, **VII:** 129; **XI:** 70, 117, 274

Pfeiffer, Johann, 19th century German composer, **X:** 108

Pfeiffer, M., 18th century composer in Vienna, **XI: 307**

Pfeilstücker, Nicolas, 18th century German, professor of clarinet & composer in Paris, **VIII:** 355 [(3) *Walzer* for military band]; **XI:** 142

Pfenninger, 18th century publisher at Wintherthur, **XI:** 259

Pffeiffer, A., 19th century (?) composer, **XI:** 69

Pfisterer, K. L., 19th century German composer, **IX:** 174

Phalèse, 17th century publisher in Antwerp, **VII:** 201ff

Phalèse, Pierre, 16th century French publisher in Leuven, **II:** 177; **VI:** 107ff, 110, 114, 124

Phébus, Gaston, 14th century nobleman, **I:** 77, 167, 210–211 [icons]

Philbert, flute player under Louis XIV, **III:** 39

Philbert, Philippe, 1650–1712, French composer, **XI:** 70

Phile, ?, 19th century American, **IX:** 139

Philiberti, ?, 19th century French composer, **IX:** 86

Philidor l'ainé André-Danican, 1726–1795, French composer, **XII:** 1

Philidor le Cadet, French composer for Hautboisten, **VII:** 92ff

Philidor, *12e suite des amusements militaries* arr. for Harmoniemusik, **VIII:** 102

Philidor, François André Danican, 1726–1795, French composer, *Ernelinde Princesse de Norvège*, opera, arr. Röser for Harmoniemusik, **VIII:** 102; **XI:** 118

Philidor, French court wind band collection, **VI:** 37

Philidor, Jacques Danican, 17th century member of the Les Grands Hautbois, **III:** 36

Philidor, Jacques, 1657–1708, Versailles, French composer for Hautboisten, **VII:** 92

Philidor, l'aisne, 1695 Hautboisten music, **VII:** 82ff, 91ff

Philidor, Michel Danican, 1683–1722, French composer, **XI:** 70

Philidor, Nicolas Danican, member in 1768 of the Les Grands Hautbois, **IV:** 64, fn. 4

Philidor, Pierre Dancan, 1681–1731, French composer, **XI:** 213

Philidor, ?, unnamed work arranged by Ozi, **VIII:** 153

Philidor, ?, **VII:** 88ff

Philippi, P., composer in 1621 German publication of English ens. music, **VII:** 23

Philip I of Spain, 1504–1506, Duke of Burgundy, **II:** 87ff

Philip II, 16th century, of Spain, **II:** 34, 73, 94ff [including his instrumental collection]

Philip III, 1270–1285, **I:** 208

Philip IV, 1285–1314, **I:** 208

Philip VI, 1328–1350, **I:** 209

Philip of Anjou, Baroque French noble, **III:** 151

Philip of Burgundy (son to Maximilian I), **I:** 140

Philip of Hesse, ca. 1534–1546, part-books, **VI:** 59

Philip the Bold, Duke of Burgundy, **I:** 103, 243

Philip the Fair, son to Maximilian I, **II:** 229

Philip the Good, Duke of Burgundy, 15th century, **I:** 103, 151, 161, 220 229, 245ff

Philip van Wilder, musician, court of Henry VIII, **II:** 23

Philippe, Edouard, 19th century French composer, **IX:** 86

Philippine Charlotte (sister to Frederick the Great), *Marches* for Harmonie, **VIII**: 324

Philipps von Hessen, 16th century, **II**: 104

Philipps, Arthur, ca. 1600, composer of English ensemble music, **VII**: 71

Philips, composer in 1600 English collection of ensemble music, **VII**: 20, 23, 25

Phillips, Lovell, 1816–1860, English composer for band, **X**: 151

Phillips, William, 18th century leader of the Litchfield militia band, **IV**: 106, fn. 4

Philostratus, Flavius, 3rd century AD biographer, **I**: 11

Phinot, Domenico, 1510–1556, French composer, **VI**: 27

Piazza, Felici, late 18th century Italian composer, **X**: 38

Piazza, Gaetano, 19th century (?) Italian composer, **XI**: 70, 27

Picchi, Giovanni, 1571–1643, Italian composer, **III**: 220, 219; **VII**: 191, 207

Picchianti, Luigi, 1786–1864, Italian composer, **X**: 231

Piccinni, Niccola, 1728–1800, Italian composer, **IV**: 209; **VIII**: 226 [*Raffael Marcia*, 1799, for Harmoniemusik]

Piccinni, Niccola, 1728–1800, as composer of works arranged for Harmoniemusik, **VIII**: 102 [*Alessandro nell'Indie, Didon*]; 103 [*Amazilia*]; unidentified works, 103, 153, 154

Picha, Frantisek, b. 1893, Czech composer, **XII**: 166

Pichl, Wenzel, 1741–1805, Czech composer in Graf Pachta Harmonie Coll., **IV**: 22, fn. 10; **VIII**: 226ff, (38) *Partitas* for Harmoniemusik; **XI**: 70, 142

Pichler, Carl, 19th century composer in Vienna, **XI**: 311

Pick, Henry, (1797), English composer for band, **X**: 32

Pick, Henry, English band composer, 1800–1805, **V**: 201; **IX**: 278

Piefke, ?, composer included in a 1871 English collection of band music, **X**: 113

Piefke, Gottfried, 1817–1884, German composer and military conductor, **V**: 19, 108; **IX**: 174; **X**: 109

Pierce, ?, 19th century English composer for band, **X**: 151

Pierkin, Lambert, 17th century Dutch composer of sonatas, **VII**: 214

Pierné, Gabriel, 1863–1937, French composer, **IX**: 86; **XII**: 64, 196, 204, 213, 214, 215

Pierne, Henri, 1863–1937 French composer of works for band, **X**: 76

Pieroni, Leopoldo, b. 1847, Italian composer for band, **X**: 231

Pierre, Constant, 18th century collector of French Revolution music, **VIII**: 273, 281

Pierson, 17th century composer, **VII**: 27, 28

Pieton, Loyset, fl. 1519–1545, French composer, **VI**: 118

Pietragrus, Gasparo, 1629, Italian composer concerti et canzoni Francese, **VII**: 207

Pietro di Boldrani, 14th century Treviso trumpet player, **I**: 124

Pigna, Alessandro, 19th century Italian composer, **X**: 232

Pignata, Pietro, 19th century Italian composer, **XI**: 118

Pignoni, 17th century publisher in Florence, **VII**: 211

Pijper, Willem, 1894–1947, Dutch composer, **XII**: 107, 167

Pilati, Mario, 1903–1938, Italian composer, **XII**: 107

Pilgrim von Puchheim, 1365–1396, Archbishop of Salzburg, **I**: 99

Pillevestre, J., 19th century French composer, **IX:** 86

Pilliard, T., 19th century French composer, conductor, 3e Rég. D'Inf. Le Marine, **IX:** 1

Pillotti, Giuseppe, 19th century Italian composer, **XI:** 126, 142

Pinault, V., 19th century French composer, **IX:** 87

Pinsuti, ?, 18th century (?) composer, **XI:** 245

Pio X, pope, **X:** 246

Pipelare, Matthaeus, 1450–1515, Flemish composer, **VI:** 9, 61

Pipelart, Maurice, 19th century French composer, **IX:** 87

Pique, Adolphe, 19th century French composer, **IX:** 87

Pirch, G., 18th century German, (7) *Märsche* for Harmoniemusik, **VIII:** 355

Pirch, George von, composer for Frederick the Great, **IV:** 89

Pirouelle, ?, 19th century French composer, **IX:** 87

Piroye, Charles, ca. 1712, French composer for Hautboisten, **VII:** 95

Pirro, 19th century publisher in Paris, **VIII:** 46

Pisapia, Raffaele, 19th century Italian composer for band, **X:** 232

Pisoni, composer in 1600 dance collection published in Heidelberg, **VII:** 180

Piticchio, Francesco, (22) works for Harmoniemusik, **VIII:** 355, 367

Pitot, ?, 19th century French composer, **IX:** 87

Pius IX, 1792–1878, pope, **V:** 157

Pius VII, 1742–1823, pope, his wind music, **V:** 195

Pivet, L., 19th century French composer, **IX:** 87

Pizzetti, Ildebrando, b. 1880, Italian composer, **XII:** 107

Pizzini, ?, *Das Mädchen von Frascati* arranged by Rosiniack for Harmoniemusik, **VIII:** 103

Pla (Plas), ?, 18th century Spanish brothers, **XI:** 118 [biographical note]

Pla, Jose, 1728–1762, French composer in London, **XI:** 213, 237

Plach, Giovanni, 18th century Italian composer, **XI:** 71

Plániczký, Joseph, composer of church music for voices and winds, **VII:** 173

Plato, 424–348 BC, **I:** 42

Platti, Giovanni, 1700–1763, Italian composer, **XI:** 71, 237

Plautus, Roman playwright, 254–184 BC, **I:** 64

Playford, H., 1695 publisher in London, **VII:** 14

Playford, J., 18th century publisher in London, **XI:** 16, 38, 188, 267

Pleyel, 19th century publisher in Paris, **VIII:** 10, 24ff, 26, 45, 47, 53, 65ff, 67, 75, 82, 252, 262, 276, 337, 341; **IX:** 17, 93, 97, 113; **XI:** 24, 48, 108, 140, 192, 299, 306

Pleyel, Ignaz, 1757–1830, Austrian/French composer, **IV:** 175; **V:** 97, 201; **VIII:** 222, 228ff, 252, (34) *Partitas* for Harmoniemusik; **IX:** 180; **X:** 18, 95; **XI:** 54, 71ff, 118, 142, 155, 214, 230, 248, 253, 277, 281, **XII:** 42 [15 works arranged for small band]

Pleyel, Ignaz, as composer of works arranged for Harmoniemusik, **VIII:** 103, 152, 153

Pliny, 1st century AD historian, **I:** 60

Pluchart, H., 19th century French composer, **IX:** 88

Plumet, composer, period of Louis XIV, **VII:** 83

Plutarch, 1st – 2nd AD historian, **I:** 10, 31, 36, 39, 40, 36, 56, 64

Pnaufnik, Tomasz, 1876–1951, Polish composer, **XII:** 106

Poessinger, Franz, 1767–1827, Austrian composer, **XI:** 72, 234, 269

Poggi, Augusto, 19th century Italian composer for band, **X:** 232

Poglietti, Alessandro, late 17th century composer in Vienna, **VII:** 4, 7

Pohl, G., 18th century composer, **XI:** 73

Pohle, David, 1620–1704, German composer of dances, **VII:** 129, 173

Poilhiot, 16th century composer, **VI:** 45

Pointz, composer in early 17th century English fantasias collection, **VII:** 20

Poisal, Johann, 1783–1865, German composer, **IX:** 174

Poisel, arr., *Harmonie für die königliche Tafelmusik,* a collection of Harmonie, **VIII:** 151

Poissl, Johann, 1783–1865, German composer, **V:** 186

Pokorny, Franz X., 1729–1794, Bohemian composer, **VIII:** 355 [*Partita,* and *Presto,* for Harmoniemusik]; **XI:** 118, 142, 172, 261

Poli, Giovanni, 19th century Italian composer, **IX:** 120

Polidori, Ortensio, 17th century Italian composer, **III:** 220; **VII:** 191; **XI:** 323

Polivka, Vladimir, 1896–1948, Czech composer, **XII:** 167

Pollet, 19th century publisher in Paris, **XI:** 243

Pollet, Jean, 18th century French composer, **XI:** 73

Polster, Amand, 19th century composer at Melk monastery, **XII:** 64

Polster, Amand, as arranger of Mozart, *Magic flute,* **XII:** 63

Polybius, 2nd century BC historian, **I:** 41, 42, 55, 57, 62

Polzelli, Antoine, 19th century composer, **XI:** 142

Ponchielli, Amilcare, 1834–1886, composer of many band works, **V:** 93, 156; **IX:** 120; **X:** 232ff; **XII:** 204, 219

Ponchielli, Amilcare, 1834–1886, composer of works arranged for band, **X:** 168 [*La Gioconda,* unidentified arranger]; 242 [*La Gioconda,* arranged by Rosi]; 176 [funeral music in honor of Ponchielli]

Pontecchi, Egisto, 19th century Italian composer, **X:** 239

Pontet, E., 19th century French composer, **IX:** 88

Pontico, Paolo Gottardo, 16th century publisher in Milano, **VI:** 103

Pontus de Tyard, French poet, 16th century, **II:** 10

Ponzo, Giuseppe, 18th century Italian composer, **XI:** 73

Poole, Geoff, 20th century American composer, **XII:** 204

Poot, Marcel, b. 1901, Dutch composer, **XII:** 167

Popp, Guglielmo, 19th century (?) Italian composer, **XI:** 73

Porpora, Nicola, 1686–1776, Italian composer of Hautboisten, **X:** 13

Porro, Pierro, 1759–1831, French composer, **XI:** 73

Porta, Bernardo, 1758–1829, Italian composer, **XI:** 270

Porta, Constanzo, 1528–1601, Padua, composer, **VI:** 104

Porter, composer in repertoire of band of George IV, **V:** 201

Porter, Quincy, b. 1897, America composer, **XII:** 108, 167

Porthaux, 19th century publisher in Paris, **XI:** 129, 243

Posch, Issak, 1611–1626, German composer of dances, **VII:** 145, 173

Poseidonius, Greek writer, 135–145 BC, **I:** 11

Posse, ?, 19th century English composer, **IX:** 278

Posse, ?, 19th century German composer, **X:** 109

Posselt, Franz, *Partitta* for Harmoniemusik, **VIII:** 230

Possenti, Pellegrino, 1628, Italian composer secular concerti, **VII:** 207

Poston, Elisabeth, b. 1905, English composer, **XII:** 167

Potot, Pierre, French oboist in Berlin in 1681, **III: 6**

Potter, Samuel, 19th century English composer for band, **X:** 151

Potter, Samuel, 19th century English composer, **IX:** 278

Pouplinière, Alexandre-Jean-Joseph Le Riche de La, 1693–1762, financier, **IV:** 65ff

Powell, Thomas, b. 1776, *Grand March and Rondo*, military, Harmoniemusik, **VIII:** 261

Prachensky, Johann, 18th century composer for military bands in Austria, **IV:** 96; **VIII:** 230, (2) *Parthias* for Harmoniemusik, (2) *Parthias* for small band

Praeger & Meier, 19th century publishers in Bremen, **XI:** 318

Praeger, Heinrich, 1783–1831, German composer, **XI:** 73, 270, 280

Praetorius, ?, 17th century composer, **VII:** 84

Praetorius, Abraham, 16th century German composer, **VI:** 74

Praetorius, B., in a 1620 Frankfurt collection, **VII:** 172

Praetorius, Christoph, 16th century German, composer, **VI:** 74ff

Praetorius, Hieronymus, 1560–1629, German composer of 6-part Fantasia, **VII:** 173

Praetorius, Michael, 1571–1621, German conductor, 1571–1621, important author on performance practice, **II:** 5, 205, 233ff, 244, 245, 251ff, **III:** 5, 13ff, 207; **IV:** 119; **VII:** 130, 145, 174; **X:** 9

Prager & Meier, 19th century publisher in Bremen, **XI:** 135

Pranzer, Giuseppe, 19th century (?), Italian composer, **XI:** 270, 281

Prati, Alessio, 1750–1788, Italian composer, **XI:** 73, 118, 155

Préau, ?, 19th century French composer, **IX:** 88

Preiner, Count, as rider in a horse ballet in 1667, **III:** 62

Preisser, M. A., 19th century French composer, **IX:** 88

Prendiville, Hayyr, 19th century American composer, **IX:** 139

Prentzl, ?, late 17th century, German composer for bsn, tpt sonata, **VII:** 130

Prescott, Caroline, 1843–1919, English composer for band, **X:** 151

Pressel, ?, composer included in a 1875 English collection of band music, **X:** 114

Preston & Son, 18th century publisher in London, **XI:** 15

Preston, 18th and 19th century publisher in London, **VIII:** 261; **IX:** 274; **XI:** 36, 47, 89, 98, 123, 150, 181, 182, 183, 197, 210, 212, 222, 228, 243

Preuss, 19th century publisher in Berlin, **IX:** 162

Prèvost, Charles, 19th century French composer, **IX:** 88

Preyz, J. des, 16th century publisher in Langres, **VI:** 56

Priess, ?, composer included in a 1880 English collection of band music, **X:** 115

Prince Eugene, 17th century, **VII:** 157

Prince Luitold v. Bayern, 19th century, **IX:** 161, 182, 185

Prince of Saxe-Meiningen, IX: 170

Prince of Wales, 1784, review of his wind band, **IV:** 73

Prince Wilhelm v. Schaumburg-Lippe, 19th century, **IX:** 247

Princiaux, fils, 19th century French composer, **IX:** 88

Princiaux, J., 19th century French composer, **IX:** 88

Prinner (Prumer) Johann Jacob, late 17th century composer, **VII:** 7

Prinster, Anton, hornist in 1801 Harmoniemusik of Prince Esterházy, **IV:** 31, fn. 57

Prinster, Michael, hornist in 1801 Harmoniemusik of Prince Esterházy, **IV:** 31, fn. 57

Printemps, J.-J., conductor of Lille civic band in 1817, **V:** 148

Prioli, Ioannis, 1618, Italian composer of canzoni and 8-part sonatas, **VII:** 143, 207

Pritchard, ?, 19th century English composer, **IX:** 278

Probst, 19th century publisher in Leipzig, **IX:** 172; **XI:** 39, 199, 283

Proch, Heinrich, 1809–1878, Austrian composer, **IX:** 240; **XI:** 316

Procházka, Leopold, bassoonist in the Joseph Schwarzenberg Harmonie, **IV:** 41, fn. 104

Procksch, ?, clarinetist for La Pouplinière, 1763, **IV:** 68, fn. 26

Proksch, Joseph, 1794–1864, German composer, **XI:** 142

Proksch, Robert, 19th century German composer, **IX:** 175

Prost, Jules, 19th century French composer, **IX:** 89

Proto (Prota), Tommaso, 18th century Italian composer, **XI:** 73, 215

Prout, Edwin, 19th century English composer, **IX:** 278

Provent, C., 19th century French composer, **IX:** 89

Provesi, Ferdinando, 19th century Italian composer, *Dies Irae,* voices and band, **X:** 239

Prowo, Pierre, 1697–1757, German composer Hautboisten, **III:** 18; **VII:** 130ff; **XII:** 2

Prudhomme, Marius, 19th century French composer, **IX:** 89

Prunier, Edoward, 19th century French composer, **IX:** 89

Pryor, Arthur, 20th century trombonist and conductor, **XII:** 201

Puccini, Domenico, 1771–1815, Italian composer, church work with band, **X:** 239

Puccini, Giacomo, 1858–1924, Italian composer, **IX:** 121; **X:** 239 [church works with band]

Puccini, Michele, 1813–1864, Italian composer, **XI:** 283, 301

Puccini, works arranged for band by Vessella, **X:** 255 [*La Boheme, Manon Lescaut*]

Puchot, L., 19th century French composer, **IX:** 89

Pucolas, ?, 18th century composer, **XI:** 215

Pugnani, Gaetano, 1731–1798, Italian composer for Military band, **IV:** 103, fn. 1

Pugni, Cesare, 1802–1870, Italian composer, **X:** 239; **XI:** 231

Pujol, Francisco, 1878–1945, composer, **XII:** 167

Pujolas, ?, French composer, numerous military marches for small band, **VIII:** 290ff

Pujolas, J., 18th century composer, **XI:** 215

Puliti, Gabriello, 1624, Italian composer, solo cornetto part for 13 works, **VII:** 191

Pumm, Johann, 1758–1760, court horn player in Olmütz, **IV:** 21

Punto, Giovanni, pseud., see Johann Stich

Purcbl, Joseph, 1768–1838, Austrian composer, **V:** 183, fn 21

Purcell, Daniel, 1664–1717, English composer, **XI:** 74, 162, 215

Purcell, Henry, 1659–1695, English composer, music for wind band, **III:** 98; **VII:** 71, 18ff; **XI:** 185 [dedication by John Blow]

Purebl, Joseph, 1768–1838, Austrian composer, arranger, **VIII:** 73; **IX:** 240ff, 256

Pureur, Chrétien, church trumpeter in Ieper in 1618, **III:** 200

Puschman, Joseph, 1738–1794, composer of Harmonie music, **IV:** 22 fn. 9, 59; **VIII:** 231ff, (7) *Parthias Turika*, ca. 1800, for Harmoniemusik

Puschmann, Giuseppe, 18th century composer in Vienna, **VIII:** 221 [see Mozart, K. C. 17.01]; **XI:** 305

Pustet, 19th century publisher in Regensburg, **IX:** 152

Pütz, Pierre, 19th century French composer, **IX:** 89

Puyau, G., 19th century French composer, **IX:** 89

Puzzi, Giovanni, 1792–1876, established quintet concerts in London in 1817, **V:** 161

PWM, 20th century publisher in Krakau, **XII:** 180

Pythagoras, 6th century BC philosopher, **I:** 29; **XII:** 91

Pythochares, ancient Greek aulos player, **I:** 40

Quagliati, Paulo, 1555–1628, Italian composer, **II:** 245, **III:** 220; **VII:** 207

Quanten, Chevalier, 18th century composer, **XI:** 74

Quantz, Johann, 1697–1773, German composer, flutist and military leader under Frederick the Great, **V:** 26, fn. 91; **X:** 9; **XI:** 74ff, 118, 215, 240, 270

Quattordici, Domenico, 1710–1740, Italian composer, **XI:** 76

Queen Anne, 1702–1727, of England, **III:** 99

Queen of Bavaria, 1827, **IX:** 154

Queen Victoria, IX: 263

Quef, Charles, 1873–1931, French composer, **XII:** 167

Queisser, famous 19th century trombonist in Leipzig, **V:** 131, fn. 8

Quentin, Alfred, 19th century French composer, **IX:** 89

Quentin, Berin, d. 1770, French composer, **XI:** 76

Queralt, Francisco, 1740–1825, Italian composer, **XI:** 76

Quilici, Domenico, 19th century Italian composer, **IX:** 121; **XI:** 289, 308

Quirici, Giovanni, 19th century Italian composer, **IX:** 121

R. O., 17th century French music critic, **XII:** 1

Rabboni, Giuseppe, 1800–1856, Italian composer, **XI:** 216

Rabe, 16th century German composer, **VI:** 65

Raben, Georg, 16th century publisher in Frankfurt, **VI:** 75

Rabitti-Sangiorgio, Giovanni, 1797–1844, Italian composer, **X:** 239

Racca, Antonio, 18th century (?) Italian composer, **XI:** 216

Racek, Fritz, b. 1911, Czech composer, **XII:** 108

Radicati, Felice, 19th century composer, **XI:** 142

Radino, Giovanni, d. 1607, Italian composer, **II:** 245, **III:** 220

Radino, Giulio, 1607, Italian composer, concerti for voices and insts., **VII:** 208

Rafael, Fr., 19th century Austrian composer, **IX:** 241

Rafelengius, 17th century publisher in Leiden, **VII:** 214

Raff, Joachim, 1822–1882, German composer of a *Sinfonietta* for winds, **X:** 109

Raff, Joseph, 1822–1882, German composer, **IX:** 175, 227 [as orchestrator]

Raffael, composer of an unidentified march arranged by an unidentified arranger, **XII:** 45

Raffara, J., 19th century French composer, **IX:** 1, 89

Rahere, English minstrel under Henry I, 1100–1135, **I:** 183

Rahter, 20th century publisher in Leipzig, **XII:** 176

Rahtgeben, Jacob, 17th century German composer, **III:** 215

Raimondi, 19th century composer, **V:** 201

Raimondi, Giovanni, 19th century Italian composer for Harmoniemusik, **X:** 240

Raimondi, Ignazio, 1737–1813, Italian, *Six grand marches,* for band, **VIII:** 261; **XI:** 76

Rajhrad, as arranger of Mozart, *Quintet,* K. 386c/407 for Harmoniemusik, **VIII:** 83

Rakow, Nikolai, b. 1908, Russian composer, **XII:** 108

Ramagini, Domenico, 19th century Italian composer, *Messe brieve* with band, **X:** 240

Ramain, J., 19th century French composer, **XII:** 64

Rambaldi, Francesco, 16th century Italian composer, **VI:** 106

Rambelli, Dario, 19th century Italian composer for band, **X:** 240

Rameau, Jean-Philippe, 1683–1764, French composer, **IV:** 65ff

Ramin, ?, fl. ca. 1800–1828, French composer, **IX:** 89

Rampezzotti, E., 19th century Italian composer for band, **X:** 240

Rampini, Domenico, d. 1816, Italian, *Kyrie* for voices and 12 winds, **VIII:** 367

Ramsdell, Eugene, 19th century American composer for band, **X:** 266

Randall, 18th century publisher in London, **XI:** 5, 68

Randall, William, ca. 1600, composer of English ensemble music, **VII:** 71

Randhartinger, Benedict, 1802–1893, Austrian composer, **IX:** 241

Ranish, John, 18th century English composer, **XI:** 76

Ranki, Gyorgy, b. 1907, Hungarian composer, **XII:** 168

Rankine, T. B., 19th century American composer for band, **X:** 266

Raphael, Gunter, 1903–1960, German composer, **XII:** 168

Rasse, François, 1873–1955, French composer, **XII:** 108

Rastrelli, Joseph, 1799–1842, German composer, **IX:** 175

Rathaus, Karol, 1895–1954, Hungarian composer, **XII:** 108, 168

Rathe, ?, 18th century celebrated clarinetist & composer in Paris, **XI:** 142, 216

Rathgeber, Johann, 1682–1750, German composer for voices and winds, **VII:** 131

Rathgen, 'Siciliano,' unknown arranger for Harmoniemusik, **VIII:** 301

Rathgen, A., English, (7) *Sonatas,* (6) *Military Divertimentos* for Harmonie, **VIII:** 261

Ratti, Leo., as arranger for Harmoniemusik, **VIII:** 64

Ratzenberger, Th., 19th century German composer, **IX:** 175

Rauchenecker, Georges, 19th century French composer, **IX:** 89

Rault, Felix, 18th century celebrated French flautist and composer, **XI:** 76, 216, 272

Rauscher, 18th century composer in a Dutch collection of marches, **VIII:** 381

Rauski, Joseph, 19th century French composer, **IX:** 90

Rauverij (1608), Venice publisher, **III:** 220

Raux, Jules, 19th century French composer, **IX:** 90

Rava, Gennaro, d. 1779, Italian composer, **XI:** 77

Ravel, Sebastiano, 16th century Italian composer, **VI:** 99

Ravenscroft, Thomas, ca. 1570–1635, English composer, **VII:** 26, 72

Raveri (Rauerij), Alessandro, 17th century Venetia publisher, **VII:** 194, 208

Ravizza, F., 19th century French composer, **IX:** 90

Rawlings, A. W. 19th century composer [see Florence Fare]

Rawlings, J. A., English, *Grand Military March,* 1780, for Harmoniemusik, **VIII:** 261

Rayder, J., 19th century American composer for band, **X:** 266

Raynaud, ?, 19th century French composer, **IX:** 90

Reali, ?, Italian, Maestro del concerto di Porto S. Giorgio, **XII:** 64

Reali, Carlo, 19th century Italian composer for band, **X:** 240

Reali, Dante, 19th century Italian composer for band, **X:** 241

Reali, M., 18th century (?) Italian composer, **XI:** 162

Rebelle, in Philidor 1690 collection, **VII:** 83

Rebenlein, 17th century publisher in Hamburg, **VII:** 158, 162, 176

Reckling, August, 1843–1900, German composer, **IX:** 175

Recourt, 16th century composer, **VI:** 120

Recoux, Charles, 19th century French composer, **IX:** 90

Redern, Count of Berlin, **V:** 122

Reed, Captain, 18th century English militia, **X:** 27

Reeves, D. W., 1838–1900, American composer for band, **IX:** 139; **X:** 267

Régent, D., 19th century French composer, **IX:** 90

Reger, Max, 1873–1916, German composer, **XII:** 108

Reggiani, Ubaldo, 19th century Italian composer for band, **X:** 241

Regiensis, Ambrosius, 16th century German composer, **VI:** 63

Regnart, composer in 1600 dance collection published in Heidelberg, **VII:** 188

Regnart, Jacob, 1540–1599, Franco-Flemish composer, **VI:** 73

Regnes, 16th century composer, **VI:** 43, 49

Regnier Canaux, 19th century publisher in Paris, **IX:** 36

Reh, Hermann, 19th century German composer, **IX:** 175

Reicha, Anton, 1770–1836, Bohemian composer in Vienna and Paris, **IV:** 51; **V:** 58ff, 151ff; **IX:** 90; **X:** 76; **XI:** 127, 156, 172, 295, 319; **XII:** 65, 204, 219ff

Reicha, Joseph, 1746–1795, composer for the Wallerstein court, **IV:** 56; **VIII:** 355ff, (12) *Partitas* for Harmoniemusik; **X:** 25

Reichardt, G. F., 18th century German composer, **XI:** 77

Reichardt, Johann Friedrich, 1752–1814, composer, writer, **IV:** 17, 36 [reviewer of the original Vienna Harmoniemusik], 51

Reichardt, Johann, 1752–1814, Der May, 1780, for voices and Harmoniemusik, **VIII:** 336

Reiche, Gottfried, 1667–1734, German trumpeter, composer, composer for civic band, **III:** 17, 163, 167ff, 171; **VII:** 132

Reichel, Bernard, b. 1901, Swiss composer, **XII:** 168

Reichelt, F. G., d. 1798, German, *Parthia* for Harmoniemusik, **VIII:** 337; **XI:** 77

Reichstadt, Duke of, as composer, **XI:** 49

Reickert, composer included in a 1885 English collection of band music, **X:** 116

Reid, John [General], 1721–1807, English, (18) original works for Harmonie, **VIII:** 261; **XI:** 77

Reidinger, Stanislaus, 1734–1794, German composer, **XI:** 156

Reill, Josef, 1793–1865, German composer, **IX:** 175

Reinagle, Joseph, 1762–1825, English, (2) *Marches,* 1776, for Harmoniemusik, **VIII:** 262

Reinards, William, 18th century flautist, **XI:** 77 [biographidal note], 216

Reinecke, Carl, 1824–1910, German composer, **IX:** 175; **XI:** 143, 242, 250; **XII:** 196, 213, 214, 215

Reiner, Karel, b. 1910, Czech composer, **XII:** 108

Reinh., 18th century publisher in Strassbourg, **VIII:** 267

Reinhardt, C., Jr., 19th century German composer, **IX:** 175

Reinioch, composer included in a 1871 English collection of band music, **X:** 113

Reis, ?, 19th century Italian composer for band, **X:** 241

Reissiger, 19th century German composer, **V:** 46

Reissiger, Karl, 1798–1859, *Die Felsenmühle zu Estalières,* arr. for Harmonie, **VIII:** 104ff

Reissigler, G. C., 19th century English composer, **IX:** 278

Reissinger, Carl, 1798–1859, German composer, **IX:** 175

Reissinger, Carlo, 19th century Italian composer, **XI:** 143

Reitano, Duca di, 18th century (?) Italian noble, **XI:** 77

Reitmayr, 19th century publisher in Regensburg, **XI:** 240

Reitter, ?, 18th century German composer, **XI:** 246

Reizenstein, Franz, b. 1911, English, **XII:** 108, 169

Relle, M., 19th century English composer, **IX:** 278

Relle, Moritz, 19th century English composer for band, **X:** 152

Rellstab, Johann, 1759–1813, German, (12) *Marches* for Harmoniemusik, **VIII:** 337

Relluzi, ?, *Parthia* for Harmoniemusik, **VIII:** 231

Reluzzy, 18th century composer in Olmütz Harmoniemusik collection, **IV:** 22, fn. 9

Renard, Pierre, 19th century French composer, **IX:** 90

Renault, ?, 19th century French composer, **IX:** 1

Rener, Adam, 16th century German composer, **VI:** 61

Requin, L., 19th century French composer, **IX:** 90

Resch, Paul, 19th century composer at the Melk monastery, **XII:** 64

Respighi, Ottorino, 20th century Italian composer, **XII:** 204

Reub, August, 1871–1935, German composer, **XII:** 109

Reuffius, Jacobus, 1643, German composer of dances, **VII:** 174

Reuland, H., 19th century French composer, **IX:** 91

Reuschel, Johann, 1667, German composer for voices and winds, **VII:** 132; **XI:** 285

Reuss, August, 1871–1935, German composer, **IX:** 175

Reuter, Fritz, b. 1896, German composer, **XII:** 169

Reutter, Georg, 1656–1738, composer, **VII:** 4, 7

Reutter, Hermann, b. 1900, German composer, **XII:** 109

Revelli, William D., former Director of Bands, University of Michigan, **XII:** 207

Reyloff, Edmund, 19th century English composer, **IX:** 278; **X:** 152

Reymann, F. G., 18th century German composer, **XI:** 118, 300

Reymann, Giovanni, 18th century Italian composer, **XI:** 77

Reynaud, J., 19th century French composer, **IX:** 91

Reynaud, Louis, 19th century French composer, **IX:** 91; **X:** 77

Reynolds, H. Robert, Director of Bands, University of Michigan, **XII:** 207

Reysser, ?, member of the 1775 Harmoniemusik of the Prince of Monaco, **IV:** 69

Reytter, Oswald, 16th century German composer, **VI:** 63

Rhames, 18th century publisher in Dublin, **VIII:** 315

Rhau, Georg, 16th century German publisher in Wittenberg, **VI:** 76

Rhein, Ferdinand, 18th century Austrian flautist & composer, **XI:** 78 [biographical note], 217

Rheinberger, Josef, 1839–1901, German composer, **V:** 211; **IX:** 175; **XI:** 172, 319; **XII:** 196

Rheinischer Musikverlag, 20th century publisher in Essen, **XII:** 73, 123

Ribaute, 19th century publisher in Paris, **IX:** 4

Riccardo, Rognoni, 1603 Italian composer of dances and canzoni, **VII:** 208

Ricci, *Crispino e la Comare,* arranged for band by Ponchielli, **X:** 235

Ricci, Francesco, 1733–1800 Italian composer **XI:** 217

Ricci, Luigi, 1805–1859, works arranged by Sedlak for Harmoniemusik, **VIII:** 104

Ricci, Niccolo, 19th century Italian composer for band, **X:** 241

Riccio, ?, Italian composer in 1619 canzoni collection, **VII:** 180, 196

Riccio, Battista, 1614, Italian composer of canzoni, **VII:** 208

Riccio, Giovanni, d. after 1621, Italian composer for wind canzoni, **III:** 219ff; **VII:** 191

Riccordi, 19th and 20th century publisher in Milan, **XI:** 225; **XII:** 109, 159, 170

Richafort, Jean, 1480–1547, Franco-Flemish composer, **VI:** 38, 63, 118, 119

Richard I, 'Coeur de Lion,' 1189–1199, **I:** 184

Richard II, 1377–1399, **I:** 191ff

Richard III, 1483–1485, **I:** 200

Richard, ?, 18th century composer, **XI:** 78

Richard, Charles, 19th century French composer, **IX:** 91

Richard, H., 19th century English composer for band, **X:** 153

Richard, J., 19th century French composer, **IX:** 91

Richart, Alfred, 19th century French composer, **IX:** 92

Richault, 18th and 19th century publisher in Paris, **XI:** 24, 62, 113, 129, 123, 129, 136, 140, 193, 238

Richault, 19th century publisher in Paris, **VIII:** 107, 110, 132ff; **IX:** 7, 61, 88, 109, 163

Richault, Janet and Cotelle, 18th century publisher in Paris, **XI:** 33

Riche, François le, French oboist in Dresden in 1699, **III:** 6

Riche, J. B., 19th century English composer, **IX:** 279

Richelieu, Cardinal, 1585–1642, statesman in France, **III:** 25

Richer, H., 19th century French composer, **IX:** 92

Richoux, L., 19th century French composer, **IX:** 92

Richter, ?, 17th century German composer of Ouvertures and an Intrada, **VII:** 174

Richter, Anton, 18th century German, (3) works for Harmonie and flute, **VIII:** 337

Richter, as arranger for Harmoniemusik, **VIII:** 55, 69

Richter, flutist, court of Mechlenburg-Schwerin, **V:** 185, fn. 4

Richter, Franz Xaver, 1709–1789, **XI:** 78, 119, 162, 172, 286, 310, 323

Richter, Pius, 19th century Austrian composer, **IX:** 241

Ricordi, 19th century publisher in Milano, **X:** 237ff

Ricordi, 19th Milano, XI: 245

Ricordi, Giulio, 1840–1912, Italian composer for band, **X:** 241

Rieck, composer in Erlebach, mss collection of Hautboisten music, **VII:** 156

Riede, ?, 19th century German composer, **X:** 109

Riedel, A., 19th century French composer, **IX:** 92

Riedel, Georg, a wedding composition with winds of 1715, **III:** 215; **VII:** 132

Riedt, Friedrich, 1710–1783, German composer, **XI:** 78, 217

Riefenstahl, C., 19th century arranger, **IX:** 257

Riegel, ?, 19th century arranger, **IX:** 256

Riegel, Henri Joseph, 1741–1799, French composer, *Parthia*, for Harmonie, **VIII:** 291

Riegel, Henri-Jean, 1772–1852, *Les Deux Meuniers*, arr. for Harmoniemusik, **VIII:** 104

Rieger, Gottfried, 1764–1855, composer, **IX:** 176, 241

Riegger, Wallingford, b. 1885, American composer, **XII:** 109, 169

Rièl, Léon, 19th century French composer, **IX:** 92

Riepel, Josef, 1709–1782, German composer, **VIII:** 337 [*Divertimento* for Harmoniemusik]; **XI:** 78 [biographical note], 143, 172

Ries, Ferdinand, 1784–1838, German composer, **IX:** 176; **XI:** 79, 143, 173, 283

Riess, ?, 19th century German composer, **IX:** 176

Riess, 18th century composer in a Dutch collection of marches, **VIII:** 360

Rieter, 19th century publisher in Leipzig, **IX:** 178

Rieter-Biedermann, 19th century publisher in Leipzig, **XI:** 310

Rieti, Vittorio, b. 1898, Italian composer, **XII:** 169

Rietz, Johann, 1767–1828, German composer, **XI:** 79, 319

Rigel, Anton, 1745–1807, compositions for flute, **XI:** 79

Rigel, pére, 18th century French, *Hymn* for chorus and small band, **VIII:** 291

Rigel, père, Henri, 1741–1799, French composer, **IV:** 201

Righini, Vincenzo, 1756–1812, Italian composer, **IV:** 60; **V:** 36; **VIII:** 231, (7) *Partitas* and *Serenati* for Harmoniemusik

Righini, Vincenzo, 1756–1812, works arranged for Harmoniemusik, **VIII:** 104 [*L'Incontro Inaspettato*]; 105 [*Armida, Enes nel Lazio, Gerusalemme liberate*]; unidentified works, 105; **XII:** 41, 46 [Sinfonia from *EinContro inAspettato*, arranged by Druschetsky]; 48 ['Larghetto,' from *Sposa Sonia*, arranged by Druschetzky for Harmoniemusik]

Riisager, Knudage, b. 1897, Danish composer, **XII:** 109, 169

Riki, Vaclav, 19th century Czech composer, **IX:** 241

Riley, 18th century publisher, London, **VIII:** 262

Rilke, German poet, **XII:** 181

Rillé, Laurent, 19th century French composer, **IX:** 92

Rimbault, Stephen, 1773–1837, English composer, **XI:** 79

Rimsky-Korsakov, Nikolai, 1844–1908, Russian composer, **V:** 7ff, 85ff, 121; **XII:** 204, 218

Rinck, Johann Christian, 1770–1846, works for band and choir, **V::** **212**

Rinck, Johann, 1770–1846, German composer, **IX:** 176ff

Rindl, Hermann, (2) *Prüfungslied*, 1799–1800, for SATB, Harmoniemusik, **VIII:** 232

Ringbom, Nils-Eric, b. 1907, Finnish composer, **XII:** 109

Risi, ?, 19th century Italian composer for band, **X:** 241

Ristic, Milan, b. 1908, Polish composer, **XII:** 170

Ristori, Giovanni, 1692–1753, Italian composer, **XI:** 119

Ritiez, B., 19th century French composer, **IX:** 92

Ritter, Fr., 19th century German poet [dedication], **X:** 105

Ritter, George, 1748–1808, German bassoonist, **VIII:** 337 [(4) *Parthien*, (12) *Kleine Stücke*, for Harmoniemusik]; **XI:** 156 [biographical note]

Rittler, Philipp Jacob, fl. ca. 1700, composer, **VII:** 8

Ritz, Jean, 19th century French composer, **IX:** 92

Riuolta, Dominico, 17th century Italian composer of canzoni, **VII:** 204, 205

Rival, L., 19th century French composer, **IX:** 92

Rivers, Walter, 19th century American composer for band, **X:** 267

Rivet, H., 19th century French composer, **IX:** 92

Rivetti, Giovanni, 19th century composer, **IX:** 92

Rivier, Jean, b. 1896, French composer, **XII:** 170

Riviere, J., 19th century French composer, **IX:** 92

Rivière, Jules, 1819–1900, French composer of numerous works for band, **X:** 77ff

Robert, A., 19th century French composer, **IX:** 93

Robert, E., 19th century French composer, **IX:** 93

Robertson, Col. 18th century officer in the British military, **VIII:** 256

Robertson, G. P., 19th century English composer, **IX:** 279

Robespierre, Maximilien, 1758–1794, French politician, **IV:** 185ff

Robinson, Alvan, 19th century American collection of military band works, **X:** 267

Robinson, H., 18th century publisher in London, **VIII:** 256

Robletti, 17th century publisher in Rome, **VII:** 200, 204

Rocca, Lodovico, b. 1895, Italian composer, **XII:** 109, 170

Roche, Gustave, 19th century French composer, **IX:** 93

Rochetin, Nicolas, faculty of the 1792 Paris Conservatoire, **IV:** 157

Rockwell, Charles, 19th century American composer for band, **X:** 268

Rode, composer, 1795 faculty of Paris Conservatoire, **IV:** 162, fn. 46

Rode, Johann Gottfried, 1797–1857, **V:** 16, 21ff

Rode, unnamed work arranged by Sedlak for Harmoniemusik, **VIII:** 152

Rodella, ?, 19th century Italian composer for band, **X:** 242

Röder, Carl, 19th century, Austrian composer, **XII:** 170

Röder, Carl, b. 1812, German composer, **XI: 156**

Röder, Georg, 19th century Austrian composer, **IX:** 242; **XI:** 143

Rodes, Oscar, 19th century French composer, **IX:** 93

Rodet, Auguste, 19th century French composer, **IX:** 93

Roedeberk, ?, 19th century English composer, **IX:** 279

Roeder, O., 19th century English composer, **IX:** 279; **X:** 153

Roellig, 17th century composer of Hautboisten music, **III:** 19

Roellig, Jun., 1762 German composer for Hautboisten, **VII:** 132

Roeser, *Presto*, arranged by Sedlak for Harmoniemusik, **VIII:** 301

Roetscher, Sen., 18th century German, (4) *Marches* and *Lied* for Friedrick Wilhelm III, **VIII:** 337

Rogalski, Theodor, 1901–1954, Romanian composer, **XII:** 109

Rogan, John, 1855–1931, English composer for band, **X:** 154

Rogat, Joseph, bassoonist, 1793 faculty of Paris Conservatoire, **IV:** 162

Roger, ?, 18th century German, (20) *Divertissements* for Harmoniemusik, **VIII:** 338

Roger, 17th century publisher in Amsterdam, **VII:** 123; **XII:** 3

Roger, 18th century publisher in Amsterdam, **VII:** 127

Roger, d'Estienne, 17th and 18th century publisher in Amsterdam, **XI:** 31, 47, 59, 61, 95, 102, 104, 115, 159, 209, 229, 230, 269, 276, 315

Roger, Jeanne, Baroque publisher in Amsterdam, **VII:** 18

Rogers, ?, 18th century English composer (24) *Divertissements* for Harmonie, **VIII:** 262

Rogers, ?, fl. 1800–1828, French composer, **IX:** 93

Rogers, composer in repertoire of band of George IV, **V:** 201

Rogier, Philippe, 1561–1595, Flemish composer, **VI:** 45, 107

Rogister, Jean, b. 1879, Belgian composer, **XII:** 109, 171

Rognoni Taeggio, Giovanni, d. 1626, Milan, Italian composer of canzoni, **VII:** 208

Rogowski, Ludomir, b. 1881, Polish composer, **XII:** 171

Rohan, Louis de, Prince, 17th century France, maintained wind band, **IV:** 69

Röhbock, 17th century publisher in Erfurt, **VII:** 111, 147

Rohde, 19th century publisher in Paris, **IX:** 5

Rohde, Michael, 19th century (?), German composer, **XI:** 270, 296, 315, 322

Rohde, Michael, Classical Period composer, **XII:** 42

Rohner, ?, 19th century German composer, **IX:** 177

Rohwer, Jens, b. 1914, German composer, **XII:** 171

Roland, nephew to Charlemagne, **I:** 261

Roldán, Amadeo, 1900–1939, Cuban composer, **XII:** 171

Rolfe, 19th century publisher in London, **XI:** 207

Rolfe, Edward, English civic musician hired in Rochester in 1640, **III:** 180

Rolla, 17th century publisher in Milano, **VII:** 198, 201, 207

Rolla, Alessandro, 1757–1841, Italian composer for band, **X:** 242; **XI:** 79, 217

Rolla, Marco, 19th century Italian composer, **X:** 242

Rolland, ?, late 19th century conductor of the Pope's band in Rome, **V:** 195

Rolle, Christian, ca. 1765, church music for brass ensemble, **VIII:** 338

Rollé, Emile, 19th century French composer, **IX:** 93

Roller, 18th century composer in Olmütz Harmoniemusik collection, **IV:** 22, fn. 9; **VIII:** 232, (13) *Partitas* for Harmoniemusik

Röllig, Carl, 19th century (?) German composer, **XI:** 261

Röllig, Johann, 1710–1790, German composer, **XI:** 79, 119, 279

Rölling, Johannes, 1624, German composer of 4-part Fuga, **VII:** 174

Rollinson, T. B., 1844–1928, American composer, **X:** 268ff

Rollison, ?, 19th century English composer for band, **X:** 154

Romain, F., 19th century French composer, **IX:** 93

Romani, unnamed work arranged by Sedlak, for Harmoniemusik, **VIII:** 150

Romano, ?, 19th century Italian composer for band, **X:** 242

Romano, composer in 1600 dance collection published in Heidelberg, **VII:** 180

Romano, L. H., 18th century, Italian composer, **XI:** 217

Romberg, Andreas, 1767–1821, **VIII:** 105 [*Simphonie,* arr. Walch for Harmoniemusik]; **XI:** 79, 132

Romberg, Bernhard, 1767–1841, German composer, **XI:** 261

Romhild, Johann, 1684–1756, German composer, **XI:** 237

Rommmann, 17th century publisher in Leipzig, **VII:** 129

Ron, Jean, 1789–1817, French composer, **XI:** 143, 157, 300

Ronalds, Mrs., 19th century English composer for band, **X:** 154

Rong, Wilhelm, 1759–1842, composer for Frederick Wilhelm II, **IV:** 90

Rong, Wilhelm, fl. 1720, German, (7) *Marches*, **VIII:** 338

Röntgen, Julius, 1855–1932, Dutch Composer, **IX:** 125; **XI:** 119, 143

Rootham, Daniel Wilberforce, 1837–1922, English composer, **XII:** 172

Roquelay, 16th century composer, **VI:** 49, 50

Rore, Cipriano de, 1516–1565, composer, **II:** 244; **VI:** 27, 83, 85, 89, 92, 107ff, 118ff; **VII:** 180

Rosati, Emile, 19th century English composer for band, **X:** 154

Rose, G., 19th century German composer, **IX:** 177

Rose, J. H., 18th century Scottish, (2) *Marches* for Harmoniemusik, **VIII:** 262

Roseingrave, Thomas, 1690–1766, English organist, **XI:** 80 [biographical note]

Rosenberg, Hilding, b. 1892, Swedish composer, **XII:** 172

Rosenkranz, Anton, 19th century Austrian composer, **IX:** 242

Rosenkranz, Fr., 19th century German composer, conductor, 27th Inf. Regiment, **V:** 132; **IX:** 177

Rosenstein, T., 19th century English composer, **IX:** 279

Rosenthal, Felix, 19th century composer in Vienna, **XI:** 319

Rosenthal, Manuel, b. 1904, French composer, **XII:** 172

Rosenzweig, composer included in a 1883 English band collection, **X:** 115

Röser, as arranger of works for Harmoniemusik, **VIII:** 39, 102

Röser, Johann Georg, 1740–1797, German composer, **VIII:** 233 [*Tantum ergo*, SATB, Harmoniemusik]; **XI:** 173, 320

Röser, Valentin, 1735–1782, French composer for the Prince de Monaco, **IV:** 70; **VIII:** 291ff, (60) original works for Harmoniemusik

Rosetti, Antonio, 1746–1792, Italian composer, **V:** 201; **XI:** 80, 119, 143, 173

Rosetti, Franz, 1750–1792, German, (49) *Partitas* for Harmoniemusik, **VIII:** 338ff, (49) *Partitas* for Harmoniemusik

Rosetti, unidentified works for Harmoniemusik, **VIII:** 151, 327, 347

Rosi, ?, 19th century Italian composer for band, **X:** 242

Rosiniack, as 19th century arranger, **IX:** 222ff

Rosiniack, as arranger for Harmoniemusik, **VIII:** 72, 75, 81, 97, 103, 144, 148

Roslawetz, Nikolai, b. 1881–1944, Ukraine composer, **XI:** 119

Rossari, ?, 19th century Italian composer for band, **X:** 242

Rossari, Gustavo, 1827–1881, civic band conductor in Milan, **V:** 156

Rossberg, G., 19th century German composer, **IX:** 177

Rosseau, Norbert, b. 1907, Belgian composer, **XII:** 172

Rossetto, Stefano, composer, **II:** 131

Rossi, ?, 19th century civic band conductor in Torino, **V:**156

Rossi, Issidoro, 1813–1884, 19th century Italian composer for band, **X:** 243ff

Rossi, Lauro, 1810–1885, Italian composer for band, **X:** 244

Rossi, Luigi, 1597–1653, Italian composer, **III:** 220

Rossi, Salamone, 1607, Italian composer of dance forms, **VII:** 209ff

Rossini, Gioacchino, 1792–1868, Italian composer for band, **IX:** 94, 143; **X:** 244ff; 203 [music for the removal of his remains from Paris]

Rossini, Gioacchino, 1792–1868, as composer of works arranged for Harmoniemusik, **VIII:** 106 [*Ciro in Babilonia, L'Inganno felice, La Scala di Seta, Tancredi*]; 108 [*Almavivas*, or *Il Barbier von Sevilla, Elisabetta, Regina d'Inghilterra, Il Turco in Italia, L'Italiana in Algeri, Torvaldo e Dorliska*]; 110 [*La Cenerentola, La Gazza Ladra, Otello*]; 111 [*Armida, Mosè in Egitto*]; 112 [*Bianca e Falliero, Eduardo e Cristiana, La Donna del Lago, Ricciardo e Zoraide, Zelmira*]; 113 [*Le Comte Ory, Le Siège de Corinthe, Semiramide*, also page 4]; 114 [*Blaubart, Die diebische Elster, Guillaume Tell, Pietro il Grando*]; unidentified works, 61, 114, 150, 151, 152; , **XII:** 66, 50 [*Blubart,* arranged for Harmoniemusik by Sedlak]; 52 [*Tancredi,* arranged for Harmoniemusik by Sedlak, *Wilhelm Tell,* arranged for Harmoniemusik by an unidentified arranger]; 66 [unidentified arrangers, movements from *La Gazza Ladra, Tancredi*]

Rossini, Gioacchino, 1792–1868, as composer of works arranged for band, **V:** 36 [arrangements by Wieprecht], 73, 87, 90, 92, 103ff, 115, 119, 133, 148, 154, 156, 168, 170, 180ff, 196, 203f, 217; **IX:** 2 [*Semiramide*]; 58 [*Italian in Algiers*]; 113 [*Barbier de Seville, La Cenerentola, Il Mose in Egitto*];142 [*Moses*]; 149 [*Marino Falieri*]; 163 [*Corradino et Moïse*]; 180 [*Tancredi, L'inganno felice, La Gazza ladra, Türk in Italy*]; 181 [*Barbier von Sevilla*]; 186 [*William Tell*]; 189 [*Le Comte Ory*]; 196 [*Trancredi, L'Italiana in Algeri*]; 199 [*Cenerentola, Guillume Tell, L'inganno felice, La Gazza ladra, Tancredi, Türk in Italy*]; 256 [*Armida, Elisabeth Königin von England*]; unidentified works arranged for band 19, 28, 166; **XI:** 143, 144 [*Zelmira*, arr.Prince Rudolph of Austria],173, 218, [unidentified theme, arr. Brod], 261, 300, 304 [unidentified opera movement, arr. Düring, J. C], 310

Rossman, ?, German, Baroque composer, **XII:** 4

Rosulek, Antonin, 19th century Czech composer, **IX:** 242

Roth, Anton, 18th century (?) German composer, **XI:** 173

Roth, Christian, 1585–1640, German composer of dances, **VII:** 174

Roth, Franz, 19th century German composer of works for band, **X:** 109

Roth, J. Cretien, French writer, 19th century, **XII:** 66

Roth, Philipp, 1779–1850, German composer, **XI:** 80, 144, 149

Roth, Sinforiano, 18th century Italian composer, **IV:** 103; **VIII:** 368, ca. 1750, military marches

Rothe, ?, fl. 1800–1828, German composer, **IX:** 143, 177

Rouart-Lerolle, 19th and 20th century publisher in Paris, **IX:** 36, 71, 94; **XII:** 158

Roucourt, Jean-Baptiste, 16th century composer, **VI:** 118

Rouget de Lissle, Claude-Joseph, 1760–1836, composer of the French national anthem, **IV:** 175; **VIII,** 153, 293 *Marche des Marseillois,* arranged for Harmoniemusik

Rouquet, Felix, 19th century French composer, **IX:** 94

Rousseau, Jean Jacques, 1712–1778, French philosopher, **III:** 36; , **IV:** 65, 99ff, 139, 168, 173ff, 176, 189; **VIII:** 292ff, original compositions for winds

Rousseau, Jean-Jacques, VIII: 284, 286

Roussel, Albert, 1869–1937, French composer, **IX:** 94; **XI:** 80; **XII:** 110, 172, 212

Roussel, C., 19th century French composer, **IX:** 94

Routier, L., 19th century French composer, **IX:** 94

Rouvayre et Leblont, 19th century publisher in Paris, **IX:** 156

Rouveirol, F., 19th century French composer, **IX:** 94

Rouveirolis, H., 19th century French composer, **IX:** 94

Rouwyzer, François, 1737–1827, church music for voices and winds, **VIII:** 361

Roux, Emile, 19th century French composer, **IX:** 95

Roux, Jacques, 19th century French composer, **IX:** 95

Rova, Giovanni, 19th century Italian composer, **IX:** 121; **X:** 245

Rovigo, 17th century Italian composer, **III:** 220; **VII:** 204, 208

Roÿ, Charles de, 19th century French composer, **IX:** 95

Royle, Thomas, 19th century English composer, **IX:** 279

Rozan, Charles, de, 19th century French composer, **IX:** 95

Rozelli, ?, 18th century Italian composer, **XI:** 218, 270

Roziere ('de Mousequetaires'), 17th century French composer for Hautboisten, **VII:** 93

Rubini, Nicolo, famous Italian cornettist murdered in early 17th century, **III:** 220

Rubinstein, Anton, 1829–1894, Russian/German composer, pianist composer, **V:** 153; **XI:** 300; **XII:** 213

Ruck ('maitre de musique'), 17th century French composer for Hautboisten, **VII:** 93

Rudel, ?, 19th century German composer of a waltz for band, **X:** 109

Rudolf II, Emperor, **II:** 103

Rudolph, Anton, b. 1742, German, (6) *Partitas* for Harmoniemusik, **VIII:** 342

Rudolph, Erzherzog of Austria, 19th century [as composer], **XI:** 144, 248

Rudolph, Johann, 1788–1831, German composer, **XI:** 144

Rudolph, Joseph, 1730–1812, German composer in Paris, **XI:** 139, 286

Ruffo, Vicenzo, 1508–1587, Italian composer, **VI:** 99

Ruge, Filippo, 18th century (?) Italian composer, **XI:** 80, 218, 233

Ruggeri, Pietro, 19th century Italian composer, *Marcia funebre for Paganini*, **X:** 245

Ruggi, Francesco, 1767–1845, Italian composer for band, **X:** 245

Ruggles, Carl, 20th century American composer, **XII:** 203

Rugni, as arranger of Weber, *Lorzing,* for Harmoniemusik, **VIII:** 133

Ruh, 20th century publisher in Adliswil, **XII:** 71

Ruhl, Hans, 19th century German composer, **IX:** 177

Ruloffs, Bartholomeus, b. 1740, *Musique militaire* for Harmoniemusik, **VIII:** 361

Rumel, German composer 1834 Hoftheater collection in Stuttgart, **X:** 95

Rumigny, Général de, friend of Sax and Berlioz, **V:** 6ff, 69

Rumler, ?, fl. 1800–1828, German composer, **IX:** 177

Rumler, Jean, b. 1780, French composer, **IX:** 95

Rummel, as arranger of works for Harmoniemusik, **VIII:** 107, 133, 150ff

Rummel, Christian, 1787–1849, German composer, **IX:** 178

Rummel, Christiano di Nassau, 19th century composer, **XI:** 144

Rupp, hornist in original Vienna Harmoniemusik, **IV**: 35, fn. 77

Ruppe, Christian, 1753–1826, German composer, **XI**: 80

Ruppert, ?, 19th century German composer, **IX**: 178

Ruscheweyn, E., 19th century German composer, **IX**: 178

Russell, W., English, *Guilford Volunteers March*, 1795, for band, **VIII**: 262

Russo, Mariano, 19th century Italian composer, a work for chorus and band, **X**: 245

Rust, ?, 18th century composer, **XI**: 81

Rustici, Alessandro, 19th century (?) Italian composer, **XI**: 162

Rutebeuf, 1245–1285, poet, **I**: 74

Rutherford, David, 18th century English composer, **XI**: 81

Ruyneman, Daniel, b. 1886, Dutch composer, **XII**: 172

Ruzitska, Georg, 19th century Hungarian composer, **IX**: 242

Ruzni, as arranger of works for Harmoniemusik, **VIII**: 11, 109, 128, 151, 156 [as arranger of works for Harmoniemusik]; **IX**: 242

Ryba, Jakub, 1765–1815, Czech composer, **XI**: 81

Ryembault, ?, 19th century French composer, **IX**: 95

Saal, Anton, 1763–1855, German composer, **XI:** 119

Sabbio, Vincenzo, 1584 publisher in Brescia, **VI:** 99

Sabel, Carl, 19th century German composer, **IX:** 178

Sacchini, Antonio, 1730–1786, as composer of works arranged for Harmoniemusik, **VIII:** 114, 153, 154

Sacchini, Antonio, 1730–1786, as composer of an unidentified work arranged by Ozi, **XII:** 51

Sacher, Josef, ca. 1770, German, *Feldpartie* for Harmoniemusik, **VIII:** 342

Sachesse, Hans, 1891–1960, German composer, **XII:** 163

Sachse, C., 19th century German composer, **IX:** 178

Saikkola, Lauri, b. 1906, composer, **XII:** 164

Sainsbury, John, 19th century English writer, **XII:** 209

Saint Jacome, L. A., 19th century English composer for band, **X:** 154

Saint-André, A., 19th century French composer, **IX:** 95

Saint-Saëns, Camile, 1835–1921, French composer, **IX:** 95; **X:** 88; **XII:** 196, 204, 212, 213, 218

Saint-Saëns, Camile, 1835–1921, as composer of a work arranged for band, **X:** 255 [*Sansone e Dalila,* arr. Vessella]

Saint-Suire, Etienne, member in 1768 of the Les Grands Hautbois, **IV:** 64, fn. 4

Sala, 17th and 18th century publisher in Venetia, **XI:** 61, 163

Sala, Eugenio, 19th century Italian composer for band, **X:** 245

Salazar, Antonio de, 1650–1715, composer of church music in Mexico, **III:** 221

Saldern, General, 18th century German, **VIII:** 301

Sale, ?, fl. ca. 1400, composer, **VI:** 4

Salieri, Antonio, 1750–1825, Italian composer in Vienna, **IV:** 35ff; **VIII:** 233, (24) original compositions for Harmoniemusik; **XI:** 81, 230, 277

Salieri, Antonio, 1750–1825, works arranged for Harmoniemusik, **VIII:** 61 [*Arbore di Diana et Azur*]; 115 [*Der Rauchfangkehrer, Il ricco d'un giorno, La Dama Pastorella* or *La Cifra*]; 116 [*La Grotta di Trofonio, Tarare,* or *Axur re d'Ormus*]; 117 [*Il Talismano*]; 118 [*Palmira, Regina di Persia*]; 119 [*Falstaff, König von England*]; unidentified works, 61, 150, 153; **XII:** 42, 48 ['Spegel arie,' from *Semire und Azor,* arranged by Druschetzky for Harmoniemusik]

Salieri, Overture to *Palmyra,* arranged for band, **IX:** 200

Salis, E., 19th century French composer, **IX:** 96

Salisbury, 'Marquiss,' 18th century British noble, **VIII:** 253

Sallaert, Anthonis, painter of 1615 visit of Isabella to Brussels, **III:** 187

Sallantin, François, oboist, 1793 faculty of Paris Conseratoire, **IV:** 64 fn. 4, 160, 162

Sallinen, Aulis, Finnish, 20th century composer, **XII:** 204

Salmier, Claudius, 16th century composer, **VI:** 107

Salner, G. P., 18th century English composer, *St. Helena March,* for band, **VIII:** 262

Salomez, Charles, 19th century French composer, **IX:** 96

Salulini, Paolo, 18th century (?) Italian composer, **XI:** 218

Saluzzi, Francesco, 19th century Italian composer for band, **X:** 245

Salzedo, Carlos, b. 1885, French harpist, composer, **XII:** 110, 173

Samamein, ?, member in 1768 of the Les Grands Hautbois, **IV**: 64, fn. 4

Sambin, V., 19th century French composer, **IX**: 96

Samfundet til Udigivelse af dansk Musik, 20th century publisher in Kopenhagen, **XII**: 112

Sammartini, Giovanni, 1700–1770, Italian composer for Harmoniemusik, **VII**: 192; **X**: 14; **XI**: 81, 218

Samuel, Adolphe, 1824–1898, Belgium composer, **IX**: 260

San Lorenzo, 18th century publisher in Venezia, **XI**: 9

San Martini, Giovanni, 18th century Italian composer, **XI**: 81, 218

San Martini, Giuseppe, 18th century Italian composer, **XI**: 82, 119, 219

Sancho IV, 1284–1295, **I**: 221

Sander, Otto, *Jubilämus Marsch* for band, **X**: 95

Sanders, Robert, b. 1906, American composer, **XII**: 110

Sandow, trumpeter in the Berlin Guard Regiment in 1805, **V**: 15

Sandra, P. A., 19th century French composer, **IX**: 96

Sandrin, Pierre, 1490–1561, composer, **VI**: 43, 44ff, 49, 50, 52, 109, 110, 114, 118

Sangiorgi, Filippo, 19th century Italian composer, **XI**: 255

Santner, Karl, 19th century Austrian composer, **IX**: 178, 242; **XI**: 310

Santoliquido, Francesco, b. 1883, Italian composer, **XII**: 173

Sarasin, Lukas, 1730 1802, *Quintetto* for Harmoniemusik, **VIII**: 374

Sarazin, Marie, bassoon faculty of the 1792 Paris Conservatoire, **IV**: **157**

Sardei, Antonio, 19th century Italian composer, *Sinfonia* for band, **X**: 245

Sargent, ?, English trumpeter at Vauxhall in 1785, **IV**: 131, note on pgs. 132–133

Saro, Heinrich, 1827–1891, German composer of works for band, **X**: 109

Saro, Heinrich, 1827–1891, German military conductor, **V**: 19

Sarocchi, G., 19th century Italian composer for band, **X**: 246

Sarrè, François, 19th century French composer, **IX**: 96

Sarrette, Bernard, 1765–1858, administrator of the Guard Band in Paris, **IV**: 152ff, 157, 160, 162, 185, 198, 209

Sarri, Domenico, 1679–1744, Italian composer, **XI**: 82

Sarrus, A., 19th century French composer, **IX**: 96

Sarsino, ?, Duet from *Nonon*, unknown arranger for Harmoniemusik, **VIII**: 119

Sarti, Giuseppe, 1729–1802 Italian composer in Vienna and Russia, **IV**: 77; **VIII**: 119, 120, 154 [as arranger of works for Harmoniemusik]; **X**: 39

Sartori, Christoph, bassoonist in the Joseph Schwarzenberg Harmonie, **IV**: 41, fn. 104

Sartorius, as arranger of works for Harmoniemusik, **VIII**: 27, 48, 54, 61, 62, 72, 78, 81, 85, 87, 95, 130, 144, 145, 147

Sartorius, Christian, b. 1797, German composer, **III**: 215; **VII**: 132

Sartorius, G., 19th century German composer, **IX**: 178

Sartorius, Paul, 1601, German comp. of canzonas in the Italian style, **VII**: 175

Sassaroli, Vincenzo, 19th century Italian composer for band, **X**: 246

Sauer, ?, 19th century German composer, **IX**: 178

Sauer, 19th century publisher in Vienna, **VIII:** 173

Sauer, Ignaz, 19th century Austrian composer, **IX:** 242; **XII:** 38

Sauers Kunsthandlung, Handschrift, 19th century publisher in Vienna, **XII:** 36

Sauguet, Henri, b. 1901, French composer, **XII:** 173

Sauvagniac, H., 19th century French composer, **IX:** 96

Sauvan, F., fils, 19th century French composer, **IX:** 96

Savari, ?, 19th century French composer, conductor Musique au 34e, **IX:** 97

Savazzini, Federico, b. 1830, Italian composer, *Sinfonia* for band, **X:** 246

Savez kompozitora Jogoslavije, 20th century publisher in Agram, **XII:** 165

Savinelli, Angelo, 19th century Italian composer, **XI:** 274

Savoia, Paolo, b. 1820, civic band conductor in Naples, **V:** 157; **X:** 246

Savoye, composer in 17th century collection, period of Louis XIV, **VII:** 83

Sawerthal, Joseph, 1819–1903, Austrian bandmaster, **V:** 45. 49; **X:** 53, 114ff

Sax, Adolphe, 1814–1894, instrument maker and publisher, Paris, **V:** 37, 46, 62ff, 74, 90, 120, 164; **IX:** 42, 97; **XII:** 61, 62, 66

Saxe, Maurice de, 1696–1750, French general, **III:** 111ff

Saxe-Meiningen, 19th century Duke of, **V:** 192

Sazenhofer, 19th century German composer, **IX:** 141

Scaglies, Angelo, 18th century (?) Italian composer, **XI:** 219

Scaglione, Antonio, 19th century Italian composer, church works with band, **X:** 246

Scala, Francis, 19th century American composer, **IX:** 139

Scaletta, Orazio, 1550–1630, Italian composer, **VI:** 101

Scandelli, Luca, 16th century Italian composer, **VI:** 65

Scandello, Antonio, 1517–1580, famous cornettist, **II:** 229; **VI:** 74

Scarlatti, Domenico, 1685–1757, original wind ensemble work, **VII:** 192

Scarlatti, Pietro Alessandro, 1660–1725, Italian composer, **XI:** 82, 219, 270

Scarron, Paul, 1610–1660, French poet, **III:** 191

Scataglia, 18th century publisher in Venezia, **VIII:** 362

Scelsi, Giacinto, b. 1905, Italian composer, **XII:** 110

Schacht, Theodor von, 1748–1823, German composer for Harmonie at Regensburg, **IV:** 58; **VIII:** 342ff, (22) original *Partitas* for Harmoniemusik; **VIII:** 3, 75, as arranger for Harmoniemusik; **XI:** 144, 242

Schaefer, Theodor, b. 1904, Czech composer, **XII:** 173

Schäfer, Karl, b. 1899, German composer, **XII:** 173

Schaffer, Paul, fl. 1617–1645, German composer of dances, **VII:** 175

Schaffner, ?, fl. 1800–1828, French composer, **IX:** 97

Schaffner, as arranger of Catel, *Zirphile et Fleur de Myrte,* opera?, for Harmonie, **VIII:** 15

Schaffner, N. A., *Chasse,* arranged by Gambaro for Harmoniemusik, **VIII:** 121

Schafgotsch, Prince at Johannisberg, employed Harmoniemusik, **IV:** 59

Schafrath, Christoph, b. 1709, German composer, **XI:** 82

Schale, Christian, 1713–1800, German composer, **XI:** 83

Schall, Claus, Danish composer, *Carasel Musique*, 1791, for Harmoniemusik, **VIII:** 249

Schallehn, ?, 19th century English composer, **IX:** 279

Schallehn, first leader of Kneller Hall in England, **V:** 83ff

Schaller, J., 19th century French composer, **IX:** 97

Schalub, 19th century publisher in Düsseldorf, **X:** 106

Schandl, Franz, 19th century Austrian composer, **IX:** 242

Scharffenberg, C., 16th century publisher in Breslau, **VI:** 64, 69, 70

Scharoch, band conductor of the Austrian IR 72 band, **V:** 111

Schauff, 19th century publisher in Pressbourg, **XII:** 41

Schedel, Hartmann, d. 1514, compiled a Liederbuch of 15th century music, **VI:** 10

Schedlich, David ('D. S.'), 17th century, German composer of dances, **VII:** 175

Scheer, ?, German, Baroque composer, **XII:** 4

Scheibe, Johann Adolph, 1708–1776, German composer, **XI:** 83

Scheibl, Johann, 19th century Czech composer, **IX:** 242

Scheidemantel, ?, German, Baroque composer, **XII:** 4

Scheidt, Samuel, 1587–1654, 1621, German composer, **VII:** 133, 144, 175

Schein, Johann, 1586–1630, German composer, **III:** 4, 161, 169, 215; **VII:** 133, 172, 176

Scheinpflug, Christian, 1722–1770, German (16) *Partiten* for Harmoniemusik, **VIII:** 344

Schelb, Josef, b. 1894, German composer, **XII:** 110, 173

Schelle, Johann, Baroque German composer for wind consort, **VII:** 133; **XI:** 277

Schenck, 17th century composer in Erlebach, mss collection of Hautboisten music, **VII:** 156

Schencker, hornist and harp for La Pouplinière, 1763, **IV:** 68, fn. 26

Schenk, Johann, 1753–1836, Austrian composer, **VIII:** 121 [*Die Weinlese*, opera, arr. Wendt for Harmoniemusik]; **IX:** 242; **XI:** 44, 250, 301

Schepper, L.-J., 19th century French composer, **IX:** 97

Scherer, ?, 19th century German composer of works for Harmoniemusik, **X:** 110

Scherer, Gottlieb, 17th century Dutch composer of sonatas for 3 flutes, **VII:** 213

Scherff, 17th century publisher in Nürnberg, **VII:** 164

Scherley, Joseph, 17th century German composer, **VII:** 24

Scherr, L., 19th century composer, **XI:** 289

Scherrer, H., b. 1865, German composer, **IX:** 178

Scherzer, ?, 19th century German composer, **IX:** 178

Scherzer, A. P., 19th century German composer, **IX:** 178

Schetky, Johann, 1740–1820, German composer, **XI:** 83, 219

Schetky, Johann, 1740–1820, Scottish, (24) *Airs & Strathspeys* for band, **VIII:** 262

Schiassi, Maria, 18th century (?) composer in Vienna, **XI:** 237

Schiavi, Corrado, 19th century Italian composer, church works for band, **X:** 246

Schicht, Johann, 1753–1823, German composer, **XI:** 290, 308

Schick, Friedrich, 1822–1847, German military band conductor, **V:** 19ff, 105; **IX:** 142

Schickhard, Johann, 18th century German composer, **XI:** 83, 119, 276, 230

Schiedermayer, arranged for band, **IX:** 256

Schiedermayr, Johann Baptist, 1779–1840, German composer, **V:** 183 fn. 21, 213; **IX:** 243; **XI:** 316; **XII:** 42
Schieferdeckern, Johann Christian, German, Baroque composer, **XII:** 4
Schield, William, 1748–1829, English composer, **XI:** 86, 221
Schier, 19th century French composer, **IX:** 101
Schiller- und Kissnerischen, 18th century publisher in Hamburg, **XI:** 62
Schiller, 19th century German poet, **X:** 105, 112
Schiller, 19th centuryFriedrich, 1759–1805, German poet, **V:** 132
Schiller, German poet, **IX:** 168, 177
Schilling, Hans, b. 1869, German composer, **IX:** 178
Schillings, Max von, 1868–1933, German composer, **IX:** 178; **XII:** 111
Schiltz, ?, 19th century French composer, **IX:** 97
Schiltz, the best cornet player in Paris, according to Wagner, **V:** 147
Schimpke, ?, 18th century German composer, **XI:** 120, 173
Schindelmeisser, Louis, 1811–1864, German composer, **XI:** 144, 304
Schindlocker, M., 19th century Austrian composer, **IX:** 243
Schinn, Georg, 18th century German composer, **XI:** 120
Schirbel, O., 19th century English composer for band, **X:** 155
Schirmer, G., 20th century publisher in New York, **XII:** 162
Schiske, Karl, b. 1916, Austrian composer, **XII:** 111
Schlegel, 16th century German composer, **VI:** 65
Schlesinger, 18th and 19th century publisher in Paris, **V:** 34, 147; **VIII:** 37, 65, 286; **IX:** 1, 35; **XI:** 303
Schlesinger, 19th century publisher in Berlin, **VIII:** 4ff, 69, 113, 133, 374; **IX:** 162, 169, 171, 173, 192; **X:** 95; **XI:** 201; **XII:** 61
Schletterer, Hans, 1824–1893, German composer, **IX:** 178
Schlick, Arnold, 1511, author on organ building, **II:** 210
Schlier, Johann, 19th century Austrian composer, **IX:** 243
Schliess, Ferdinand, clarinetist in Prince Liechtenstein Harmonie, **IV:** 39
Schloeger, Mathaeus, 1722–1766, Austrian composer, **XI:** 83
Schlosser, Augsburg, IX: 162
Schmacht, F., 19th century German composer, hornist, Füsilier-Bataillion de Duke de Braunsweig Inf. Reg. Nr. 92, **IX:** 179
Schmatz, 18th century publisher in Erlangen, **XI:** 85
Schmeidt & Rau, 19th century publisher in Leipzig, **XII:** 41
Schmelzer, Johann Heinrich, 1620–1680, Austrian composer for Leopold I, **III:** 62, 169; **IV:** 21; **VII:** 4, 156
Schmid, Erich, b. 1907, Swiss composer, **XII:** 111
Schmid, Heinrich Kaspar, 1874–1953, German composer, **XII:** 174
Schmid, J. C., 17th century composer in Erlebach, mss collection of Hautboisten music, **VII:** 156

Schmid, Josef, b. 1868, German composer, **IX:** 179

Schmidbauer, ?, (2) *Partitas* for Harmoniemusik, **VIII:** 234

Schmidt, ?, 18th century German, *Parthia* for Harmoniemusik, **VIII:** 344

Schmidt, ?, 19th century English composer for band, **X:** 155

Schmidt, A., 19th century publisher in Boston and Leipzig, **IX: 160**

Schmidt, E., 19th century German composer, **IX:** 179

Schmidt, Franz, 1874–1939, Austrian composer, **XI:** 144, 145, 270; **XII:** 111

Schmidt, G., 19th century English composer, **IX:** 279

Schmidt, Henri, 19th century French composer, **IX:** 97

Schmidt, Johann, trumpeter in band of George IV, **V:** 203, fn. 10

Schmidtbach, C., 18th century (?) Austrian composer, **XI:** 157

Schmidt-Wunstorf, Rudolf, 20th century German composer, **XII:** 204

Schmiedecke, A., 19th century German composer, **IX:** 179

Schmitt, ? 18th century German, *Scherzo* for Harmoniemusik and flute, **VIII:** 344

Schmitt, Alois, 19th century German composer, **IX:** 179

Schmitt, as arranger for Harmoniemusik, **VIII:** 25, 54, 85, 87, 105, 127, 131

Schmitt, Florent, 1870–1958, French composer, **XII:** 111, 204, 212

Schmitt, Geo., as 19th century arranger, **IX:** 391

Schmitt, J., 18th century publisher in Amsterdam, **XI:** 20, 202, 225

Schmitt, Joseph, 1734–1791, German composer, **XI:** 83, 220

Schmitt, Nicol, 18th century French bassoonist & composer, **XI:** 157

Schmitt, Nicolas, b. 1779, arranger of Haydn string quartets for Harmoniemusik, **XII:** 50

Schmittbaur, Joseph, 1718–1809, (8) works for Harmonie or band, **VIII:** 344; **XI:** 84, 120, 157, 162, 173, 220

Schmotzer, Jacob, 19th century (?) composer, **XI:** 84

Schmügel, Johann, 1727–1798, German composer, **XI:** 84, 271

Schnabel, Joseph Ignaz, 1767–1831, German composer for choir and winds, **V:** 242; **IX:** 179; **X:** 110 [*Missa* for voices & band]; **XII:** 42

Schneider, ?, 18th century German, (18) *Harmonien* with 2 flutes, **VIII:** 344ff

Schneider, ?, 18th century German composer, **XI:** 84

Schneider, ?, German composer, *Partita* for Harmoniemusik, **X:** 25

Schneider, Anton, 19th century German composer, and leader, **IX:** 179, 180

Schneider, Franz, 19th century German composer, **XI:** 312

Schneider, Friedrich, 1786–1853, German composer, **IX:** 181; **XII:** 67

Schneider, Georg Abraham, 1770–1839, head of Prussian military music, **V:** 19ff, 26; **IX:** 141

Schneider, George, 19th century German composer, **XI:** 145, 174

Schneider, Harmann, b. 1862, German composer, **IX:** 181

Schneider, Johann, German composer in 1745 of a church music, **III:** 211

Schneider, Julius, 19th century German composer, **IX:** 182

Schneider, Louis, 19th century French composer, **IX:** 97

Schneider, trombonist in band of George IV, **V:** 203, fn. 10

Schneitzhoeffer, Jacques, flute, oboe faculty of the 1792 Paris Conservatoire, **IV:** 156

Schneitzhoeffer, Jean-Madeleine, 1785–1852, French composer, **XII:** 67

Schneklud, Ad., 19th century French composer, **IX:** 97

Schnell, Johann, 1687–1754, German composer, **XI:** 85

Schnellinger, 16th century composer, **VI:** 76

Schnept, Josef, b. 1785, Czech (?) composer, **XI:** 85

Schnittelbach, Natanael, 1633–1667, German composer of dances, **VII:** 176

Schnyder von Wartensee, Franz, 1786–1868, Swiss composer, **XI:** 246

Schoeck, Othmar, b. 1886, Swiss composer, **XII:** 112, 174

Schoeps, ?, 18th century German, *Partiten*, for Harmoniemusik, 345

Scholl, Nickolaus, as arranger of *L'Arbore di Diana*, overture for Harmonie, **VIII:** 12

Scholl, Nikolaus, 18th century German composer, **X:** 25

Scholl, W., 19th century German composer, **IX:** 182

Scholz, Bernhard, 1835–1916, German composer, **IX:** 182

Scholz, Gottfried, composer in 1622 German collection of dance music, **VII:** 145

Schön, ?, 18th century German, (2) *Parthias*, for Harmoniemusik, **VIII:** 345

Schön, ?, 18th century German composer, **X:** 22

Schön, ?, 18th century Swiss, *Parthias* for Harmoniemusik, **VIII:** 374

Schönberg, 20th century Austrian composer, **XII:** 204

Schonebeck, C. S., 1758–1800, composer, **XI:** 85

Schönemann, ?, 19th century German composer, **IX:** 182

Schönenberger, 19th century publisher in Paris, **XI:** 164, 235, 286

Schönfeld, Johann Ferdinand von, 1750–1821, diarist, **IV:** 22, 41

Schonfelder, 16th century German composer, **VI:** 62

Schöniger, bassoonist, 19th century court at Rudolstadt, **V:** 186, fn. 8

Schop, Johann, d. 1667, German cornett, trombone player, composer, **VII:** 176

Schöringer, Carl, *Parthia* for Harmoniemusik, **VIII:** 234

Schott, 18th 19th and 20th century publisher in Mainz, **VIII:** 27, 47, 49, 69, 107, 114, 132ff, 150, 159, 274, 350, 358; **IX:** 90, 148ff, 155, 159, 162, 163, 164, 165, 172, 183, 185, 186, 188, 189, 192, 195, 234; **XI:** 22, 39, 132, 134, 136, 138, 139, 144, 244, 246, 318, 319; **XII:** 133, 151, 153, 161, 174, 175, 180

Schoulenbourg, 17th century General, [dedication], **XII:** 4

Schoulenbourg, 17th century General, **VII:** 125

Schouwman, Hans, b. 1902, Dutch composer, **XII:** 174

Schramm, 17th century publisher in Neustadt an der Hardt, **VII:** 178

Schramm, Melchior, 1553–1619, German composer, **VI:** 65, 75

Schrammel, J., 19th century French composer, **IX:** 97

Schreck, Gustav Ernst, 1849–1918, German composer, **IX:** 182; **XII:** 112, 174

Schreck, P., 19th century German composer, **IX:** 182

Schreiner, Adolf, 19th century German composer, **IX:** 182

Schreuder, Frédéric, faculty of the 1792 Paris Conservatoire, **IV:** 157

Schröder, F., 19th century German composer, **IX:** 182

Schroeder, H. B., English (7) *Marches*, ca. 1795, for band, **VIII:** 263ff

Schroeder, Hermann, b. 1904, German composer, **XII:** 175

Schroeter, Johann, 1752–1788, German composer, **XI:** 85

Schroeter, John Samuel, 1752–1788, composer, **XII:** 42

Schroll, Ludwig, 19th century German composer, **IX:** 182

Schröter, 17th century composer of canzoni, **VII:** 208

Schubart, Christian F. Daniel, 1739–1791, German critic, **III:** 110

Schubart, Ludwig Albrecht, critic, **IV:** 54ff

Schubert [Rimsky-Korsakov as arr.], **V:** 86

Schubert, A., 19th century English composer for band, **X:** 155

Schubert, Anton, composer included in a 1887 English band collection, **X:** 116

Schubert, F. L. (brother to Franz Schubert), as arranger, **IX:** 198

Schubert, Ferdinand, 1794–1859, Austrian composer, **IX:** 244; **XI:** 302

Schubert, Ferdinand, 1794–1859, Austrian composer, as arranger of Mozart *Alma dei,* K. 277, **VIII:** 223 [Mozart *Alma dei,* K. 277]; **XI:** 132 [unidentified theme arr. Devienne], 239 [unidentified theme, arr. Sinigaglia]

Schubert, Franz, 1797–1828, Austrian composer, **IX:** 14, 62, 243; **X:** 53 [6 minuets for Harmoniemusik]; **XII:** 198, 199 [arranged for band by Stokowsky], 204, 213, 215

Schubert, Johann Fredrich, 1770–1811, German composer, **XI:** 240, 248

Schubert, Joseph, 1757–1837, German, many works for Harmoniemusik, **VIII:** 345ff; **XI:** 85

Schubert, Raoul, 19th century French composer, **IX:** 98

Schuberth, 19th century publisher in Hamburg, **XI:** 259; **XI:** 300

Schuberth, 19th century publisher in Leipzig, **XI:** 300

Schuester, ?, (9) *Parthias* for Harmoniemusik, **VIII:** 234

Schultes, 17th century publisher in Augsburg, **VII:** 150, 166

Schulthess, Walter, 1894–1956, Swiss composer, **XII:** 175

Schultz, ?, 19th century German composer, **IX:** 182

Schultz, Johannes, 1582–1653, 1617, German composer of dances, **VII:** 145, 177ff

Schültz, Lebrecht, 18th century German composer, **XI:** 85; **XI:** 220

Schultz, Svend, b. 1913, Danish composer, **XII:** 112, 175

Schultz, Th., 19th century French composer, **IX:** 98

Schultze, G., Baroque composer, **XI:** 200

Schültze, J. C., 18th century German composer, **XI:** 85, 220

Schulz, 17th century composer, **III:** 17; **VII:** 133

Schulz, as arranger of works for Harmoniemusik, **VIII:** 124, 131

Schulz, Christian, 1773–1827, German composer, **IX:** 182

Schumann, Christoph, 1726 Stadtpfeifer contract, **III:** 165

Schumann, Clara, **V:** 131

Schumann, Erich, b. 1989, composer, **XII:** 112

Schumann, Friedrich, 18th century, German composer, **XI:** 86

Schumann, Robert, 1810–1856, **V:** 5, 131; **IX:** 55, 182; **XII:** 204

Schumann, William, 20th century American composer, **XII:** 204

Schürer, 17th century publisher in Wittenberg, **VII:** 176, 179

Schurer, heirs of, 17th century publishers in Leipzig, **VII:** 155

Schüster, Joseph, 1748–1812, composer in Olmütz Harmoniemusik coll., **IV:** 22, fn. 9; **XI:** 86

Schutz, 17th century composer in Erlebach, mss collection of Hautboisten music, **VII:** 156

Schütz, Heinrich, 1585–1672, German composer, **II:** 246, **III:** 16, 214ff; **VII:** 134ff

Schuyt, Cornelis, 1557–1616 Dutch composer of instrumental dances, **VII:** 214

Schwann, 20th century publisher in Düsseldorf, **XII:** 83, 116, 118

Schwarer, Ph., 19th century French composer, **IX:** 98

Schwartz, ?, 19th century French composer, **IX:** 98

Schwartz, Ad., 19th century French composer, **IX:** 98

Schwartz, an *Adagio* in a Swiss manuscript, **VIII:** 371

Schwartz, K., 19th century French composer, **IX:** 98

Schwartzkoff, 17th century comp. in Erlebach, collection of Hautboisten music, **VII:** 156

Schwartzkopff, Theodor, 1659–1732, German composer, **XI:** 220

Schwarz, ?, (11) *Märsche für die ganze Türkische Musick oder Harmonie*, **VIII:** 235

Schwarz, A., 19th century German composer, **IX:** 182

Schwarz, *Adagio*, unknown arranger for Harmoniemusik, **VIII:** 151

Schwarz, M., 19th century Austrian composer, **IX:** 244

Schwarzenberg, Joseph Adam, Prince, 1722–1782, of Vienna, **IV: 37, 40**

Schwarzenberg, Joseph Johann, 1769–1833, Prince, **IV:** 40

Schwarz-Schilling, Reinhard, b. 1904, German composer, **XII:** 112, 175

Schwegler, German composer 1834 Hoftheater collection in Stuttgart, **X:** 95

Schwegler, Johann, 18th century German, (4) *Quartuors* for flutes, horns, **VIII:** 345

Schweickard von Kronberg, Johann, of Mainz in 1604, **III:** 57

Schwemmer, d. 1696, German composer, **III:** 215

Schwemmer, Heinrich, 1621–1696, German composer for voices and winds, **VII:** 135

Schwencke, C. F. G., as arranger of Mozart K. 361, **VIII:** 219

Schwencke, Christian, 1767–1822, German composer, **IX:** 182; **XI:** 120, 249

Schwenckenbecher, Gunther, 1651–1714, German comp. for Hautboisen, **VII:** 135

Schwenke, Christian Friedrich Gottlieb, 1767–1822, German composer, **XII:** 42

Schwent, Guillaume, horn faculty of the 1792 Paris Conservatoire, **IV:** 156

Schwent, Philippe, faculty of the 1792 Paris Conservatoire, **IV:** 156

Schweska, H., 19th century French composer, **IX:** 98

Schwiegerauen, 18th century publisher at Rostock, **VII:** 125

Schwindel, Friedrich, 1737–1786, German composer, **XI:** 86, 145, 220, 261

Sciacca, Vittoro, 19th century Italian composer for band, **X:** 247

Sciers, Dominique, 19th century French composer, **IX:** 98

Scimpke, ?, 18th century composer, **XI:** 157

Sciroli, Gregorio, 1722–1781, Italian composer, **XI:** 120

Scontrino, Antonio, 1850–1922, Italian composer, **IX:** 121; **XII:** 113, 175

Scott, Cyril, b. 1879, English composer, **XII:** 175

Scotti, 19th century publisher in Milan, **XI:** 16, 131

Scotto, Girolamo, 16th century publisher in Venice, **VI:** 100

Scottum, Hieronymum, 16th century publisher in Venice, **VI:** 101

Scouris, André, b. 1899, French composer, **XII:** 177

Scrépel, Carlos, 19th century French composer, **IX:** 98

Sebastiani, Giuseppe, 19th century Italian composer for band, **X:** 247

Sedlak, Wenzel, 1767–1835, as arranger of works for Harmoniemusik, **V:** 177ff, 180ff; **VIII:** 4, 5, 6, 8, 9, 12, 16, 18, 23, 25, 31, 34, 35, 42, 43, 47, 48, 49, 52, 53, 58, 63, 65, 66, 68, 69, 88, 89, 91, 92, 101, 102, 103, 104, 106, 107, 108, 109, 112, 113, 114, 118, 128, 129, 132, 142, 146, 147, 148, 150, 152, 154; **XII:** 50 [biographical note]; 45 [Cherubini, *Faniska*]; 50 [Gyrowetz, *Die Hochzeit der Thetis und des Peleus;* Hummel's *Helene e Paris*, for Harmoniemusic; Rossini *Blubart*]; 52 [Persuis, *Nina*, for Harmoniemusik; Rossini *Tancredi*, for Harmoniemusik]

Seebach, hornist in the Duke of Sondershausen Harmonic, **V:** 185, fn. 2

Seelicke, 19th century German composer, **IX:** 142

Seeling, 19th century publisher in Dresden, **IX:** 165

Sega, A., 19th century French composer, **IX:** 98

Segario, Francisco, 17th century Pavan for consort, **VII:** 135

Seghers, Frédéric, 19th century French composer, **IX:** 98

Segneri, Vincenzo, 19th century Italian composer for band, **X:** 247

Segni, Giulio, 1498–1561, Italian composer, **VI:** 46

Sehlbach, Erich, b. 1898, German composer, **XII:** 113, 176

Seiber, Mátyás, 1905–1960, Hungarian composer, **XII:** 175

Seidel, ?, 19th century Austrian composer, **IX:** 244

Seidel, Arthur, 19th century German composer, arranger, **IX:** 183, 198

Seidl, Anton, 1850–1898, protégée of Wagner, **V:** 123

Seifer, R., fl. 1800–1828, German composer, **IX:** 183

Seifert, Anton, 19th century English composer, **IX:** 279

Seiff, J., 19th century German composer, **IX:** 183

Seiffert, ?, 19th century Austrian composer, **IX:** 244

Seiling, 19th century publisher in Regensburg, **XI:** 311

Seiller, A., 19th century Italian composer for band, **X:** 247

Seiller, Franz, 19th century German composer, **IX:** 183

Seipoldsdorf, serpentist, court of Mechlenburg-Schwerin, **V:** 185, fn. 4

Seitz, 19th century publisher in Leipzig, **XI:** 319

Sekles, Bernhard, 1872–1934, German composer, **XII:** 113, 167

Selich, Daniel, 1614, German composer of dances, **VII:** 136, 177

Selijuk Sultan, 17th century, **III:** 106

Selim III, 1789–1807, Sultan, **III:** 104

Selim, 1512–1520, Sultan, **III:** 104

Selle, Thomas, 1599–1663, German composer of 6-part Ritornellorum, **VII:** 177

Sellenik, Ad., 19th century French composer, conductor Musique 2e Regiment de Voltigeurs de la Garde Imperiale, **IX:** 1, 98

Sellner, Josef, 19th century Austrian composer, **IX:** 244

Sellner, Joseph, 1787–1843, German oboist & composer, **XI:** 120, 237

Selma Y Salaverde, Bartolomeo, Spanish bassoonist, composer of canzoni, **VII:** 219

Selmair, Franz, d. 1888, German composer, **IX:** 183

Selmer, Johan, 1844–1910, Norway composer, **IX:** 127

Selneccer, Nicolaus, b. 1539, German composer, **VI:** 65

Selter, H., 19th century French composer, **IX:** 99

Selva, ?, as 19th century arranger, **IX:** 254

Senart, 20th century publisher in Paris, **XII:** 143, 159

Seneca, Roman historian 1st century AD, **I:** 64

Senée, Henri, 19th century French composer, **IX:** 99

Senfer, Luigi, 19th century Italian composer, **XI:** 281

Senfl, ?, 19th century (?) Italian composer, **X:** 247

Senfl, Ludwig, 1486–1543, German composer, **II:** 97; **VI:** 27, 62, 63, 64, 77

Senofonte, Giovanni, 19th century Italian composer for band, **X:** 248

Serfert, A., 19th century French composer, **IX:** 99

Sergiusi, Anselmo, leader of Torino town band in 1580, **II:** 197

Serini, Giovanni, b. 1710, Italian composer, **XI:** 86

Sermisy, Claudin de, 1490–1562, French composer, **VI:** 39ff, 43ff, 49ff, 63, 92, 109, 114, 119

Serocki, Kazimierz, b. 1923, Polish composer, **XII:** 168

Serpette, Gaston, 19th century French composer, **IX:** 99

Serria, Giovanni, 1787–1876, Italian composer for band, **X:** 248

Servandoni, Chevalier, late Baroque English fireworks mechanic, **III:** 100

Setaccioli, Giacomo, 1868–1925, Italian composer, **IX:** 121

Setti, Giacomo, 19th century Italian composer for band, **X:** 248

Sévérény, H.-A., 19th century French composer, **IX:** 99

Seydel, Oscar, ?, 19th century English composer, **IX:** 279

Seydelmann, Franz, 1748–1806, German composer, **XI:** 86

Seyeller, ?, 18th century composer, **XI:** 86

Seyfert, Johann, 1731–1772, German composer, **XI:** 86

Seyffert, 17th century publisher in Dresden, **VII:** 111, 157, 199

Seyfried, Ignaz Ritter von, 1776–1841, works arranged for Harmoniemusik, **VIII:** 121 [*Saul, Konig in Israel*]; 122 [*Marpissa, Mitternacht, Alamar der Mare, Richard Löwenherz*]; unidentified work, 152

Seyfried, Ignaz von, 1776–1841, Viennese composer and arranger, **V:** 182ff; **VIII:** 77, [as arr., Mozart, *La Clemenza di Tito*, opera, for Harmoniemusik]; **IX:** 245, 254; **X:** 53

Seyler, Josef, 19th century Austrian composer, **IX:** 245

Sezza, Gratiano Fido di, 16th century composer, **VI:** 30

Sezza, Paolo Gigli di, 16th century composer, **VI:** 30

Shakespeare, William, 1564–1616, English playwright, **II:** 4, 55ff, **III:** 145

Shakespeare, XII: 204

Shepherd, John, 1520–1563, English composer, **VI:** 35

Shipman, W. H., 19th century American composer, **IX:** 139

Sibelius, Jan, 20th century composer, XII: 199 [arranged for band by Stokowsky]; 204

Sibelius, Jan, b. 1865, Finnish composer, **IX:** 123

Sibillot, Charles, 19th century French composer, **IX:** 100

Sibold, John, 19th century English composer for band, **X:** 115, 155

Sidney, Sir Philip, 1554–1586, **II:** 3, 45 [funeral]

Siebenhaar, Malachias, 1661, German composer for voices and winds, **VII:** 136

Siebenkas, conductor of the Bavarian Infantry band at the 1867 competition, **V:** 115

Sieber and Bailleaux, 19th century publisher in Paris, **XI:** 173

Sieber, 18th and 19th century publisher in Paris, **VIII:** 15, 19, 23, 26, 27ff, 29, 33, 37, 39, 44ff, 48, 56ff, 61ff, 65, 67, 75, 90, 95, 130, 153, 196, 220, 240, 276ff, 291; **IX:** 31, 48, 62, 77; **XI:** 28, 14, 50, 57, 70, 106, 115, 130, 132, 151, 192, 227, 243, 244, 247, 251, 273; **XII:** 52

Sieber, Ferdinand, 19th century Berlin music professor, **V:** 33

Sieber, père, 19th century publisher in Paris, **VIII:** 77, 82ff

Sieber, père, Jean, 17th century French publisher, **IV:** 71

Siebert, E., 19th century German composer, **IX:** 183

Siede, C., conductor of an 19th century Austrian band playing in Hamburg, **V:** 110

Siefert, Paul, 1586–1666, 1651, German composer of an 8-part canzona, **VII:** 177

Siegbert, S., 19th century composer for choir and brass, **V:** 209

Siegbert, S., 19th century German composer, **IX:** 183

Siegel, 19th century publisher in Leipzig, **XI:** 49

Siégrist, ?, 19th century French composer, **IX:** 100

Sigefrid, Cornelius, 1607 German composer, **VII:** 178

Sighicelli, Vincenzo, 1830–1892, Italian composer for band, **X:** 249

Sigismund, Emperor, Holy Roman Empire, **I:** 266ff

Sigl, Georg, 18th century composer in Olmütz Harmoniemusik collection, **IV:** 22, fn. 9; **VIII:** 345ff, (11) *Partitas,* and *Messe* with Harmoniemusik

Signard, P., 19th century French composer, **IX:** 100; **X:** 89

Signorucci, Pompeo, 1608, Italian composer of church concerti, **VII:** 209

Siklós, Albert, 1878–1942, Hungarian, **XII:** 113, 177

Siluani, 17th century publisher in Bologna, **VII:** 187; **XI:** 160

Silva, de, 16th century composer, **VI:** 63

Silverstolpe, Fredrik, Swedish Ambassador to Vienna, 1796–1802, **IV:** 14

Simes, Thomas, 1768 search for a military conductor, **IV:** 111

Simiot, André, 19th century French composer, **IX:** 100

Simmes, William, early 17th century, composer of English ensemble music, **VII:** 72

Simon, 18th century composer, **IV:** 24, 90; **VIII:** 235, (4) *Partitas* for Harmoniemusik

Simon, 19th century publisher in Paris, **IX:** 5

Simon, Anton, b. 1851, French composer, **IX:** 100

Simon, Johann, 19th century German composer, **XI:** 145

Simon, Martin, Baroque composer, **XII:** 5

Simonet, as arranger of Solié, *Le jockey,* opera, for Harmoniemusik, **VIII:** 123

Simonet, F. M., 19th century (?) composer, **XI:** 253

Simonet, François, bassoon faculty of the 1792 Paris Conservatoire, **IV:** 156

Simonetti, ?, ca. 1767, *Dresdner Menuetten* for band, **VIII:** 346

Simoni, arr., Kunzen, *Das Fest der Winzer,* opera, for Harmoniemusik, **VIII:** 56

Simonich, Anna, 19th century Turkish composer (wife of the sultan) for band, **X:** 263

Simpkins, 18th century publisher in London, **VIII:** 202

Simpson, 18th century publisher in London, **XI:** 4, 37, 76, 87,102, 163, 198, 199, 210

Simpson, J., early 18th century publisher in London, **XI:** 190

Simpson, Thomas, 1582–1628, English composer, **VII:** 23ff, 72ff, 144, 163, 172

Simpson's Musick Shop, 18th century publisher in London, **XI:** 213

Simrock, 19th century publisher in Bonn, **X:** 18; **XI:** 145, 173, 201,246, 288, 300, 319; **XII:** 53

Simrock, 19th century publisher in Berlin, **IX:** 165

Simrock, 19th century publisher in Bonn and Paris, **VIII:** 82ff, 99, 126, 200, 206, 218, 229, 339; **IX:** 90, 147, 155, 160, 183, 186, 235

Simrock, 20th century publisher in Paris, **XII:** 168

Simrock, Henry, horn faculty of the 1792 Paris Conservatoire, **IV:** 156

Singer, Pater Peter, 19th century composer in Vienna, **XI:** 289

Sinigaglia, Leone, 1868–1944, Italian composer, **XI:** 174, 239

Sinoquet, E., 19th century French composer, **IX:** 100ff

Sinsoilliez, Adolphe, 19th century French composer, **IX:** 101

Sixt, Johann (Giovanni), Italian composer, 1757–1797 (6) *Allemandes* for Harmoniemusik, **VIII:** 346 [(6) *Allemandes* for Harmoniemusik]; **XI:** 221

Skacel, as arranger of Rossini, *Bianca e Falliero,* opera, for Harmoniemusik, **VIII:** 117

Skalkotas, Nico, 1904–1949, Greek composer, **XII: 177**

Skalkotas, Nicos, 1878–1942, Greek composer, **XII:** 113

Skandinavisk Musikforlag, 20th century publisher in Kopenhagen, **XII:** 153

Skillern, 18th century publisher in London, **VIII:** 264

Skotscoffsky, G. V., 18th century composer, **XI:** 87

Skroup, Jan, 1811–1892, Austrian composer, **IX:** 245

Smancini, ?, 19th century Italian composer for band, **X:** 249

Smart, G., 18th century publisher in London, **VIII:** 256ff, 260, 264

Smart, Peter, preacher in Durham in 1630, opposed to winds in church, **III:** 203

Smart, Timothy, 18th century English, (24) *Select military pieces for Harmonie,* **VIII:** 264

Smith, 18th century publisher in London, **XI:** 210

Smith, A., 19th century English composer for band, **X:** 156

Smith, Mr., court trumpeter of Charles I, **III:** 91

Smith, R., 20th century publisher in London, **XII:** 91, 92

Smyth, James, 19th century conductor of the Royal Artillery band, **V:** 83

Snel, Joseph, 1793–1861, Belgium composer, conductor, Société Royale de la Grande-harmonie (1831), **IX:** 260

Snelling, H.J., 19th century German composer, **X:** 110

SNKLHU, 20th century publisher in Prag, **XII:** 182

Sobeck, Johann, 1831–1940, German composer of works for band, **X:** 110

Socrates, 469–399 BC, **I:** 35

Socrates, V: 54

Soderini, Agostino, 1608, Italian composer of canzoni, one 14-parts, **VII:** 209

Sofie von Mecklenburg, German, 16th century bride, **II:** 6

Sohier, Henry, 19th century French composer, **IX:** 101; **X:** 89

Sola, Charles, b. 1786, composer, **XI:** 87

Soland, 19th century French composer, **IX:** 2

Solar, Francisco, 1625–1688, Spanish composer, **III:** 221

Soldi, 17th century publisher in Roma, **VII:** 198

Soler, Francisco, 1625–1688, Spanish composer for voices and winds, **VII:** 219; **IX:** 131

Solère, Étienne, 1753–1817, clarinet faculty of the 1792 Paris Conservatoire, **IV:** 156; **VIII:** 293, *March* for small band; **IX:** 101; **XI:** 145

Solié, Jean Pierre, 1755–1812, *March* for small band, **VIII:** 293

Solié, works arranged for Harmoniemusik, **VIII:** 123

Soller, ?, 18th century Austrian composer, **XI:** 145

Soller, Antonio, 1729–1783, as arranger for Harmoniemusik, **XII:** 52

Solomon, E., 19th century English composer for band, **X:** 156

Sombrun, Alexis, 19th century French composer, **IX:** 101

Somervell, Arthur, 1863–1937, English composer, **XII:** 177

Somis, Giovanni, 1686–1763, Italian violinist & composer, **XI:** 87, 120, 162

Sommer, Johann, 1619, German composer, **VII:** 144, 166, 178

Sommer, Johann, ca. 1780, *Pieze* for Harmonie, 2 violas (?), **VIII:** 347

Sondershausen, 19th century Duke of, **V:** 185

Sonneleiter, Antonius, 19th century Austrian composer, **IX:** 245

Sonnenleitner, 18th century composer in Olmütz Harmoniemusik collection, **IV:** 22, fn. 9

Sonntag, Gottfried, colleague of Wagner, **V:** 123

Sophocles, ancient Greek playwright, **I;** 49; **II:** 133

Sor, Joseph Fernando, 1778–1839, Spanish composer, **IX:** 131; **XII:** 67

Sorcsek, Jerome, 20th century American composer, **XII:** 204

Sorge, Georg Andreas, 1703–1778 German composer, **XI:** 87, 120, 125, 221; **XI:** 87

Sostratus, aulos player, 280–261 BC, **I:** 11

Souillard, Jean, member in 1768–77 of the Les Grands Hautbois, **IV:** 64, fn. 4

Souliaert, Carolus, d. 1540, Dutch composer, **VI:** 12

Sousa, J. P., XII: 199 [arranged for band by Stokowsky], 200, 201, 205

Sousa, John Philip, 1854–1932, American composer, **IX:** 139; **X:** 116, 271

Southerton, Leonard, 16th century English composer, **VI:** 35

Southworth, W., 19th century English composer for band, **X:** 156

Souyeux, E., 19th century French composer, **IX:** 101

Sowerby, Leo, b. 1895, American composer, **XII:** 177

Sowinski, A., arr. Berr, 1800–1828, German composer, **IX:** 183

Soyer, Adolphe, 19th century French composer, conductor Musique 109e de Ligne, **IX:** 101

Spaet (Spath?), Andrea, 19th century composer, **XI:** 246

Spalek, Ignac, 1758–1760, court bassoonist in Olmütz, **IV:** 21

Spalenza, Pietr' Antonio, maestro di cappela in Treviso, **II:** 243

Spandau, ?, 18th century composer, **XI:** 242

Sparano, Giuseppe, 19th century Italian composer for band, **X:** 249

Späth, André, 1790–1876, German composer, **V:** 211; **IX:** 183

Spazier, ?, reports on Harmoniemusik in Bonn in 1793, **IV:** 51

Speer, Daniel, 1636–1707, German composer for civic music, **III:** 17, 168ff, 227ff; **VII:** 136ff

Spehr, early 19th century publisher at Braunschweig, **XI:** 175

Spellerberg, oboist in band of George IV, **V:** 203, fn. 10

Spencer, Capt. John, English, *Oxfordshire Militia March*, 1793, for band, **VIII:** 264

Spencer, John, (1795) English composer for band, **X:** 32

Speranza, ?, 19th century Italian arranger, **X:** 169

Spergen, ?, *Parthia*, 1799, for Harmoniemusik, **VIII:** 235

Sperger, Johannes, d. 1812, Czech composer of Harmoniemusik, **IV:** 33, 59; **VIII:** 347ff, (77) *Partitas* for Harmoniemusik; **XI:** 87, 174, 221

Spergher, Ignaz, 18th century, Austrian composer, **XI:** 261

Spforad, 20th century publisher in Paris, **XII:** 164

Spiegler, Matthias, 1631, German composer for church ens., **VII:** 137

Spieringk, 18th century publisher in Hamburg, **VII:** 157

Spiller, ?, 18th century German, *Partia* for Harmoniemusik, **VIII:** 352

Spinas, 19th century publisher in Vienna, **XI:** 90

Spisak, Michal, b. 1914, Polish composer, **XII:** 113, 177

Splichal, Jan, 19th century Czech composer, **IX:** 245

Spohr, Ludwig, 1784–1859, German composer **IV:**78 [review of the Russin horn band]; **V:** 102, 152ff, 156, 185, 192, 195, 205; **IX:** 180, 184; **X:** 110; **XI:** 145, 288, 300; **XII:** 215, 220

Spohr, Ludwig, 1784–1859, composer of works arranged for Harmoniemusik, **VIII:** 123, 124

Sponga, Francesco, 1561–1641, Italian composer, **VI:** 101

Spongia, canzona composer in Venice, 16th century, **II:** 245

Spontini, Gaspare, 1774–1851, Italian composer in Berlin, **V:** 22, 27,30, 36 [arr. by Wieprecht], 61, 63, 73, 122, 148, 191

Spontini, Gaspare, 1774–1851, works arranged for Harmoniemusik, **VIII:** 124 [*Julie, Milton, La Vestale*]; 125 [*Dieux Rivaux, Fernand Cortez,*]

Spontini, Gasparo, 1774–1851, Italian composer, **IX:** 184; **X:** 249

Spontini, works arranged for band, **IX:** 141 [*Vestalin, Cortez*]; 180 [*Vesttalien, Fernand Cortez*]

Sporck, Franz Anton, Count, 1662–1738, (re the arrival of the horn indoors), **III:** 10

Spourni, Wenceslaus, 18th century Czech composer, **XI:** 87

Springer, ?, 19th century Austrian composer, **IX:** 246

Sprongl, Norbert, b. 1892, Austrian composer, **XII:** 177

Sramek, Vladimir, b. 1923, Czech composer, **XII:** 178

St. Augustine, I: 91, 92

St. Clair, W., 19th century English composer for band, **X:** 157

St. Felis, composer in 1600 dance collection published in Heidelberg, **VII:** 180

St. Francis of Assisi, I: 95 (fn. Nr. 4)

St. Julien, Paris wind guild, music of, **VI:** 37

St. Leger, W. N., 19th century English composer, **IX:** 279; **X:** 157

Stabile, composer in 1600 dance collection published in Heidelberg, **VII:** 180

Stablingher, Mathias, 1750–1815, Italian composer, **XI:** 87, 221

Stackelberg, 19th century German composer, **IX:** 141

Staden, Johann, 1581–1634, German composer, **VII:** 144, 145, 163, 178

Stadler, Anton, 1753–1812, clarinetist in orig, Vienna Harmoniemusik, **IV:** 35 fn. 77, 42, 46ff; **VIII:** 235, *Partitas* for Harmoniemusik

Stadler, Giuseppe (di Praga), Austrian composer, 18th century, **XII:** 43

Stadler, J. Dominicus (Maximilian Abbé), Austrian composer, **XI:** 221

Stadler, J., fl. 1800–1828, Austrian composer, **IX:** 246

Stadler, Johann, 1756–1804, clarinetist in original Vienna Harmoniemusik, **IV:** 35 fn. 77, 42

Stadler, Josef de Wolfersgrun, (12) *Tadeschi pour Musique d'Harmonie,* **VIII:** 235

Stadler, Joseph, 1725–1765, German composer, **XI:** 88

Stadler, Maximilian, 1748–1833, Austrian composer, *Hoch du mein Vaterland,* chorus and Harmoniemusik, **VIII:** 236; **IX:** 246

Stadlmayr, Johann, 1575–1648, German composer, **III:** 215; **VII:** 137

Staempfli, Edward, b. 1908, Swiss composer, **XII:** 114, 178

Stager, 19th century French composer, **IX:** 72

Stahel, 16th century German composer, **VI:** 64

Stahl, H., 19th century English composer for band, **X:** 157

Stainer & Bell, 20th century publisher in London, **XII:** 145

Stamitz, ?, 18th century German composer, **XI:** 88, 120

Stamitz, Anton, 1754–1809, German composer, **XI:** 88, 120, 281

Stamitz, Carl, 1745–1801, German composer, **XI:** 88, 121, 174, 222, 279

Stamitz, Fr., 18th century German composer, **XI:** 261

Stamitz, Franz, horn player at Esterházy, **IV:** 29

Stamitz, Johann Carl, 18th century German composer, **XI:** 88

Stamitz, Johann Wenzel Anton, 1717–1757, German composer in France, **IV:** 66ff, 70; **XI;** 88, 121, 146

Stamitz, Karl, 1745–1801, German composer, ca. (77) works for Harmoniemusik, **VIII:** 352ff; **XI:** 146, 242

Standhaft, H. F., 19th century English composer, **IX:** 279

Stanford, Charles Villiers, 1852–1924, English composer, **XII:** 114, 178; **IX:** 279

Stanislaus, ?, composer included in a 1889 English collection of band music, **X:** 116

Stanley, John, 1713–1786, English composer, **XI:** 89

Stappen, A., 19th century French composer, **IX:** 102

Starbe, 19th century arranger, **X:** 18

Stark, ?, composer included in a 1878 English collection of band music, **X:** 114

Starke, as arranger for Harmoniemusik, **VIII:** 5, 43, 44, 49, 106, 108, 110, 111, 112, 114, 138, 152, 154, 159

Starke, Friedrich, 1774–1835, Austrian composer, arranger, **IX:** 196, 246, 254

Starker, Liberato, 19th century German composer, **XI:** 290

Starzer, Joseph, 1726–1787 Austrian composer, Harmonie composer for Count Palm in Vienna, **IV:** 19, 42; **VIII:** 126 [*Adelheid von Ponthieu,* ballet, arr. for Harmoniemusik]; 236, (5) compositions for Harmoniemusik; **XI:** 262

Stasny, ?, 19th century English composer, **IX:** 279

Stasny, ?, 19th century German composer, **X:** 111

Stebbing, E., 19th century English composer for band, **X:** 157

Stechi, Antonine, 19th century Austrian composer, **IX:** 247

Stefani Jean l'aine, French, 1746–1829 (6) *Parties* for Harmoniemusik, **VIII:** 369

Steffani, ?, (6) *Parthien,* Op. 1, for Harmoniemusik, **VIII:** 236

Steffens, Fr., 19th century German composer, **IX:** 184

Stegman, composer in repertoire of band of George IV, **V:** 201

Stegmann, Carl, 1751–1826, German tenor & composer, **XI:** 241

Steibelt, Daniel, 1765–1823, German composer, works arranged for Harmoniemusik, **VIII:** 126 [*Bataille d'Austerlitz, Cinquième pot-pourry, Combat naval, La Journée d'Ulm, March and trio*]; **IX:** 141; **XI:** 89; **XII:** 53 [*Combat Naval,* arranged for small band by Carl Andreas Göpfert]

Stein, 17th century publisher in Frankfurt, **VII:** 161, 162, 170, 171

Steinacker, 19th century German composer, **IX:** 180

Steiner, 19th century publisher in Vienna, **V:** 101; **VIII:** 6ff, 8, 49, 51, 78, 122, 125, 133, 136ff, 157ff, 194; **IX:** 209, 211, 218, 219, 220ff, 227, 240, 243, 254; **XI:** 144

Steiner, Ernst, 19th century Austrian composer, **IX:** 246

Steiner, Franz, bassoonist, in Prince Liechtenstein Harmonie, **IV:** 39

Steinfeld, Albert, 1741–1815, German composer, **VIII:** 353 [(6) *Quartets* for Harmoniemusik]; **XI:** 89, 222, 306

Steinmüller, ?, 18th century Austrian, **XI:** 174 [biographical note]

Steinmüller, Thaddaus, hornist in 1761 for Prince Esterházy, **IV:** 27

Stengel, F. von, 18th century German, untitled work for Harmoniemusik, **VIII:** 353

Sténosse, Ed., 19th century French composer, **IX:** 102

Stepan, Josef, 1726–1797, (9) works for Harmoniemusik, **VIII:** 236ff

Stephan, Wilhelm, successor to Wieprecht, **V:** 122

Stéphanie, 19th century Grande Duchesse de Bade, **XII:** 10

Stephann, 18th century composer in Olmütz Harmoniemusik collection, **IV:** 22, fn. 9

Stephen Mahu, 16th century composer, **VI:** 63

Stephen, composer in a 1609 Hamburg collection, **VII:** 166

Sternberg, Erich-Walter, b. 1891, German composer, **XII:** 178

Steuccius (Steucke), Heinrich, 1602, German composer, **VII:** 179ff

Stevens, Bernard, b. 1916, English composer, **XII:** 114, 178

Stevens, Richard, 1757–1837, English, (2) *Marches* for band, **VIII:** 264ff

Stevenson, composer in 1615 English ensemble part-books, **VII:** 23

Stewart, 18th century publisher in Edinburgh, **VIII:** 257

Stich, Johann, 1748–1803 (pseudo. Punto, Giovanni), composer, **XI:** 74, 172, , 217, 234, 261, 283, 286

Stich, Josef, 19th century German composer, **IX:** 185

Stiglitz, Georges, d. 1799, faculty of the 1792 Paris Conservatoire, **IV:** 156

Stivori, Francesco, 16th century composer in Venice, **II:** 245; **VI:** 101

Stivorio, Francesco, 1603 Italian composer of 8 canzoni, **VII:** 209

Stock, Christoph, b. 1862, German composer, **IX:** 185

Stockaert, Adrien, Flemish, composer, **VI:** 114

Stöckel, chief Stadtpfeifer in Altenburg (early 18th century), **III:** 162ff

Stockhausen, Karlheinz, b. 1928, German composer, **XII:** 179

Stokes, Eric, 20th century American composer, **XII:** 205

Stokowsky, Leopold, conductor, **XII:** 199

Stoltzer, Thomas, 1480–1526, German composer, **II:** 109; **VI:** 27, 62, 63, 74, 76, 77

Stölzel, Gottfried, 1690–1749, German composer, **III:** 17; **XI:** 89, 121, 237, 242

Stölzel, Heinrich, 1815 inventor of a modern valve for brass, **V:** 4

Storace, collaborator in a *Divertimento* with Pleyel, Attwood, **VIII:** 252

Storace, Stephen, 1763–1796, English, works arranged for Harmoniemusik, **VIII:** 127, 252; music for voices and 10 winds, **VIII:** 264

Storaro, ?, 18th century Italian composer, *March* for 11 winds and organ, **VIII:** 368; **X:** 39

Storch, Anton, 19th century German composer, **IX:** 185; **XI:** 174

Storck, ?, 19th century German composer, **IX:** 185

Storck, 18th century German publisher, **VIII:** 295

Störl, Johann, 1675–1719, German composer for Hautboisten, **III:** 17, 131; **VII:** 138ff

Stössel, ?, fl. 1800–1828, German composer, **IX:** 185

Stoupan, F., 19th century French composer, arranger, **IX:** 102

Strabo, 1st century BC geographer, **I:** 33, 40

Stranensky, ?, ca. 1800, German, (6) *Partitas* for Harmoniemusik, **VIII:** 353

Strasser, William, 1875–1944, American, composer, **XII:** 190ff

Strastegier, Herman, b. 1912, German composer, **XII:** 179

Strauss, ?, a work arranged by Lindpainter, **X:** 105

Strauss, ?, *Krapfenwaldelwalzer*, unknown arranger for Harmoniemusik, **VIII:** 127

Strauss, ?, late 19th century Austrian composer, **X:** 53

Strauss, composer in a collection of Harmoniemusik by an unknown arranger, **VIII:** 152

Strauss, E., 19th century Austrian composer, **IX:** 247

Strauss, Eduard, 1835–1916, Austrian composer, **X:** 54

Strauss, J., composer included in a 1878 English collection of band music, **X:** 115

Strauss, J., IX: 253

Strauss, Joh., composer included in a 1874 English collection of band music, **X:** 113

Strauss, Johann, 1804–1848, **IX:** 247

Strauss, Johann, arranged for band by Stokowsky, **XII:** 199

Strauss, Johann, arranged for band, **VIII:** 151; **IX:** 186, 256, 257

Strauss, Johann, Jr., 1825–1899, Viennese composer, **V:** 55, 111ff, 177; **X:** 54ff, 115

Strauss, Johann, Sr., V: 136

Strauss, Josef, 1827–1870, Austrian composer, **IX:** 247; **X:** 58ff

Strauss, Richard, 1864–1949, German composer, **V:** 132; **IX:** 185; **XII:** 205, 207, 215

Stravinsky, Igor, 20th century Russian composer, **XII:** 205

Strazer, Josef, 1726–1787, composer in Vienna, Russia, **IV:** 17

Streck, ?, composer included in a 1873 English collection of band music, **X:** 113

Streck, P., 19th century Austrian composer, **IX:** 246

Streck, Peter, 19th century German composer, **IX:** 186

Streicher, Nanette (née Stein), fl. 1800–1828, German composer, **IX:** 186

Strepponi, Feliciano, 1767–1832, Italian composer, **IX:** 121

Stricker, Augustin, 1675–1720, German composer, **XI:** 89, 121

Striegler, Kurt, 1886–1958, German composer, **XII:** 179

Striggio, Alessandro, 1536–1592, Italian composer, **II:** 131ff; **VI:** 84, 88

Strobe, Heinrich, 19th century Austrian composer, **IX:** 247

Strogers, 16th century composer, **VI:** 32

Strogers, composer in 1613–1619 Tregian ensemble collection, **VII:** 23

Strouhal, Padre Bernard, (18) *Parthias* for Harmoniemusik, **VIII:** 237ff

Strube, Gustav, 19th century German violinist living in Boston, **XII: 192**

Struck, Paul, 1776–1820, German composer, **XI:** 89, 146, 262, 287

Strum, 17th century publisher in Augsburg, **VII:** 166

Strunck, Nikolaus, 1640–1700, German composer for recorder consort, **VII:** 138

Strungk, Delphin, 1601–1694, German composer for voices and winds, **VII:** 138

Strunz, Georg, 1781–1852, German composer, **XI:** 89, 174

Strutius, Thomas, 1658, German composer of church concerti, **VII:** 179

Stüber, clarinetist, 19th century court of Mechlenburg-Schwerin, **V:** 185, fn. 4

Stückel, as arranger of Weigl, *Richard Löwenherz*, ballet, for Harmoniemusik, **VIII:** 139

Stückel, Ferdinand, Classical Period composer, **XII:** 43

Studer, Hans, b. 1911, Swiss composer, **XII:** 114, 179

Stühl, ?, German Baroque composer of music for bassoons, **X:** 9

Stumpf, as arranger for Harmoniemusik, **VIII:** 29, 61, 75, 76ff, 78ff, 80ff, 90, 91, 94, 99ff, 117, 118, 135, 144, 148, 159; **XII:** 53 [*Les Visitandines* (opera) by Devienne, for Harmoniemusik; Martin's opera *Capricciosa* for Harmoniemusik; Paër, *la Camilla;* Peter Winter's *Das unterbrochene* (opera) for Harmoniemusik]; 54 [Paër's, *Il morto vivo,* for Harmoniemusik]

Stumpf, band leader in Strassburg, **V:** 209; **X:** 95

Stumpf, Johann Christian, d. 1801, (2) *Partitas* for Harmoniemusik, **VIII:** 353ff; **IX:** 180, 186

Stuntz, Joseph, 1793–1859, German civic militia composer, **V:** 125, 132; **IX:** 186; **XI:** 90, 121, 146

Stupan, 17th century composer in Erlebach, collection of Hautboisten music, **VII:** 156

Stupfler, Ph., 19th century French composer, **IX:** 102

Sturzenegger, Richard, b. 1905, Swiss composer, **XII:** 115, 179

Stutschewsky, Joachim, b. 1891, German composer, **XII:** 115

Sudessi, P., 19th century French composer, **IX:** 102

Sudre, Jean-François, 19th century violinist, teacher and inventor of a language based on music, **V:** 58; **IX:** 102; **XII:** 67

Suetonius, 1st – 2nd century AD, Roman historian, **I:** 57

Suise, Étienne, member in 1777 of the Les Grands Hautbois, **IV:** 64, fn. 4

Sul, ?, late 17th century, German composer for 3 flutes, **VII:** 138

Suleiman the Great, 1520–1566, **III:** 104

Sumner, hornist, 19th century court at Rudolstadt, **V:** 186, fn. 8

Suppé, Franz von, arranged for band, **IX:** 257

Suppé, Franz, 1819–1895, 19th century Austrian composer, **IX:** 247; **X:** 59, 115; **XI:** 90, 174, 262

Supries, Joseph, 1761–1822, composer, **XI:** 253

Surinach, Carlos, 20th century Spanish composer, **XII:** 205

Susato, Tielman, 1510–1570, composer, publisher and leader of Antwerp town band, **II:** 166, 175ff, 213; **VI:** 63, 109, 118, 119, 120, 121

Süssmayer, Franz Xaver, 1766–1803, **VIII:** 238 [(3) works for Harmoniemusik]

Süssmayr, Franz Xaver, 1766–1803, as composer of works arranged for Harmoniemusik, **VIII:** 56 [as arranger of Kürzinger, *Robert und Caliste,* for Harmoniemusik]; 127 [*Der Spiegel von Arkadien*]; 128 [*Der Retter in Gefahr, Soliman der Zweite*];];**XI:** 146, 222, 230, 234, 238; **XII:** 48 [, movements from *Aus dem Spiegel von Arcadien,* arr. Druschetzky for Harmoniemusik]; **XII:** 48 [movements from *Aus dem Spiegel von Arcadien,* arr. Druschetzky for Harmoniemusik]

Suter, Robert, b. 1919, Swiss composer, **XII:** 115, 179

Sutermeister, Heinrich, b. 1910, Swiss composer, **XII:** 115, 180

Sutton, W. W., b. 1793, English composer, **XI:** 90

Suvini Zerboni, 20th century publisher in Milan, **XII:** 184

Suwarrow, General, 18th century English militia, **X:** 28

Suzanne, Marius, 19th century French composer, **IX:** 102

Swart, Willem, 1603 Dutch composer of works for voices or winds, **VII:** 215

Sweelinck, Jan, 1562–1621, Dutch composer, **VI:** 118

Swoboda, ?, 19th century Austrian composer, **IX:** 247

Sydow, ?, composer included in a 1878 English collection of band music, **X:** 114

Sydow, ?, director, 1750, of Prussian army music school, **IV:** 90

Sydow, Herr von, German composer, **V:** 101 [1804 announcement of a collection of military music]; **IX:** 192

Sydow, Samuel, 17th century composer, **VII:** 100; **XII:** 5

Sykora, Franz, arranged for band, **IX:** 257

Sylvani van, Dutch student of Mozart, composer, **IX:** 125

Syringus, Jacobus, 16th century German composer, **VI:** 75

Szabelski, Bolslaw, 1896, Polish composer, **XII:** 115

Szabo, Xaver, 19th century (?) Hungarian composer, **XI:** 239

Szalowski, Bonifacy, 1867–1923, French composer, **XII:** 180

Székely, Endre, b. 1912, composer, **XII:** 180

Szekeressy, Antal, early 19th century Hungarian composer, **XII:** 43

Szeligowski, Tadeusz, 1896–1963, Polish composer, **XII:** 180

Szervánszky, Endré, b. 1911, composer, **XII:** 180

Taaffe, Den., Capt., of regiment at St. Helena, **VIII:** 262

Tabeteau, Marcel, Principal oboe, Philadelphia Orchestra, **XII:** 189

Tacet, Joseph, 18th century, English composer, **XI:** 90, 121

Tacitus, 1st century AD Roman historian, **I:** 58

Tadolini, Giovanni, 1785–1872, Italian composer, **X:** 249; **XI:** 90, 241, 299

Taeggio, Francesco Rognoni, d. 1626, Italian composer, **III:** 220; **VII:** 205

Taffanel, Paul, 1844–1908, founder, chamber wind society in Paris, **V:** 153; **IX:** 67; **XI:** 90; **XII:** 196, 212, 213, 216

Tag, Christian, 1735–1811, German composer of church music with winds, **IV:** 124; **VIII:** 353, church music for voices and winds; **IX:** 187; **XI:** 302

Tagietti, Luigi, late Baroque Italian composer, **III:** 14

Täglichsbeck, Thomas, 1799–1867, German composer, **XI:** 147

Taglioni, Marie, 1804–1884, Swedish ballerina, 'Pas de Deux,' arranged by Triebensee for Harmoniemusik, **VIII:** 128

Taillard, l'aine, 18th century, first flautist at the Concert Spirituel in Paris in 1760, **XI:** 90

Taillefer, minstrel to William the Conqueror, **I:** 181

Takáscs, Jenö, b. 1902, Hungarian composer, **XII:** 180

Talbot, James, 1700 reference to the new oboe, **III:** 225

Taliano (the 'Italiano'?), Baroque composer, **XII:** 5

Talini, Giuseppe, 19th century Italian composer for band, **X:** 250

Talleyrand, Charles Maurice, 1754–1838, Bishop of Autun, 18th century France, **IV:** 141

Tallis, Thomas, 1505–1585, English composer, **VI:** 31, 35

Tanejew, Alexander, 1850–1915, Russian composer, **IX:** 135; **XI:** 147

Tarchi, Angelo, 1760–1814, works arranged for Harmoniemusik, **VIII:** 13, 128, 129, 152, 153

Tardos, Béla, b. 1910, Hungarian composer, **XII:** 180

Tartagnini, Luigi, 19th century Italian composer, **XI:** 157, 253

Tartini, Giuseppe, 1692–1770, Italian, composer, **XI:** 91

Tassoni, Clemente, ?, late 18th century Italian composer, **X:** 39

Tate, Phyllis, b. 1911, English composer, **XII:** 181

Tauber, J. F., d. 1803, flautist & composer, **XI:** 91

Tauchmann, Johann Friedrich, fl. ca. 1700, **VII:** 8

Tausch, F., as arranger of Righini, *Pièces d'harmonie,* for Harmoniemusik, **VIII:** 105

Tausch, fils, Mr., **XI:** 139 [dedication]

Tausch, Franz, 1762–1817, clarinetist, **V:** 16, fn. 45; **VIII:** 354, (17) *Marches,* (14) chamber works for Harmonie; **XI:** 147, 246

Tausch, German composer in 1834 Hoftheater collection in Stuttgart, **X:** 95

Tautwein, 19th century publisher in Berlin, **V:** 34

Tavernar, 16th century composer, **VI:** 35; **VII:** 22

Tchaikowsky, Peter, 19th century Russian composer, **XII:** 205

Tebaldini, Giovanni, 1864–1952, Italian composer, **IX:** 121; **X:** 250; **XII:** 115

Tebay, J., English, *The Bath Volunteer's March,* ca. 1785, for Harmoniemusik, **VIII:** 264

Tedeschi, 18th century publisher in Bologna, **XI:** 61

Teike, Carl, 1864–1922, German composer, **IX:** 187

Teimer, Ignaz, oboist in the Joseph Schwarzenberg Harmoniemusik, **IV:** 41, fn. 104

Teimer, Johann, oboist, English hornist, **IV:** 33, 41 fn. 104

Teimer, Philip, oboist, English hornist, **IV:** 33, 41 fn. 104

Teissier, A., 19th century French composer, **IX:** 102

Telemann, Georg, 1681–1767, German composer, **III:** 11, 19, 21, 123, 215; **IV:** 7, 19; **VII:** 107, 138ff; **X:** 10; **XI:** 91, 121, 125, 222, 237, 275; **XII:** 5

Tempia, Stefano, 1832–1878, Italian composer works for band, **X:** 250

Terry, le C. de, 18th century composer, **VII:** 88

Terschak, Adolf, b. 1832, Czech composer, **XI:** 91

Tertre, Estienne, 16th century publisher of danceries, **VI:** 52

Tessarini, Carlo, 1690–1766, Italian composer, **XI:** 91, 122, 222

Textor, Caspar, early 17th century, German composer of dances, **VII:** 180

Teyber, Anton, 1756–1822, German composer, **XI:** 174

Thayer, Alexander, 1817–1897, American early biographer of Beethoven, **IV:** 51

Theen, hornist, 19th century court of Mechlenburg-Schwerin, **V:** 185, fn. 4

Theile, Johann, 1646–1742, instructor of Hautboisten bands, **III:** 125

Theny, Jan, 19th century Austrian composer, **IX:** 247

Theodore of Cyrus, churchman, d. 460 AD, **I:** 92

Theon, 4th century BC Greek painter, **I:** 37

Therese, 19th century Queen of Bavaria, **IX:** 182

Théret, G., 19th century French composer, **IX:** 102

Thern, Carl, *Wachtparade* for Harmoniemusik, **VIII:** 238

Therstapen, Hans Joachim, 1905–1950, German composer, **XII:** 181

Thesselius, Johann, 1609, German composer of dances, **VII:** 140, 180

Theuss, ?, fl. 1800–1828, German composer, **IX:** 143, 187

Thiabot, Victor, 19th century French composer, **IX:** 102

Thiel, 19th century publisher in Leipzig, **XI:** 272

Thiele, Eduard, 19th century Austrian composer, **IX:** 247

Thilman, Johannes Paul, b. 1906, German composer, **XII:** 115, 181

Thiriet, André, b. 1906, French composer, **XII:** 181

Thisio, composer in 1600 dance collection published in Heidelberg, **VII:** 180

Thomas Aquinas, Church philosopher, 1225–1275, **I:** 95

Thomas de Cabham, d. 1313, **I:** 96

Thomas, 19th century French composer, **XII:** 218

Thomas, A., composer, [judge of the 1867 world competition in Paris], **V:** 114

Thomas, C. S., 19th century English composer, **IX:** 279

Thomas, J., 19th century French composer, **IX:** 103

Thomas, P. J., von, 19th century German composer, **IX:** 188

Thomas, P., 19th century French composer, **IX:** 103

Thompson & Son, 18th century publisher in London, **XI:** 199

Thompson, 18th century publisher in London, **XI:** 4, 47, 102, 163, 195, 218, 252

Thompson, C. and S., 18th century publisher in London, **XI:** 187, 191, 193, 199, 270

Thompson, R., 18th century publisher in London, **XI:** 193, 194

Thomsen, Magnus, trumpeter and scribe, 16th century, **II:** 110

Thomson, Virgil, b. 1906, American composer, **XII:** 115, 181

Thornowets, ?, 18th century composer, **XI:** 92

Thorowgood and Horne, 18th century publisher in London, **XI:** 101

Thorowgood, 18th century publisher in London, **XI:** 101

Thouret, Georg, 1855–1924, German composer of works for band, **X:** 90

Thucydides, 5th century BC historian, **I:** 45

Thuille, Ludwig, 1861–1907, German composer, **XI:** 319; **XII:** 214, 216

Thusius, in a 1616 Nürnberg collection, **VII:** 163

Tiburtino, Giuliano, 1510–1569, Italian composer, **VI:** 101

Ticci, Rinaldo, 19th century civic band conductor in Siena, **V:** 157

Tidewell, J., 19th century English composer for band, **X:** 157

Tiersmith, Richard, in the 1775 Harmoniemusik of the Prince of Monaco, **IV:** 69

Tiessen, Heinz, b. 1887, German composer, **XII:** 182

Tillard, ?, 19th century French composer of band works, **V:** 151

Tilliard, Geroges, 19th century French composer, **IX:** 103ff

Tinctoris, Johannes, 15th century theorist, **I:** 162, 173

Tinet, Charles, 19th century French composer, **IX:** 104

Tini & Lamazzo, Heirs of, 17th century publishers in Milan, **VII:** 195, 198ff, 208, 209

Tini, Francesco & Simon, 1594 publishers in Milano, **VI:** 93

Tinney, F. G., 19th century English composer, **IX:** 280; **X:** 157

Tipsly, unnamed work arranged by Triebensee for Harmoniemusik, **VIII:** 152

Tischer, Johann, 1707–1774, German composer, **XI:** 122

Tischler, Conrad, author of a *Flöten-Schule*, **XI:** 92

Titl, Anton, 1809–1882, German composer, **VIII:** [*Der Zauberschleier*, arr. Wajacek, for Harmoniemusik]; **IX:** 188, 257

Titoff, ?, 19th century German composer, **IX:** 141

Tittel, Ernst, b. 1910, German composer, **XII:** 116

Tittl, ?, composer included in a 1871 English collection of band music, **X:** 113

Tobi, F. J., 18th century composer in Paris, **XI:** 147

Tobias, Michael, 17th century German composer for voices and winds, **VII:** 140

Todt, Johann, 1833–1900, German composer, **XI:** 92, 175, 223, 262

Toeschi, Carlo, 1724–1788, *La Chasse royale* for Harmoniemusik, **VIII:** 354; **XI:** 92

Toeschi, Giovanni, 1735–1800, Italian composer, **XI:** 92, 223

Toja, Giovanni, 18th century Italian, *Serenata* for Harmonie and flute, **VIII:** 368

Tollar, Pater, fl. ca. 1700, composer, **VII:** 8

Toller, ?, composer included in a 1875 English collection of band music, **X:** 114

Tollet, A.-E., 19th century French composer, **IX:** 104

Tollet, Edouard, 19th century French composer, **IX:** 104

Tollet, Thomas, late Baroque English composer, **III:** 98; **VII:** 14; , **XI:** 93 [author of a treatise on playing flute]

Tollot, J., 19th century French composer of works for band, **X:** 89

Tolou, A., 18th century French composer, **XI:** 93

Tomaschino, ?, 18th century composer, **XII:** 43

Tomásek, Vaclav, 1774–1850, 19th century Czech composer, **IX:** 247

Tomasi, Henri, b. 1901, French composer, **XII:** 182

Tomkins, Thomas, d. 1656, composer of English ensemble music, **VII:** 20, 25, 72ff

Töpffer, Christian, 17th century German composer, **VII:** 24

Topham, William, 18th century, English composer, **XI:** 93

Torelli, Giuseppe, 1655–1709, Italian composer, **III:** 13ff, 14; **XI:** 163, 241, 255, 262

Torlez, C., 18th century French composer, **XI:** 93

Török, Francesco, 19th century, as arranger, **IX:** 257

Torri, Pietro, 1650–1737, 17th century Italian composer for voice with oboe, **III:** 220; **VII:** 192

Torricella, 18th and 19th century publisher in Vienna, **VIII:** 184ff, 209

Torti, Giuseppe, 18th century (?), Italian composer, **XI:** 223

Toschi, ?, 19th century Italian composer for band, **X:** 251

Toski, ?, 19th century English composer for band, **X:** 158

Tosoroni, ?, author of Instrumentation book (1851), **X:** 251

Tost, Frantisek, 19th century Czech composer, **IX:** 247

Tostolo, Giulian, 16th century composer, **VI:** 30

Touchemoulin, Joseph, 1727–1801, *Divertimento* for Harmonie, 2 violas (?), **VIII:** 354

Toulouze, ?, publisher before 1496 of basse danse melodies, **VI:** 18

Tourey, Charles, 19th century French composer, **IX:** 105

Tourneur, L., 19th century French composer, **IX:** 105

Tournier, 19th century publisher in Paris, **IX:** 1

Touront, Johannes, fl. 1450–1480 composer in Prague, **VI:** 7

Tovey, Cécile, 19th century English composer for band, **X:** 158

Tovey, Donald, 1875–1940, English composer, **XII:** 116, 182

Townley, Charles, 1737–1805, English composer for band, **X:** 158

Tradate, 17th century publisher in Milano, **VII:** 195

Tradate, Heirs of, 17th century publishers in Milan, **VII:** 208

Traeg, A., 18th century composer, **XI:** 93

Traeg, as publisher, Vienna, **VIII:** 218

Traeg, Johann, 1799 *Catalog* [of manuscripts] published in Vienna; **IV:** 35, 49; **VIII:** 19, 33, 36, 37, 46, 54, 60ff, 77ff, 83, 85, 95ff, 98ff, 103, 115, 116ff, 120ff, 127ff, 138ff, 140ff, 145, 148ff, 163ff, 177ff, 187, 193, 196ff, 207, 210ff, 218, 221ff, 225ff, 231, 235, 238, 244, 312, 319, 325, 341, 358; , **XI:** 3, 4, 5, 6, 8, 10, 13, 14, 15,18, 19ff, 21, 25, 26, 28, 29, 30, 34, 36, 39, 40, 41, 43–46,

50, 51, 54–56, 58, 60, 64, 65, 67, 70ff, 77, 79, 80, 81, 83, 86, 88, 90, 91, 93, 95, 96, 100, 102, 103, 107, 109, 110112, 115, 117–120, 122, 123, 126, 127, 132, 135, 141, 145, 151, 152, 154, 157, 159, 163, 167, 170, 171, 173, 182, 184, 186–188, 192–194, 197, 198, 200, 201, 202, 204, 205, 209, 211, 215, 216, 217, 219, 220–222, 224, 226, 231, 232, 239, 242243, 246, 248, 249, 251–153, 190, 256, 258, 260, 261, 262, 268, 270, 272, 274, 277, 281, 283, 284, 288, 295, 298, 299, 300, 301, 303, 305, 307

Traut, M., 19th century French composer, **IX:** 1

Trautwein, 19th century publisher in Berlin, **IX:** 181; **XII:** 67

Trautzl, Jacob, 19th century Austrian composer, **IX:** 247

Trave, D., 19th century French composer, **IX:** 105

Trebbi, ?, 19th century Italian composer for band, **X:** 251

Tréfouel, E., 19th century French composer, **IX:** 105

Trefz, V., 19th century French composer, **IX:** 105

Tregian, Francis, Jr., 1613–1619, copied English ensemble music in prison, **VII:** 23

Trento, Giuseppe, 19th century Italian composer for band, **X:** 251

Trento, Vittorio, 1761–1833, Italian composer, **XI:** 93

Treu, Daniel, 1695–1749, German composer, Partitas for winds, **VII:** 140

Trichet, Pierre, French 17th century treatise on the military, **III:** 144

Triebensee, Georg, 1746–1813, oboist, **IV:** 35 fn. 77, 41 fn. 104; **XI:** 157

Triebensee, Joseph, 1772–1846, Bohemian composer in Vienna, leader of Prince Liechtenstein's Harmonie, **IV:** 18ff, 32 fn. 67, [performing Beethoven *Quintet* with Beethoven in 1798], 39ff; **V:** 177ff; **IX:** 248, original compositions for winds; **XI:** 93, 122, 271, 307

Triebensee, Joseph, as arranger for Harmoniemusik, **VIII:** 6, 10, 12, 16, 17, 22, 30, 32, 33, 34, 36, 38, 39, 43, 44, 46, 47, 48, 49, 51, 53, 54, 55, 56, 57, 59, 62, 63, 65, 67, 68, 70, 74, 77, 78, 84, 87, 88, 90, 92ff, 103, 104, 122, 124, 126, 127, 128, 129, 130, 131, 136, 137, 143, 144, 145, 146, 147, 148, 150, 151, 152, 156, 157

Triébert, 19th century double reed maker, **V:** 5

Triébert, 19th century publisher in Paris, **XI:** 122

Triébert, Charles, 1810–1867, French composer, **XI:** 122

Triébert, Frédéric, 1813–1878, French composer, **XI:** 122, 277

Trietto, unnamed work arranged by Ozi for Harmoniemusik, **VIII:** 153

Trofeo, Italian composer in 1617 collection of canzoni, **VII:** 204

Troiano, M., 16th century Italian singer, **VI:** 78

Troilo, Antonio, canzona composer in Venice, early 17th century, **II:** 245, **III:** 220; **VII:** 210

Troisano, Massimo, singer, diarist in court at Munich, 16th century, **II:** 98ff

Trojan, Václav, b. 1907, Czech composer, **XII:** 182

Trombetti, 19th century Italian composer for band, **X:** 252

Tromlitz, Johann, 18th century German author of a flute treatise, **XI:** 94

Troop, A., 18th century Scottish (3) *Scotch Marches* for band, **VIII:** 264

Trost, J. G. M., 18th century German, *Parthia* for Harmoniemusik, **VIII:** 354

Trost, Johann Kaspar, 17th century German composer for bassoon ensemble, **III:** 8; **VII:** 140

Trottier, A., 19th century French composer, **IX:** 105

Troupenas, 19th century publisher in Paris, **VIII:** 51ff, 53; **XI:** 260

Trousseau, Charles, 19th century French composer, **IX:** 105

Truelove, J., 19th century French composer, **IX:** 105

Trugnet, Jean, member in 1777 of the Hautbois et Musettes du Poitou, **IV:** 64, fn. 5

Truschetzky? (Georg Druschetzky), **XI:** 147

Trusson, A., 19th century French composer, **IX:** 105

Tschaikowsky, Peter, 1840–1893, Russian composer, **IX:** 135

Tschemberdshi, Nikolai Karpowitsch, 1903–1948, Russian composer, **XII:** 116

Tscherepnin, Nikolai Nikolajewitsch, 1873–1945, Russian composer, **XII:** 182

Tschirch, Ernst, 19th century German composer, **IX:** 188

Tschirch, Rudolf, 19th century German composer, **IX:** 188

Tual, Théophile, 19th century French composer, **IX:** 105

Tubal, A., 16th century composer, **VI:** 27, 108, 123

Tuberville, George, Baroque composer of music for hunting horns, **VII:** 19

Tucek, Vincenc, 19th century Czech composer, **IX: 250**

Tuch, Heinrich, 1766–1821, German composer, **IX:** 188; **XI:** 94, 262

Tucsek, Vincenz, 19th century (?) composer, **XI:** 249

Tudway, Thomas, contemporary review of Purcell wind music, **VII:** 19

Tuerlinckx, Corneille, 1783–1850, Belgium composer, conductor in Mechlin, **IX:** 260

Tulon, ?, 19th century French composer, **IX:** 105

Tulon, Louis, d. 1799, bassoon faculty of the 1792 Paris Conservatoire, **IV:** 156

Turck, ?, 18th century composer in Vienna, **XI:** 284

Turina, Joaquin, 1882–1949, Spanish composer, arr. Strasser, **XII:** 182

Turine, V., 19th century French composer, **IX:** 105

Turner, Sir James, comments on 17th century English military trumpet, **III:** 147ff

Turnhout, Gerard de, 16th century Flemish composer, **VI:** 113, 114

Turnhout, J., 16th century composer, **VI:** 114

Türrschmiedt, Carl, 1753–1797, German composer, **XI:** 262

Tushratta, 1,400 BC, **I:** 10

Tutsch, Georg, 19th century German composer, **X:** 90

Twenger, Johann, artist in Germany, 1577, **II:** 193

Tye, 16th century composer, **VI:** 32

Tye, 17th century English composer, **VII:** 22

Tyther, 18th century publisher in London, **XI: 42**

Uber, Alexander, 1783–1824, German composer, **XI:** 94, 175

Uccelli, Giovanni, Italian composer, **XI:** 94

Uhl, Alfred, 20th centuryAustrian composer, **XII:** 116

Ulbrecht, F. J., Baroque German composer for Hautboisten, **VII:** 140

Ulbrecht, Franz, 18th century German, (5) Sätze for Harmoniemusik, **VIII:** 354

Ulich, Johann, b. 1634, German composer, **VII:** 112, 141

Ulrich Paser, wind player at Memmingen in 1501, **II:** 191

Ulrich, ?, 19th century English composer for band, **X:** 158

Ulrich, E., fl. 1800–1828, German composer, **IX:** 188

Umberto I, 1844–1900, of Italy, **V:** 196; **X:** 173, 174, 176, 224, 233, 247, 252, 253, 256

Umlauf, Ignaz, 1746–1796, Austrian composser, original Harmonie within an opera, **VIII:** 239; **XI:** 94

Umlauff, Michael, 1781–1842, Austrian composer, as composer of works arranged for Harmoniemusik, **VIII:** 129 [*Aeneas in Carthago, Das eigensinnige Landmädchen, Don Quixotte, Paul et Rosetta, Die schöne Schusterin,* arranged for winds]; **XI:** 282, 306

Umstatt, Joseph, d. 1762, German composer, **XI:** 255, 306

Universal Edition, 20th century publisher in Vienna, **XII:** 83, 87, 106, 120, 152, 158, 169

Unrath, ?, 19th century French composer, **IX:** 105

Unrath, ?, 19th century German composer, **X:** 90, 113ff

Unterholtzer, Rupert, 16th century composer, **VI:** 62, 63

Unterlegner, F. A., 19th century, German composer, **X:** 90

Urania, Greek goddess, VII: 196

Urban IV, pope, 13th century, **I:** 102; **V:** 216

Urban, Emil, bandmaster of the IR 9th Regiment in Austria, **V:** 52

Urbano VIII, 1568–1644, Pope, trumpets in 1623, **III:** 72

Urbanus, Gregorius, 17th century composer of Italian church music with winds, **III:** 220; **VII:** 192

Urbridge, Earl of, 18th century English noble, **VIII:** 258

Ursino, H. F., Baroque Italian composer, **XI:** 279

Usper (or Spongia), Francesco, 1561–1641, Italian composer, **III:** 220; **VII:** 192, 210

Utendal, Alexander, b. 1543, German composer, **VI:** 65, 75

Utrecht, Heinrich, 1624, German composer of dances, **VII:** 180

Vaet, Jacob, 1529–1567, Flemish composer, **VI:** 108, 123

Vaillant, ?, fl 1800–1828 French composer, **IX:** 106

Vala, Do., fl. 1430–1440, composer of wind motet, 'O Thoma Didime,' **VI:** 13

Valdes (or Baldes), Francesco de, head of court minstrels, 17th century Spain, **III:** 75

Valen, Fartein, 1887–1952, Norway composer, **XII:** 182

Valenta, Bedrich, d. 1934, Bohemian composer, **IX:** 251; **XII:** 68

Valenti, A., 19th century French composer, **IX:** 106

Valentin ?, (1844), as arranger, **IX:** 255

Valentin, Léon, 19th century French composer, **IX:** 106

Valentine, ?, composer included in a 1888 English collection of band music, **X:** 116

Valentine, Robert, 1680–1735, English flautist, **XI:** 94, 223, 238

Valentini, Giovanni, 1681–1753, Italian violinist, composer, **III:** 16; **VII:** 210

Valer, composer in a 1620 German collection, **VII:** 172

Van Ammelsvoort, Jos., 20th century, Dutch composer, **XII:** 202

Van Beer, ?, 19th century Dutch (?) composer, **XI:** 177

Van Berghe, Carl, 19th century French composer, **IX:** 106

Van Buggenhout, Ed., 19th century French composer, **IX:** 106

Van Campenhout, François, 19th century French composer, **IX:** 106

Van der Muelen, 16th century composer, **VI:** 114

Van Eyk, Jan, 1646 Dutch composer of instrumental dances, **VII:** 213

Van Maanen, ?, composer included in a 1871 English band collection, **X:** 113

Van Ranst, Philippe, church bassoonist in the Netherlands, in 1619, **III:** 199

Van Rossum, 20th century publisher in Utrecht, **XII:** 162

Van Vincle, Jehan, wind player in church services for Margaret of Austria, **II:** 215

Van Wedingen, J., 19th century French composer, **IX:** 106

Van Winckle, Cornelis, member of the Ghent town band, **II:** 165

Vandenbroeck, Othon, horn faculty of the 1792 Paris Conservatoire, **IV:** 157

Vandergahen, Armand, 1753–1822, Belgian clarinetist, as arranger for Harmoniemusik, **VIII:** 9, 20, 21, 24, 40, 47, 49, 50, 58, 70, 73, 75, 95, 102, 153, 157, 159, 160; **X:** 25; **XI:** 95, 232, 246; **XII:** 51 [Nicolo's Du Médicin Turc]

Vanerovsky, ?, 18th century Bohemian composer, **IV:** 123; **VIII:** 239, (2) Parthias and (2) works for voices and Harmoniemusik

Vanhal, Johann Baptist, 1739–1813, (19) original works for winds, **VIII:** 239ff; **XII:** 45 [unidentified march arranged by an unidentified arranger]

Vaninetti, Giuseppe, b. 1849, Italian composer for band, **X:** 252

Vannacci, Biago, 18th century (?), Italian composer, **XI:** 224

Vanremoortel, A., 19th century French composer, **IX:** 106

Vanremoortel, Michel, 19th century French composer, **IX:** 106

Vantura, Ceslav, d. 1736, Baroque Czech composer, **VII:** 4

Varlet, A., 19th century French composer, **IX:** 106

Varro, Roman scholar, 1st century BC, **I:** 60

Vartl, Ludwig, oboist in the Joseph Schwarzenberg Harmoniemusik, **IV:** 41, fn. 104

Vasely (Wessely), Thad, 19th century Czech composer, **IX:** 251

Vassal, 16th century composer, **VI:** 45

Vasseillière, fils, 19th century French composer, **IX:** 106

Vasseur, J., 19th century English composer, **IX:** 280

Vaubourgoin, Sohn Mare, 1887–1952, France, composer, **XII:** 182

Vauchelet, Nicolas, trumpet faculty of the 1792 Paris Conservatoire, **IV:** 157

Vaughn Williams, Ralph, 1872–1958, Ralph, England, **XII:** 116

Vecchi, ?, composer in 1600 dance collection published in Heidelberg, **VII:** 180

Vecchi, G., 19th century Italian composer, **X:** 252

Vecchi, Orazio, 1550–1605, composer, **VI:** 102

Vechi, Horatio, 1608 Italian composer of *Dialoghi* in 9-parts, **VII:** 210

Veillard, Gaspard, serpent faculty of the 1792 Paris Conservatoire, **IV:** 157

Veit, Wenzel, 1806–1864, German composer, **XI:** 175

Vellones, Pierre, 1889–1939, French composer, **XII:** 183

Vencenti, 17th century publisher in Venice, **VII:** 186, 188

Vencenti, Giacomo, 16th century publisher in Venice, **VI:** 93, 105

Venturini, Francesco, 1675–1745, Italian composer of Hautboisten music, **III:** 9, 19; **IV:** 7; **VII:** 141ff; **XII:** 49 [*Variation sur le Menuet par Mademeiselle Venturini a Vienne*, arranged by Druschetzky for Harmoniemusik]

Verbonet, Johannes, 16th century composer, **VI:** 63

Verbregge, Auguste, 19th century French composer, **IX:** 107

Verdelot, Philippe, 1495–1552, Flemish composer, **VI:** 63

Verdi, Giuseppe, 1813–1901, **V:** 5, 121, 155 [as band conductor], 174, 211; **IX:** 28, 257 [works arranged for band]; **X:** 55 [unidentified work arr. by Johann Strauss]; 165 [unknown Italian arr. of *Ballo in Maschera*]; 169 [unknown Italian arrangers of *Giovanna d'Arco* and *La Traviata*]; 221 [*Fantasia on Otello* by Neri]; 229 [*Don Carlos*, arr. Petrali]; 234 [*Rigoletto* and , *I due Foscari*, arr. Ponchieli]; 238 [*Luisa Miller*, arr. Ponchielli]; 251 [*Ballo in Maschea*, arr. Toschi]; 255 [*Aida*, *La Forza del Destino* and *Rigoletto*, arr. Vessella]; **X:** 88 [dedication]; **XI:** 159 [*Trovatore*, themes) arr. Capanna]; **XII:** 56 [*Atila*], arranged by Debali]; 205

Verdier (Werdier), Pierre, 17th century Dutch composer of sonatas, **VII:** 215

Verdier, J., 19th century French composer, **IX:** 107

Verdonck, Cornelis, 1563–1625, Flemish composer, **VI:** 113, 118

Verèse, Edgar, b. 1885, Franco-American composer, **XII:** 116

Verhulst, Johannes, 1816–1891, Dutch composer, **IX:** 125

Verlag der Ges. Rumän Komp., 20th century publisher in Bukarest, **XII:** 109

Verleye, ?, 19th century French composer, **IX:** 107

Vermont, Pierre, 16th century composer, **VI:** 39

Vern, ?, fl. 1800–1828, century French composer, **IX:** 107

Vern, Auguste, 19th century German composer, **IX:** 180, 188; **X:** 90 [*Nocturne* for small band]; **XI:** 95, 224, 246

Vernazobres, C. Z., 19th century French composer, **IX:** 107

Vernet, H., 19th century French composer, **IX:** 107

Verneville, Monsieur de la, XI: 246 [dedication of a clarinet work by Vanderhagen]

Verso, Antonio, 1565–1621, Italian composer, **VI:** 103

Vesque von Püttlingen, Johann, 1803–1883, *Johanna d'Arc*, for Harmnonie, **VIII:** 130

Vessella, Alessandro, 1860–1929, Roman band conductor and historian and author of *La Banda*, **I:** 125; **II:** 123, 132; **V:** 155, 158; **X:** 252ff

Viadana, Giacomo, 1604, Italian composer of church concerti, **VII:** 196, 210ff

Viadana, Lodovico, 1560–1627, Italian composer, **II:** 254, **III:** 14; **VI:** 102

Viala, political hero of the French Revolution, **VIII:** 271

Viallon, Justinien, 19th century French composer, professor of composition at the Gymnasse Musical Militaire and the College de Vaugirard, **IX:** 1, 107

Vicentino, Nicoló, 1511–1576, Italian composer, **VI:** 103

Victor Amadeus III of Turin, Italy, **IV:** 103, fn. 1

Victoria, Queen of England, **V:** 83, 189ff, 205; **IX:** 192; **X:** 130

Vidal, H., 19th century French composer, **IX:** 107

Vidal, Paul-Antoine, 1863–1931, French composer, **IX:** 107; **XII:** 117

Videix, Paul, 19th century French composer, **IX:** 107

Vié, L., 19th century French composer, **IX:** 107

Vierdanck, Johann, 1641, German composer for wind consort, **VII:** 141

Vierne, Louis, 1870–1937, French composer, **XII:** 117

Vieuxtemps, 19th century composer, **V:** 22

Vieweg, 20th century publisher in Berlin, **XII:** 89

Vignali, Gabriele, late 18th century Italian, church music with winds, canzoni, **VII:** 192ff; **VIII:** 368ff; **X:** 39

Vignati, Milos, 1897–1966, Czech composer, **XII:** 183

Viking, 20th century publisher in Kopenhagen, **XII:** 147

Vilhaver, Urban, 17th century, Italian composer, **III:** 215 **VII:** 192

Villa-Lobos, 1887–1959, Heiter, Brazil, **XII:** 117, 183, 205

Villebichot, P., 19th century French composer, **IX:** 108

Villeroy, Duke of, 17th century France, maintained wind band, **IV: 69**

Villette, Charles, nephew to Voltaire, **IV:** 154

Villiers, Pierre, 1532–1560, Italian composer, **VI:** 43ff, 49

Vincent, Henri, 19th century French composer, **IX:** 108

Vincent, R., 19th century French composer, **IX:** 108

Vincent, Thomas II, 1720–1783, composer, **XI:** 230

Vincenti, 17th century publisher in Venice, **VII:** 191ff, 195ff, 200ff, 202, 205ff, 209ff; **XI:** 150, 322, 323

Vincenzi, Giacomo, 16th century publisher in Venice, **VI:** 89, 99, 101, 103

Vinci, ?, 18th century Italian composer, **XI:** 287

Vinci, Pietro, b. 1515, Sicilian composer, **VI:** 103

Vincini, ?, 19th century Italian composer for band, **X:** 256

Vinders, Hieronymus, composer, **VI:** 27, 63, 120

Vineux, P.-E., 19th century French composer, **IX:** 108

Viney, Victor, 19th century French composer, **IX:** 108

Vinit (Vény), Michel-Joseph, as faculty of the 1792 Paris Conservatoire, **IV:** 156

Vintz (Wintz), Georg, 1630, German composer of dances, **VII:** 180

Violanti, composer in 1600 dance collection published in Heidelberg, **VII:** 180

Violetta, Gregorio, 19th century French composer, **IX:** 108

Violot, Antony, 19th century French composer, **IX:** 108

Viotti, composer in repertoire of band of George IV, **V:** 201

Viotti, unnamed works arranged for Harmoniemusik, **VIII:** 153

Virdung, composer of a treatise discussing instruments in 1511, **I:** 289; **II:** 264

Virenque, ?, 19th century French composer, **IX:** 108

Virgil, 1st century BC, poet, **I:** 30, 37, 50, 65

Vitali, Filippo, 1617, Napoli composer, **VII:** 205, 211

Vitaliti, Sebastiano, 19th century Italian composer, *Sinfonia* for band, **X:** 256; **XII:** 205

Vitásek (Witasek), Jan, 1770–1839, Czech composer, **IX:** 251

Vittorio Amadeo II, son-in-law of Louis IV (his military music), **III:** 71, 151

Vittorio Emanuele III, 1869–1947, of Italy, **V:** 196

Vivaldi, Antonio, 1678–1741, Concerto grossi with winds in concertino, **III:** 16; **X:** 14 [music for Hautboisten]

Vivian, L., 19th century English composer, **IX:** 280

Viviani, Giovanni, 17th century Italian composer, **XI:** 163

Vivier, A., 19th century French composer, **IX:** 108

Vivola, Alphonso dalla, composer, court of Ercole d'Este, 16th century, **II:** 125

Vobaron, ?, fl. 1800–1828, 19th century French composer, **IX:** 109

Vocet, Jan, 1777–1843, Bohemian composer, **XI:** 147

Vogel, ?, 18th century composer, **XI:** 95, 245, 246

Vogel, 19th century German composer, **IX:** 141

Vogel, Cajetan, 1750–1794, Bohemian composer, **VIII:** 72 [as arranger of Mozart, *Le Nozze di Figaro*, opera, for Harmonie; *Démophon Overture* for Harmoniemusik]; **XI:** 123, 147, 175

Vogel, Friedrich Wilhelm, 1807–1892, **XI:** 261

Vogel, J., 19th century (?), composer, **XI:** 253

Vogel, Johann, 1756–1788, 18th century French composer, **IV:** 150 fn. 27, 197; **XI:** 147, 224, 249

Vogel, Johann Christoph, 1756–1788, composer of works arranged for Harmoniemusik, **VIII:** 130ff [*Démophon*, arranged for Harmoniemusik]; **XII:** 54 [*Overture de Démophon*, unidentified arranger for Harmoniemusik]

Vogel, Louis, 18th century flautist & composer, **XI:** 54

Vogel, Vladimir, b. 1896, Russo-German composer, **XII:** 184

Vogelin, 1600 publisher in Heidelberg, **VII:** 180

Vogler, C., 19th century English composer, **IX:** 280

Vogler, Georg, Abbé, 1749–1814, composer of church music with winds, **IV:** 124; **V:** 36, 98; **VIII:** 130, 355, church works for voices and winds

Vogt, August, 1861–1926, German organist, **XI:** 123, 238

Vogt, Gustave, 1781–1870, French composer, arranger, **IX:** 109, 180

Voight, ?, 19th century composer published in England, **IX:** 263

Voigt, Marie, 19th century French composer, **IX:** 109

Voisin, Louis, clarinet faculty of the 1792 Paris Conservatoire, **IV:** 157

Vojácek, as arranger of Mozart, *Cosi fan tutte*, opera, for Harmoniemusik, **VIII:** 76

Vojacek, H, 19th century Czech composer, arranger, **IX:** 251, 254, 255, 256

Volbach, Fritz, 1861–1940, German composer, **XII:** 184

Völckel, Samuel, 1606, German composer for wind consort and hunting, **III:** 61 **VII:** 142, 181

Volke, ?, 19th century German composer, **IX:** 188

Volkert, Frantisek, 19th century Czech composer, **IX:** 251

Vollmar, Heinrich, 1839–1915, German composer of works for band, **X:** 90

Vollstedt, Robert, 1854–1919, German composer, **IX:** 188

Vols, ?, 19th century (?) composer, **XI:** 147

Voltaire François-Marie, 1694–1778, French philosopher, **IV:** 64ff, 168ff, 171ff

Voltaire, VIII: 282

Vos, Camille, 19th century French composer, **IX:** 109

Voss, ?, 19th century German composer, **X:** 112

Vuastch, 17th century publisher in Frankfurt, **VII:** 188

Vuataz, Roger, b. 1898, composer, **XII:** 184

Vuckovic, Vojislav, 1910–1942, Yugoslav composer, **XII:** 184

Vulder, J. de, 19th century French composer, **IX:** 109

Wace, 12th century poet, **I:** 159

Wachs, Paul, 19th century Italian composer, **IX:** 121; **XII:** 68

Wacker, Charles, 19th century French composer, **IX:** 109

Waddell, James, 19th century English composer, **IX:** 280; **X:** 158

Wadkovskoi, Prince of 18th century Russia, **IV:** 78

Waele, Ed., de, 19th century French composer, **IX:** 109

Waelput, Hendrik, 1845–1885, Flemish composer, **XI:** 96, 312

Waelrant, H., 16th century publisher in Antwerpen, **VI:** 123

Waelrant, Hubert, 1517–1595, Flemish composer, **VI:** 27, 107, 108, 114, 123

Waetzig, J. G., bassoonist in band of George IV, **V:** 203, fn. 10

Waetzig, trumpeter in band of George IV, **V:** 203, fn. 10

Wagenaar, Johan, 1862–1941, Dutch composer, **XII:** 118

Wagenführ, 19th century publisher in Berlin, **V:** 34

Wagenmann, 17th century publisher in Nürnberg, **VII:** 163, 172ff, 181ff

Wagenseil, Georg, 1715–1777, Austrian composer, **III:** 20ff; **IV:** 8, 41; **VII:** 5ff; **XI:** 96, 157, 177

Wagner, ?, 18th century composer, **XI:** 96

Wagner, ?, fl, 1800–1828, German composer, **IX:** 189

Wagner, Albert, 1799–1874, English composer for band, **X:** 159

Wagner, B., 18th century composer, **XI:** 96

Wagner, Carl, 1772–1822, *March* for trumpets, ca. 1790, **VIII:** 355

Wagner, Eduard, 19th century Austrian, *Militar-Messe* with band, **X:** 59

Wagner, Eugéne, 19th century composer, **XII:** 196

Wagner, F. A., 19th century German composer, **IX:** 189

Wagner, Franz J., 19th century Austrian composer, **IX:** 252, 254

Wagner, Guillaume, 19th century composer, **XI:** 147

Wagner, J. F., 19th century composer, **XII:** 200

Wagner, Jakob Karl, 1772–1822, 'Liebe und Freundschaft,' arr. for Harmonie, **VIII:** 130

Wagner, Joseph Franz, 19th century, Austrian military band leader, **V:** 453

Wagner, Karl Jakob, 1772–1822, German composer, **XI:** 96, 241, 262

Wagner, Richard, 1813–1883, German composer, **V:** 5, 19 fn. 61, 26, 36 [Wieprecht as arr], 81, 86 [Rimsky-Korsakov as arr.], 108ff, 117, 121, 122ff, 145 [on the Berlioz *Symphony for Band*], 156, 172ff, 193ff, 236; **IX:** 161, 189

Wagner, Richard, 1813–1883, German composer, music arranged for band, **IX:** 39 [*Die Walküre*]; 94 [*Die Walküre*]; 113 [*Lohengrin, Rienzi*]; 122 [*Tannhäuser*]; 200 [*Faust* Overture, *Der Fliegende Holländer, Götterdämmerung, Lohengrin, Die Meistersinger, Parsifal, Rheingold, Siegfried, Tannhäuser, Walküre*]; 258 [*Lohengrin, Tannhäuser*]; **X:** 256 [arrangements by Vessella: *Lohengrin, L'Oro del Reno, Sigfrido, Tannhäuser, Tristano e Isotta, Il Vascello Fantasma, Die Walküre, Il Crepuscolo Degli di Dei*]; **XII:** 68 [unidentified arranger, march from *Tannhäuser*]; 199 [arranged for band by Stokowsky]; 205

Wagner, P. Basilius, d. 1813 at Melk monastery [dedication], **XII:** 59

Wagner, Siegfried Richard, 1869–1930, German composer, **XII:** 118, 184
Wailly, Paul de, fl. 1882–1900, French composer, **XII:** 192
Wajacek, as arranger of Titl, 1809–1882, *Der Zauberschleier,* for Harmoniemusik, **VIII:** 129
Walch, as arranger of Romberg, *Simphonie,* for Harmoniemusik, **VIII:** 105
Walch, Johann, as 19th century arranger, **IX:** 189
Walckiers, ?, 18th century (?), composer, **XI:** 224
Walckiers, Eugene, 1793–1866, French composer, **X:** 90
Waldeck, Karl, 19th century Austrian composer, **IX:** 252
Waldek, Prince, 18th century, **VIII:** 152
Waldteufel, Émile, 1837–1915, French composer of works for band, **IX:** 280; **X:** 90ff
Waley, Simon, 19th century English composer, **IX:** 280
Walker, 19th century publisher in London, **XI:** 48, 54, 59, 205
Walker, George, 19th century English composer for band, **X:** 159
Wallace, 19th century band composer in England, **V:** 82
Wallentin, as arr. of Lortzing, *Czaar und Zimmermann,* opera, for Harmoniemusik, **VIII:** 59
Wallerstein, Anton, 1813–1892, German composer of works for band, **X:** 112
Wallerstein, F., 19th century French composer, **IX:** 109
Wallerstein, Prince, 18th century German, **VIII:** 356ff
Wallis, 18th century Prince of England, **VIII:** 302
Wallner, Vinzenz, 1769–1799, a collection of Hamoniemusik, **VIII:** 240
Walpole, Horace, English historian, politician, **IV:** 131, fn. 17
Walrand, J., 19th century French composer, **IX:** 109
Walsh and Hare 17th and 18th century publisher in London **XI:** 12, 18, 37, 59ff, 62, 83, 92–96, 110, 116, 119, 182, 190, 208, 211, 212, 230, 223, 255, 267, 269, 276, 295
Walsh, 18th century publisher in London, **XI:** 11ff, 23, 28, 40, 41, 42, 59, 75, 76, 81, 82, 91, 95, 97, 111, 118, 122, 151, 181, 184, 195, 199, 200, 203, 208, 218, 219, 222, 224, 215, 223, 238, 256
Walsh, I., 18th century publisher in London, **XI:** 16, 18, 188, 190
Walsh, J., 1733, London publisher, **VII:** 13
Walsh, Randall and Hare, 18th century publishers in London, **XI:** 4, 5, 69, 93, 213, 233
Walter, ?, 18th century German composer, **XI:** 246
Walter, ?, 19th century German composer, **IX:** 253
Walter, Albert, d. 1860, French composer, **IX:** 109
Walter, August, 1821–1866, German composer, **XI:** 148, 310
Walter, G., ca. 1797, (7) *Partitas* for Harmoniemusik, **VIII:** 355
Walter, Johann, 1755–1822 German composer, **XI:** 96, 247
Walter, Karl, 1862–1929, Austrian composer, **XII:** 118
Walther, Johann, 1496–1570, wrote wind fugues for Martin Luther, **II:** 232; **VI:** 27ff, 65, 78
Wanerzovsky, as arr. of Müller, *Die Schwestern von Prag,* opera, for Harmonie, **VIII:** 86
Wangemann, ?, fl. 1800–1828, German composer, **IX:** 190
Wanhal, Jan, 1739–1813, Bohemian composer, **XI:** 96, 123, 148, 157, 224, 387
Wanhall, composer in an anonymous collection for Harmoniemusik, **VIII:** 151

Wanisek, Otto, 19th century Austrian composer, **IX:** 252

Wannenmacher, Johannes, 1485–1551, Swiss composer, **VI:** 28, 63

Ward, John, d. 1640, composer of English ens. music, **VII:** 20, 22, 23, 25, 41, 73ff

Warlen, Georg, clarinetist in 1801 Harmoniemusik of Prince Esterházy, **IV:** 31, fn. 57

Warmuth, C., 19th century German composer, **IX:** 190

Warneford, Harry, 19th century English composer for band, **X:** 159

Wassermann, Heinrich, 1791–1838, German composer, **XI:** 97, 158

Wassman, 17th century publisher in Leipzig, **VII:** 171

Waterson, James, 19th century French composer, Bandmaster 1er Life Guards, **IX:** 109; **X:** 92

Watier, ?, 19th century French composer, **IX:** 109

Watson, William, 19th century English composer, **IX:** 280

Wätzold, 17th century publisher in Oels [Poland], **VII:** 167

Waylet, H., 18th century publisher in London, **XI:** 18, 190

Wayser, W., ca. 1600, composer of English ensemble music, **VII:** 77

Webb, William, 19th century English/American composer, **VIII:** 264; **IX:** 139, 280

Weber, ?, 18th century German, (11) *Partien* for Harmoniemusik, **VIII:** 355

Weber, 'Lützows wilde Jagd, und Schwerdtlied,' arr. Neithardt for brass, **VIII:** 133

Weber, Bernhard Anselm, 1766–1821, German composer of works arranged for Harmoniemusik, **VIII:** 124 [arr. by Schulz; for Harmoniemusik; 131 [*Die Jungfrau v. Orleans*, unknown arranger]; **IX:** 190; **X:** 112 [as arrangner]; **XII:** 44

Weber, Carl Maria von, 1786–1826, German composer, **V:** 6, 23 fn. 84, 27, 36 [Wieprecht as arr.], 73 fn. 24, 82, 98, 107, 114, 118, 125, 134, 168, 192, 205; **IX:** 190

Weber, Carl Maria von, 1786–1826, works arranged for Harmoniemusik, **VIII:** 131 [*Der Freischütz, Johanna, Preciosa*]; 132 [*Euryanthe*]; 133 [*Lorzing, Oberon*]; unidentified works, 133, 150, 151, 195; **XII:** 43, 54 [*Der Freischütz*, arranged by Flachs for Harmoniemusik], 205

Weber, Carl Maria von, 1786–1826, music arranged for band, **IX:** 114 [*Freischütz*]; 163 [*Der Freischütz*]; 178 [*Ouverture jubilaire*]; 180 [*Freischütz, Symphony in C*]; 186 [*Oberon*]; 196 [*Preziosa*]; 201 [*Euryanthe, Der Freischütz, Jubel Overture, Oberon, Preciosa*]; unidentified works arranged for band, 55, 149, 177, 189, 201

Weber, Friedrich, 1766–1842, Austrian composer, **IX:** 252

Weber, Jacob, 1779–1839, German composer, **IX:** 192

Weber, Ludwig, 1891–1947, German composer, **XI:** 247; **XII:** 119, 184

Weber, S. J., as 19th century arranger, **IX:** 197

Weber, Wilhelm. 19th century Austrian composer, **IX:** 252

Weber, XI: 182 [*Der Freischütz*, arr. anon.]; 304 [unidentified opera movement, arr. Düring, J. C.]

Webster, Mauritz, 17th century German composer, **VII:** 24

Weckmann, Matthias, 1621–1674, German composer, **XI:** 163

Weelkes, Thomas, ca. 1573–1623, composer of English ensemble music, **VII:** 20, 77ff

Weger, 19th century publisher in Brixen, **IX:** 169

Wehrli, Werner, 1892–1944, Swiss composer, **XII:** 119, 185

Weichlein, Romano 17th century composer in Innsbruck, 1695, **VII:** 8

Weichmann, Johann, 1620–1652, 1646, German composer of dances, **VII:** 181

Weichowicz, Stanislaw, b. 1893, Polish composer, **XII:** 119

Weichsel, Carl, German wind player plays in London in the 1750s, **IV:** 105, fn. 2

Weideman, Carl, d. 1728, German composer, **X:** 26

Weideman, Charles, d. 1782, English, *Old Buffs March*, ca. 1760, for Harmonie, **VIII:** 265;
 XI: 97, 224

Weidinger, Anton, 1766–1852, inventor of the keyed trumpet, **IV:** 33, fn. 68

Weidner, 17th century publisher in Jena, **VII:** 114, 169

Weigart (Weigerth), Francesco, 18th century composer in Olmütz collection, **IV:** 22, fn. 9

Weigart, Francesco, (8) *Partitas* for Harmoniemusik, **VIII:** 240ff

Weigel, Ch., engraving of Hautboisten band of Frederick William in 1720, **III:** 127

Weigel, Christoph, 1654–1725, German composer, **XI:** 97

Weigh, John, 18th century, English (2) *Marches* for Harmoniemusik, **VIII:** 265

Weigl, ?, 19th century composer, **IX:** 216

Weigl, ?, *Tiroler Jahrmarkt,* ballet, unknown arranger for Harmoniemusik, **VIII:** 143

Weigl, J., as arranger of Méhul, *Joseph,* opera, for Harmoniemusik, **VIII:** 66; **IX:** 252

Weigl, Joseph, 1740–1820 (3) original works for Harmoniemusik, **VIII:** 241; **XI:** 123, 297

Weigl, Joseph, 1740–1820, composer of works arranged for Harmoniemusik, **VIII:** 133 [*Das
 Petermännchen*]; 134 [*Giulietta e Pierotto, I solitari, Il pazzo per forza, La Principessa d'Amalfi*];
 135 [*L'Amor marinaro, Kaiser Hadrian, Die Uniform*]; 136 [*Adrian von Ostade, Das Waisenhus,
 Die Schweizerfamilie*]; 138 [*Das Sinnbild des menschlichen Lebens, Die Reue des Pygmalion,
 Nachtigall und Rabe*]; 139 [*Richard Löwenherz*]; 140 [*Insel Christina, Der Raub der Helena, Die
 Verbrennung und Zestörung der Stadt Troja*]; 141 [*Alcina, Alonzo e Cora, Clothilde, Prinzessin
 von Salerno*]; 142 [*Alceste, Die Atheniensische Tänzerin, Die Spanier auf der Insel Christina*]; 143
 [*Palmira, Piolla*]; 144 [*Ginevra di Scozia*]; unidentified works, 144, 151, 152; **X:** 18 [*Nachtigall
 und Raabe*]; **XII:** 54 [*Die Uniform,* arr. unidentified arranger for Harmoniemusik]

Weigl, Josef, 1740–1820 composer of works arranged for band, **IX:** 201

Weigl, Thadeus, fl. 1797–1804, works arranged for Harmoniemusik, **VIII:** 143 [*Bachus et
 Ariadne, Die Huldigung, Die Vermählung im Keller*]

Weigl, ?, *Vesta's Feuer,* opera, unknown arranger for Harmoniemusik, **VIII:** 135

Weill, Kurt, 1900–1950, German composer, **IX:** 280; **XII:** 119

Weilland, ?, ca. 1797, German, (3) *Harmonie* for Harmoniemusik, **VIII:** 355

Weilland, 19th century English composer, **IX:** 280

Weinberger, Joseph, 19th century composer in Austria, **XI:** 316

Weiner, Leo, 19th century German composer, **XI:** 148

Weinlich, ?, 19th century, as arranger, **IX:** 256

Weinzweig, John, b. 1913, Canadian composer, **XII:** 119, 185

Weis, Flemming, b. 1898, Danish composer, **XII:** 185

Weise, Christian (pseud. ?), 17th century German composer, **VII:** 115

Weismann, Julius, 1879–1950, German composer, **XII:** 185

Weiss, ?, *Amphion*, ballet, arr. Triebensee (one movement) for Harmoniemusik, **VIII:** 144

Weiss, Carl, 18th century German composer, **XI:** 225, 271

Weiss, composer in a collection of Harmoniemusik by an unknown arranger, **VIII:** 152

Weiss, Franz, 1778–1830, German composer, **XI:** 98, 225, 247, 274

Weiss, G., 18th century (?), composer, **XI:** 98

Weiss, Heinrich, 19th century German composer, **IX:** 192

Weiss, Johann Sigismund, 1690–1737, German composer, **XI:** 123, 225

Weiss, Karl I, 1735–1795, flautist & composer, **XI:** 98 [biographical note]

Weiss, Karl II, 1777–1845, English composer, **XI:** 98, 225, 271

Weiss, Wenzel, 18th century German, *Marsch und Echo* for Harmoniemusik, **VIII:** 356

Weissensteiner, Raimund, b. 1905, Austrian composer, **XII:** 185

Weissheimer, Wendelin, 1838–1910, German composer, **XI:** 272

Weiwanosky, Paul Joseph, late 17th century composer in Vienna, **VII:** 8

Welack, Matthias, 16th century Wittenberg publisher, **VI:** 73

Welcker, 18th and 19th century publisher in London, **XI:** 4, 6, 7, 26, 28, 36, 77, 88, 92, 107, 123, 181, 188, 197, 207, 213, 216, 220, 236

Weldon and Gasperini, early 18th century publishers in London, **XI:** 204

Weldon John, 1676–1736, English composer, **XI:** 225

Welker, James, 19th century leader of the Wold Band of York, **V:** 168

Weller, ?, 19th century composer, **IX:** 142

Weller, as arranger of works for Harmoniemusik or band, **VIII:** 5, 133ff

Weller, F., fl. 1800–1828, German composer, **IX:** 192

Weller, Friedrick, German military conductor, 1840–1844, **V:** 19ff, 105

Wellesz, Egon, b. 1885, Austrian composer, **XII:** 186

Welter, Louis, ?, 19th century French composer of church music for choir and band, **V:** 215; **IX:** 110

Wenck, 16th century German composer, **VI:** 62

Wenck, August, d. 1814, German composer, **XI:** 158

Wend, Johann, 16th century German composer, **VI:** 75

Wendling, Johann, 1720–1797, German composer, **XI:** 98, 123, 225

Wendt, (Went, Vent), Johann, 1745–1809, oboist and leader of the Emperor's Harmoniemusik, **IV:** 17, 24, 35 fn 77, 37 (& fn. 85), 41 (and fn. 104), 44ff; **V:** 181; **VIII:** 241ff, (99) *Parthias* for Harmoniemusik; **XI:** 123, 195, 271, 226; **XII:** 34

Wendt, as arranger for Harmoniemusik, **VIII:** 19, 30, 32, 37, 38, 41, 42, 54, 61, 71, 72, 75, 76, 80, 90, 93, 95, 96, 97, 99, 101, 104, 115, 116, 117, 118, 120, 121, 127, 129, 134, 138, 139, 140, 141, 142, 143, 146, 155, 156, 157, 160

Wenkel, Johann, 1734–1792, German composer, **XI:** 99, 226

Wenusch, arr., *VIII Stücke aus opern und Ballets*, a collection for Harmonie, **VIII:** 150

Wenusch, Stanislaus, 19th century Austrian composer, **IX:** 252; **XI:** 255, 322

Wenzel, Eberhard, b. 1896, German, **XII:** 186

Wenzel, Edovard, 19th century German composer, **IX:** 192

Werckmeister, 18th century publisher in Orangeburg, **VIII:** 354

Werckmeister, Andreas, 1645–1706, composer, introduced Bach to equal tuning, **III:** 66

Werkmeister, Rudolf, 19th century German composer, **IX:** 192

Werner, Christoph, 1617–1650, German composer for voices and winds, **VII:** 142

Werner, Gregor, 1695–1766, German composer of Hautboisten music, **X:** 10

Werttig, Joseph, 18th century German, (30) *Märches,* (12) *Pièces,* Harmonie, **VIII:** 356

Weschke, Paul, 19th century German composer, **IX:** 192

Wesley, Samuel, English, *March,* 1777, for Harmoniemusik, **VIII:** 265

Wessel, W., 1604 publisher in Kassel, **VII:** 181

Wessely, Johann, 1762–1810, German composer, **XI:** 148, 175, 226

Wessil, 19th century publisher in London, **XI:** 47

West, Alfred, 19th century English composer, **IX:** 280

Westenholz, Friedrich, 1756–1802, German composer, **XI:** 99, 231, 241

Westerhoff, Heinrich, 1760–1806, German composer, **XI:** 99, 148, 158, 226, 249

Westerholt, Friedrich von, Count, had Harmoniemusik in 1793, **IV:** 51

Westmeyer, Wilhelm, 19th century leader in Austrian band music, **V:** 52

Westmoreland, Earl of, composer of a Battle Symphony, **V:** 28

Wettge, Gustave, 19th century French composer, conductor of the Musique de la Garde Républicaine, **V:** 75, **IX:** 110

Wettge, Léon, 19th century French composer, conductor, Musique du genie en retraite, Chavalier de la legion d'Honneur, **IX:** 110

Wettich, 19th century bassoonist, court at Rudolstadt, **V:** 186, fn. 8

Weyr, F. W. 19th century as arranger, **IX:** 257

Wheatstone, 19th century publisher in London, **XI:** 192, 202, 203, 205

Wheatstone, C., 18th century publisher in London, **XI:** 20, 191

Whishaw, Frederick, 1854–1934, English composer for band, **X:** 159

Whitaker, 18th century publisher in London, **XI:** 191

White, William, early 17th century, English composer, **VII:** 22, 23, 25, 78ff

Whittaker, William Gillies, 1876–1944, English, **XII:** 186

Whitwell, David, 20th century conductor, composer, **XII:** 205

Widder, as arranger for Harmoniemusik, **VIII:** 4, 113, 151

Widerkehr, Jacob, 1759–1823, (10?) *Simphonie concertantes,* 6 winds & cello, **VIII:** 293 [(10?) *Simphonie concertantes,* 6 winds & cello]; **XI:** 99, 273, 275

Widerkehr, Philippe, trombone faculty of the 1792 Paris Conservatoire, **IV:** 156

Widmann, Erasmus, 1572–1634, collections of German dances, **VII:** 145, 181

Widmann, Wilhelm, 19th century German composer, **X:** 112

Widmer, Ernst, Brazilian 20th century composer, **XII:** 205

Widor, ?, 19th century French composer, **XII:** 212

Widor, Charles, 1845–1937, French composer, **IX:** 110

Wiedeman, 18th century composer, **VIII:** 264

Wiedemann, Josef, 19th century Austrian composer, **IX:** 252

Wiedner, Johann, 1714–1783, German composer, **XI:** 99, 124

Wiegand, George, 19th century English composer for band, **X:** 159

Wieland, ?, 19th century English composer for band, 159

Wieland, Philipp, ca. 1700, German composer for Hautboisten, **III:** 19; **VII:** 142

Wieprecht, Wilhelm, 1802–1872, Head of Prussian bands, composer, **V:** 4ff, 17, 19ff, 23ff, 323ff, 38ff, 46ff, 51, 80, 108, 115, 118, 185, 189ff; **IX:** 143, 170, 192ff; **X:** 107 [as arranger of works by Meyerbeer]; **XII:** 34, 62, 68

Wiese, Fr., 19th century German composer, **X:** 95

Wieweg, 20th century publisher in Berlin, **XII:** 123

Wigglesworth, instrument maker at Otley, England, **V:** 168

Wigthorpe, William, early 17th century compiler of ensemble books, **VII:** 20

Wilbye, John, 1574–1638, composer of English ensemble music, **VII:** 22, 79

Wilche, Cyriacus, 1659, German composer of 6-part *Battaglia Sonata*, **VII:** 182

Wilder, Philip van, late 16th century composer, **VI:** 119, 122 ; **VII:** 23

Wildgans, Friedrich, 1913–1965, German composer, **XII:** 120

Wilhelm I of Germany, 19th century, [dedication], **XII:** 61

Wilhelm I, Kaiser, IX: 152 [funeral, 1864], 171, 175

Wilhelm II, Kaiser (1891), **IX:** 160

Wilhelm von Prussia (and Princess Auguste von Saxe-Weimar, 1829), **IX:** 184

Wilhelm, 19th century Kaiser [dedication], **X:** 104

Wilhelm, 19th century Prince of Prussia, **XII:** 68

Wilhelm, J., in an anonymous arrangement for Harmoniemusik, **VIII:** 151

Wilhelm, Landgraf von Hessen, d. 1663, composer of a Sarabande, **VII:** 182

Wilhelmus von Nassau, 18th century, **VIII:** 298

Wilk von, ?, 19th century German composer, **IX:** 194

Wilkinson, 19th century publisher in London, **XI:** 44

Willaert, Adrian, 1490–1562, Flemish composer, **II:** 244; **VI:** 28, 46, 63, 64, 84, 92, 102, 119, 120, 122

Willi, 20th century publisher in Cham, **XII:** 88

William 'the Red,' 1087–1100, **I:** 182

William and Mary, 17th century England, **III:** 98

William IV, of England, **V:** 204

William the Conqueror, 11th century, **I:** 181

William V of Munich, 16th century, **II:** 98ff

Williams, Warwick, 19th century English composer, **IX:** 280; **X:** 159

Williamson, 18th century publisher in London, **XI:** 199

Willman, Samuel, 1780–1813, German composer, **XI:** 99, 236

Willy, Jean, 18th century composer in Olmütz Harmoniemusik collection, **IV:** 22, fn. 9; **VIII:** 244, (7) *Parthias*, ca. 1766, for Harmoniemusik

Wilms, Johann, 1772–1847, German composer, **XI:** 99, 148, 273, 275

Wilson, Thomas, ca. 1600, composer of English ensemble music, **VII:** 79

Wineberger, Paul, 1758–1821, German Harmoniemusik composer at Wallerstein court, **IV:** 56; **VIII:** 356ff, (22) *Partitas* for Harmonie with flutes

Winer, Leo, 19th century composer, **XI:** 148

Winkelmayer, ?, fl. 1800–1828, German composer, **IX:** 194

Winkler, E., 19th century German composer, **XI:** 158

Winkler, Johann, 19th century Austrian composer, **IX:** 252; **XI:** 262, 291

Winkler, Martin, 19th century Austrian composer, **IX:** 252

Winn, Roland, 1820–1893, English composer for band, **X:** 160

Wintelroy, Jan van, 1520–1576, Franco-Flemish composer, **VI:** 107, 114

Winter, 18th century publisher in Berlin, **VIII:** 338; **XI:** 183, 215

Winter, Paul, 1894–1971, German composer, **XII:** 120

Winter, Peter von, 1754–1825, (9) original works for Harmoniemusik, **VIII:** 245; **X:** 18, 95; **XI:** 100, 124, 158, 283, 287

Winter, Peter von, 1754–1825, composer of works arranged for Harmoniemusik, **VIII:** 144 [*Helena und Paris, Henry IV, Das unterbrochene Opferfest*]; 146 [*Babylone Pyramiden, Das Labirint, Marie von Montalban*]; 147 [*Brüder von Stauffenberg, Elise Graefin von Hilbur, Tamerlan*]; 148 [*Oboe Quartet*]; unidentified works, 148, 151; **XII:** 44, 53 [*Das unterbrochene,* arranged for Harmoniemusik by Stumpf]; 54 [*Vologesus* (ballet), unidentified arranger of Harmoniemusik]

Winter, Peter, 1754–1825, composer of works arranged for band, **IX:** 158, 258; **X:** 18 [*Das Labyrinth*]

Winterbottom, William, 1838–1889, English composer for band, **X:** 161

Winterhalter, Valentin, civic band conductor in Baden, **V:** 135

Winterle, Edmund, 19th century composer, **XI:** 148

Winton, S., 19th century English composer for band, **X:** 161

Winzer, trumpeter, 19th century court of Mechlenburg-Schwerin, **V:** 185, fn. 4

Wirth, Helmut, b. 1912, German composer, **XII:** 186

Wismes, Nicholas de, fl. 1554–1564, Dutch composer, **VI:** 28, 107, 108, 109

Wiss, H. B., 19th century French, composer, **XII:** 69

Withy, John, late 17th century, composer of English ensemble music, 79

Witmann, G., French, 19th century band conductor, **XII:** 69

Witt, ?, fl. 1800–1828, German composer, **IX:** 194

Witt, as arranger of Paisiello, *L'Olimpiade,* opera, for Harmoniemusik, **VIII:** 98

Witt, Christian, 1660–1716, German composer for Hautboisten, **VII:** 142, 182

Witt, Friedrich, 1660–1717, German composer of Hautboisten music, **III:** 19

Witt, Friedrich, 1770–1836, German Harmoniemusik composer at Wallerstein court, **IV:** 56; **VIII:** 358, (5) *Partitas* for Harmonie with flutes; **X:** 26; **XI:** 100, 175, 263

Wittassek, August, 19th century Austrian composer, **IX:** 252

Witte, Johann, 19th century Austrian composer, arranger, **IX:** 253, 255

Wittel, Martin, 17th century publisher in Erfurt, **VI:** 70

Wittelsbach, Rudolf, b. 1902, composer, **XII:** 186

Witter, leader, 19th century military band in Munich, **V:** 107

Wittmann, ?, 19th century French composer, **IX:** 111

Wittmann, G., fils, 19th century French composer, **IX:** 111

Wittmann, J.-B., 19th century French composer and band conductor, **IX:** 111; **XII:** 69

Witvogel, 18th century publisher in Amsterdam, **XI:** 201

Witzleben von, ?, 19th century German composer, **IX:** 195

Witzleben, Colonel of a Prussian regiment, **IX:** 27

Wivill, Zarubbabel, English, *Berkshire March*, 1793, for band, **VIII:** 265

Wode, Thomas, 16th century composer, **VI:** 31

Woelfl, Joseph, 19th century German composer, **XI:** 100

Woestijne, David van de, b. 1915, Belgian composer, **XII:** 186

Wohlfahrt, Frank, b. 1894, German composer, **XII:** 120, 187

Wohlmuth, Andreas, 1809–1884, German composer, **IX:** 195

Wöhning, S. C., fl. 1800–1828, German composer, **IX:** 195

Wolcken, Andreas 16th century publisher in Breslau, **VI:** 66, 68, 70

Woldemar, N., 18th century violinist & composer in Paris, **XI:** 149

Wolf, Cyrill, 19th century Austrian composer, **IX:** 253

Wolf, Ernst, 1735–1892, German composer, **XI:** 100, 231,273

Wolf, Franz, ca. 1799, German (4) works for Harmoniemusik, **VIII:** 358

Wolf, Friedrich, 1750–1824, German composer, **XI:** 175, 234

Wolf, Josef, 19th century Austrian composer, **IX:** 253

Wolff, Martin, 16th century German composer, **VI:** 62

Wölfl, Joseph, 1773–1812, composer, (6) *Sonatas* for Harmoniemusik, **VIII:** 358; **IX:** 253; **XI:** 281

Wolfram von Eschenbach, 1170–1220, **I:** 261

Wolsey, English Cardinal, 1473–1530, **II:** 22, 23, 217, 225

Wood, James, 19th century English composer, **IX:** 281

Wood, John, 1769 eyewitness report of the Bath band, **IV:** 129

Wood, Ralph, b. 1901, English composer, **XII:** 120, 187

Wood, Thomas, 1892–1950, English composer, **XII:** 120

Woodcock, composer in 1600 English collection of ensemble music, **VII:** 20

Woodesonn, Leonharde, d. 1604, composer of English ensemble music, **VII:** 80

Worgan, James, English composer for militia band, **IV:** 106, fn. 7

Worgan, James, Jr., 1715–1753, English composer, **VIII:** 265 [(2) *Marches* and a *Song* with Harmoniemusik]; **X:** 32 [work for band]; **XI:** 226

Work, Thomas, early 17th century, composer of English ensemble music, **VII:** 80

Wormser, Andre, 1851–1926, French composer, **IX:** 111

Wöss, Josef Venantius von, 1863–1943, Austrian composer, **XII:** 120

Woyrsch, Felix, 1860–1944, German composer, **XII:** 187

Woytowicz, Boleslaw, b. 1899, Polish composer, **XII:** 187

Wragg, 19th century publisher in London, **XI:** 171, 215

Wragg, J., 18th century English composer, **XI:** 100, 124, 266, 231

Wranitzky, ?, 18th century composer, **XI:** 124, 226

Wranitzky, Anton, 1761–1820, (12) *Marches* for Harmoniemusik, **VIII:** 245

Wranitzky, Anton, Jr., 19th century Austrian composer, **IX:** 253

Wranitzky, Paul, 1756–1808, Austrian composer, **IV:** 37, fn. 85 [on Wendt]; **X:** 19

Wranitzky, Paul, 1756–1808, works arranged for Harmoniemusik, **VIII:** 148 [*Das Waldmädchen, Oberon*]; unidentified works, 150, 246

Wranitzky, Wenzel, 18th century Austrian composer, **X:** 19; **XI: 281**

Wranizky, Paul, 1756–1808, Moravian composer, **XI:** 100, 227, 231

Wratni, J., as arranger of *Messano* (composer unidentified) for Harmoniemusik, 156

Wright, early 18th century publisher in London, **XI:** 223, 238

Wright, Thomas, 1763–1829, English, (5) *Marches* for Harmoniemusik, **VIII:** 265ff

Wüllner, Franz, 1832–1902, German composer, **IX:** 195

Wulstan, 10th century English deacon, **I:** 95

Wunderer, Anton, 19th century composer in Vienna, **XI:** 310

Wunderlich, Christian Friedrich, b. 1722, oboist and clarinetist, **XI:** 124 [biographical note], 149 [biographical note]

Wunderlich, Johann 1755–1819, German, **XI:** 101 [biograhical note], 227

Wurst, M. L. F., 19th century German composer, **IX:** 195

Wust, 17th century publisher in Frankfurt, **VII:** 129, 145, 146

Wynne, David, b. 1900, Welsh composer, **XII:** 187

Xenophon, 4th – 5th century BC, **I:** 30, 35

Yost, Michel (pseudo. Josef Michel), 1754–1786 Fr. clarinetist & composer, **VIII:** 359 [*Suito* for Harmoniemusik]; **XI:** 139, 149, 247

Zabala, Nicola, 19th century Italian composer, **XI:** 302; **XII:** 69

Zaccheus, 16th century composer, **VI:** 107

Zach, Johann, 1699–1773, German composer, **XI:** 101, 124

Zächer, Johann Michael, d. 1712, composer, **VII:** 9

Zaininger, Benedikt, 19th century German composer, **IX:** 195

Zaluzan, Johann, 19th century Austrian (?) composer, **XI:** 284

Zampieri, 19th century Italian composer, **X:** 244

Zanchi, Francesco, 19th century Italian composer, **X:** 256

Zandonati, Giovanni, 1754–1838, Italian composer, **X:** 257

Zangius, Liberalis, 1619, German composer, **VII:** 144, 145, 183

Zangl, Josef, 19th century Austrian composer, **IX:** 253

Zani, Andrea, 1696–1757, Italian composer, **XI:** 101

Zannetti, 17th century publisher in Rome, **VII:** 193, 200

Zannetti, Francesco, b. 1740, Italian composer, **XI:** 101, 227

Zanti, Alessandro, 19th century Italian composer, **X:** 257

Zapf, Johann Nepomuk, *Parthia* for Harmoniemusik, **VIII:** 246

Zarlino, Geoseffo, Italian theorist, 16th century, **II:** 13

Zarth, Georg, 1708–1778, German composer, **XI:** 101, 227

Zavertal, Josef, 1819–1893, Austrian composer, **IX:** 253

Zavertal, Ladislao, 1849–1942, Austrian composer, **IX:** 253

Zavertal, Vaclav, 19th century Austrian composer, **IX:** 253

Zbinden, Julien-François, b. 1917, Swiss composer, **XII:** 120

Zech, Markus, 1727–1770, church music for voices and winds, **VIII:** 374

Zedler, Johann Henrich, 1705–1751, German encyclopedist, **III:** 119

Zelenka, Jan Dismas, 1679–1745, Bohemian composer, **VII:** 5

Zellbell, Anders, 1680–1727, German composer, **XI:** 101, 158

Zender, Hans, b. 1936, German composer, **XII:** 121, 187

Zenemükiadó Vállalat, 20th century publisher in Budapest, **XII:** 159

Zerboni, S., 20th century publisher in Milan, **XII:** 175

Zerezo, Isidore, 19th century Belgium composer, **IX:** 260

Zetter, 19th century publisher in Paris, **IX:** 90; **XI:** 164, 257, 286, 309; **XII:** 66

Zetterquist, L. J., 19th century German composer, **IX:** 195

Zeutschner, 17th century composer, **VII:** 183

Ziani, Pietro, ca. 1630–1715, composer of sonatas, **VII:** 183

Zichy, Graf Geza, 1849–1924, German composer, **IX:** 195

Ziegler, ?, 19th century French composer, conductor, Musique, 1er Hussards, numerous works for large band, **IX:** 111ff

Ziegler, Benno, 1891–1965, German composer, **XII:** 121

Ziegler, Johannes, 19th century novelist, in Vienna, **V:** 112

Ziehrer, ?, 19th century English composer, **IX:** 281

Ziehrer, Carl, 1843–1922, Austrian composer, **IX:** 253; **X:** 59 [German Waltzes for band]

Zielche, Johann, 18th century, flautist to the King of Denmark, **XI:** 102

Zierfuss, 19th century publisher in Munich, **IX:** 175

Zifra, Antonio, 19th century Italian composer, **IX:** 121

Ziha, ?, (5) *Partittas* for Harmoniemusik, **VIII:** 246ff

Zikoff, ?, 19th century English composer, **IX:** 281

Zillig, Winfried, 1905–1963, German composer, **XII:** 121, 187

Zillmann, 19th century Kapellmeister in Dresden, **V: 23**

Zimmerman, Michael, b. 1833, Austrian military band leader, **V:** 43, 115

Zimmermann, ?, 18th century composer, **XI:** 102, 124, 253

Zimmermann, 19th century French composer, **IX:** 112

Zimmermann, 19th century publisher in Leipzig, **XI:** 308

Zimmermann, Anton, 1741–1781, Bohemian composer, **IV:** 41; **VIII:** 247, (6) *Parthias* for Harmoniemusik

Zimmermann, Carl, 19th century German composer, **IX:** 195

Zincarelli, arranged for band, **IX:** 258

Zinck, Bendix, 1743–1801, German composer, **XI:** 227

Zingarelli, Nicola Antonio, 1752–1837, works arr. for Harmoniemusik, **VIII:** 149, 150, 154; **IX:** 141; **X:** 257

Zinke, Friedrich, oboist under Liechtenstein in Vienna, **IV:** 39

Zinzendorf, Count, Vienna, diary entries of 1761–1793, **IV:** 13ff, 41

Zitek, ?, 19th century Austrian composer, **IX:** 253

Zobl, ?, 18th century German, *Partita* for Harmoniemusik, **VIII:** 359

Zoëdler, ?, *Parthia* for Harmoniemusik, **VIII:** 247

Zöllner, Richard, b. 1896, German composer, **XII:** 188

Zoncada, Giovanni, 18th century Italian, *Partita*, solo oboe, Harmoniemusik, **VIII:** 368

Zoras, Leonidas, b. 1905, Greek composer, **XII:** 121

Zuber, Gregor, 1649, German composer of dances, **VII:** 183ff

Zucchi, Giacomo, 1750–1850, Italian (?) composer, **XI:** 231

Zuckert, Johann, 18th century German composer, **XI:** 227

Zulehner, 18th century publisher in Mainz, **VIII:** 219

Zulehner, 19th century publisher in Mainz, **XI:** 45

Zulehner, band conductor at Mainz, **V:** 46

Zulehner, Georg, 1770–1841, German composer, **V:** 133; **IX:** 195

Zumpe, ?, composer included in a 1874 English collection of band music, **X:** 113

Zumsteeg, Jan, 19th century Austrian composer, **IX:** 253

Zumsteeg, Johann, 1760–1802, German, (6) works for winds, **VIII:** 359; **XI:** 102, 227

Zurlo, Giuseppe, 19th century Italian composer for band, **X:** 257

Zweckstetter, Christoph, 1772–1836, composer for choir and brass, **V:** 209; **IX:** 195

Zwing, M., 18th century German, (9) works for small band, **VIII:** 359

Zwirzina, hornist in 1780 for Count Palm in Vienna, **IV:** 42

Zwyssig, Alberich, 1808–1854, German composer, **XI:** 289

Zyrler, Stephen, 16th century German composer, **VI:** 63

About the Author

Dr. David Whitwell is a graduate ('with distinction') of the University of Michigan and the Catholic University of America, Washington DC (PhD, Musicology, Distinguished Alumni Award, 2000) and has studied conducting with Eugene Ormandy and at the Akademie fur Musik, Vienna. Prior to coming to Northridge, Dr. Whitwell participated in concerts throughout the United States and Asia as Associate First Horn in the USAF Band and Orchestra in Washington DC, and in recitals throughout South America in cooperation with the United States State Department.

At the California State University, Northridge, which is in Los Angeles, Dr. Whitwell developed the CSUN Wind Ensemble into an ensemble of international reputation, with international tours to Europe in 1981 and 1989 and to Japan in 1984. The CSUN Wind Ensemble has made professional studio recordings for BBC (London), the Koln Westdeutscher Rundfunk (Germany), NOS National Radio (The Netherlands), Zurich Radio (Switzerland), the Television Broadcasting System (Japan) as well as for the United States State Department for broadcast on its 'Voice of America' program. The CSUN Wind Ensemble's recording with the Mirecourt Trio in 1982 was named the 'Record of the Year' by The Village Voice. Composers who have guest conducted Whitwell's ensembles include Aaron Copland, Ernest Krenek, Alan Hovhaness, Morton Gould, Karel Husa, Frank Erickson and Vaclav Nelhybel.

Dr. Whitwell has been a guest professor in 100 different universities and conservatories throughout the United States and in 23 foreign countries (most recently in China, in an elite school housed in the Forbidden City). Guest conducting experiences have included the Philadelphia Orchestra, Seattle Symphony Orchestra, the Czech Radio Orchestras of Brno and Bratislava, The National Youth Orchestra of Israel, as well as resident wind ensembles in Russia, Israel, Austria, Switzerland, Germany, England, Wales, The Netherlands, Portugal, Peru, Korea, Japan, Taiwan, Canada and the United States.

He is a past president of the College Band Directors National Association, a member of the Prasidium of the International Society for the Promotion of Band Music, and was a member of the founding board of directors of the World Association for Symphonic Bands and Ensembles (WASBE). In 1964 he was made an honorary life member of Kappa Kappa Psi, a national professional music fraternity. In September, 2001, he was a delegate to the UNESCO Conference on Global Music in Tokyo. He has been knighted by sovereign organizations in France, Portugal and Scotland and has been awarded the gold medal of Kerkrade, The Netherlands, and the silver medal of Wangen, Germany, the highest honor given wind conductors in the United States, the medal of the Academy of Wind and Percussion Arts (National Band Association) and the highest honor given wind conductors in Austria, the gold medal of the Austrian Band Association. He is a member of the Hall of Fame of the California Music Educators Association.

Dr. Whitwell's publications include more than 127 articles on wind literature including publications in Music and Letters (London), the London Musical Times, the Mozart-Jahrbuch (Salzburg), and 39 books, among which is his 13-volume *History and Literature of the Wind Band and Wind Ensemble* and an 8-volume series on *Aesthetics in Music*. In addition to numerous modern editions of early wind band music his original compositions include 5 symphonies.

David Whitwell was named as one of six men who have determined the course of American bands during the second half of the 20th century, in the definitive history, *The Twentieth Century American Wind Band* (Meredith Music).

A doctoral dissertation by German Gonzales (2007, Arizona State University) is dedicated to the life and conducting career of David Whitwell through the year 1977. David Whitwell is one of nine men described by Paula A. Crider in *The Conductor's Legacy* (Chicago: GIA, 2010) as 'the legendary conductors' of the 20th century.

'I can't imagine the 2nd half of the 20th century—without David Whitwell and what he has given to all of the rest of us.' Frederick Fennell (1993)

About the Editor

CRAIG DABELSTEIN began studying the piano at age seven and took up the saxophone at age twelve. Mr Dabelstein has Bachelor of Arts (Music) and Bachelor of Music degrees from the Queensland Conservatorium of Music, where he majored in the performance of classical saxophone repertoire. He also has a Graduate Diploma of Learning and Teaching and a Graduate Certificate in Editing and Publishing from the University of Southern Queensland.

He has held the principal alto and tenor saxophone chairs in the Australian Wind Orchestra and has been an augmenting member of the Queensland Philharmonic Orchestra, the Queensland Symphony Orchestra, and the Queensland Pops Orchestra. For many years he was also a member of the Queensland Saxophone Quartet.

He has been a casual conductor of the Young Conservatorium Symphonic Winds, and has previously been a saxophone teacher at the Queensland Conservatorium of Music. He is a regular conductor of the Queensland Wind Orchestra, having served as their artistic director and chief conductor from 2004 to 2009.

Craig Dabelstein is a research associate for the *Teaching Music Through Performance in Band* series of books, contributing analyses to volumes 7, 8, 1 (rev. edn), and the *Solos with Wind Band Accompaniment* volume. He served as the copyeditor and layout designer of the *Australian Clarinet and Saxophone Magazine* from 2007 to 2009 and he has written many CD and book reviews for *Music Forum* magazine. He is the editor of the second editions of the books by Dr. David Whitwell including *A Concise History of the Wind Band*, *Foundations of Music Education*, *Music Education of the Future*, *The Sousa Oral History Project*, *Wagner on Bands*, *Berlioz on Bands*, *The Art of Musical Conducting*, and the *Aesthetics of Music* series (8 volumes) and *The History and Literature of the Wind Band and Wind Ensemble* series (13 volumes). From 1994 to 2012 he was a staff member at Brisbane Girls Grammar School. He now teaches woodwinds and conducts bands at St. Joseph's College, Gregory Terrace, Brisbane.

www.ingramcontent.com/pod-product-compliance
Lightning Source LLC
Chambersburg PA
CBHW080236270326
41926CB00020B/4257